BACKYARD
HORSEKEEPING

ALSO BY JOAN FRY

The Beginning Dressage Book (with Kathryn Denby-Wrightson)

BACKYARD HORSEKEEPING

THE ONLY GUIDE YOU'LL EVER NEED

JOAN FRY

THE LYONS PRESS
Guilford, Connecticut
An imprint of the The Globe Pequot Press

The Lyons Press is an imprint of The Globe Pequot Press.

10 9 8 7 6 5 4 3 2 1

Printed in the United States of America

Designed by Maggie Peterson

ISBN 1-59228-249-0

Library of Congress Cataloging-in-Publication data is available on file.

DEDICATION

For John, who never lost faith in me.

TABLE OF CONTENTS

ACKNOWLEDGMENTS

My greatest debt and most heartfelt gratitude go to all the horses who taught me—Playboy, Bachelor, Sinjun, and Prim in particular. This is their book too.

Many people helped me bring *Backyard Horsekeeping* to life. First and foremost I want to thank my husband John Fry, longtime professional horse trainer, my first reader, and on-call 24/7 tech support. Special thanks to Gina Cresse, whose exact and graceful drawings illustrate this book. A mystery writer and horse lover as well as an artist, she also took many of the photographs and read every chapter—twice, in some cases—pointing out necessary corrections she tactfully disguised as "just a few suggestions."

Special thanks also to Mark Williams, DVM, who is not only my horse and goat veterinarian, but who devoted a lot of his nonexistent spare time to make sure I got my medical facts straight and spelled them correctly. More special thanks to Judy Reynolds, PhD, PAS, for helping me revise the two chapters on feed. She also provided the "Nutrients in Common Horse Feeds" chart, helped me research material relating to the "Horse Condition Scorecard," and took new photographs to illustrate it.

More thanks go to: my horse-loving friend Gayle Lampe of William Woods University, who somehow managed to take time out of her own busy schedule to answer my nonstop questions; my literary horse-loving friend Gail Lofdahl, who went over this book chapter by chapter with pen in hand offering advice and clarification; Alan Balch, for his friendship and support; Jamie Alder, for *his* friendship and support; my other horse-loving friends including Barbara Davis, artist, chocolate maker, dog breeder, and best friend since childhood; Avis Girdler, horse photographer extraordinaire; Kimry Bassett, who at age eleven was one of John's equitation riders; Kelly Vela; Lisa Heres-Rosenberger; Kathy Boddicker; Peggy Touchstone; and Raphaella Goodwin. Thanks to Rick, Charmaine, Matthew, Luke, Josh, and Brielle Jimmink, for being the best neighbors imaginable; the entire staff of Sweetwater Veterinary Clinic for patiently forwarding and/or answering questions; Cynthia Heck of the American Saddlebred Horse Association; my Internet friends who helped me with research at The Barn Book (www.thebarnbook.com); Steven M. Jones, Livestock/4-H Extension Specialist at the University of Arkansas; Shirley S. Winer; Peg Greiwe; James Kim of One-

Hour Photo, for his help in all matters photographic; and the personnel of Horse Shows in the Sun (HITS) for arranging interviews and photo sessions.

A very special thank you to my agent Pamela Malpas for her generous heart, and editor and fellow horse lover Steve Price for his patience and quick humor.

I'm grateful to the Board of Trustees of Antelope Valley College, who awarded me financial assistance through Staff Development to do additional research.

This book is the result of a collaboration of many minds, not all of them human. The information is as true as I can make it. Any errors are mine.

Joan Fry
Acton, California

INTRODUCTION

Consider the following scenario: You're single, and you keep your horse at a boarding stable—not cheap. One day, as you're out trail riding, you meet somebody. Since both of you are headed in the same direction, you and the other rider start talking. *This is fun*, you think. *A pretty day, and an interesting new person who's also a horse lover.* But sooner than you'd like, you have to head back—your job, a schedule you have to keep, errands you have to run. You ask the other rider where he or she boards his/her horse, and the rider responds cheerily, "Oh, he lives with me." You and your new friend agree to meet for another trail ride—next week, same time, same place. As you head back to the stable, you think, *What would it be like to ride* my *horse home? To end every trail ride that way—not by surrendering him to strangers, but by riding him home and keeping him there, so close that I can see him out the window?*

Or this one: You're married, your kids have finally flapped out of the nest, and you and your wife (or husband) decide to buy that piece of land you've always wanted. Your wife can't stop talking about all those roses she wants to plant. You can't stop thinking about how much fun it would be to have a do-anything, go-anywhere horse you could sling a saddle on and take to the hills with, just like when you were a kid.

Or this: Your kids are definitely, although defiantly, still in the nest. The oldest, a teenager, has been replaced by the Adolescent from Hell—tattoos, nose ring, purple hair, and an attitude. You and your husband (or wife) decide to move to a rural area. You think if you buy some horses and go trail riding together as a family, your teenager will morph back into somebody you actually want to claim kinship with.

Or this: Your marital status is nobody's business. You want a horse, you want him in your backyard, and you want him *now.*

Whoa there, pilgrim. Keeping a horse in your own backyard is a big step. How hard is it to do all that—buy a horse and all the tack, feed, and equipment that go along with him so you *can* keep him on your own property? Is your property big enough? Are you zoned for horses? How much time does caring for a horse take? How much will it cost? And how do you know if you're taking proper care of him? Who do you turn to for advice—the guy at the feed store? A neighbor? A video about horse training?

Owning a horse is more complicated than owning a dog or cat. It also requires a lot more work. Cats in particular are pretty self-reliant, and if you're a lousy pet owner and get bored with them, they can usually fend for themselves. But horses are completely dependent on humans to give them food and water—the basics of their existence. If you get bored with your horse and expect him to fend for himself, he will die.

But for many horse lovers, taking care of their horse—their best buddy, their friend—is a big part of the pleasure of ownership. The emotional bonds that humans forge with horses, and vice versa, can be very strong—even though horses haven't been domesticated as long as our other "pets." Compared to dogs, in particular, horses still retain most of their wild traits. But the more time you spend with your horse—and the more you learn how he sees, hears, and reacts to what happens around him—the stronger that bond will be, and the more the two of you will enjoy each other's company.

Even though I just lumped horses into the same category as dogs, cats, and the rodent of the moment (around here it's tumbling mice), please remember that horses are *not* "pets" in the same sense that other human-friendly creatures are. Because of the relatively short time they've been domesticated, horses still carry a lot of unpredictable (from a human's point of view), wild-child genes. As your horse's caretaker, you have to make allowances for that fact.

Backyard Horsekeeping is not for beginning riders or first-time owners whose experience with horses has been limited.

This book is for people like you. You had starter pets like parakeets and gerbils when you were a kid. After demonstrating your reliability—you fed and watered and exercised and cleaned up after your pets—your parents allowed you to graduate to cats and dogs. You are, in other words, a *responsible* owner. You've ridden horses before, even if you haven't ridden lately, and you may even have owned one or two. You're not a complete greenhorn, and when I say *backyard horse*, what you hear is, a horse I own and take care of by myself, without a trainer, on my own property.

You're just not 100 percent sure how to go about doing that.

Backyard Horsekeeping will explain how.

For simplicity's sake I'm going to call your horse *he*, no matter what his or her real gender might be. For the same reason I'm going to assume that *you* are an adult, male or female. I will also assume that you ride for relaxation and enjoyment—that is, your main interest is trail and recreational riding. Lastly, I will assume that you personally—not your housemate or your kids—are responsible (there's that word again) for taking care of your horse or horses.

So, reader, do you still want to know how to take care of a horse in your own backyard?

Good. The first thing I want you to do is carry this book to the counter and pay for it, so you can finish reading it at home, at your leisure. We'll go from there.

The Horse Owner's Most Important Rule of Thumb:

If you're faced with a question you can't answer, or a situation you can't handle, *ask for help*.

CHAPTER 1

PROPERTY, TIME, AND MONEY: HOW EXPENSIVE IS A BACKYARD HORSE?

Many horse lovers dream about owning a horse and caring for it by themselves. But they're reluctant to act on it because they don't think they know enough. Three questions—more accurately, the answers to these questions—stop them in their tracks. The questions are always the same, and I might as well answer them before we go any further.

One: How much property do I need to keep my horse in my backyard?

Two: How much time will at-home horsekeeping take?

Three: How much will it cost?

Please keep in mind that the answers here are mini-answers. You'll find the unabridged versions in the following chapters. I'll use my experience with Prim, my American Saddlebred trail horse, as a baseline. (Prim is her barn name because *prim* describes her finicky personality. Her registered name is Pacific Belle.) Ask your horse-owning friends for input, too.

How about horses—do *they* need friends? You bet your pet ferret they do. Horses are herd animals. A horse stabled by himself, out of sight or sound of other horses, can get bored, depressed, cranky, and/or self-destructive. The ideal stablemate is another horse. But since I'm the only person in my family to ride, and I only have time for one horse, I bought Prim a neutered, dehorned 4-H goat named Kyle. (For information about other barn buddies, see Chapter 12.)

Feed me!

Prim and Kyle share a twenty-four foot by twenty-four foot pipe corral. As a result, you can probably shave a few minutes off my time estimates because I have to tie up the goat before I lead Prim into or out of their corral. Otherwise my husband and I wouldn't have any landscaping left around our house.

THE BACKYARD HORSE—A DEFINITION

A backyard horse is one that you own and care for on your own property and ride for fun. In other words, you didn't buy your horse in order to race, play polo, or compete in shows. You bought him primarily for pleasure—to trail ride.

Before you go on a buying spree for the horse *or* the property, do enough fact-finding to answer these two questions. How much property do you need to keep a horse? Is it zoned for horses?

HORSE PROPERTY

In most states, horse owning falls under county jurisdiction, and most counties want you to own at least half an acre, or 21,780 square feet, per horse. Even though I live in a remote area of the California high desert, it's still in Los Angeles County, and I abide by the same LA County code that horse owners in Hollywood abide by. The code stipulates that anyone who owns 15,000 square feet of property—considerably less than half an acre—can keep one horse, as long as the property is zoned for horses. If you want more than one horse, you need an additional 5,000 square feet per horse.

Cities often have their own regulations, which supersede county regulations. If you live in Fullerton, California—which is in Orange County—the city stipulates that "horses, cattle and sheep are generally permitted in residential areas when the following conditions are met: Two adult animals may be kept on a lot containing not less than 32,670 square feet of land. One additional animal may be kept for each additional 15,000 square feet of land." The county of Orange becomes involved only if you buy property in an unincorporated area (outside city limits). According to Orange County Planning and Development Services, you can keep a horse in any unincorporated area zoned for residential use as long as all corrals, barns, stalls, etc. are no closer than twenty-five feet to your nearest neighbor's closest window. There are no acreage requirements.

To find out about property in your part of the country, open your telephone book and look under the heading County. (Government listings are in the first section of the white pages.) Look for Planning Department or Regional Planning. If that doesn't work, try Public Health or Veterinary Public Health. If *that* doesn't work, try Animal Care, Animal Regulations, or Animal Control.

Or, let your computer do the walking and research local codes using the Internet. (Once you get into sub-headings, look for Livestock Kept As Pets.) For additional suggestions, see Appendix II.

The Roaming Zone

Make sure the property is zoned for horses. If you reach a live person when you call about acreage requirements, don't let that person escape until you find out who to contact about zoning.

Suppose that person doesn't know?

Turn to the County listings in your phone book again and look under Zoning. If you live in Charles County, Maryland, it will take you less than ten minutes to find that you need two acres to keep one horse (for each additional horse, add another acre) and whether or not a particular piece of property is zoned for horses.

If you live in Los Angeles County, look under Regional Planning again. Since the department is available to the public only Monday through Thursday between the hours of 7:30 A.M. to 11:30 A.M., be persistent. Before you call, choose a comfortable chair and make sure you have a project of some sort to keep you occupied between busy signals. You might, for example, want to get a head start on next year's income tax.

According to LA County code, you can keep a horse in your backyard as long as you live in an agricultural zone. Some residential and industrial areas are also zoned for horses. In Compton, deep in the urban heart of Los Angeles, a group of black horsemen raise and train their own horses on their own property, where they hone their skills as cowboys. Not many inner-city residents keep a horse in a backyard lot, but you can if you live in LA.

Since not all counties list a phone number under Zoning, you may have to play detective again. If Regional Planning doesn't work, try Planning and Development Services, Planning Division, or Planning and Growth Management.

Or, give the Internet another try.

Call first, buy later: Play it safe and find out about acreage and zoning requirements *now*, especially if you already own a horse and are keeping him at a boarding stable while you look for property. You may find the perfect piece of land, only to find it's not quite big enough or isn't zoned for horses. By doing a little preplanning you can save yourself a big disappointment.

Don't rely on your realtor to tell you these facts. And don't rely on the seller's say-so either, even if the property is represented as horse property and the seller has horses on it. He may be keeping them there illegally.

How You Can Do It

For ideas on how to fit a house *and* a horse on half an acre and still have room for a riding ring, a garage, and a backyard, see the plot plan on the next page and read Chapter 4. For additional suggestions, see Appendix II.

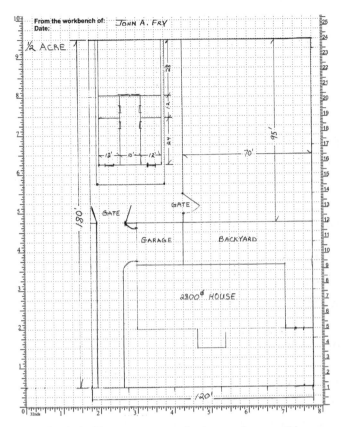

A plot plan for building a 2,800 square-foot house and a two-stall barn on half an acre, with enough room to ride. (Drawing by John Fry)

Hay bales break apart into "flakes"; the weight varies from hay to hay and bale to bale.

TIME

You must—with no excuses (such as, "But I have pneumonia!" and/or "But I'm on crutches!") and without exception—feed your horse at least twice a day. You *must*. Many owners insist that you feed at exactly the same time every day, but I'm not that much of a stickler. For one thing, I've never figured out how to explain daylight saving time to a horse.

Speed Feeding

Our house is approximately 300 feet from Prim's corral. (In this book I use the terms corral, pipe corral, stall, and paddock interchangeably to refer to a horse's living quarters. I also use the terms arena, ring, and riding ring interchangeably to refer to a fenced turnout area, where you can turn your horse loose to romp and roll.) The hay shed, which is right next to the corral, is also right next to my tackroom but in a separate building. In the morning, as soon as I'm dressed but before I'm fully awake, I sleepwalk to the corral, check Prim's feeder for leftover hay (there shouldn't be any—healthy horses clean their plates), throw one flake of hay in her feeder and about a quarter of a flake in Kyle's, clean the corral, check the water to see if anything strange is floating in it, collect Prim's nightly contributions to my compost heap using a pitchfork and a wheelbarrow, and spread them out on the other side of the hill.

If the waterer needs filling, I turn on the water and stand there and watch until it's full. If you're ever tempted to do something else—check the tackroom to see if you need fly spray, for example—and then happen to look out the window of your house two hours later and see water cascading down your driveway, you'll understand why I stand and stare at the water: so I remember to turn it off. By the time I'm back in the house, I'm ready to face the day. (Can you tell I'm a night person?)

Total elapsed time: eighteen minutes.

A confined horse is a bored horse. I feed Prim a midday snack of mini-carrots and hay to give her something to do—and because nutritionally, it's a smart move. Carrots also happen to be one of the few foods Kyle refuses to eat.

Total elapsed time: five minutes.

After John and I finish dinner, we walk to the hay shed and turn on the outside lights if necessary. While John waters, I check for uneaten feed, throw a flake of hay in Prim's feeder and another quarter of a flake in Kyle's (yes, he's a very round goat), and eyeball both animals to make sure they're walking on all fours and have no scrapes or bite marks they didn't have at noon. Then we turn off the water and the lights and walk back to the house.

Total elapsed time: seven minutes.

Turnouts

Ideally—and all horse owners will tell you this—you *should* turn your horse out once a day to exercise. I don't mean you have to ride every day—just make sure your horse gets exercised every day. Those owners are right. You should. Many people turn their horse loose in the arena and walk away, expecting him to self-exercise. After a brief fit of bucking and galloping, most horses will hang their heads over the gate and nicker until you return them to their stall. That's why so many owners exercise their horse by putting him on a longe line and asking him to walk, trot, and canter for a specific length of time. I free longe Prim using only a longe whip (no longe line) and I count strides. In other words, first I ask her to trot (or jog, as

The easiest way to exercise a horse: free longe him. (Photo by Gina Cresse)

Western riders say) for fifty strides. Nothing strenuous, just a warmup. Then I ask her to lope (or canter, as English riders say) for a hundred strides. Then I reverse her and count a hundred canter strides and fifty jog strides (to cool her down) going in the opposite direction. A turnout like this takes about ten minutes.

Why don't I just say, "I longe my mare ten minutes every day"? Horse owners here in the high desert face some unusual weather conditions: nearly constant wind, nine percent humidity, one hundred-degree summers, and one-day winter snowstorms. How long I longe Prim depends on the weather and how she feels. Full-gallop turnouts on a windy, twenty-degree morning take much less time than lethargic, hot-weather turnouts. But even a lethargic turnout gets Prim's heart pumping and her legs moving and her lungs working, which is exactly what a turnout is supposed to do. If I have time, I leave her in the ring while I clean the corral again, dump the manure, and top off the water. Once she's back inside, I turn Kyle loose and feed them.

Total elapsed time: thirty minutes (on the average).

Since I work at home most of the time, I often turn Prim out before her midday meal, especially if I've spent the morning sitting in front of my computer. It breaks up my day and gives us both something to look forward to.

No time for turnouts? If you work full-time, you may not be able to turn your horse out every day. In that case, arrange for your spouse, kids, or a reliable friend to do it.

Weather can play a part. If it's raining and your turnout ring is either dangerously slippery or has turned into Lake Erie, don't turn your horse out. If the daytime temperature is over ninety-five degrees, most professional trainers will not work horses. Take a tip from them and either turn your horse out very early in the morning (4–5 A.M.), or after the temperature has dropped in the evening. If it's below freezing and snowing so hard you can't see the barn from your house, don't turn your horse out to exercise, especially if he lives outdoors. Give him extra hay instead.

But now that I've given you these two tiny loopholes, don't take advantage of them. If I can't turn Prim out every day, I turn her out every other day. You can too. Unless your vet tells you otherwise, *do not* leave a horse standing in a stall or corral longer than three days. If a whole week has gone by and you couldn't find ten minutes to turn your horse out, pay a neighbor's horse-savvy kid to do it for you. If you can't afford that, sell your horse.

Dress for success: If you do work full-time away from home, turn your horse out in the morning before you feed, or before you feed at night. Change into your "horse" clothes first.

Several years ago I boarded Sinjun, my first Saddlebred trail horse, at a local stable. The stable had a huge riding ring with good footing and two light poles in the center for night riding, which is not the safest arrangement (safest is having the poles *outside* the ring). Late one afternoon I watched a woman who had obviously driven straight from work try to longe her horse. She was wearing a skirt, matching jacket, a blouse, stockings, and high heels. Predictably—since heels sink into horse-friendly footing and sometimes disappear entirely—she ended up wrapping her horse around one of the light poles. The horse, demonstrating more intelligence than his owner, simply stopped when he couldn't go any farther and waited to be untangled.

A Horse Owner's Rule of Thumb:

The smaller the enclosure you keep your horse in, the more time he needs to spend in a big fenced area so he can stretch his legs and gallop and buck and do stupid horse things.

Grooming

Horses stay healthier and happier when you groom them on a regular basis; the shine on their coats will tell you the same thing. Although I don't always succeed—sometimes I only have time to clean her feet—I *try* to groom Prim every other day. I also groom her whenever I ride.

Here's what I consider basic, no-frills, maintenance grooming. First, brush your horse's forelock, mane, and tail. If you encounter knots, use your fingers and a "hair polish" product for horses. If you just rip a comb through them, the hair will break. Then, making small circles, curry your horse's entire body (face and legs included) with a rubber curry mitt, the kind that slips over your hand. Be careful around his head in case the horse is headshy. A lot of people untie their horse to brush his face and head. Then go over him using an oval rubber curry comb, but skip his face, legs, and backbone. (Curry combs don't bend around a horse's joints the way a mitt does.) After that, go over his entire body with a brush, always brushing towards his tail. Clean your horse's feet, apply a hoof moisturizer or thrush medication as needed, and check for loose shoes.

Total elapsed time: twenty minutes.

Total elapsed time per day (feed three times, clean once) without turnout: thirty minutes.

Total elapsed time per day (feed three times, clean once) *with* turnout: forty minutes (on the average).

Total elapsed time on a day that you turn your horse out and groom him (feed three times, clean once): add twenty minutes.

My recommendation: While the following schedule works for me and Prim, I'm not suggesting that you adopt it. Establish your own—a realistic schedule, not an "I wish" one.

Our schedule: Monday I longe her; Tuesday I clean her feet and groom her; Wednesday, longe; Thursday, clean feet and groom; Friday, I longe or ride her—as long as we both shall live.

Groom your horse daily. Most of them soak it up like sunshine. (Photo by Gina Cresse)

MONEY—ALWAYS MONEY

The short answer to the question "how much will it cost?" is, there *is* no short answer. Your biggest expense—*after* you buy or build a shelter for your horse, *after* you buy the horse and tack, and *after* you buy horse property (provided you don't already own some)—will be feed. What I'm about to describe is what horse people call maintenance feeding. In other words, a horse that's ridden only once a week and eats this food in these quantities will not lose or gain weight.

Hay

Because I live in an area of California where alfalfa is local, top quality, freshly baled, and relatively cheap, I feed Prim alfalfa. It's not "local" in the sense that I can call a nearby farmer and order directly from him. But the hay doesn't have to travel far before it arrives at my feed store. Like most food items, hay is cheapest if you can buy directly from the grower. If you buy it at a feed store, it had to be shipped there—and guess who pays for the shipping. (There's also a hay broker involved, but if you only have a few horses, you don't need to know what he does—only that he exists, and that he gets his cut too.)

Around here, alfalfa is sold in heavy (about 120 pound) rectangular bales. If you feed your horse one flake of alfalfa in the morning and another at night, your bale will last about a week. Premium alfalfa hay (referred to as number-one alfalfa) costs me about $10.45 a bale. (The price will vary depending on where you live.) Until I bought Kyle, a bale lasted me almost a week. As a troubled adolescent—Prim was three when I bought her—she walked the fence line all day, shedding pounds with each stride. That's why I feed extra hay, to keep her occupied (the boredom factor again). That's also why we own Kyle. At the other extreme is the easy keeper, the horse who gets fat on two flakes of alfalfa a day even if you ride him seven days a week.

Hay Helpers

Like many owners, I supplement a straight alfalfa diet with a grain-based feed. Oats are every old-timer's first choice, but not all horses *need* grain. You've probably heard the expression, "He's feeling his oats." If you grain a horse but don't ride very often, he'll feel good. When you do ride, such a horse will often misbehave—not out of meanness, but because he's so full of energy he doesn't know what to do with himself.

I grain Prim daily—that is, I give her slightly more than half of a thirty-six-ounce coffee can of a pelleted, grain-based supplement. Twice a week I add psyllium, which prevents sand colic. (Your horse may not need it.) The feed supplement I use costs about $12 a bag and lasts about two months.

Salt of the Earth

Horses also need salt. Since Prim and Kyle have separate feeders, I buy four-pound trace-mineral salt bricks, one for each feeder. A brick costs $2, and how often I replace it depends mainly on the weather. When it's cold, horses consume very little salt. When it's hot, they consume much more. You can also buy a 50-pound block for $5.95.

All together now: Adding the cost of pellets, psyllium, and salt to the $42 a month I spend on hay, I spend *approximately* $52 a month to feed Prim.

Greener Pastures

In some parts of the country, horse owners have pastures with real grass in them—at least during the summer—and simply open the barn door in the morning and turn their horse out to graze. Sounds simple enough. It's not. Planting and maintaining a pasture that provides your horse with all the essential nutrients in the correct balance is not a project for beginners. To do it correctly, you need a degree in agriculture and a lot of free time. Most backyard horse owners have neither, and even horses on pasture usually need supplemental feed.

Gayle Lampe, Professor of Equine Science at William Woods University in Fulton, Missouri, used to turn the school horses out to pasture every summer without additional feed. No more. Once classes started in the fall, the horses were too thin, and it took too long to get them back in shape. Now, even though most of the horses still spend their summer vacation at pasture, Gayle makes sure they also get hay. "And sometimes we grain them," she added. "It depends on the individual horse."

Feeding by weight: Many owners, particularly those who have more than one horse, and all trainers feed by weight, not bulk. It's much more accurate to weigh what your horse eats than to feed him hay by the "flake" and grain by the "coffee can." But if you only have one or two horses, you can pretty much eyeball them and judge for yourself if they're losing weight, gaining weight, or maintaining. (To check the accuracy of your eyeballs, check the "Horse Condition Scorecard" in Chapter 8.)

Regional Expenses

Because of the soil composition in many Western states, and because of the nature of horses—who are greedy and love the tender little alfalfa leaves and pale lavender flowers better than the stems, and are willing to eat dirt in order to get them—sand colic is, unfortunately, very common. Most of the dirt doesn't pass through their digestive tract. Instead, it builds up until it forms an impaction and the horse colics.

The good news: Prevention is easy and fairly inexpensive. Buy your horse some solid rubber pads (available at most feed stores), especially if your horse lives outside in a pipe corral. If he doesn't already have a metal feeder, buy one of those too. After you install the feeder, lay the pads directly under it. When you feed, toss the hay into the *feeder* instead of on the ground.

More good news: For additional insurance—and comfort—bed your horse's corral with wood shavings so he *can't* eat dirt. (Some owners, especially if they stable their horse indoors, prefer straw bedding.) It will take you a couple of months and many bags of shavings to establish decent bedding in a pipe corral. After that, shavings are a minor expense (I buy four "big blue bags" of shavings for $7.50 each, once a month)—especially if you compare it with the vet bill you'll get after your horse comes down with sand colic.

Other Regional Expenses

If you live in a humid climate, insects will be a problem. Any New Englander, horse or human, goes through gallons of insect repellent every summer, especially during black fly season. In the South molds and fungus are a concern, both in the feed and on the horse. In Northern states famous for their long, bitter-cold winters, owners face their own specialized problems, as do owners in the Midwest. Horses in southern California are rarely electrocuted during thunderstorms because we rarely *have* thunderstorms. But where thunder and lightning are common, you may want to replace the wooden posts that hold your wire fencing with metal stakes. Pipe corrals are grounded automatically.

Don't Forget the Veterinarian

Some owners budget $300 a year for vet expenses. In my experience, if you're a conscientious owner and your horse isn't accident-prone, that's high. Prim sees the vet once a year, twice if she needs her teeth floated (a dental procedure that grinds down the sharp edges of her teeth). Even if your horse is in good health, you still want a vet to check him once a year and keep his vaccinations up to date. A horse's yearly checkup is similar to your yearly checkup, and the shots are cheap insurance against various expensive-to-treat and often fatal diseases. I pay my vet, Dr. Mark Williams, $85 for his annual visit. The last time he floated Prim's teeth he charged me $132, and he usually repeats the procedure every two to two-and-a-half years.

Worming: This is your responsibility, not your vet's. How much it costs to worm your horse depends on the climate, how many horses you have, and how much contact they have with other horses. In this arid climate, since Prim seldom comes into physical contact with other horses, I spend about $42 a year for commercial paste wormers that I buy at the feed store and administer myself at three-month intervals.

Or the Farrier

Some horses have good, sturdy feet and can go barefoot—in other words, they don't need shoes. (Both Prim and Sinjun went barefoot.) Every six to eight weeks, depending on how often I ride, I call Mark Stallings, my shoer, to trim Prim's feet. But most horses require shoes, and fitting a shoe to a horse's hoof is very physical, labor-intensive work. Mark charges $35 for a trim, $60 to shoe the front feet only, and $80 to shoe all four feet. He doesn't do re-sets—in other words, he won't trim the horse's feet and nail the old shoes back on—because the process is almost as labor-intensive as putting on new shoes. (Other farriers will do re-sets; they're usually a little less expensive.) Unless your horse stands in a stall most of the day, he'll wear his shoes down at about the same rate of speed he would wear his hooves down if he went barefoot. In other words, a shod horse needs to be re-shod every six to eight weeks (sooner if a shoe pulls loose or the horse manages to lose one completely) because his feet continue to grow whether he's shod or not.

WHERE DO ALL THE ROAD APPLES GO?

There's really a fourth question, and this is it—although most people weighing the pros and cons of backyard horse-keeping usually forget to ask. The average horse on a maintenance diet produces a pile of manure every four to five hours for a total of five-plus piles a day. What are you going to do with it? The closer your neighbors are, the more important the answer becomes.

The best way to dispose of manure is to spread it in a thin layer over a large area, let it age for a year, and dig it into your garden as compost. Your non-horse-owning acquaintances who garden (tomatoes *love* composted horse manure) will become your new best friends the instant you buy a horse. Organic gardening acquaintances will bond even faster. (If you bed your horse on shavings, remind your gardening friends to add nitrogen to the soil.) Many boarding stables allow neighbors—or just about anybody with a pickup truck—to haul away manure. Consider posting a sign that reads Free Garden Fertilizer.

Don't have the room to spread it out? Contact your waste disposal company—the folks who pick up your trash—and ask if they accept horse manure. If they don't, call around to local nurseries. Your best bet, if you can find one, is a mushroom grower. Many commercial growers contract with horse-show facilities to clean up during and after shows.

Can't find Mushroom Grower in the yellow pages? Ask your horse-owning friends what *they* do with their horse's road apples. The easiest solution might be your local landfill.

Dr. Mark Williams and Prim having a heart-to-heart.

THE BOTTOM LINE

In very round numbers, at-home horsekeeping costs me $130 a month, a figure that includes feed, shavings, worming, Prim's annual vet check, and the cost of trimming her feet every six weeks.

The 2004 *Arabian Horse Experience*, a brochure put out by the Arabian Horse Association (which graciously granted me permission to use these figures), estimates that the average owner spends $4–$7 per month on grooming supplies; $17–$25 per month on veterinarian care and supplies; and $25–$58 per month on shoeing. That total, *which excludes feed and bedding*, is $46–$90 per month.

The $130 a month total I gave you includes both feed *and* bedding and is one of the most compelling arguments for backyard horsekeeping. Keeping your horse

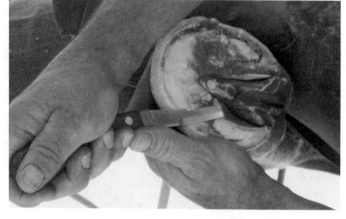

Farrier Mark Stallings trims the sole of Prim's front hoof.

at a stable at full board—which means the stable owner provides the stall or outdoor corral and the hay, and pays somebody to clean up after your horse—costs between $200–$500 per month. These figures, also courtesy of the Arabian Horse Association, are consistent with prices here in California. If you buy a young horse—a three-year old, for example, but nothing younger—and put him in training, which I strongly suggest you do, it will cost you even more.

You'll have to do some research and a little math to estimate how much keeping a backyard horse in your area of the country will cost. And the prices I gave you are for the California high desert, and they apply right now—today. Next week Mark Stallings might decide to raise his rates. Dr. Williams might too. Or we might have an abnormally rainy spring and the price of hay will go up. (It rarely goes down.) Suburban horse owners will also have to factor in the cost of water.

PREPARE YOURSELF

If you don't already own a horse and your experience with them has been limited in recent years, I suggest that you take riding lessons—at least once or twice a week for at least eight weeks. Find a hands-on barn where *you* do the catching and grooming and tacking up and walking the horse to cool him out after your lesson. You may discover that you still enjoy the riding part but not the caretaker part, and that if you do buy a horse, you'd rather board him than keep him in your backyard.

That's fine—as long as you and your horse are happy. Not every horse lover is cut out to be a backyard owner.

Get Ready

By now you should have a pretty good idea of what backyard horsekeeping involves. If you're still game—and still reading—you've decided that you have enough property (or are prepared to buy it) to keep a horse, that it's zoned for horses, that you're willing to spend the time to care for a horse, and that you can afford him.

If you don't already own a horse, you have a few more decisions to make. Once they're out of the way, get set. Your dream is about to come true.

CHAPTER 2

CHOOSE A RIDING STYLE

When horse people talk about a *seat*, they're not talking furniture. They may be talking about your ability: a rider with a good seat is a good rider. But more often than not they're talking about the saddle you use, and the style of riding associated with that saddle. Your seat and the horse you ride define you.

THE FIRST GREAT DEBATE: COWBOYS VERSUS FOX HUNTERS

The show horse world recognizes four seats, or riding styles: Western (also called reining seat or stock seat), hunter seat (commonly called hunt seat), dressage, and saddle seat.

In the real world your choice is much simpler. You can be a cowboy or you can ride English, a category that includes the other three seats. Horse people will instantly recognize who you are, a cowboy or a fox hunter—or who you want to be—just by looking at your saddle. Which one do *you* want to be?

Our Heros Have Always Been Cowboys

Today's Western saddle is a uniquely American invention that was designed for one purpose: to rope cattle. Although the days of the open range are long gone, you can still find cowboys who rope cattle, and the saddles they use attest to that fact.

Form follows function: In the frontier days, every scrap of saddle leather had a function. For the most part that's still true today, even though most people who ride Western will never rope a cow and wouldn't know what to do with it if they caught one. All Western saddles have a horn, because the first thing a cowboy does after roping a cow is dally (wrap) the other end of

A New Mexican cowboy riding a Morgan mare. Morgans are generally considered an "English" breed. (Photo courtesy of the American Morgan Horse Association)

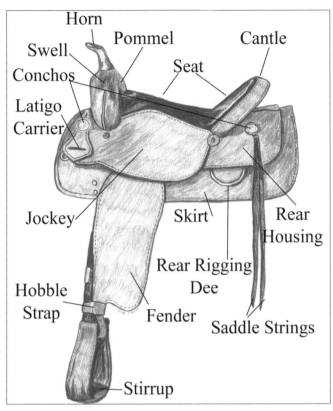

A Western saddle—what that thingamajig is called and where to find it. (Drawing by Gina Cresse)

his braided rawhide *reata* around the horn (unless he's using a rope, which is fastened to the horn). If you browse through tack catalogues, you'll see two measurements for the horn. The catalogue I'm looking at as I write shows a "trail and pleasure" saddle that has a 3¼ inch horn with a diameter of 1⅞ inches. The first measurement tells you how high the horn is. On roping saddles, the horn is much sturdier—usually 3¾ inches high and 3 inches wide—to make sure it stays on the saddle when half a ton of steer hits the other end of the cowboy's rope, or *reata.*

Saddles designed for pleasure and trail have lower, smaller horns. They're mainly designed to give you something to hang on to as you mount your horse. Please note that once you're in the saddle, grabbing the horn is only for emergencies. Once the emergency is over, you're expected to let go. If you trail ride clutching the reins in one hand and your saddle horn in the other, other riders will laugh at you. Just so you know.

- On either side of the horn are immovable leather swells that help you stay put. Most saddles have a suede seat (and in this case, *seat* means where you park your rear end) to make you feel even more secure, since smooth leather can be slippery.
- At the rear of the seat is the cantle. Roping saddles usually have a 4-inch cantle for fast dismounts. Pleasure and trail saddles have higher cantles. Again, the objective is to keep you securely and comfortably in place.

- All Western saddles have thick leather fenders that end in wide, heavy stirrups. They're wide on purpose, to keep you from accidentally sliding your foot completely through the stirrup.

- Some old-time Western saddles have only one cinch, which you will probably have to lift up the fender to find. Modern saddles have two cinches, in other words, full double rigging. The front cinch is usually a wool/synthetic blend that you fasten to the billets on the right side (or off side) of the saddle. The rear cinch is leather, even on pleasure and trail saddles. Its original function was to keep the back end of the saddle from lifting up when the steer hit the rope. Most riders leave both cinches attached to the off-side of the saddle; it makes saddling your horse a lot easier.

- Western saddles weigh about forty pounds. They're much heavier than English saddles because the leather is thicker and sturdier, and the tree of a Western saddle—which determines its size and shape—is bigger and heavier than the tree of an English saddle. Originally, saddle makers used wood for the tree. Most modern saddle trees are synthetic.

- While you can buy a Western saddle for comparatively little money (pound for pound, English saddles are much more expensive) every extra raises the price. A simple leather saddle carries the lowest price tag. Once you get into tooling—designs stamped into the swells, fenders, and skirts—the price goes up. German silver conchos, which are small metal decorations on the skirt, also raise the price—even though "German silver" isn't real silver and it's not imported from Germany. (It's an alloy composed of nickel, copper, and zinc.) If the saddle is custom-made and handtooled, the price will go *way* up. And once you start looking at custom-made, handtooled parade saddles detailed with real silver, your only limit is the one on your credit card.

Synthetic cowboys: If you like the whole-body security of a Western saddle but don't like dragging forty pounds of wood and leather from the tackroom and slinging it over your horse's back, lightweight saddles made entirely of various space-age synthetics are becoming more and more popular. From a distance, these twenty-pound saddles look exactly like their all-leather counterparts.

Ride 'em Cowboy: the Advantages

Many people, especially if they haven't ridden for a while, prefer Western because the sheer physical bulk of the saddle makes them feel safe.

Being John Wayne: The cowboy image itself is a powerful draw. The glory days of the long cattle drives, when the cowboy was king of the West, lasted less than thirty-five years—from 1865, the end of the Civil War, to the turn of the century. Once Joseph Glidden patented barbed wire (called the Devil's fence), in 1874, the open range began to disappear. So did the cowboys. The appeal of a Western saddle is similar to the appeal of a mustang—a way to participate, in your imagination, in one of the most colorful eras of American history.

The practical saddle: Today's Western saddle is almost as functional as its Old West counterpart. Most pleasure saddles have saddle strings, two on either side of the horn and two more on either side of the cantle. If you plan to picnic on the trail, sling your horse's halter and leadrope over the horn, tie your canteen to the saddle strings on one side of the horn and your lunch on the other. Hint: try this at home first. Some horses don't like being swatted on the shoulder at every stride, and because they don't know what's swatting them, they might try to buck it off.

If you find you like trail riding well enough to go on an overnight ride, you can use the rear saddle strings to tie your sleeping bag behind the cantle. (Read Chapter 12 before you set out.)

The Disadvantages

Bad backs: As comfortable as they are to sit in, Western saddles do have their drawbacks. I've already discussed their weight. Another disadvantage: most modern saddles feature a Cheyenne roll, a cantle that angles straight up from the deepest part of the seat and is outlined by a flat, decorated rim. If you have back problems, a Cheyenne roll can aggravate them because the angle causes most people to roll their hips *behind* them instead of *under* them. Big tack stores and some catalogues carry a few old-fashioned saddles without a Cheyenne roll. These saddles also have deep seats, but the angle is different and the cantle has a curved, half-moon shape that cups your rear end very securely.

Not exactly close contact: The limited amount of contact you have with your horse is another drawback. In this sense *contact* doesn't mean sending him postcards when you're on vacation. It means how much of your horse you can feel between your thighs and under your seatbones. Western saddles have several layers of leather between you and your horse—and then there's the saddle pad, which goes on under the saddle. When you ride, can you feel, through your seat and legs, how the horse is moving? Not very well. Although a few Western saddle makers now market a close-contact saddle, even some die-hard cowboys riders agree that the only *real* close-contact saddle is an English one.

Oops: What happens if you're trail riding and come to a shallow creek or other obstacle? When I rode Western, I owned a big black Quarter Horse/Thoroughbred cross named Bachelor. One day when we were trail riding we came to a dead tree that had fallen across the trail. Bachelor was a leggy 16½ hands, and I thought he would simply step over it.

Wrong. One second I was on *this* side of the dead tree. The next second I was on the *other* side—sitting on Bachelor's neck. He had jumped from a standstill; luckily for me, he had bumped me off his back far enough that I slid right over the horn. If you're a guy and that happens, you might not be so lucky.

How to Measure a Western Saddle

A correctly fitted saddle is necessary for your horse's health and safety, and for the comfort of you both.

Your horse: It's important that the bars of the tree that span your horse's back fit properly. The widest bars (they're almost horizontal) are *full Quarter Horse.* Other trees have *semi-Quarter Horse* bars, which have a steeper slope.

Bachelor, my crossover horse from Western to dressage, investigating scary sights at a construction site. (Photo by Anne Steinbach, courtesy of Western Horseman*)*

You: Most Western saddles have a fourteen- to seventeen-inch seat (the size should be on the price tag). If the salesperson knows his (or her) job, he'll take a good look at you—your general build, weight, and the length of your legs—and suggest a size. Pick out a few saddles in that size and in a price range you can afford and ask to sit in them. If you feel cramped, the saddle—more specifically the *seat* of the saddle—is too small. If you could fit a week's worth of groceries between you and the horn, the saddle is too big.

- With a deposit, most tack stores will let you take the saddle home to road test it on your horse before you agree to buy it. If you order from a catalogue, make sure you know what their return policy is.
- Since the salesperson might be the only employee and might be helping other customers, go shopping with a tape measure in case *you* have to figure out what size you need. Start at the front of the seat and measure it straight across to the midpoint of the cantle. There's an empty space between the swells and the front of the seat. Start measuring *past* that space, where the seat actually begins, and keep the tape measure straight. Do not measure from the base of the swells, and do not measure the dip in the seat. Don't measure the Cheyenne roll, either.

My recommendation: All Western saddles have a horn, cantle, and fenders, and fall into one of the following categories: trail and pleasure, barrel racing, roping, or reining. Even if the inner you is a cowboy, you'll probably spend most of your time on the trail. Choose the pleasure or trail saddle.

For more information about Western saddles and how to ride cowboy-style, see Appendix II.

Shall We Fox Hunt?

The English saddle as we know it today was invented by the British in order to hunt foxes. On a hunt you and your horse follow the hounds, which follow the fox. If an obstacle stands in your way—a fence, a hedge, a stream—you jump it. If you decide not to, you have the option of going around it. But you're not *herding* the fox, and you seldom ride in conditions that cowboys face on a daily basis (ravines, rock outcroppings, dense, low-growing brush, etc.). In other words, you don't need a saddle to prop you up and keep you there while your horse navigates rough terrain. You need a saddle you can balance yourself on and allows you to take a jump that looks inviting.

Although an English saddle doesn't have a horn, it does have a raised pommel that keeps you from sliding too far forward. Park (or saddle seat) saddles traditionally have a flat pommel with a notch in it. These cutback saddles can accommodate any horse's withers, no matter how high or pronounced. The dressage saddle I use is also a cutback saddle.

Hunt seat and dressage saddles have pronounced cantles, which are designed, like Western cantles, to keep you from sliding back. Instead of fenders, English saddles have narrow stirrup leathers; instead of stirrups, they have stirrup irons. If you ride English you use a leather girth instead of a cinch, with buckles on both ends that are sometimes connected to

A fox hunter in training. This poised young rider awaits her turn in the show ring.

Gina Cresse on Buster, her Appaloosa gelding. Another crossover— Appaloosas are generally considered cowgirl horses. (Photo by J. LeRoy Weathers)

stretchy material (sewn directly to the leather) that provides additional "give" and makes life a little more pleasant for your horse.

Riding English: The Advantages

No matter what kind of saddle you use, you should be able to balance yourself without depending on the saddle to do it for you. Suppose you're out riding when a plastic bag blows across the trail. What happens next? Most horses will shy, especially if they're young or don't have much trail experience. Where does that leave you? Unless you have a good seat, it leaves you sitting in the dirt feeling stupid—because you were riding with your feet in front of your rear end instead of under it. When your horse shied, you fell off.

Close to you: Although riding English may or may not require better balance than riding Western—a debate that has been going on for years—an English saddle definitely allows you more contact with the horse. As a result, you can influence your horse very subtly by using your legs, seatbones, and other natural aids.

For many people, women in particular, the main advantage of an English saddle is how little it weighs. Compared to the thirty- to fifty-pound heft of a Western saddle, English saddles weigh a mere thirteen to seventeen pounds. Synthetic saddles, which weigh even less, are tremendously popular among trail riders on the East Coast.

Follow that fox: If you're trail riding and your horse decides to jump a stream or a tree across the trail, you won't mutilate yourself on the horn when you land.

Spare parts: If Western saddles are practical, English saddles are stripped nearly to the tree, which is another way of saying that an English saddle has more replaceable parts than a Western saddle. There's the saddle itself, and the girth, stirrup leathers, and stirrup irons are sold separately. The rubber stirrup pads inserted into the irons (also sold separately) "grab" the sole of your boot and keep your foot positioned correctly. The only replacement parts I've seen in tack stores for a Western saddle are stirrups and the front and rear cinches.

The Disadvantages

The only real disadvantage of an English saddle is that it resembles a pancake with a dent in the middle. The dent is the seat. If you're insecure about your riding ability, you'll probably feel safer in a Western saddle.

The Aussie Alternative

Although not officially recognized as a separate "seat," Australian saddles have become very popular among trail riders because they offer the best of both worlds. They're sturdier and

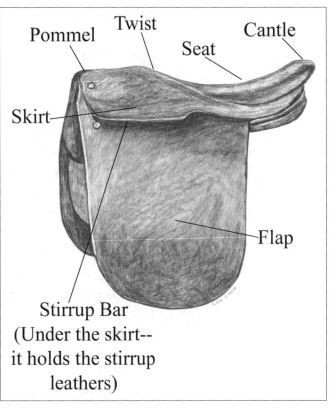

A park saddle, one of the three English saddles, broken down part by part. You can see why they're called "flat" saddles. (Drawing by Gina Cresse)

Pommel Twist Seat Cantle
Skirt
Flap
Stirrup Bar (Under the skirt-- it holds the stirrup leathers)

offer the rider more support than an English saddle, but they're not as heavy as a Western saddle. Some have a horn and swells, others do not. Still others have an elevated pommel similar to the one on an English saddle, except it's open front and back to form a handle. A pommel like this is useful for most of the same reason a horn is useful, but it has none of the horn's drawbacks.

How to Measure an English Saddle

As with a Western saddle, consider your own size and build as well as your horse's conformation. Saddles for adult riders start at 16½ inches and progress by half-inches to an 18-inch seat. To measure an English saddle, measure from the rivet (there's one on either side of the pommel) to the center of the cantle.

■ English saddles also have a tree that determines the width of the seat. If you plan to buy a warmblood or a big, stocky Quarter Horse, you want a wide. If you plan to buy anything else, you want a regular.

Hunt Seat

Of the three English seats, hunt seat is the most popular. This saddle is sometimes referred to as a forward seat saddle because of the rider's position as she (or he) takes a jump. To see an extreme example of a forward seat, watch a horse race. The jockey crouches directly over the horse's center of gravity (his withers) so that nothing about her position interferes with how the horse moves. For more information about hunt seat, see Appendix II.

Dressage

Because dressage requires you to ride with a long, nearly straight leg, the flaps drop in a nearly vertical line from the pommel to the stirrup irons. Since it's also important to ride with a deep seat, the cantle of a dressage saddle is more elevated than the cantle of a hunt-seat saddle.

Some expensive dressage saddles are so well padded that the rider's legs might as well be glued in place: it's impossible to ride in anything *but* the correct position. If you spend a lot of time in the show ring, don't use the same saddle to trail ride. There's no way to comfortably shorten your stirrups, and why risk banging up your expensive show saddle when you can bang up a cheap one just as easily? Buy a second saddle and shorten your stirrups so you won't lose them, which is easy to do riding over uneven terrain. For more information about riding dressage, see Appendix II.

Saddle Seat

American Saddlebreds, Standardbreds (also known as roadsters or road horses), Arabians, Morgans, Tennessee Walkers, Welsh ponies, and occasionally Andalusians and Friesians— collectively called show horses—compete in a barely-there park saddle with no saddle pad. The reason for riding such a low-profile saddle is to show off the horse's high knee and hock action.

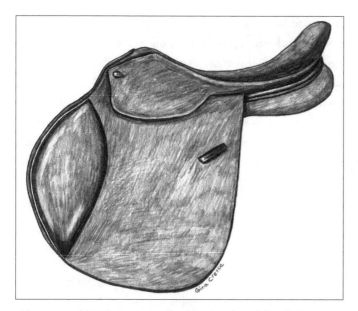

A hunt seat saddle. The most versatile of the three flat saddles, they're most "English" trail riders' first choice. (Drawing by Gina Cresse)

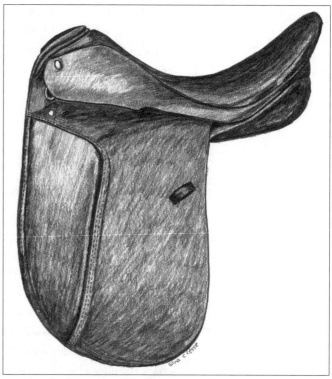

A dressage saddle. (Drawing by Gina Cresse)

In the show ring, saddle seat riders dress in dark suits so they don't distract the judge's eye from what's important: their horse's animation. Riders who show in roadster under saddle classes wear racing silks, like jockeys.

Because a park saddle's primary function is to highlight the horse's performance, it has very little padding. If you own a show horse and show from time to time, replace your saddle with a more comfortable one (anything that has padding) when you hit the trail. Be sure to put a saddle pad on first; it's easier on your horse's back and *it* gets dirty instead of your saddle. And shorten your stirrups. For more information about riding saddle seat, see Appendix II.

Imported or American-Made?

Since horse care isn't cheap, you will probably be tempted to cut corners at some point. Don't cut this particular corner. Good tack, Western or English, will literally last you a lifetime. I still ride a French-made dressage saddle with minimal padding that I bought in 1978 and have used on four of my own horses, including Prim and Sinjun, as well as numerous leased and lesson horses. I've replaced the girth and stirrup leathers many times and the stirrup irons twice. But I repaired the saddle only once, five years ago, when the stitching around the gullet (the underside of the pommel) pulled apart. I took it to a Western saddle maker who told me, "This is a beautifully made saddle and you've taken good care of it. It will outlive you." He replaced the original hand-stitched flax with hand-stitched synthetic thread that he described as "industrial-strength dental floss."

There are several good American saddle makers, although not all tack stores carry their products. Shop around. Buying imported tack isn't a problem as long as it was imported from England, Ireland, Germany, Italy, or France. It's just more expensive. You should be able to find the country of origin on any saddle, including one you buy through a catalogue. If it was made in England, the description will say that. But half the tack in catalogues is simply described as "imported." Before you place your order, find out where the saddle was imported *from*. If you can't get that information—or if the answer is Korea, Japan, India, or someplace in Latin America—don't buy it. Be especially wary if the price is so low it seems too good to be true.

If a Western saddle says "imported," keep looking. We *invented* the Western saddle, remember?

New versus Used

If you can't afford a high-quality new saddle, there's nothing wrong with buying a high-quality used saddle. In fact, I'd recommend it over buying a cheap import. It will last longer.

Test that tree: If you're looking at used saddles, make *sure* the tree is intact. A broken tree isn't always obvious. If the horse fell with his rider, the tree might have split even though both horse and rider walked away unhurt. Since a saddle that's out of alignment can cause back problems for both you and your horse, some owners try to sell the saddle without revealing that the tree is broken.

You don't want a saddle with a broken tree any more than the person who's trying to get rid of it does. Reputable tack stores won't accept a saddle with a broken tree for resale unless they do so by mistake. (As with any business, tack stores depend on satisfied customers who keep coming back.) Turn an English saddle upside down with your palms against the flaps so you can both feel and see the tree. Try to squeeze the flaps together with your hands. If the tree is intact, you shouldn't be able to. But a saddle with a broken tree will bend, and you can often see (and hear) where the break is. A Western saddle with a broken tree is harder to detect because of all that leather, but you test it the same way.

Decide on a size: The best way to buy a used saddle is to sit in a few new ones and see what size and style you like best. Once you've narrowed your choices down—you've measured the seat and know what size tree your horse needs—visit a tack store with a wide selection of used saddles. When you find one you like, check out the tree. Then look for the weak points of the saddle itself—the areas with the most wear, especially around buckles. Are the stirrup leathers or the billets so worn and cracked they look ready to break? Look at the stitching; can you see loose threads? Can you pull them out? How big are the stitches? The saddle will last longer if the stitches are small and close together.

Trail test it: Once you decide on a saddle, take it home and introduce it to your horse. Hand-walk him or longe him to see what he thinks about it. If he pins his ears and seems reluctant to move, the saddle is probably pinching him. But if his ears are forward and he looks happy and alert, mount him and slide your hand under the pommel. You should be able to fit at least two fingers, one on top of the other, between the pommel and your horse's withers. Your next step is to ride him in an enclosed area. Do you feel anything shift beneath you even though the horse is just walking?

If you answered no and your horse has no objections, ride your horse fifteen or twenty minutes, hard enough that he sweats. Before you dismount, see if you can still fit two fingers between his withers and the pommel. If you can't, the tree may be broken. An intact saddle shouldn't settle as you ride.

Remove the saddle and saddle pad. Check your horse's withers first; you shouldn't see rub marks, pink skin, or loose hair. If you do, the tree is too narrow (or too wide) or your saddle pad was too tight. The next time you ride, make sure the saddle pad doesn't press against the horse's withers. Since the saddle should never rest directly on your horse's spine (it should rest on the muscles on either side of his spine), his sides should be sweaty, but you should see a dry line running the length of his backbone.

Your comfort: Consider yourself, too. Did you feel cramped in the saddle? If so, it's probably too small. Did you feel you had to lean forward or back in order to sit up straight? Either the saddle is too big for you or the bars are too narrow for your horse, which may cause the cantle to tilt up.

A poorly fitted saddle can give you physical aches and pains and cause behavioral problems in your horse—such as running around to the other side of the hitching rail as soon as he sees you carry your saddle out of the tackroom. As I said earlier, buy the horse first. *Then* buy the saddle. That way you'll know your saddle fits both of you.

■ If the saddle passed all the tests, buy it—even if it has superficial blemishes. Dry, stiff leather, for example, is acceptable as long as it's not cracked. A good slathering of pure neatsfoot oil, preferably heated, will soften up dry saddles.

My recommendation: If you decide to join the landed gentry and ride English, look for an all-purpose saddle. An offshoot of the hunt-seat saddle, an all-purpose saddle is the most versatile of the three English saddles because it has longer flaps than a hunt-seat saddle, less padding in the knee area, and the seat is a little deeper. It's a comfortable saddle that lets you balance yourself so your horse *could* jump a stream or other obstacle (some owners like to set up jumps in their backyard) without leaving you behind. For information about buying saddles and tack over the Internet, see Appendix II.

Bridle Styles

Bridles come in many diverse sizes and styles. Again, buy the horse before you buy either the bridle or the bit. Different horses have different needs.

Some riders have no qualms about riding in a Western saddle using an English bridle with rhinestones on the browband (a recent trend in dressage circles). The purists insist that if you ride English, you use English accessories—but hold the rhinestones, please. If you buy a horse accustomed to being ridden in a double bridle—a former show horse, for example, or an upper-level dressage horse too old to be competitive—you'll probably want to replace the bridle with a headstall designed for a single bit. As long as your main interest is trail riding and the horse responds to either the snaffle *or* the curb, there's no reason to complicate your life with two reins. You'll probably need a different snaffle though, because the one in a double bridle is a very thin snaffle that wasn't designed to be used alone.

Western wear: Although a Western saddle has more parts than an English saddle, the reverse is true when it comes to bridles. You need only two parts: a headstall to keep the bit in your horse's mouth, and reins.

- Western headstalls come in two sizes: horse or pony. Since both cheek pieces are adjustable, a horse size will fit almost any adult horse. Some headstalls are composed of a single piece of leather with a lopsided hole on the top for one of your horse's ears. These are split-ear or one-ear headstalls. Others have a leather loop that slides from one side of the crownpiece to the other; in other words, *you* decide which ear you want to put through it. These are sliding-ear headstalls.

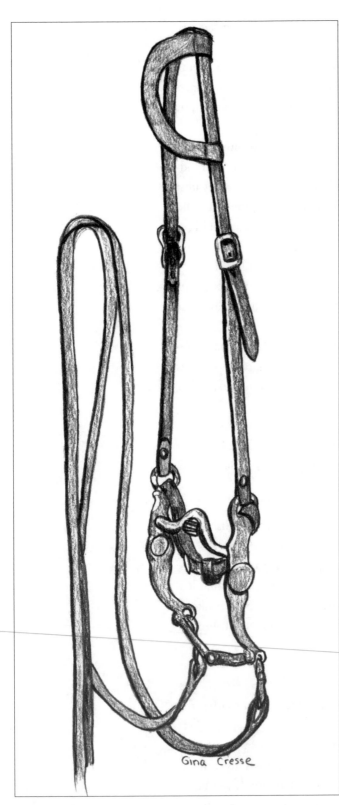

A Western bridle stripped to the essentials: headstall, bit, and reins. (Drawing by Gina Cresse)

How a Western bridle should fit a horse. (Drawing by Gina Cresse)

- Western headstalls that lack ear holes sometimes have throatlatches, but not always. Since Western riders traditionally favor a curb bit, designed to hang vertically in the horse's mouth, nothing happens until you pull on the reins—that is, the port doesn't come in contact with the roof of the horse's mouth, and the curb chain doesn't tighten under his jaw. Correctly positioned, the curb is usually heavy enough to keep the headstall on without a throatlatch.

- Western bridles sometimes have browbands. Their main purpose is to keep the cheekpieces away from one another and prevent the headstall from sliding off.

- With the exception of a mechanical hackamore, Western bridles rarely have nosebands. Since a noseband's primary function is to keep the horse's mouth closed, cowboys outside the show ring have little use for them. Unless they're traditionalists who start a horse using a bosal and finish him so he carries a spade bit, they don't care if their horse's mouth gapes.

- The reins are attached to the bit by Chicago screws (which can very easily unscrew and fall out), tie ends (leather lacing tied into a knot), or double-ended snaps. Since the headstall and reins are usually sold separately, stay away from split reins held together by a keeper, a small leather square big enough to "keep" the reins together. The advantage of split reins is that you can shorten or lengthen them by sliding the

A poised young Western rider. Her horse's bridle has a throatlatch and browband, but no noseband. Note the Cheyenne roll on the cantle.

An English bridle with a raised leather browband and noseband. (Drawing by Gina Cresse)

keeper forward or back. The disadvantage is that the keeper often slides off completely, and not because you wanted it to. As a result, you may have just lost a rein.

■ Other reins are joined before they reach your hand and are called romals. A romal has two advantages. One, you can't lose a rein; you're only holding one piece of leather (Most romals are made of braided rawhide). Two, you can use the romal as a quirt. At the end of the joined rein are two leather straps called *slappers*, and if you slap them against your palm, you'll know why. The noise itself works on most horses as well as actual contact.

■ Synthetic Western headstalls come in a variety of colors and patterns; most have a browband and throatlatch but no noseband. The ones made of braided nylon rope have round, braided reins. Wear gloves to minimize rope burn.

My recommendation: I've heard about horses in shows who "lost" their bridles because they shook their head to get rid of a fly. Because the bridle didn't have a throatlatch, it slid completely off. Unless you want this to happen to you on the trail—especially if your horse tends to jump off his feet every time something rustles in the underbrush—buy a bridle with a throatlatch and a romal.

English bridles: In addition to the headstall itself, an English bridle has a browband, noseband, and a throatlatch. All are available in flat or raised leather. Most come in four sizes: pony, cob (which fits horses with small heads), horse, and Quarter Horse.

■ Specialty nosebands. If your horse likes to slide his tongue over the bit—easy to do if the bit is a snaffle—buy a figure-eight (sometimes called a crossed) noseband, a flash noseband, or a dropped noseband. All three prevent the horse from opening his mouth, and if he can't open his mouth, he can't get his tongue over the bit (some horses' favorite evasion). A horse wearing a plain, flat leather cavesson can open his mouth wide enough to snack on grass or bushes, but do you want him to? Buy one of the specialized nosebands. If you trail ride and your horse likes to nip the pony in front of him because the pony isn't going fast enough, a specialty noseband is a must.

■ Many English riders like laced or braided reins because they don't slip. They're particularly useful if your horse sweats heavily on the neck or you get caught in an unexpected downpour. These reins evolved from the hunt and show ring, not trail riding. Although they look good, braided reins collect dirt and are hard to clean. Laced reins are easier to clean, but the lacing is made of thin leather that breaks easily.

The drawback to both types is that they *won't* slip, which makes it hard to lengthen your reins and then get them back when you want more contact. If you ride with smooth leather reins, you can give your horse his head and let him find his own balance by letting the reins slip through your fingers. You get the reins back the same way, by spreading your hands and letting the reins slip through your fingers until you have the contact you want—even if you ride one-handed.

All English reins fasten with a buckle, so you don't have to worry about losing them.

■ On the trail I usually ride with the reins completely slack—called riding *on the buckle*. By doing so, I give Prim her head and let her carry herself and choose her own footing.

Most recreational riders, Western and English, prefer to ride with a little slack in the reins because it's more comfortable for the horse. A loose rein tells him that trail riding is fun—something he can look forward to. If you try to keep his head and neck in correct hunt-seat position, or if you've been reading dressage books that tell you your horse should be *on the bit* at all times, what does your horse have to look forward to? Nothing. You might as well be doing ring work. If you want your horse to think trail riding is fun, let *him* choose the head and neck position he's comfortable with.

Riding with a loose rein also tells your horse, especially if he's flighty or high-strung, that you won't keep him boxed between your legs and hands with every stride, that you trust him enough to give him his head. Once he knows that, he's more apt to relax and trust you.

But if you'd feel safer with more contact, shorten your reins until you can just feel his mouth.

My recommendation: Pay the money for a high-quality American-made bridle or one imported from England or Europe; they last so long that they pay for themselves many times over. The only time I bought a cheap import, it looked terrific for about a month—then the stitching pulled apart. (The thread is usually bright red or yellow cotton.) Since the last thing I wanted was a bridle that would unravel while I was off-roading, I had it repaired. A month after that, the throatlatch crumbled like wet particle board, which I suspect it was. In the end, I paid more to buy and repair that "bargain" bridle than I would have if I'd bought a reputable name brand in the first place. Choose one of the tight-fitting nosebands, so your horse won't be tempted to snack while you ride, and smooth reins.

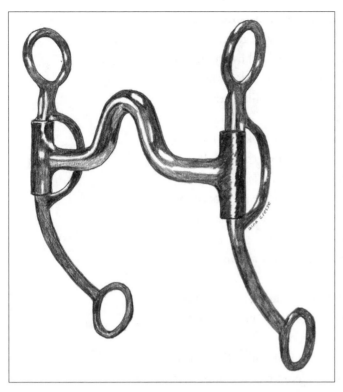

A curb bit with a mild port and short, curved shanks sometimes called a grazing bit. (Drawing by Gina Cresse)

Emily Louise the donkey wearing a Western headstall and a curb bit over her halter.

Bits and Pieces

Use the mildest bit your horse will respect. There's no sense in putting five pounds of hardware in his mouth if all you need is a grazing bit or a smooth, straight snaffle. Unless you have to influence every step your horse takes during a trail ride—and I just explained why that's not a good idea—there's no reason to use anything stronger.

Cowboy bits: Most Western riders use a curb. The mouthpiece is straight and has an upside-down U called a port that lies vertically over the horse's tongue when the reins are slack. The higher the port, the more severe the bit.

■ The same is true of shanks, the parts of the bit you can see on either side of the horse's mouth when he's bridled. (Attach the headstall to the top ring of the shank and the reins to the bottom ring.) A curb bit is used either with a curb chain or a leather strap; if you use a chain, make sure the links lie flat. (Attach the chain or strap to the top ring of the shank and fasten it under the horse's chin.)

If the horse is wearing a curb with a high port, long shanks, and a curb chain, you exert a tremendous amount of pressure on the horse's tongue, bars, the roof of his mouth, his lower jaw, and his poll (behind his ears, where the crownpiece of the bridle rests) every time you pull back on the reins.

Some curbs are called grazing bits. These have low ports and short, curved shanks that allow the horse to graze while the bit is in his mouth.

Pieces: Many Western riders use a breastcollar; they "dress up" a horse and are very practical if you ride in hilly terrain where your saddle might slip.

■ Some riders also like a running martingale, especially with young horses, to remind them where their head ought to be. The best martingales are leather with surgical rubber tubing, sometimes called training forks. Each fork ends in a metal loop. The reins pass through the metal loop so the horse teaches himself that if he flings his head, he'll bump his mouth against the bit. (Some English trainers make their own side reins using surgical rubber tubing, which works on the same principle; see Chapter 16.)

■ A tie-down (English riders call this item a standing martingale) is a simple leather strap attached from the noseband to the cinch that prevents the horse from raising his head above a certain point.

Fox hunter bits: English riders prefer snaffles because they're very mild, even in the hands of an inexperienced rider. Some like a straight bar snaffle, others prefer a jointed one.

■ If you pull back on the reins of a horse wearing a straight bar snaffle, you're pulling a piece of metal over his tongue until it encounters the corners of his mouth. In other words, there's a direct relationship between how hard you pull and how far the bit moves. But if you use a jointed snaffle and pull back, the joint has a slight nutcracker effect on the horse's tongue. As a result, you don't have to pull quite so hard. Like all bits, a snaffle also exerts pressure on the horse's lips. If you look inside your horse's mouth while he's wearing a bit, you'll see that the bit rests on the fold of his lower lip as well as on his tongue and bars.

If you want to see how a bit acts, fasten it to a headstall and a set of reins. Hang the headstall from some vertical object—a post or a doorknob, for example—and pull on the reins. The bit will move the same way in your horse's mouth.

■ Quarter Horses between the ages of two and five can show in certain classes wearing either a snaffle bit or a hackamore. No curbs. But more and more Western riders are using snaffles outside the show ring for the same reason English riders do: they're easy on a horse's mouth.

■ English riders start most of their young horses in a snaffle bit. Because most horses respond to it so well, they never wear any other kind. Prim was started in a very fat, smooth, jointed rubber snaffle. When she got too strong in it, I replaced it with a smooth, jointed eggbutt snaffle that I still use. (No, I don't know why it's called an eggbutt and not a fixed-ring snaffle.)

■ Loose-ring snaffles are popular with some riders because the horse can play with the bit by rolling it around in his mouth, which relaxes his jaws. I don't like them because they're apt to pinch the corners of his mouth, and if you pull too hard on one rein, the

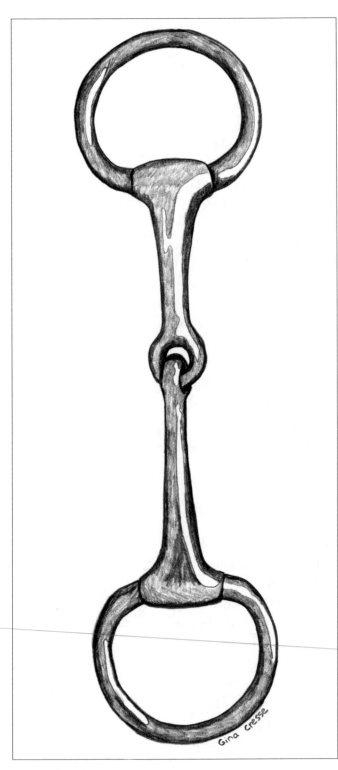

An eggbutt snaffle. (Drawing by Gina Cresse)

snaffle will slide completely through the horse's mouth, no matter how big the rings are. I know; I've done it.

- I like a copper mouthpiece because it helps a horse salivate. Whether he has a bit in his mouth or not, a relaxed horse rolls his tongue over his teeth, opens and closes his mouth, sucks on the inside of his lips, and makes slurping noises. (If you're not sure what I'm talking about, watch your horse at the end of a ride after you remove his bridle.) Because the copper encourages a horse to mouth the bit, he'll relax sooner. A horse with a wet mouth is also more responsive to your hands.

- All snaffles exert some pressure on the sides of the horse's mouth. If your horse is wearing an eggbutt snaffle and you tighten your left rein, the horse will bend his head to the left because you're pulling it in that direction, but also because the fixed ring of the eggbutt exerts pressure on the *right* side of his mouth. If you want more power steering, try a D-ring or a full-cheek snaffle.

How to measure a bit: Lay it flat and measure the mouthpiece. A 5-inch bit will fit most horses that take a cob or a horse-sized headstall. Most snaffles are available in 4½ to 6 inches.

My recommendation: I've ridden all my horses in a jointed snaffle, even Bachelor, who was started in a bosal (I'll explain in a minute). If you use a snaffle and ride Western, *please* buy a bridle with a throatlatch to make sure the bridle stays put.

If you buy a horse and the owner tells you to use the bit the horse is wearing and no other, ask why. If the answer makes sense, follow the owner's advice. Once you and your horse get to know each other, you might want to experiment to see if he'll respond to a milder bit.

Other Pieces

Both Western and English riders use hackamores with horses that can't (because of tongue or dental problems) or won't (because of psychological problems) tolerate a bit.

- There are two types of hackamores. One is a bosal, a teardrop-shaped oval made of rawhide that fits over the horse's nose and is held in place by a single piece of leather that slides behind his ears. A rope called a *mecate* (sometimes made from braided horse hair) is wrapped through, over, and under the point of the teardrop to form a long loop (the reins) and a loose end (the leadrope). The other end forms a tassel under the horse's chin.

A bosal acts on both sides of the horse's face, primarily his lower jaw. Years ago, California *vaqueros*, or cowboys, started all their young horses in a bosal to teach them the basics of sliding stops, rollbacks on their haunches, etc. without hurting their mouths. Once the horse knew what he was doing, he graduated to a "straight up" spade bit. Like any curb, a spade hangs vertically in the horse's mouth; it's a heavy bit with a high, solid port and so much potential for misuse that it's rarely seen anymore. Good reinsmen can still perform near-miracles with a bosal, although their finished horses now usually wear a grazing bit.

A braided rawhide bosal with a mecate. (Drawing by Gina Cresse)

- The second type of hackamore, commonly called a mechanical hackamore or a curb hackamore, has shanks, a curb chain or strap, and a reinforced noseband. The hackamore exerts pressure on the horse's nose (from the noseband and shanks) and lower jaw (from the curb chain). If it has short shanks and a curb strap instead of a chain and is loosely fastened, this type of hackamore can be relatively mild.

A mechanical hackamore also makes bridling easy, since you don't have to coerce your horse into opening his mouth and accepting the bit. If you're young and athletic, you can slide a mechanical hackamore over your horse's head, climb the fence, hop on him bareback, and you're off. Instant gratification. But since steering is a little difficult—although stopping is not—most riders use a mechanical hackamore only if they have to.

VICTORIA'S LITTLE SECRET

Let's talk about underwear.

But first, let's talk about outerwear.

Western Wear

If you ride Western, you probably dress like a cowboy because denim jeans are sturdy, comfortable, and hug your hips. Most riders team their jeans with T-shirts, long-sleeved dress shirts, sweatshirts, and a waist-to-chin zippered windbreaker, depending on the weather. Cowgirls like decorated, form-fitting Western shirts that button or snap up the front, and fringed chaps over form-fitting denim jeans. Don't ride wearing slacks. They'll slide up your legs, crease, and give you road rash you'll never forget.

Most people prefer to ride in boots.

Hats are optional unless you have kids who ride, and one is fourteen or younger. As of this writing, the state of New York, some cities, and most parents require children—whether they ride Western or English—to wear ASTM/SEI-certified headgear (the initials stand for American Society for Testing and Materials/Safety Equipment Institute).

Grownup cowboys seem to think that safety helmets are for kids and sissies, and they wear cowboy hats. So do most cowgirls.

In general, avoid fluttery, loose-fitting clothes. They won't be comfortable, and they might spook your horse.

Grace Arnold enjoys a ride along the shore of the Pacific on Snow Job, her American Saddlebred. (Photo by Avis Girdler)

Dude Duds

People who ride saddle seat generally wear flared riding pants (or jeans) and jodhpur boots (or rubber-soled athletic shoes) when they trail ride. Jod boots are only ankle high because the riding pants are designed to cover them. They're much less expensive than the knee-high leather dress boots favored by other English riders.

Lace-up, ankle-high paddock boots have become very popular lately, especially worn with suede or leather half chaps. Half chaps don't look anything like the chaps cowgirls or bull riders wear. They cover your leg from the heels of your paddock boots to your knees; most fasten with a zipper. Like their knee-high leather counterparts, half chaps protect your legs from the briars and the brambles when you off-road.

The rest of us wear black leather dress boots like the ones motorcycle cops wear, and stretchy, form-fitting breeches (pronounced "britches"). Some boots lace over the upper arch of the foot, which makes them field boots. Since the lacing is adjustable and provides additional give, these boots are easier to pull off than dress boots; for many people field boots are easier to break in and more comfortable to wear.

Some owners, particularly if they plan to ride after they've mucked out and cleaned their horse, like to wear boot covers or rubbers over their riding boots. When they're ready to ride, they peel the boot covers off.

A last-minute yoga stretch before hitting the trail. I'm wearing black leather dress boots because I like black leather dress boots. I ride using a French-made dressage saddle for the same reason. (Photo by Gina Cresse)

English trail riders also wear T-shirts, sweatshirts, and warm windbreakers. Most wear safety helmets—especially the ones disguised to look like black velvet hunt caps.

Work Clothes

Footwear: Steel-toed rubber boots are a must, especially if your horse lives outside and you muck out his corral while it's raining or snowing. Some people worry that if their horse steps on their foot, the steel will bend and squash their toes instead of protecting them. In my opinion there are more important things to worry about—too many backyard-bred horses killed for meat, for instance, or too many humans for the planet to support. If a horse has ever stepped on you when you *weren't* wearing boots, I don't think the possibility of getting your toes squeezed by steel-toed boots will ever cross your mind.

A hint for first-time users: put on two pairs of socks. If you only wear one pair and your boots are slightly large, your socks will slide off your feet before you reach the barn. Pull the second pair over the first pair *and* over your pant legs. That way your socks won't slip and your pant legs will stay cleaner.

Cold weather wear: If you live in snow country, you already know about layering. But if you just moved there from someplace else—someplace warm and sunny, like Atlanta—here are a few tips for keeping warm. (The first winter I spent in New Hampshire, the temperature went down to twenty below zero and stayed there a week. Unless I walked or skied, I couldn't go any place—the transmission of my truck had frozen.) Wear cotton next to your skin for breathability, although some people prefer silk. Others prefer synthetic fabrics. My usual "work" outfit consisted of a cotton tank top, turtle-necked shirt, sweatshirt, ski jacket, and a snug, ear-covering hat. I rode wearing leather gloves—pigskin or deerskin are the warmest and most pliant. If you have cold hands, take a tip from the skiers and layer using pure silk gloves next to your skin.

■ Bachelor didn't live in my backyard in those days (he lived outside, with other horses) so while I would longe or briefly ride him once or twice a week, I didn't spend as much time working outside as I do here in California. If it rains or snows here, I pull on a pair of farmer's striped overalls *over* my denim work pants and pull the second pair of socks over the overalls to do chores. When I scrub Prim's waterer, I wear fuzzy wool gloves inside big yellow dishwashing gloves.

■ When I ride in cold weather and the winds that blow off the surrounding snow-covered mountains pick up, the windchill factor can drop to thirty below. In these conditions, a cotton tank top or T-shirt still goes on first. Then I add a lightweight, long-sleeved, windproof shirt designed for skiers, a vest, and a heavy sweatshirt. Last, I pull on a lightweight, water-repellent riding jacket.

■ I personally want a fleecy scarf around my neck and a fleecy cap to cover my ears.

■ If you ride when it's cold, don't forget to warm your horse's bit before you ask him to wear it.

Back to Underwear

Most men prefer the support of cotton briefs when they ride because boxer shorts slide up and cause blisters. Ladies, wear *cotton* underpants—they breathe and you won't get friction burns. If you wear a bra, make sure it's a sport or athletic bra. They're much more comfortable than the dress-up kind. They're also safer.

A friend of mine—I'll call her "Victoria" for legal reasons—put a Western saddle on her two-year-old colt, led him to the bull ring, and got on him for the first time. She walked and jogged the colt both directions, and the first few minutes were uneventful. But then Victoria asked him to lope. Since young horses aren't sure how to balance themselves with a rider on their back the first few times, she crouched and clucked to get him started.

At this point I should mention that it was summer. Victoria wore jeans, boots, a loose sleeveless shirt that buttoned down the front, and a bra—a plain-Jane bra with elastic between the cups. When Victoria leaned down and clucked, the colt threw in a little crow-hop before getting down to the business. But "business" didn't happen. Instead, Victoria found herself unable to straighten up. The colt—feeling her weight shift when he bucked—panicked.

So did Victoria. Why couldn't she sit up?

Many bucks and bruises later and only partially dressed, she discovered what had happened. A button on her blouse had popped, and when she leaned forward, the saddle horn snagged on the elastic of her bra.

The moral of this story? Don't ride wearing loose-fitting clothes. And if your horse bucks, keep your shirt on.

TACK FOR YOU AND YOUR HORSE—A CHECKLIST

If you currently own a horse or have owned one in the past, you may already have some of these items, particularly a saddle. But if you don't have a saddle (most owners' biggest expense after the horse himself), buy the horse first. The same is true of halters and bridles because they come in so many different sizes.

What follows is a list of necessary items and a brief explanation of why they're necessary. I've discussed most earlier in this chapter. Must-have items are indicated by a check mark.

YOUR HORSE
✓ A halter, either leather or a breakaway halter—one for each horse you own or plan to buy.

✓ A leadrope—one per horse.

An extra leadrope, just in case.

✓ A saddle—one per horse.

✓ Two machine washable saddle pads per horse, so you always have a clean one. Don't reuse a dirty saddle pad; the dirt will chafe your horse's back.

✓ A leather punch. The throatlatch never has enough holes, and neither do your stirrup leathers.

✓ A bridle—one per horse.

An extra set of reins.

✓ A bit—one per horse.

✓ If the bit is a curb, you need either a curb chain or curb strap.

A breastplate, especially if you live in rugged country or plan on doing a lot of off-roading.

✓ A longe whip.

A riding whip.

A small plastic bucket—half fill it with stones or sand to hold your whips upright. In warm weather you can use it as a doorstop.

A mechanical hackamore with a curb chain or curb strap, and reins.

A bosal instead of a headstall.

A *mecate* instead of reins and a leadrope.

Extra Chicago screws.

Extra double-ended snaps.

✓ Fly spray.

✓ A fly mask. Fasten it loosely enough so your horse can swallow—you should be able to fit your thumb between his jaw and the mask. Remove it before you halter him and at night.

A blanket, if your horse truly needs one (see Chapter 16).

✓ A clock—like many riders, I prefer not to wear a watch when I ride. But when I get back to the barn it's helpful to know how much time I have left to spend with my horse.

YOU

✓ Gloves to protect your hands. I use one set of gloves for barn work and to groom my horse. When I ride, I wear leather riding gloves.

✓ Tight-fitting riding pants that don't chafe.

✓ Whatever top you feel comfortable wearing.

✓ A safety hat or helmet.

✓ Sunglasses.

✓ A visor, for any outdoor work.

✓ Sun screen.

✓ Fly repellent.

✓ Corn Huskers Lotion. If you live in a dry climate, nothing beats this oil-free hand lotion. No more sticky hands or greasy leather gloves.

✓ Riding boots.

✓ Knee-high, steel-toed rubber work boots when you muck out, to save your "good" riding boots.

✓ Snug cotton underwear.

✓ Snug cotton socks.

✓ A boot jack, to get your boots off, especially if you ride wearing English dress or field boots.

✓ Boot pulls, if you wear dress or field boots. Otherwise you can't get them on.

✓ Plastic grocery bags, if you wear dress or field boots. Use them together with the boot pulls (also useful if you have to improvise a longe whip).

CHAPTER 3

CHOOSE A HORSE

If you already own a horse and keep him at a local boarding stable, you probably can't wait until Moving Day. To you, that means the day your horse moves to your own property, not when *you* move—which is, as we all know, stressful, traumatic, and (if you're a woman) good for about a ten-pound weight loss. Temporarily.

But if you intend to buy a horse, especially if you've never kept one in your backyard before, your biggest challenge will be to keep your objectivity long enough to write a check. You've already made up your mind who you want to be—a cowboy or a fox hunter—and what kind of tack you want. But before you actually buy the tack, and definitely before you start looking for a horse, take some time to think about what kind of horse you want. Do you want a specific breed? A specific color? How big? How old?

By making at least most of these decisions in advance, you can save yourself the emotional pain of buying a horse that isn't suitable for you as a rider, or isn't suitable for pleasure riding on the trail.

Keep this simple truth in mind: buy a horse that fits your personality *and* your ability.

HORSE BREEDS: AN OVERVIEW

Although each individual horse is unique, a few broad generalizations can be made about breeds. If you tend to be nervous and high-strung, you might get along best with an even-tempered, kindly, Golden Retriever sort of horse—a Quarter Horse, Buckskin, Appaloosa, or one of the other Western breeds. These horses tend to be calm and reliable—useful qualities in a trail horse. But if you're the one with the unflappable, easygoing temperament, you might enjoy the challenge of one of the "hotter" breeds like a Thoroughbred, American Saddlebred, or Arabian.

YOU AS A RIDER

Be realistic about your level of ability. People who think they don't need lessons because as kids they could ride "anything with hair" might be in for a surprise. As with any activity, practice makes perfect; if the last time you swung a leg over a horse was ten years ago, you're out of practice. Take lessons, or risk finding yourself aboard a horse you can't control.

While you might enjoy riding a breed of horse you've never tried before, you'll probably feel safer riding what you know. In her book *Riding for Success,* Gayle Lampe, who developed this country's first four-year academic degree program in equestrian science at William Woods University in Fulton, Missouri, put it like this: "Over the years I've taught many good jumper riders who will bravely jump a six-foot fence, but are terrified to ride the safest Saddlebred because he will not flat walk. [Saddlebred show horses are not trained to flat walk.] Their line of reasoning is that if a horse will not flat-foot walk, he surely is not even broke. This goes along with the same line of reasoning that makes hunt seat riders afraid the saddle seat horse is going to rear because his neck is so high, and makes the saddle seat rider fearful that the western horse is going to buck because his head is held so low" (112).

Other riders are perfectly capable of handling a "hot" horse and would enjoy him much more than they would a trustworthy plodder, but they lack confidence in their ability. (For some reason this is particularly true of women.) Lessons will restore your confidence, and if you ride at a big stable, you'll probably have the opportunity to ride several different horses. Who knows—the one you like best might be for sale!

Stay away from barns with only one sour, over-ridden lesson horse. It's not fair to the horse, and the experience might be unpleasant enough to sour you on the entire idea.

Who's Responsible?

No matter what kind of horse you buy, the other bottom line (the first one was money) is, who will take responsibility for this horse?

You're single: If you live by yourself and only plan to buy one horse, the answer is obvious. But it wouldn't hurt to have a short list of neighbors and horse-owning friends you can call on to feed in an emergency—if you get caught in traffic driving home from work, for instance, or get caught in a late-season blizzard.

You're married, no kids: If you're married but don't have children, and only one of you wants a horse, the answer is also obvious: *you* want the horse, *you* take care of it. But if you're a wage earner who commutes, you too will occasionally face delays caused by traffic and weather. Does your spouse like horses well enough to feed for you?

Sit down and talk about it. Some spouses, husbands in particular, don't really like horses. Unless you ask, they probably won't volunteer to do *anything* horse-related. Get a commitment out of them—yes, they will occasionally feed if necessary, or no, they will not. If they won't, draw up a list of neighbors and horse-owning friends and their phone numbers. Make sure the list is in your purse.

You're married with a kid: If you don't fall into either of the previous categories, you have at least one kid—possibly one with purple hair and a nose ring. Since your goal is to ride together as a family, you need three horses.

In this case, a discussion about who's responsible for what becomes a necessity. Make it clear to your teen what you expect of him (or her). And then stick to it.

■ Swapping off is usually the best solution. You feed all three horses in the morning. Your teen mucks out, even if you keep your horses in a field or pasture. Your spouse feeds at night. The schedule rotates every week: now your teen feeds in the morning, your spouse cleans, and you feed at night. The following week your spouse feeds in the morning, you clean, and your teen has night duty.

More than one kid: Here's where life really gets interesting, especially if you have young children.

■ If they're old enough to go to school, include them in the discussion, even though they won't be feeding or mucking out unless they're "helping" you or your spouse. Make sure they understand that under *no* circumstances are they to go into a stall, pipe corral, field—wherever you confine your horses—by themselves. They *must* be accompanied by an adult. Even if you allow them to sit on your horse's back while you lead him around the corral, be sure the kids understand they cannot do this unless they're under direct parental supervision.

■ If they're in the eight to eleven range, give them something to do. Make them responsible for cleaning the tackroom once a week, or helping you feed in the morning before you leave for work and they leave for school. Kids this age are still too young to ride unsupervised, no matter how big they are or how well they ride.

To forestall unauthorized stealth rides, lock the tackroom. Even if your pre-teen whines or begs or throws a tantrum or gives you the sullen treatment, don't back down. Do decide on a specific age: "When you turn twelve [or fourteen—any age you consider realistic], you can ride without one of us being with you." Make sure your teen understands that with the privilege of riding comes the responsibility of taking care of his (or her) horse by including your teen in the rotating chore schedule. Without being obvious about it, check up on him. If one day he gallops his horse all the way home and then pulls the saddle off and turns the horse out—and when you see the horse, the outline of a sweaty saddlepad is still visible—ask him to return the key to the tackroom. He *isn't* old enough to be responsible. Make sure he understands that's why you're taking away his riding solo privileges and give him a review date. If he does his chores faithfully for the next six weeks, for example, you'll allow him to ride by himself again.

PRICEY BUT A PUREBRED

All the horses I mentioned earlier belong to specific breeds. In the world of dogdom, a Golden Retriever is a specific breed—a purebred. When you buy one, you should receive the dog's registration papers. If the owner claims not to have the dog's papers, or won't give them to you, the dog is probably not a purebred. Don't pay purebred prices for an unregistered dog.

And don't pay purebred prices for an unregistered horse. The words *purebred* and *registered* are often used interchangeably, but they have different meanings. If you decide to buy a Quarter Horse and the owner tells you he's registered, ask to see the horse's papers. What you'll usually get is a single sheet of paper stamped by the breed association, but for some reason people still refer to this as a horse's "papers." A horse's registration papers will physically describe him—his coat color, the markings on his face or body, how many white socks or stockings he has, etc. It will give his date of birth (when he was foaled) and track his pedigree. In other words, you can see who he was sired by (who his father is) and who he's "out of" (his dam). Other information usually includes the names of the sire's sire and dam, the names of the dam's sire and dam, and who begat those four horses.

When you buy a registered horse there will be a transfer of ownership form to fill out that must be signed by both parties—the person who currently owns the horse and is legally entitled to sell him, and you, the new owner. If the name of the person you're buying the horse from does not appear on the chain of ownership, ask why. Because there's usually a fee associated with a change of ownership, some owners skip this little formality. If there's a miss-

An afternoon trail ride. Right to left: Raphaella Goodwin on her Quarter Horse mare. Her daughter Ally riding a grade mare. Bringing up the rear is son Chris on Emily Louise, and Brian riding Cowboy Justin, an Appaloosa.

ing link in the chain of ownership but you go ahead and buy the horse anyway, some registries will not allow you to reregister the horse. Other registries will, but only for an additional charge.

Prim is a purebred American Saddlebred, registered with the American Saddlebred Horse Association (ASHA). Her sire and dam are also registered with the ASHA. This registry is closed—in other words, no horse can be registered as an American Saddlebred unless his sire and dam are both registered American Saddlebreds. This fact makes Prim a purebred. A horse with only one American Saddlebred parent, even if the other parent is a registered something else— an Arabian, for example—is not eligible for registration in the American Saddlebred Horse Association because he's not a purebred. But a Saddlebred/Arabian cross *would* be eligible for registration in both the National Show Horse Registry and the International Arabian Horse Association, which registers Half-Arabs. As long as a registry is open, the horses in them are registered but not purebred.

Hallie McEvoy with Juliet, her eight-year-old Thoroughbred. The mare is remarkably calm after her first longeing lesson. (Photo by Thom McEvoy)

I bought Prim because of her eagerness to please and her affectionate nature. Sinjun had a very similar personality; he loved people and was endlessly curious about them. I'm hooked on the breed because I've never ridden horses with smoother gaits. Sitting to Prim's trot is like swinging in a hammock.

Plenty of Purebreds

According to Kathie Luedeke, director of administration of the American Horse Council, the three top Western breeds in order of popularity are Quarter Horses, Paints, and Appaloosas. Even though these breeds are considered "cowboy" horses, plenty of owners ride and show them English. Quarter Horses account for more of the pie chart than any other breed, with 156,199 new horses registered in a single year (2002). There are approximately three times as many Quarter Horses as there are Thoroughbreds, the top English breed. The English runners-up—accurate numbers are hard to come by—are Arabians, Tennessee Walkers, and Standardbreds, although these breeds also "cross over" and do just fine as Western horses.

The American Horse Council lists over a hundred different breed associations, but not all are breed *registries*. Some are associations or clubs. Some breeds have multiple listings. Both Buckskins and Lipizzans, the "dancing" white horses of the Spanish Riding School of Vienna, are represented by two associations.

To find out more about horse breeds, especially if you're in the market for something exotic—a Nonius, for example—look for books on horse breeds. See Appendix II, visit the library, or check the Internet.

Advantages of buying a purebred: The main reason people want a purebred, registered horse is the same reason they want a purebred, registered dog: they know what they're getting. As I said earlier, each horse has his own take on the world (i.e. he is an individual), but most major breeds have been confined to a limited gene pool long enough that you can make some generalities about their disposition, size, and what they do best.

- Quarter Horses are famous for their calm dispositions. Originally bred to herd cattle, they're stocky, muscular horses; most stand around fifteen hands. They're equally famous for their agility and quick bursts of speed.
- Paints and Appaloosas are both discussed in depth later in this chapter.
- Thoroughbreds are famous for being high-strung and fast. A Thoroughbred has less bone density and muscle than a Quarter Horse—his legs and neck are longer and more refined—and most stand 16 to 17 hands. Thoroughbreds were bred for racing and that's what most of them want to do—run. The best candidates for backyard horses are the ones who never make it to the track (too slow) or lose interest in running as soon as another horse passes them. Many trainers and horse dealers specialize in re-educating racing Thoroughbreds into pleasure horses suitable for trail riding.
- Tennessee Walkers and Standardbreds are discussed later in this chapter.

Just Say No to Backyard Breeding

Please do not breed your backyard horse. Most owners don't know enough to select and work with a breeding stallion, or handle a newborn foal or an overly protective dam. If you don't own a stallion but plan to ship your mare to one, ask yourself why. We already have too many horses in this country—more than 50,000 of them end up in European meat markets and restaurants as "the other red meat" every year. If you can't tell a poorly conformed horse from a good one, and you know nothing about genetics but are determined to breed your mare because you just *know* "she wants a baby," you don't know enough. Leave breeding to the responsible professionals who understand what they're doing and why.

Disadvantages of buying a purebred: A registered horse generally costs more than an unregistered one, since the mare owner had to pay a stud fee to breed her (or his) mare to a stallion. Then the owner brings her mare back home and feeds her for eleven months until the foal—a colt, if he's male—is born. For the next two years the owner has two horses to feed until she's able to sell the colt as a three-year-old. Add the stud fee and the cost of additional feed to the time the owner spent starting the colt (getting him used to handling, introducing him to a saddle and bridle, and teaching him the basics of carrying a rider), and translate the time into money. To make a profit, this owner has to put a pretty hefty price tag on her three-year-old—and the price may be more than you're willing to pay.

- But if you're patient and get to know the right people, buying a purebred, registered horse doesn't have to reduce your bank account to a series of zeros. Often professional breeders will sell culls, which are horses deemed unfit for racing or showing or whatever they were bred to do, at bargain prices—just to get them off their account books. If you decide to buy such a horse, ask about his registration papers. Some breeders will hand them over in exchange for more money. Others won't hand them over at all, particularly if the horse is a mare. If they're serious breeders, they don't want their culled mares to pass on an undesirable bloodline or a "nick" between bloodlines that carries unwanted traits. Freer shoulder action (more range of motion), for example, often occurs with bad feet: they're too small, they're crooked, or they're so fragile that the mare has barely enough hoof to hold a shoe on. That's why she was culled in the first place.

Another disadvantage: Open registries accept horses of other breeds. As a result, it's next to impossible to characterize these horses. The Racking Horse Breeders Association of America, for instance, is open to any horse that racks *naturally*. Prim does not rack—she comes from generations of three-gaited horses who walk, trot, and canter. (Although the breed as a whole has a tendency towards lateral gaits, the ability to slow-gait and rack naturally, without training, runs strongly in families.) Prim would not be eligible for registration in the Racking Horse Association, but a natural-gaited part-Thoroughbred (and I knew a part-Thoroughbred who racked) would be eligible. Nearly any horse can be *taught* to rack, but the ones the Racking Horse Association is looking for are natural-gaited horses. Registries like this include horses of all breeds, sizes, colors, conformations, and personality types. The only genetic trait they have in common is their natural ability to rack.

Grade A

A grade horse is the equine equivalent of a mutt and is not registered with any breed, color, or gait-specific registry. Although many people look down their noses at grade horses, their thinking often changes when they find out how much a registered horse costs. Like mutts, grade horses tend to be easy keepers, require minimal vet care, and make sensible trail horses.

Advantages: The main reason to buy a grade horse is cost. In the not-so-distant past you could buy a sound, good-thinking, good-looking grade horse for $200. Those bargain horses are still out there, but now they sell for around $1,200—slightly under the price you can expect to pay for a cull. In addition, a cull might not have made the cut not because of any physical or genetic abnormality, but because he's a head case.

Disadvantages: What you see is what you get. You can't rely on the horse's registration papers to tell you anything about his breeding or disposition. And if you buy a green-broke grade horse, by the time he matures, he might not look the way he did when you bought him.

Horses of Another Color

To some people, the horse's color isn't important. To others, it's essential. Their horse *has* to be black, or a palomino, or white with blue eyes. Although black horses occur in most of the popular riding breeds, there is no color-specific registry open only to black horses. Friesians, those showy black horses with the arched necks and waterfall manes, have been bred for centuries in the Netherlands, first as war horses and most recently as show horses. But the Friesian Horse Association of North America registers only purebred Friesians, not black horses.

They may look like Friesians, but their papers say they're black Percherons.

A palomino.

Show your colors: All horses fall into one of several well-defined color categories.

■ Pure black horses are common in breeds such as Thoroughbreds, Arabians, and Saddlebreds, but rare or nonexistent in others. A black horse has a black coat and a black mane and tail. He sometimes has white on his face (a star, blaze, snip, snip and a stripe, or he's bald-faced) and/or on his legs (socks or stockings).

■ Many so-called "black" horses are really seal brown, which means the color around their eyes, muzzles, the insides of their legs, and their underbelly shades from dark brown to light brown.

■ Most horses, for complicated genetic reasons I don't plan to discuss, are chestnut—sorrel to some Western riders. A chestnut horse has a red coat. It can be a light red with yellow highlights—Quarter Horses are famous for their brilliant, copper-red coats—or dark-red liver chestnut, or red shading into light brown. Unlike black horses, who have completely black manes and tails, the tail of a chestnut is usually some combination of gray, red, white, and black hair. A chestnut with a mane and tail lighter than his coat color is said to have a flaxen mane and tail.

A bald-faced stud with a glass eye. This horse and the palomino are owned by Gary Jensen. (The Percherons are sold.)

■ Although a bay can have nearly the same coat color as a chestnut, red shading to a dark, gleaming brown, he always has a black mane and tail and black points— meaning that his legs, from his knees and hocks down, are also black. Like blacks

As a youngster, Prim had a flaxen mane. Haflinger ponies, all of them chestnuts, often have pure white manes and tails.

A bay Paso Fino gelding with a star on his face and four short white stockings. (Photo by owner Jean Johnson)

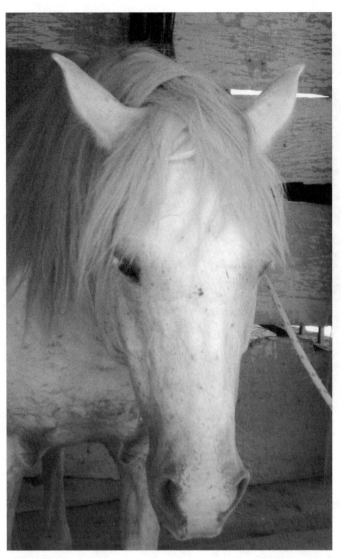

One of the white horses indigenous to the Camargue region of France. Like Lipizzans, they're born black with brown eyes; their coat color starts to fade almost immediately.

and chestnuts, a bay can have white facial markings and assorted white legs, but he will still have black on his knees and hocks and often little snippets of black (called ermine markings) that extend upwards from his coronet.

- Gray horses also occur in most of the popular riding breeds. Usually born a dark, iron-gray, their coat color lightens with age. Dapple grays are eye-catching because of the contrasting patterns of light and dark gray dapples, but nearly all horses—particularly bays and chestnuts—will "dapple" if they're in tip-top physical shape. If the dapples of a gray horse show a tinge of chestnut, he's a rose gray.

- True white horses (as opposed to albinos) are born white and have brown eyes, not blue or amber. Lipizzans are born black and have brown eyes; by the time they're fully mature, they have pure white coats, manes, and tails.

- A roan horse—usually found in the Western breeds—is a blend of colors. A red or strawberry roan is predominantly chestnut mixed with white and gray. The coat color of a blue roan is black with white and gray hairs mixed in. Manes and tails usually match the coat color.

- Buckskins, duns, and grullas (pronounced GREW-yas) are all members of the same genetic extended family and also occur mainly in the Western breeds. These horses have coat colors that range from dark tan to a light palomino color (buckskin), a faded reddish-brown to a smokey yellow (dun), and mouse-gray (grulla). Like bays, buckskins have black manes and tails and black points. But according to geneticists, buckskins with a black dorsal stripe down their back, a black stripe across their withers, and/or horizontal black slash marks across their knees and hocks are actually zebra duns. Red duns—sometimes called claybanks—also have a dorsal stripe, although theirs is a darker red than their coat color. The same is true of their lower legs, and their ears are often outlined by darker red hair. Grullas have a dark gray or black dorsal stripe. All are eligible for registry in the two color-specific buckskin associations. The American Quarter Horse Association also registers certain buckskins.

- Palominos, familiar to most people as parade horses, have flashy golden coats of varying hues and snowy white manes and tails. Although they occur in many breeds, they also have their own color-specific registry. The Palomino Horse Association and the American White & American Creme Horse Registry (if you insist on having a blue-eyed white horse) register horses according to their color, not their breed.

This welcome committee includes, from left to right, a red dun, a bay with a heart-shaped star on his forehead, and a buckskin. Note that the buckskin's ears are outlined in black. Owned by Vickie Sharp.

A grown-up buckskin.

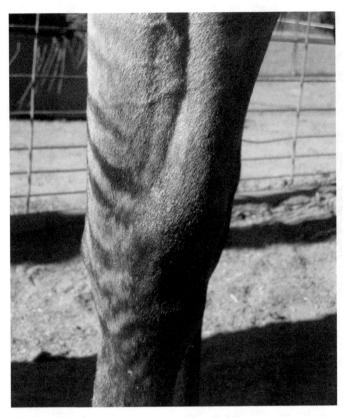

The knee of a zebra dun.

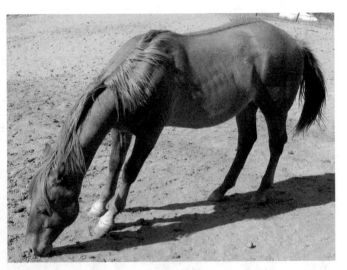

You can just make out the dorsal stripe on this youngster's back—one of the traits that make him a red dun.

These black beauties, owned by Lin Roberts, have an intriguing past. The filly in the foreground is Sky, a breeding stock Paint; her twin brother (not pictured), is a registered Paint. Behind her is Stormy, an Appaloosa. Sky and Stormy are out of the same dam, an Appendix-registered Quarter Horse. Twins are extremely rare in horses. (Photo by Mike Hays).

Want Lotsa Spots?

The United States has cornered the market on spotted horses—in fact many of these colorful horses originated in North and South America.

Polka-dot spots: All spotted registries are color-specific, but some are also breed-specific.

An Appaloosa owned by Lori Jensen.

- Appaloosas are both. Similar-looking spotted horses can be found in pre-Christian Chinese artwork. Spotted Danish horses, the Knabstrup, were bred for their markings during Napoleonic times up to the end of World War II. But today's Appaloosas are a genuine, made-in-America product. The Nez Percé, a native American tribe living along the Palouse River in the Pacific Northwest, selectively bred their colorful, exotic spotted horses to other horses with similar polka-dot spots. Modern Appaloosas are the result of crosses with Quarter Horses, Thoroughbreds, and Arabians. Most Appaloosas have a multitude of small spots, especially on their rumps, and the Appaloosa Horse Club recognizes several distinct colors and patterns.

- Paints and pintos both have large, splashy spots—sometimes round, sometimes jagged. A Paint has two registered Paint parents, or one Paint parent and one Quarter Horse or Thoroughbred parent. (A Quarter Horse with white above the knees or hocks can't be registered as a Quarter Horse but can be registered as a Paint.) A registered Pinto has papers that show he belongs to the National Pinto Horse Registry, which accepts all two- or three-colored spotted horses of any breeding as long as one of the colors is white. Bi-colored pintos can be either black and white or brown and white. Tri-colored pintos are black, brown, and white.

This handsome tri-colored horse (white, brown, and black) could be registered either as a Paint or a Pinto, depending on how his sire and dam are registered.

Although Paints can look exactly like pintos, the difference is in the breeding. This brown and white spotted horse could likewise be registered as a Paint or a Pinto. (Drawing by Gina Cresse)

Go Gaited!

For some owners, the gait of the horse is what's important.

Rack on!: Many American Saddlebreds are natural-gaited, which means that they rack naturally, without being trained to do so. A rack is a four-beat, lateral gait. It's often called the single-foot, because only one foot is on the ground at any given time. Some Saddlebreds perform five gaits: the walk, trot, canter, rack, and slow-gait (a hesitant, highly animated rack). Natural-gaited horses prefer not to trot, although some can be taught.

Because the single-foot is a very smooth gait, many riders who can't tolerate the bouncy, up-down motion of the trot prefer gaited horses, particularly the ones that don't trot at all. Other gaited breeds include the Rocky Mountain Horse, the Missouri Fox Trotting Horse, the Paso Fino, and the Peruvian Paso.

Walkers: In a class by themselves are Tennessee Walking Horses. Instead of doing a single-foot, with only one leg on the ground at a time, these horses truly "walk"—that is, they

Imperator, four-time 5-Gaited World's Grand Champion, performs a true rack: only one foot is on the ground. Photographer Avis Girdler is the rider. (Photo by Howard Schatzberg)

have only one foot in the air at any given time, with the other three on the ground. Horse people refer to the gait as a running walk, and it too is extremely comfortable. Like most of their gaited cousins, Tennessee Walkers rarely trot. With their easy gaits and good dispositions, they're becoming increasingly popular as all-round pleasure horses—even cow horses. If you buy one that's been shown, be sure to have a veterinarian check the horse for soundness. Unfortunately some owners and trainers resort to unscrupulous (and illegal) practices in order to win.

Standardbreds: Standardbreds are another gaited breed gaining in popularity as pleasure horses. Bred to race as harness horses (pulling a sulky, which is a light, two-wheeled cart), Standardbreds either pace or trot. A pace is a lateral gait: both the horse's left front foot and left hind hit the ground at the same time, then his right front and right hind hit the ground, whereas the trot is a diagonal gait. These horses have very willing natures. Although they descend from Thoroughbreds, as do Morgans and American Saddlebreds, they have shorter necks and legs than Thoroughbreds and more muscular hindquarters. Commonly shown at horse shows in driving competitions and under saddle, many Standardbreds have also competed successfully as jumpers.

A Standardbred mare in the show ring—she just won a blue ribbon in the roadster under saddle class. Helmets for riders are now a must. (Photo by Jack Schatzberg)

Want a *Real* Cowboy Horse?

Bands of wild horses (most are technically feral, i.e., escapees from civilization) still roam the West just as they did in the frontier days. These mustangs are protected by law, and the Bureau of Land Management (BLM) periodically rounds them up, sorts through them, quarantines the keepers for a couple of months, and then ships them to adoption centers throughout the country. Mustangs are not for inexperienced owners. In fact BLM screens you as a prospective parent before allowing you to even bid on a horse, and you must have owned horses previously. (There are additional restrictions.)

Keep in mind that most of these horses have been touched by human hands only a time or two in their entire lives. If you pass the qualifying test and buy one, be prepared to spend a lot of time with your horse before you even think about riding him. When he's ready, take him to a professional trainer.

My suggestion: Buy another horse first. After you've ridden him for a while, you're in a much better position to judge whether you have the ability to handle a mustang.

How Big?

For some owners, the horse's size is the main consideration—never mind looks or papers. Big people, even medium-sized people with long legs, feel funny riding small horses. Many short people, especially children, feel safer on ponies or small horses.

A mustang stallion, foreground, with a mustang mare. Both are bay; their heavy manes hide a white freeze brand.

Pony breeds: Any "horse" standing 14.2 hands and under is technically a pony. Many of the popular riding breeds come in pony sizes, including Quarter Horses, Arabians, Morgans, Paints, and American Saddlebreds.

- The Pony of the Americas is the result of a cross between a Shetland pony stallion and Appaloosa mares. These ponies have the spotted coats of Appaloosas and are known for their docile nature and athletic ability. They make very good jumpers.
- Other ponies suitable for pleasure and trail riding include the Welsh pony, a very attractive breed with arched necks and flowing manes and tails. They can be ridden or driven.
- Haflingers, another attractive breed that originated in the foothills of the Alps, are exclusively chestnuts with white manes and tails. They're noted for their docility, sure-footedness, and endurance. The first cloned horse was a Haflinger pony.
- Shetland ponies bred in this country only slightly resemble their shaggy, opinionated British cousins. With their slight build, arched necks, and excitable temperament, most are not good candidates for trail riding, particularly for children.
- Icelandic ponies, also known to be opinionated, have a fast, ground-covering *tolt*, or rack. These ponies have a strong, muscular build and are easy keepers.
- Irish-bred Connemaras are good-natured ponies with a finer build than Icelandics. Their stamina and docile temperament makes them ideal for riding. They also do very well as jumpers.

How to measure a horse or pony: Although various contraptions are available to measure horses—including the most obvious, a tape measure—most horses don't like them. (*Way* too scary.) Luckily, it takes very little time to develop an eye for a horse's height.

Horses are measured by how many hands they are. A hand equals four inches—the approximate width of a man's hand—and you measure a horse from his withers down. To find his withers, use your hand to follow his top line (his back) from his tail forward. The bony projection that marks the end of his back and the beginning of his neck is his withers. Or, run your hand down his neck, starting from behind his ears, until you reach bone. Measure from the highest point of the horse's withers straight down to the ground. Divide that number by four and you'll have his height. Most riding horses suitable for adults range from pony-size, 14.2 (fourteen hands, two inches), to 16.2 hands.

If you see an ad for a 15.2 mare, that means she's fifteen hands, two inches—or fifteen-and-a-half hands, or sixty-two inches. To train your eye for a horse's height, measure his withers against your own height. Stand next to him. Are his withers higher than your head? Unless you're a skilled rider, he's probably too big. Are his withers on the same level as your elbow? Unless you're seven feet tall, he's a pony. Some pony breeds are as small as ten hands. But if you're a small person, or are buying a horse for a young child, a pony may be exactly what you want.

He, She, or It?

Most people who ride for fun believe that geldings, or castrated males, are the gentlemen of the horse world. Their temperament remains the same—moment to moment, season to season, year after year. Don't buy a horse past the age of six who has "just been gelded." He usually doesn't *know* he's just been gelded.

And do not buy a stallion. Stallions can be dangerous, especially if they've been used for breeding, and most backyard owners simply don't know enough to handle one. It's true that individual stallions, particularly in some of the calmer breeds, can be as docile as geldings. But most stallions are bossy, territorial, and not a whole lot of fun to work with or ride.

Mares can also be opinionated, and many owners don't like them for that reason. When mares come in season—usually every thirty days except in the winter—they can be obnoxious. If you're riding such a mare and use your leg to move her over, she'll squeal and kick at your leg instead of responding. (A sideways maneuver called a cow kick.) Other, more flirtatious mares stop and squat and flag their tails at anything that remotely resembles a stallion. But many mares, Prim among them, don't get PMS-ish. I know she's in season only because her urine turns cloudy and leaves a chalky residue behind.

Some mares get so belligerent and unpredictable when they're in season that it's impossible to get near them, let alone ride them; they're too dangerous. If hormone injections don't work, some owners resort to spaying their mare—a surgical procedure similar to spaying a female dog except more expensive.

How Old?

Pairing a young, inexperienced, or timid rider with a young horse is not a good idea—no matter how docile the breed. If you or your children fall into any of these categories, your best bet is an older horse.

If you just want to saddle up and ride as the mood strikes you, you'll also be happier with a more mature horse. Thanks to advances in nutrition and deworming, horses are living longer than they used to, and staying sound longer. It's not uncommon any more to see or hear about thirty-year-old horses. With good care, most horses live well into their twenties. I've ridden fifteen-year-old mares so sassy I wouldn't want to own them. A "mature" eight-year-old gelding, on the other hand, is likely to be a good citizen—solid, dependable, and easygoing.

How Young?

However: if you know what you're doing, there are undeniable advantages to buying a young horse—specifically a green-broke three-year-old. Nothing younger. The phrase green-broke usually means that the horse knows how to lead and tie, has been saddled, ridden at all three gaits, and responds to the bit—but hasn't been ridden *much*. Most of these horses are like the proverbial blank slate. They've had good treatment their whole lives and rarely exhibit the bad habits (or vices) that older horses so easily acquire—usually from inexperienced owners.

They spook: Be especially careful around young horses; they take fright easily. (Some spook at their own shadow the first time they see themselves with a rider on their back.) Whenever you're around a young horse, move slowly and make sure he knows where you are at all times. He isn't sure how you figure into his world yet, and if something scares him, he may run you over trying to escape from it. An older horse will rarely trample you unless it's by mistake: he just didn't see you.

They take time: You'll also have to put more time and effort into a green-broke horse, because it will be up to you to *finish* him—in other words, to finish training him. Your smartest move would be to put him in training for a couple of months while you get to know each other under the supervision of a trainer.

I've bought most of my horses as green-broke three-year-olds. Except for one part-Thoroughbred gelding and a grade mare who never spooked at anything, I put them all in training for a few months. Your vet—the one you call to do a prepurchase exam (more about that in Chapter 10)—can probably recommend some trainers. Or ask the riding instructor you've been taking lessons from. Once you feel comfortable riding your horse and confident that you can handle him by yourself, take him home. He'll teach you the rest.

Have You Decided?

By now you probably have some idea of the kind of horse you want. As a potential buyer, learn all you can. Many books have been written exclusively about horse breeds; you can find additional information in Appendix II and on the Internet. Learn about the breeds for sale in your area; join a local trail club, for example. The more you know, the more successful you'll be at finding a horse who suits you.

My recommendation: Unless you absolutely *must* have a registered horse, don't be a breed snob. Many breeds aren't suitable for trail riding: they're too flighty or unpredictable.

A few exceptions:

- You want a gaited horse. The trot is not an easy gait to ride, either for children or graying adults. As this country's population ages, gaited horses are growing in popularity across the board with people riding them both English and Western.
- You want ponies for your kids. Some ponies have very friendly, docile dispositions, while others are ornery, stubborn bullies. If you buy a grade pony, you can't tell much about his temperament unless you know the owners and have seen children actually ride him. A bomb-proof pony is worth his weight in canary diamonds because so many people want one—trainers with juvenile riders, riding instructors, and other parents. In the long run you might be better off buying a pony with papers from a breed known for its amiability.

Follow Your Heart

Sometimes even the best-informed, most skeptical shopper ends up choosing a horse he or she "just likes the looks of." As with a marriage, there has to be some chemistry involved, even though from an outsider's perspective the horse is all wrong for you. In my experience, if you're that committed, the "marriage" will probably work.

MORE TACK—A CHECKLIST

If you decide you want a purebred, contact the breed registry (see Appendix II for how to do that). Explain you want to trail ride the horse. (If you query the Standardbred registry, for example, the person on the other end may assume you plan to race him.) Ask for brochures that discuss buying and taking care of a Standardbred, desirable conformation, specific traits to look for (you want a horse who trots, not one who paces), etc. This information is usually free for the asking. Ask if the registry publishes a magazine. Most do, and may be willing to send you a sample copy. Even though you haven't bought the horse yet, reading about the breed will be a good introduction.

If you have a spouse and three kids and can only afford grade horses, subscribe to a magazine anyway; some of the most popular are available at bookstores and newsstands. Since you've made up your mind that you want to be a cowboy, look for magazines that show Western riders on the cover, or have the word *Western* or *Cowboy* in the title. For additional suggestions see Appendix II.

As you look through the pictures, think about tack again—what you have and what you'll need to buy once the horses arrive. Again, check marks indicate necessary items.

✓ A self-contained tackroom or tack shed that you can lock if necessary.

A mounting block. Buy or build a sturdy wooden one that won't blow over and has non-skid steps.

✓ Saddle racks, one per horse. The wall-mounted types are sturdier than the rolling-basket types.

✓ Bridle brackets or headstall holders curved to hold the shape of the crownpiece.

An inexpensive wooden coat rack to store extra bridles, cinches, tie-downs, reins, etc.

A two-pronged tack hook suspended from a beam in the ceiling. It makes cleaning tack, especially saddles, a lot easier.

A sawhorse.

✓ Tack cleaner and conditioner. Many owners prefer a two-in-one combination.

✓ Pure neatsfoot oil to soften and restore stiff leather (works best when heated slightly).

A piece of lamb's wool to apply the neatsfoot oil.

✓ Sponges (or old washcloths) and towels. Use these only to clean tack. Even after machine washing, most contain too much oil or dye to make good horse-grooming rub rags.

✓ A mildly abrasive pot-scrubber designed to clean nonstick cookware. Good for cleaning bits and removing greasy black scurf (crud) from your reins, bridle, girth, and hard-to-reach areas of your saddle.

✓ A medium-sized bucket you use exclusively for cleaning tack and nothing else (the buckets tend to develop a greasy residue along the sides).

CHAPTER 4

WHERE TO KEEP YOUR HORSE: GIMME SHELTER

There are few things more soul-satisfying than sauntering down the aisleway of a big, well-lit, carefully tended barn lined on both sides with horses. As you walk, the horses pop their heads over the bottom half of their Dutch doors, and you can hear their throaty nickers of inquiry: *Who's this? A human? Does she have food?*

This dream barn has a twelve-foot-wide center aisleway, sometimes called a breezeway, that ends in a covered arena measuring 100 feet by 150 feet—big enough to practice your sliding stops or set up some jumps without going outside in bad weather. At the other end of the aisleway is a covered bull ring 50 feet in diameter. Both the bull ring and the arena have skylights.

Each twelve-foot by twelve-foot stall has Dutch doors that face the aisleway. During the day, the top of each door is open, held in place by eye screws and a double-ended snap. At night, to encourage peaceful snoozing, the top and bottom doors are closed and fastened with bolts.

At the back of each stall is another set of Dutch doors. When they're open, each horse can leave his stall and roam around his own twelve-foot by twelve-foot outdoor paddock at will. Each paddock is a three-rail pipe corral six feet high with an eight-foot-wide back gate for easy manure cleanup. (In other words, you can back a pickup through the gate, swing a full muck bucket into the bed of the truck, and drive it away.)

Not far from the barn is another fenced riding ring and a few one-acre pastures, shaded by big, spreading trees. (Not oak, red maple, or black walnut, though; see Chapter 9.)

This barn, or something like it, is every horse owner's dream. But at some point you have to face reality. The reality in this case is—you're only going to buy one horse.

Where in your backyard will you keep him?

Even if you plan to buy three or four horses, the question doesn't change. You have to keep these horses *someplace*; they can't live in the garage while you figure out what to do with them. In this chapter I'll discuss why some living arrangements are better than others by looking at:

Design

Ventilation

Insect/Pest Control

Footing

Lighting

Weather

Water

Feed

Fire Protection

INSIDE OUT

As you discovered in Chapter 1, most counties have legal codes that pertain to horse ownership. Buried somewhere in the "ifs" and "musts" and "therefores" is a definition of shelter. In Los Angeles County, shelter can be anything that protects a horse from the extremes of weather. In my case, that means the hot, high-desert sun in the summer and icy winds blowing off snowy mountaintops in winter. Even a tree can qualify as shelter as long as it's big enough to shade the horse in hot weather and offer him protection from wind and snow in winter.

But to any conscientious horse owner, shelter is more than a tree. It's the place your horse will call home.

From Stall to Pasture

You have three basic choices: you can stable your horse inside, in a stall; outside in a corral or field; or outside in a pasture. Or you can combine aspects of both, as in the indoor/outdoor stalls I just described. I've seen a few barns partially enclosed in a pasture, so when the owner opened the back of the horses' stalls, the horses stepped outside into pasture. The usual practice is to keep the horses inside during the day for fly control during the summer, and turn them out at night. In winter most owners reverse the procedure.

Real *backyard horsekeeping—home, your backyard, the barn, and your horse. (Photo courtesy of the American Morgan Horse Association)*

A beautiful old wooden barn with a hay loft built above the main aisleway. Don't store *hay in it; it's a fire hazard.*

Inside usually means a roofed barn separated into individual stalls. Outside can mean anything from a neat, utilitarian pipe corral, to an overgrown field defined by a few strands of wire, to grassy pastures filled with stands of trees.

There are usually fire code restrictions about what kind of barn you can build; they vary from region to region. In fire country you may be prohibited from storing hay in the top of a two-story barn—or from building such a barn in the first place. In other parts of the country you can build whatever kind of barn you want to, using whatever materials you please: wood, adobe bricks, cinder blocks, pre-engineered metal frames designed to hold panels of prefinished wood that—according to the manufacturer—won't burn.

INDOOR LIVING—STARTING FROM SCRATCH

Before you even make an offer on horse property, check with your local zoning department. There might be restrictions on the property, such as, you can have horses but you can't build a barn, usually for environmental reasons. Another possibility: you can build a barn as long as it's not a "permanent structure."

Design

As long as you have the right permits, you can usually build whatever kind of barn you please. And if you only plan to buy one horse, you *can* build a one-stall barn. But why would you want to? Horse people always run out of room. As long as you're paying a contractor to build a one-stall barn, build a two-stall barn. Unless you plan to build a separate hay shed (and you might), you can keep your horse in one stall, your hay and grain in the other, and your tack in the open area behind them.

If you intend to buy four horses, build a six-stall barn. Keep everybody's tack in the fifth stall and leave the sixth vacant, in case one of your trail riding buddies decides to spend the night.

Wood barns: If you're any kind of carpenter, or are married to one, build the barn yourself—especially if a simple, old-fashioned wooden barn (sometimes called a pole barn) appeals to you. These are easy to modify. You can, for example, support the barn (and discourage termites) by using concrete columns instead of wooden posts or poles.

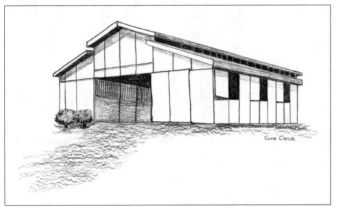

A six-stall modular barn with an elevated breezeway. Inside, the stall doors are on runners. The back exits are Dutch doors. Since horses are curious about what's going on around them, if you let them look, they're much less likely to be bored. (Drawing by Gina Cresse)

Modular barns: Another option: consider buying a pre-engineered or modular barn from a company that specializes in building them. While they're spacious and attractive, they don't look at all traditional. But in some aspects, ventilation in particular, these barns are a big improvement over wooden barns. They can also be less expensive, since everything is twelve feet long (each stall measures twelve by twelve) and can easily be mass produced.

A wash rack: In some barns, one stall—usually an end stall—is built with concrete flooring and a drain in the

An outdoor wash rack; this one has cross-ties. (Photo courtesy of the American Quarter Horse Association and America's Horse, Becky Newell)

center and designated as a wash rack. Other owners, reluctant to give up the stall space, prefer to build wash racks outside. Unlike an indoor wash rack, which usually has cross-ties, most outdoor racks use metal piping that encircles your horse's body to keep him from moving around; you tie him by the halter to the pipe in front of him.

Rubber pads: All stalls must have a manger (also called a feed bin or feeder) and provide water for your horse. For the sake of your horse's legs and feet, put solid rubber pads down that completely cover the floor of the stall, and bed his stall with shavings or straw. Instead of rubber pads, some owners prefer asphalt. (See pages 64–65.)

If you want bars on the stall door, make sure they're no wider than three inches apart. Otherwise an active horse can wedge a foot between them. Since sliding doors are more popular than Dutch doors at the moment, your horse can't see out of his stall unless you have bars.

Your horse gets cast: Horses love to roll, and there's no way to design a barn to prevent them from doing it. For reasons known only to your horse, he'll usually decide to roll right next to a wall. Most horses are physically capable of rolling over. In other words, they sink down on their left side and squirm around on their back for a few seconds before rolling over to their right side and scrambling to their feet. Other horses roll on their left side, then stand up. Then they sink down on their right side and repeat the procedure. Some old-time horsemen believe that a horse capable of rolling completely over is more athletic than one who can't.

■ What if the horse rolls completely over and then finds he's too close to the wall to get up? This horse is cast and requires human intervention to get up on his feet again. The problem is more serious than it first appears, because if nobody notices the horse's predicament, he's in trouble. While struggling to free himself he can colic, pull an abdominal muscle, or injure his spine.

■ Don't try to help a cast horse to his feet if you don't know how. You risk getting kicked by a frantic, thrashing horse, even though he may be lying quietly (he's already thrashed; now he's exhausted) when you first see him. Instead, call all the knowledgeable horse people you know, starting with your vet and your shoer, until somebody says, "I'll be right there." When help arrives, watch what the person does, and help him (or her) if he'll let you. The next time your horse gets cast, you may have to pull him away from the wall and get him back on his feet by yourself.

■ I once worked in a barn that had tail boards—they're like a chair rail in a house but wide enough to set a grooming box on. A mare in one of the stalls got herself cast. Not because of the usual reason, but because while she was rolling, she managed to jam a hind foot into the angle created by one of the brackets holding up the tail board. It took three men, one kneeling on her neck, and a shot of tranquilizer to free her—a victim of poor barn design.

Entryways and exits: Unless you have a single row of roofed stalls, called a shed row, your barn should have sturdy doors front and back so you can close it up completely in bad weather. (If you like the idea of a barn with a center aisle, the usual arrangement is an equal

A Horse Owner's Rule of Thumb:

If a horse can hurt himself, he will.

number of stalls on both sides.) If possible, both doors should be ten feet high, so your horse won't brain himself—or you—if he rears at the wrong time. For exterior doors, many owners prefer two doors with runners on the top and rollers on the bottom; the doors meet in the center and fasten with bolts. Doors like these are attractive but more expensive than the other option, which is one long sliding door that will shake, rattle, and roll whenever the wind catches it just right.

Stall doors: Make sure the stall door is either in the center of the stall as you face it or on the extreme right (center is best). That way you can lead a horse through the doorway and immediately step to the left, still facing him, so your back is against the aisleway wall as he continues through. If something frightens the horse, he'll run past you, not over you.

If you lead a horse into a stall designed with the door on the left, you can still move to the side so your back is against the aisleway wall. But your left arm will be pressed against the wall that separates this stall from the next one. If your horse gets rambunctious, you're trapped—you have nowhere to go.

Ventilation

Even in climates where it rarely (if ever) snows, build a barn with a pitched roof. In snow country a steep slope is vital because you want the snow to slide off the roof, not rest on it and collect moisture until your whole roof collapses. Why pay for a pitched roof in a hot climate ? Because heat rises. The hot air collects around the eaves, but the air at ground level—where your horse is—can be several degrees cooler. If you build anything bigger than a two-stall barn, consider a raised, center-aisle roof for ventilation. Adding two big exhaust fans, one at each end of the barn, will also help.

Most wooden barns have very little ventilation: that's what keeps them so snug and warm during the winter. In hot weather, they're less inviting. Unless you install exhaust fans, all you can do to move the air around is open the doors at either end and aim a portable fan at your horse. Be sure to unplug it when you leave.

Odor: Without ventilation, the smells have no place to go. Very few horse people find the smell of manure offensive—in fact many of us enjoy it. Urine-soaked bedding, however, is another story. It stinks, and in older barns with dirt floors the ammonia in the urine will come back to haunt you.

I once spent the better part of a year working in a stall that had been converted into an office by laying wood flooring over the dirt. (It was a working barn—a horse lived in the stall next to me.) Most of the time the ammonia smell was barely noticeable. But as much as I love horses, whenever it rained, I moved into the main office.

■ Ventilation is one area where a modular barn with a raised, center-aisle roof really outshines other barns. These barns are attractive, practical, and safe. And as long as you don't add too many extras (an extra-wide barn aisle; blanket holders on each stall door; all-brass fixtures and hardware), they don't have to cost a fortune.

Insect and Pest Control

They fly: Blister beetles (see Chapter 9) are the only toxic insect that can contaminate your horse's feed. But numerous not-so-nice bugs and other lowlifes love to hang around horse barns.

- Mosquitos are the most dangerous because they transmit viruses, including Eastern and Western encephalomyelitis and West Nile virus. To cut your risk, eliminate the insects. Use whatever means necessary—fly spray on your horse, a fly sheet if he's indoors (not a blue one—researchers claim mosquitos are drawn to the color blue), and/or a drop or two of mineral oil on the surface of his water.

- Flies can pester your horse half to death; they also transmit disease and multiply rapidly in horse manure. The most efficient way to control mosquitos and flies is an automatic mister, which releases a fine spray of insect repellant at timed intervals. But for a small barn, the price is prohibitive. There is another disadvantage, especially if you water your horse using buckets or a barrel: as the droplets of fly spray descend on your horse, they also descend on his water. (The problem isn't as acute if you use automatic drinkers, since the cups are small and shallow and hold very little water.)

- Fly bait traps, the plastic ones you fill with water and hang on trees or from the barn ceiling, are your best bet for price. Hang them downwind; the bait smells foul.

- Fit your horse with a fly mask during the day. When you fasten it, make sure it's loose enough so the horse can eat and swallow, but snug enough so an insect can't crawl under it. To reduce irritation, remove the mask at night. Except for mosquitos, most biting insects take the night off.

- When wasps, hornets, and bees congregate around your barn, it's usually because they intend to take up residence there. Honey bees that have been interbred with killer bees have notoriously short tempers. All bees can be dangerous in the spring, when they swarm. Spring is when the new queen leaves the hive with part of the old queen's entourage, looking for a place to set up her own hive. Check your pasture— bees often settle in dead, hollow tree trunks. But since they like protected areas, they can also settle under the eaves of your barn. If you find a swarm, the standard advice used to be to call a beekeeper. But given the bees' current bad reputation, you might not be able to find a beekeeper willing to come out. In that case, contact a local pest-control company. This is not a do-it-yourself project. Wasps and hornets also like to nest under the eaves; if you find a nest, call pest control.

They lurk: Black widow spiders hang out in damp, dark crannies where they spin webs to capture flies, moths, and other insects. The biggest black widow I ever saw was in a southern California barn. She had built her web under a hose bib and crept into the space between the water pipe and the surrounding wood. I had turned that water faucet on and off all summer, but when I reached for it one morning, I heard a telltale crinkling noise. Black widows' webs are messy to look at and crackle like cellophane when you disturb them. As I yanked my hand back, the spider rushed out of hiding, poised to kill whatever had blundered into her web. I finished her off with my horse's fly spray.

■ You don't want to be bitten by a black widow—the bite is extremely painful because it's so full of venom. Scientists still aren't sure why a spider that size needs a toxin that strong. Your horse doesn't want to be bitten by one either.

Footing

While some owners like to groom and saddle their horse in his stall, others prefer the barn aisle. When you build the barn, provide for cross-ties—two heavy ropes, one on each side of the aisleway. Each rope ends in a snap that you attach to your horse's halter. The ropes shouldn't be tight, but make sure they're not so slack that your horse can hook a leg over one. If you build a six-horse barn, you'll probably have enough room for four cross-ties.

In the aisleway: Since most center aisles are packed dirt, cleanup is easy. Some owners like to put down solid rubber pads, especially on either side of the cross-ties, which makes cleanup even easier—scoop up the road apples and hose down the pads.

In the stalls: Your best choice for flooring is four inches of lightly-packed asphalt. *Lightly packed* means you tamp it down using hand tools, not a machine. (Look in the

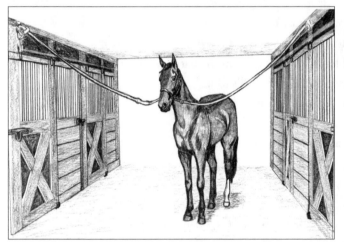

Most owners like to cross-tie their horse in the barn aisle for grooming and saddling. The stall doors, designed to look like Dutch doors, slide on runners. (Drawing by Gina Cresse)

Real Dutch doors. Many owners wouldn't consider anything else. In nice weather you can open the top and keep the bottom closed. In hot weather you can keep both doors open and snap a stall guard across the lower half of the stall. In bad weather you can close the stall completely. (Drawing by Gina Cresse)

yellow pages under the heading Asphalt.) Other owners prefer a stall base of two or three feet of gravel topped with one or two feet of sand, then bedding with straw or shavings. (I would lay rubber pads down under the feeders before adding bedding.) The key to no-stink maintenance is to make sure you remove *all* urine-soaked bedding every day.

- Asphalt flooring is low maintenance. Horses can't dig holes in it the way they do in dirt; you don't have to strip the stall once every year using lime to clean and air it out; and if you install it when you build the barn, it's cheaper than rubber pads.
- But if you only own one horse, dirt flooring is most owners' first choice because it's so inexpensive. I do recommend that you put down rubber stall pads because they'll help keep odors under control, even though urine can still seep between them. Pick up a load of DG (decomposed granite)—look in the yellow pages under Landscaping Equipment and Supplies. Fill the stall *to grade*—in other words, so it's level with the barn aisle—and tamp it down. The disadvantage is that without pads, some horses *will* paw holes in the flooring, usually in a corner. You will have to strip the stall once a year and repack it with DG—and you *must* be prompt (and thorough) about removing urine-soaked bedding.
- Wood shavings and straw are the most commonly used bedding materials. Some owners use sawdust, which I don't recommend. It's too dusty, especially if the barn is poorly ventilated.

Lighting

Ideally you want overhead lights the length of the aisleway. If the ceiling is ten to twelve feet high, you have room to install fluorescent lighting that's well out of range of most rearing horses.

- For the tackroom, figure on at least one ceiling light—preferably a combination light/ceiling fan. You'll also want three or four electrical outlets, because no tackroom is complete without a coffeemaker, microwave, and a refrigerator for carrots, manure samples you're saving for the vet (double-wrapped in zippered plastic freezer bags), and to keep your bottled water and Gatorade cold. Mini-refrigerators, intended for apartment dwellers, are the size of the freezing unit on top of most conventional refrigerators and are most owners' first choice.

  Many people like to play music to relax their horse. Buy a plug-in radio/CD player that will also run on batteries in case of a power failure.

  Depending on the season, space heaters and portable fans come in handy.
- You want electrical outlets in the barn aisle with safety-snap covers. If you have a six-horse barn, you want four outlets, two on either side. For a two-horse barn, two outlets are sufficient. You can cross-tie your horse and use plug-in clippers, which tend to be sturdier than the battery-operated kind, to trim his bridle path and clip his hairy fetlocks. If you just bathed him with soap and water to prepare for a show, you can plug a hair dryer into a heavy-duty extension cord to blow-dry his tail (more about show grooming in Chapter 18).

- Immersible water heaters come in handy if you want to heat a bucket of water but the barn isn't plumbed for hot water.
- As soon as you're finished using any appliance, unplug it from the wall socket and snap the cover closed. *Never* leave fans or space heaters running unless you're right there with them. (The exception is exhaust or ceiling fans that you turn off and on with a switch.) Even though most space heaters will turn themselves off if they tip over, nothing mechanical is foolproof. Among horse owners, the real F-word is fire.

Weather

Many owners bring their horse inside in very bad weather; others prefer to turn their horse out and let him make his own decisions about protecting himself. If Prim lived outside (and I had a barn), and the wind picked up and it started to sleet, I'd bring her and Kyle inside simply because of her age. I'd bring them inside during a thunderstorm, too. Where there's thunder, there's lightning.

Because most barns are higher than their surroundings, lightning can strike a barn for the same reason it often strikes the tallest tree in the area. More horses are killed by lightning when it strikes metal fencing (the horses must be physically touching the fence) than when it strikes a barn. But that's no reason to tempt fate. Tell your contractor you want the barn grounded, and follow up by asking the electrician how he intends to do that. A lightning rod on one end of the barn that runs directly into the ground is usually the easiest solution.

Water

Plumb the barn for running water, install a hose bib at both ends, and buy heavy-duty, kink-free hoses. Coil hoses on hose hangers (sometimes called hose caddies) *outside* the barn to keep the aisleway free of unnecessary clutter.

Automatic waterers: To water your horses, if you plan to buy more than one, an automatic drinker system is probably your best bet. There are three types.

The first is gravity-fed and involves a water tank and a float that automatically fills all the drinkers to a certain level and then shuts off. This system will only work if your water tank is level with all the drinkers. (Another version is an automatic float valve that's threaded to fit a garden hose or water line and can be attached to any water tub or barrel.)

The second is a pressure system that involves a paddle, or lever. In order to drink, the horse has to press the paddle with his nose so water flows into the drinker. If your horse has never seen one of these before, make sure there's a little water in the bottom. In order to drink it, he'll *have* to push the paddle. If he's not thirsty, lure him to the drinker with a carrot. While you splash it around the bowl, push the paddle down for him, then give him the carrot. He'll get the idea.

The third and most expensive is a sleek, stainless steel tank that releases water only when activated by a sensor.

- Once you install an automatic drinker system it's usually maintenance-free, unless your horse decides to deposit a load of road apples in it (I owned a mare who did that once), or you live where it's cold enough to freeze the water in the pipes. In that case your horse won't have any water except what you haul in to him—possibly carrying it from your house—until the pipes thaw. If your system is plumbed with PVC pipe (an inexpensive and extremely durable plastic) instead of copper, the PVC is guaranteed to break if the weather falls below freezing and stays there any length of time. (Most owners even insulate copper pipe.) If you're a gambler, wrap your PVC with insulation and hope Lady Luck blows you a kiss.

The bucket brigade: In parts of the country where automatic waterers aren't commonly used, owners hand-water their horses. I've also heard of owners who hand-water so they can monitor their horse's water intake. The only reason to do that is if you think your horse is sick, and a sick horse will usually go off his feed before he stops drinking. If you suspect your horse is sick, record his vital signs (see the following chapter) and test him for dehydration. If you're still not sure, call the vet.

■ The most practical stall buckets have flat backs and come with their own custom-fitted metal wall-mounts. Hand-watering is much cheaper than any kind of automated system, but for your horse's sake—especially if you have a full-time job away from home—install two buckets. Otherwise he could run out of water on a hot day.

Barrels: If your horse lives in an indoor/outdoor stall, most owners put a fifty-gallon plastic water barrel, or half a barrel, in a corner of his paddock. Barrels don't require filling as often as buckets, you can refill them using a hose, your horse won't step in them (they're too big), and you can easily tell how much water he's drinking.

The drawbacks are: waterers this big are hard to clean, especially the full-sized barrels; and any standing water (including the water in buckets) will absorb odors from the rest of the barn, which might make your horse reluctant to drink. Most owners use the half-barrels.

Feed

Wooden mangers are occasionally found in old barns, where they were usually built into the corner of the stall. Modern mangers are usually brisket-high for safety, so the horse won't step in them if something frightens him. But I watched a panicky two-year-old, just in from the pasture, climb into hers in a desperate attempt to go over the top and into the stall next door; she probably thought she could get out that way.

Most feeders are made out of metal and have bars on the front, so the hay won't fall out, and a bin or well in the bottom so you can grain your horse at the same time. The bin is also the ideal place for a salt brick.

Hay nets—no way: You've seen them for sale in the tack catalogs and may have wondered, can they do double-duty as feeders? Not on your horse's life. Nylon hay nets are only useful if you're trailering your horse and feed him to keep him occupied. If your horse manages to catch his foot in a nylon net and can't pull it out again, he's stuck. The nylon won't break.

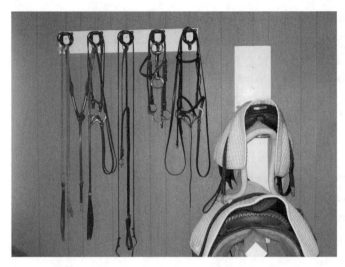

A neat tackroom, free of clutter, is a good safety precaution.

Storing your horse's hay in the barn makes feeding easier, but you don't want rodents anywhere near your tack. This tackroom is a free-standing, rodent-proof outbuilding.

Outbuildings: The advantage of storing your feed in the same building that houses your horse or horses is obvious. But for many owners, especially those who feed cereal-grain hay, there are two big disadvantages.

■ Horses can—and will, given the opportunity—eat themselves to death. Whatever kind of lock you use to secure the door of the stall or feed room, make sure your horse can't figure out the combination. Some horses are better escape artists than Houdini, especially if their "reward" for picking the lock is being able to gorge on grain all day. Chain the feed room closed, if you have to, and padlock it. If you arrive home from work to discover your horse has been binging on grain all day, call your vet immediately. You have an emergency.

■ Do not, for *any* reason, allow your horse free access to hay, either to indulge him or reward him or for any other reason. I've seen owners at boarding stables open their horse's corral gate and allow him to run over to the hay barn and snack for ten or fifteen minutes. These owners have never considered the possible consequences. If they continue this practice, the next time they open the gate, their horse may run over them on his way to the hay. If the owner decides to skip the "snack" step, the horse may be extremely reluctant to leave the barn area and in such a hurry to get back that his owner can't control him.

Rodents: Mice can be cute, but not when they shred your saddle blankets to make nests, urinate on your saddle, and reduce the bristles on your brushes to a five-o'clock shadow. You also don't want their droppings contaminating your horse's hay.

Rats are even worse—they're bigger and not at all cute.

■ Before you use poison to rid your barn of rodents, pick up a couple of kittens (preferably litter mates) from your local animal shelter. (Rodent bait should be your last resort. It's attractive to dogs and cats, and if your pet gets into it or eats a poisoned rodent, he can die.) Neuter the kittens immediately and arrange for rabies shots. Make sure they have someplace safe and warm to sleep, like a box lined with a bath towel on top of your filing cabinet—the one in your tackroom. Keep their food and water bowls on the filing cabinet too, so your dog won't get into them. The myth that hungry cats make better hunters is just that: a myth.

■ Make sure your cats are flea-free. If you start scratching every time you feed, the cats have probably been sleeping on the hay bales, which are now swarming with cat fleas. Your vet can tell you how to get rid of the fleas, but birth control is the most effective. This product chemically sterilizes all the fleas on your cat's body.

■ If you still plan to store feed in the barn, designate an end stall without an outside paddock but with a back entrance. If you designate one of the middle stalls as your feed room, the delivery man is not going to drag your hay there, one bale at a time, from his truck.

They slither: No discussion of feed-related pests would be complete without mentioning snakes, particularly rattlesnakes. I met my first one in a barn in Del Mar, California. I was walking across the floor of the hay barn, which opened into the stable area, to look at a horse. When I heard a soft whirring noise that sounded very much like the rustle of dry leaves, I stopped and looked around, too ignorant to be scared. When the noise stopped, I continued walking. I didn't see the rattler until I was on my way out. Most rattlers will avoid you if you give them the chance.

■ Although I've heard about rattlesnake sightings in New York and Florida, most rattlers congregate in hot, dry areas throughout the Southwest. Nearly every horse owner I know has at least one rattlesnake story. A friend of mine, Lin Roberts, was bitten on the hand by a rattler as she reached over her head to pull down a flake of hay for her horses. "My kidneys felt the aftermath of the venom for months," she noted wryly.

■ Then there are the yarns an old feed store owner used to tell me about Mojave greens —a highly venomous and unusually aggressive rattler (translation: if you run, they'll chase you). He claimed the snakes were sometimes baled with alfalfa, only to be sprung, still alive and spitting mad, when some unsuspecting horse owner broke open a new bale.

■ What draws rattlers to your barn? The same thing that attracts good-guy snakes like gopher and king snakes. Both lack the distinctive triangular head and segmented tail of a rattlesnake, but they all come to your barn for the same reason—because that's where you store hay and grain. Rodents eat grain. Snakes eat rodents.

Hay sheds: Many rural owners prefer to store their hay in a separate building because shed-sized outbuildings usually don't require a building permit. Hay sheds and barns (a barn is bigger) are both open in front, so the person who delivers your hay has room to unload and stack the bales. The open side usually faces away from prevailing winds. If rain or snow comes from all directions, designate the "open" side of the shed as the one nearest your horse. Buy a sheet of clear polyvinyl (if your feed or tack store doesn't carry it, look in one of the tack catalogs) to hang across the open side. Leave it in one piece or slit it into vertical strips for easy access. Other owners use blue plastic tarp, but it won't hold up as long.

■ Don't think you can store your hay outside on pallet-racking, to keep it off the ground, and cover it with a tarp in

Waiting for a hay delivery. My hay shed is right next to my tackroom.

bad weather. Tarps are tough, but after they've been exposed to sunlight, rain, and snow for a few months, they disintegrate. As a result, the next time it rains your hay will get wet. Wet hay molds, and you'll have to discard it or risk colicking your horse. Spend the money to build a hay shed.

Fire Protection

In case of fire, a barn is your third safest bet. (Acres of pasture with a river running through them is your safest; next safest is keeping your horse outside in a corral.) Because of how fast fire travels and how hot it can burn, a barn is not safe. Horses panic easily, and a scared horse who's not paying attention to you is hard to handle. Most horses resist efforts to evacuate them from a burning barn. To them, it's home—and home is safe. If you ever find yourself in this situation, blindfold your horse with whatever you can lay your hands on—your shirt, if necessary—*then* lead him out.

Treated wooden stalls advertised as fire-retardant are better than untreated wood, but if you can't get your horse out of the barn, the smoke will kill him before the wood ignites.

Overall Approval Rating

Barns offer the best protection against extremes of weather, and your horse's feet will be in better shape. But you must be diligent about turning him out at least once a day (without his blanket, even if it's cold out) to exercise and soak up his daily dose of vitamin D. For comfort, looks, and practicality, a barn is hard to beat.

Comfort, unfortunately, comes with a price tag. Compared with outdoor living, the average stall isn't big enough unless it opens directly into an outdoor paddock. If you build your own barn you *can* build twenty-four-foot by twenty-four-foot stalls, although roofing gets more complicated. But if you build a modular barn, the best you can do is leave out every other partition so you have twelve-foot by twenty-four-foot stalls. Wooden barns offer little ventilation or fire protection unless they're very carefully designed. And last but not least, a barn costs more to build than any "outdoor living" facility.

RUNNING RINGS AROUND YOU

In addition to the barn, hay shed, and a tackroom, most owners want some kind of arena where they can longe their horse or turn him out to self-exercise. The ring I have is about sixty feet in diameter—a good size for a turnout ring but a little too small to ride in. (Since I don't do much ring work, I chose the small size on purpose.) It's enclosed by a four-foot-high wooden fence with three rails. The posts are four-by-four, and the rails, or stringers, are two-by-six. Each post-and-rail section is ten feet long, except for some shorter sections near the gate. The gate itself, built with an **X** between the uprights so it won't sag, is eight feet long. It's hinged so I can open it completely and leave it that way in order to ride in and out of the ring without dismounting.

Most owners prefer an arena big enough to use as a turnout *and* riding ring. The 100-foot by 180-foot arena my neighbors let me use is a luxury; most riders would be happy with an arena half that size.

Backyard horsekeeping in the high desert. Left to right: hay shed with the tackroom behind it; pipe corral with shader; turnout ring.

Design

Arenas can be round or oval-shaped.

Others are rectangular, although these have four drawbacks—each corner. If you own more than one horse and turn them all out together, it's easy for the dominant horses to bully the weak or submissive one into a corner and kick the daylights out of him. You can avoid the problem by turning the horses out separately. If that's not feasible, nail a board across each corner, to round it off. That usually gives the picked-on horse enough leeway to escape.

Veterinarians, on the other hand, love rectangular rings, especially if they're dealing with an uncooperative horse. They just back him into a corner and do what they have to do.

Entryways and exits: Whatever size or shape you decide to build your arena, make sure the gate is wide enough to allow a tractor, ATV (all-terrain vehicle—also called a quad or four-wheeler), golf cart, jeep, or pickup inside. An eight-foot gate is wide enough for a quad, pulling a tine harrow, to enter and exit. Periodically John breaks up the dirt and softens the footing for me, then reverses the harrow and drags the ring. A tine harrow is the most versatile and usually the cheapest way to maintain good footing, and most do reverse into a drag.

Fencing: John and I moved to Los Angeles when he accepted a job with a private owner who wanted a string of show horses and a big new barn. He also wanted John to design the barn. John drew up plans for a thirty-six-stall barn that included a twenty-foot-wide barn aisle (so he could work horses in bad weather), an outdoor bull ring, turnout rings and pastures, and a jogging track—all on twelve acres.

Traditional white fencing; note the "cage" around the tree. A bull ring is visible in the lower right.

The first turnout ring to go up had the stringers, or rails, on the *outside* of the posts. John immediately tracked down the contractor, who said he had built it that way on purpose—for aesthetic reasons. John pointed out that the ring wasn't safe. A horse could lean against the top rail trying to reach grass on the other side and easily pop it out, leaving sharp, pointy nails exposed. The contractor, after reluctantly admitting he hadn't thought about that possibility, rebuilt the ring.

As a rider, you want the stringers inside too. If they aren't, the posts will be on the inside—and it's very easy to bang your knee against a post that juts out into the ring. You only want to do that once. (You really don't want to do it at all.)

Footing: Make sure your arena is slightly higher than the land that surrounds it. Hire somebody who does tractor work—or if you know how to drive a tractor, rent one—to elevate and level the pad. Look under Grading or Excavating Contractors in the yellow pages.

A raised ring usually drains by itself—that is, the rising water spills out at the lowest point and cuts its own channel. If you want the ring to drain faster, dig the channel deeper and wider with a trenching shovel. If possible, channel the water next to a post; you don't want to create a permanent hole along the fence that your horse can stumble into.

Since you probably won't be spending much time doing ring work—most backyard owners use their arena primarily to turn their horse out or to longe him—whatever dirt is already in the arena is usually sufficient. Before your horse arrives, prepare the footing using your tine harrow; then drag the ring.

Clay, however, is another story. If your soil is clay, you need additives to loosen and aerate it. Because each particle of clay is so tiny, the clay packs down so tight and hard it's like riding on a sidewalk. No matter how little time your horse spends in the arena, cement-like ground isn't good for his feet or legs; you risk shin splints, bruising the sole of his hoof, and other injuries. Clay is also extremely slippery when it's wet (your horse could take a spill, with you riding him) and is very slow to drain.

- Add two inches of coarse sand (it has bigger, more irregularly shaped particles than smooth desert sand, which is also slow to drain) and half a dozen muck baskets of dried manure and shavings. Using your tine harrow, dig them into the soil. After that, drag the ring whenever the footing starts to compact and add additional dried manure/shavings once or twice a year. You want footing that "gives" but isn't so deep that your horse risks bowing a tendon.

  Before you ride, turn on the sprinklers (placed outside the arena) to keep the dust down.
- Some people insist on a recipe for arena footing—this much sand, loam, ground-up rubber crumbles from the soles of athletic shoes, etc. But they're usually amateur owners who spend more time in the show ring than on the trail. All *you* need is footing that's comfortable for your horse and drains well.

OUTDOOR LIVING—SEMI-ROUGHING IT

There are degrees of outdoor living. The one favored by the majority of horse owners is a corral. A corral is any fenced area where your horse lives. Although it has no fixed dimensions, it must provide your horse with water, feed, and shelter. There are two main types: pipe corrals and wooden-fenced corrals. Whichever type you choose, build the corral on level ground.

Design
Pipe corrals: These are stall-size, twelve feet by twelve feet. Like modular barns, they come in sections. Since it's cheaper to put up a corral than it is to build a barn, give your horse some moving-around room and make the corral twenty-four feet by twenty-four feet, whether you build it out of premeasured metal pipe or wood.

- In most parts of the country, pipe corrals are physically and legally portable, which means you don't have to rent a posthole digger in order to "build" one. Because the corral rests *on* the ground, not *in* the ground, you can take it apart and reassemble it anywhere on your property, any time you want to. That, in turn, means you probably won't need a permit.
- If you own or intend to buy more than one horse, another advantage of a pipe corral is how easily you can expand it. Each outside "fence" can become a divider between

Winter weather, the only serious downside to a pipe corral. Note the two lidded feeders and the shader, which is far from leak-proof. The water barrel is in the far corner, behind Prim.

the existing corral and a new one. You can add as many corrals as you want, or create an aisleway as wide as you want and put more pipe corrals on the other side. Some manufacturers even build roofed storage sheds where you can keep hay and tack, although they're far from rodent-proof. I personally wouldn't risk keeping my tack in one, although I would keep feed.

- Most pipe corrals have four or five rails. Because I reinforced mine by adding two-inch by four-inch wire mesh (sometimes called stud wire) to keep Kyle from climbing out, Prim's corral has three rails. The spacing between each rail is three feet; the entire corral is six feet high.

The welded wire mesh keeps Kyle safe. It also keeps him from climbing out of the corral.

- Horses can't chew metal, although they can crib on it, and it takes a very determined kicker to dent metal pipe. In other words, pipe corrals are sturdier than wood ones. If your horse kicks, put him in a pipe corral. A chewer is another good candidate for a pipe corral.
- If you buy a new pipe corral from a local manufacturer, the company will assemble it for you. Sometimes you can find panels of used pipe corral that are in pretty good shape, but you'll have to put them together yourself. You might want to buy some additional sections in order to build an arena. Be sure one of the sections is a gate.

Wooden corrals: These corrals, on the other hand, are usually considered permanent structures. Because of those posts you sunk in the ground, you might need a permit. Check with the zoning department.

- Most wood corrals have three or four rails and aren't as high as pipe corrals.
- If you add another horse to your corral, you'll have to rip some stringers out and dig more postholes to make the corral bigger. At some point, you'll no longer have "a corral." If you keep half a dozen horses in a dusty field, that's what you have—a dusty fenced field. It's not a corral and it certainly isn't a pasture, no matter how big it is. Pastures have grass.
- Know exactly where you want your wooden corral and what shape you prefer. Once it's built, you can't pick up a circular corral and turn it into a rectangle.

Wooden post corrals reinforced with electric fencing, commonly called hot wire.

Entryways and exits: Whichever type of corral you choose, install the gate either in the center of the corral or the extreme right as you face it as a safety precaution. If you can, install a gate that swings both ways.

Hitching rail: Since you don't have a barn aisle, you need some way to fasten your horse while you groom him and saddle him up. The easiest solution is a chest-high hitching rail just outside the corral. If it's lower and something scares your horse, he might be tempted to jump it. Build it too high and he might walk under it.

- Make sure the rail is heavy-duty metal. My preference is two-inch galvanized pipe. If you want the rustic look, use sturdy cedar posts. The hitching rail I have is about forty-two inches off the ground.
- If you don't have, or don't want, a wash rack, lay down rubber pads on either side of the hitching post, so your horse won't splash himself with mud when you bathe him.

A 16.3 backyard jumper tied to the hitching rail. Dakota is an Oldenburg, one of the German warmblood breeds. (Photo by owner Patty Jakobi-Stopper)

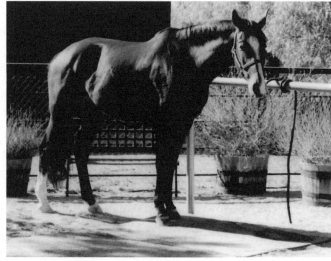

Disadvantages: No matter what type of corral you choose, your horse can rub his mane off (or worse, *part* of his mane), especially in the spring when he's stretching his neck out as far as possible to nibble on that tender new grass on the other side.

- A horse can also get cast in a corral. He's in more danger here than in a stall because he has probably managed

This is how horses get cast.

to stick at least one leg between the rails. In addition to pulling *him* away, you have to make sure his legs come with him.

Ventilation

There's no way to regulate the temperature of a corral or to completely protect your horse from the elements. If you buy a pipe corral, do buy a shader to protect him from the sun. Shaders aren't leak-proof or big enough to keep your horse completely dry when it rains. If they were, a gust of wind could pull your entire corral over.

To protect your horse from the weather, you would have to build a roof over the front of the corral. It should completely cover the feeders, and be a real roof—with tar paper, shingles, the works. If you do that, you'll probably have to provide additional support, and a post in the middle of your horse's corral isn't the safest way to do that.

Smells: Odor won't be a problem with only one horse as long as you clean the corral daily and spread the manure in six-inch layers so it can dry. Cleaning is easy—pick up your pitchfork, open the gate, and wheel your wheelbarrow in. When you're finished, open the gate and wheel your wheelbarrow out. Unless you live in an area with very high humidity, manure and urine dry faster in a pipe corral than they do in a stall, since the corral is open to the elements.

Because manure freezes and you can sift through it without picking up shavings, cold-weather cleanup is easy. When it's raining, cleanup isn't as much fun. Don't postpone it more than once.

Insect and Pest Control

Some flies are attracted to manure. Others are attracted to your horse. Still others are attracted to parts of your horse, like face flies. A few, like deer flies, are attracted to you both. You can't install an automatic insect sprayer in a corral, but you have other options.

In combination: Most owners use a combination of fly masks, fly bait, insect spray that you apply directly on the horse, and fly predators. These pint-sized flies, which are much smaller than the average pest flies, live on the larvae of pest flies. They themselves don't bite, sting, carry disease, or present any health hazard. They live only to prey on the unhatched eggs of other flies—that's their job. (You'll see ads for them in horse magazines.) Fly predators have been given the seal of approval by veterinarians, and they work just as well in your backyard as they do in a million-dollar Thoroughbred breeding operation.

■ Wash your horse's fly mask periodically, and inspect it for rips or tears where he could catch it on something. Remember to remove it when you feed at night.

■ Hang the fly bait bags on nearby trees. When they're full, dispose of the bags carefully. They're not leak-proof, and the smell isn't one you want lingering in your trash can. The easiest way to dispose of them is to leave them on the tree until autumn, when all you'll have left is a plastic bag full of dried-out fly carcasses. No smell. If your summers are too humid to allow the liquid in the bags to evaporate, deposit them into two heavy-duty zippered freezer bags, one inside the other.

Footing

By keeping your horse in a barn, you bypass one problem completely—mud. If you buy or build a corral for your horse, consider adding a two- to four-inch layer of coarse sand or DG (decomposed granite). You'll raise the level of the corral, which will improve the drainage, and both sand and DG drain more quickly than other soils.

Before your horse moves in, add several bags of shavings. Once the sand and the shavings mix together, your horse will have good, absorbent, comfortable footing. Most owners prefer shavings for outdoor horses because shavings are more absorbent and tend to dry out a horse's feet slightly. Make sure to moisturize them when the frog feels dry.

Mud: Whenever it rains, be scrupulous about cleaning your horse's feet. Standing in mud, no matter how deep, can result in medical problems like scratches, thrush, or even founder.

■ If your corral floods, figure out where the water's coming from. When you do, dig a ditch to divert the water so it bypasses the corral.

Water inside the corral will puddle in the deepest spot, usually where your horse rolls. Dig another ditch from the low spot to someplace outside the corral, being careful not to dig so deep your horse can stumble into it and hurt himself. As soon as the water drains, distribute three or four bags of shavings inside the corral. That should solve the mud problem.

If it doesn't, and if it continues to rain, see what you can do about getting your horse inside—even if you have to ride him to a neighbor's barn and board him there until his corral dries out.

Water

Automatic drinkers: Many owners, and I'm one of them, don't like automatic drinkers for horses stabled outdoors. Even if the drinker is shaded, the water sits in such a small, shallow container that during the summer it can get hot enough to brew coffee. Why spend the money to install an automatic system if the water gets too hot for your horse to drink? Another disadvantage is that in full summer sun, automatic drinkers turn slime-green with algae overnight. Be prepared to scrub yours daily.

Barrels: Most owners prefer heavy-duty, fifty-gallon plastic drums or barrels. I prefer half-barrels because they're easier to clean. To thoroughly scour a full-size plastic drum, you can't just bend over and scrub. You have to climb inside it. And they do require frequent cleaning.

■ Check your horse's waterer daily. You'd be surprised at what you can find floating in it. The usual suspects include live hornets, half-drowned wasps, bees, and grasshoppers. I've also found dead birds and rodents.

Feed

If you buy a metal feeder—which you can attach to your pipe corral or, with a few minor adjustments, to your wooden corral—do you want a lid? Yes. If it's raining, a lid on your feeder will keep your horse's feed dry. Your salt will last a lot longer too. If you hang an S-hook on the fence above the lid (another reason wire fencing comes in handy), the lid will stay open while you drop the hay inside. When you're done, slide the hook out and drop the lid.

Ground-level feeding: The only problem with feeders is that most horses don't like them. They're accustomed to eating at grass level and will usually reach into the feeder, yank out some hay, and drop it. Once the hay is where they want it—on the ground—they'll eat it. That's why I'm such a stickler about laying down rubber pads under feeders.

Overall Approval Rating

The advantages of controlled outdoor living are better ventilation, low maintenance, and low price. By *price* I mean both the initial cost of putting up a corral and the ongoing cost of maintaining it. Well-made pipe corrals last a long time.

Looking at a metal feeder from the horse's point of view. John had to bend the center bar in both feeders because Kyle kept getting his head stuck.

The disadvantage: if you live in a cold climate, a corral doesn't offer your horse the protection a barn does. On the other hand—horses do grow winter coats and have been getting along without additional protection (a category that includes blankets) for thousands of years.

My recommendation: Horses stay warmer when they can move around, the same way humans do. Build your horse a twenty four-foot by twenty four-foot pipe corral with a shader. If you plan to buy your horse a goat- or sheep-sized stable buddy, add a second feeder and ask the manufacturer to weld two-inch by four-inch stud wire or three-inch by three-inch field wire around the entire corral. I sleep better at night knowing that Kyle can't escape and nothing can crawl through the bars of the corral and drag him off. Although I haven't mentioned it to Prim yet, we do have cougars and bobcats roaming these canyons.

OUTDOOR LIVING—*REALLY* ROUGHING IT

A field or pasture gives your horse room enough to roam around in *and* provides shelter, especially if you were smart enough to incorporate a couple of trees and a hillside within

Electric fencing in a pasture.

the fence. Your horse can stand under the trees for shade during the summer, and he'll use the side of the hill as protection from rain and snow.

Design

Don't fence a fruit grove inside your pasture. I've seen horses pastured in old apple orchards peacefully cropping grass while the apples rotted on the ground under their feet, the air smelling like cider vinegar and humming with hornets and yellow jackets. But I'd never pasture my own horse there. Most horses love apples and can gorge themselves until they colic. Any fruit with a pit—peaches, plums, apricots—are even more dangerous. If the horse swallows the pit, he risks choke or an impaction. If he chews the pit, he can colic.

Also avoid red maples, all oaks that shed their leaves in the fall, and all nut-bearing trees, especially black walnuts. Everything about the black walnut—including shavings from the wood, which can cause a horse to founder (see Chapter 9)—is toxic except the nut. But to get to the nut, the horse has to crack the hull around it, which is also poisonous. A mature black walnut tree is so toxic it kills earthworms and most vegetation within a fifty- to eighty-foot radius of its trunk.

Water

If your horse is pastured, problems with ventilation, insects, footing, lighting, and weather are all beyond your control. You can deal with insects to a certain extent by a combination of

One type of commonly-used metal stock tank.

prompt manure removal, fly predators, and rotating the pastures—more accurately, rotating the horses out of one pasture and into a new one. You do have to figure out how to get water and additional feed to your horses.

If you live in a cold climate, your horse's water will freeze. Check his waterer every time you feed, and if there's ice on the surface, break it up and remove it. Consider buying one of those plug-in gadgets designed to keep your horse's water from freezing without electrocuting him.

Bathtubs: Some owners like to use an old fashioned claw-footed bathtub for their pastured horses. Just make sure to remove all the fixtures—although if your horse is wearing a halter, he can probably find something to snag it on. (*Always* remove your horse's halter before you turn him out to pasture unless it's a leather or breakaway halter.)

Stock tanks: Another option is a livestock waterer—some people call them stock tanks. Modern tanks are made out of galvanized steel or heavy, flexible black rubber, although occasionally you'll still see an old-fashioned wooden horse trough. They're all tough and durable, but they too require cleaning, especially in hot weather. Mark Stallings, my farrier, stocks his field tanks with catfish. They not only eat the mosquito larvae, but—because they're bottom feeders—they also take care of the algae that forms on the bottom of waterers.

Stainless: And then there are the round, state-of-the-art stainless steel drinkers that probably cost more than your horse did.

Culverts: As an alternative, convert part of a concrete drainage culvert—the kind used to divert water under a road—as a waterer. These have two drawbacks. One is their weight. They're so heavy that you better be absolutely sure where you want yours when it's delivered. The second is, they're hard to clean. I've seen products on the market that claim to keep outdoor waterers odor-free and sludge-free without adding chemicals. Ask your vet. If you just bought the property and the concrete waterer *and* the water that came in it, drain and scrub the waterer with industrial-strength steel-wool before you let your horse drink out of it. During the summer some owners add goldfish to eat mosquito larvae. (No, I've never heard of a horse accidentally drinking a goldfish.)

Off! To cut the risk of West Nile virus and other mosquito-borne diseases, pour a few drops of mineral oil into your horse's waterer. The oil will float on top and smother the mosquito larvae without endangering your fish.

Feed

If you own four horses—one for each family member—and you keep all four in a pasture, don't buy a feeder designed to hold hay for multiple horses. Instead, buy five separate feeders—one for each horse plus one extra—attach them to the fence, and space them as far apart as possible.

A moveable pasture feeder. (Drawing by Gina Cresse)

You'll reduce mealtime bickering, and even the timid horse on the very bottom of the pecking order will get enough to eat.

The Bottom Line: The Fence Line

No matter where you live, your main consideration will be fencing. Most of the Southwest was originally fenced with barbed wire because it was cheap, effective, and easy to put up. No, cowboys did not use post hole diggers. Many of them didn't even use posts. They used whatever was handy—and you don't have to look very far even today to find barbed wire wrapped around trees, rocks, even cactus.

Get rid of it: Barbed wire is dangerous. It was designed to contain livestock, and the "barbs" insured that. But horses sometimes don't see barbed wire, especially if they've had no experience with it. One summer when I knew I wasn't going to have time to ride Bachelor, I turned him out with half a dozen other horses in a three-acre pasture fenced with barbed wire. In his excitement he was off and running even before I pulled his halter completely off, kicking up his heels with his new buddies in hot pursuit. The inevitable happened—Bachelor ran into the fence. I will never forget the sight of my big, beautiful, pitch-black horse with blood streaming down his chest and side. Luckily his wounds were so superficial he didn't need stitches.

Many owners like to take the precaution of walking a new horse along the fence line before they turn him loose.

If your property has barbed wire on it, remove it. Make sure there are no stray pieces half-buried in the dirt. If your horse doesn't get his foot caught in one, he might inadvertently eat a tiny portion of wire along with a mouthful of grass. That's how enteroliths—intestinal "stones"—can get their start.

What do you replace barbed wire with?

Green acres, white fences: If you have a lot of money you don't know what to do with, you can fence your pastures with the traditional three-rail white wood fencing so common on Kentucky and Virginia horse farms. These fences are very high maintenance. For one thing, you have to paint them every year. For another, horses who chew love wooden fences. Make sure you have plenty of extra rails.

Split-rail: Don't like painting? Go rustic with an unpainted split-rail fence. Version one: the posts have slots in them, so you can slide the rails in. No nails required. Version two: the zigzag fence. You don't use nails *or* posts—only the rails, one piled on top of the next until the fence is as high as you want it. How do you keep it from collapsing if your horse leans on it or tries to scratch himself on it? You don't. Some owners run a single strand of electric fencing just far enough from the wood to keep the horse from physically touching it, but the look just isn't the same.

Metal: You can use sections of pipe corral, but an entire pasture fenced with pipe would be costly and not particularly attractive.

The safest fencing, and many horse owners use it, is three-inch-square wire, often called field wire, supported by stout wooden posts. But a wire fence is almost as expensive as a wooden zig-zag fence, and you *have to* bury the bottom. Otherwise your horse is guaranteed to wedge a foot under it when he's rolling. Other owners prefer heavy-gauge chain link, capped with pipe.

Metal fences have another drawback: they're prime targets for lightning, which means you have to be sure the fence is grounded. The best way to do that is to build it using metal stakes instead of wooden posts to support the wire. If the fence is already there, you can leave most of the wooden posts, but replace them with a metal stake every fifty feet or so. Another alternative: drive a stake into the ground every fifty feet so it *touches* the post.

Hot wire: Electric fencing is another option. (Some people like it hot.) There's a wide variety on the market—look through any horse magazine. If possible, buy the kind that pulsates. Otherwise some small hapless animal, including your dog or cat, can bite the wire out of curiosity—and then can't let go. If you grab a strand of hot wire in both hands, you probably won't be able to let go either.

If your barn opens directly out into pasture, you can plug the electric fence into an outlet in your barn. Other electric fences are battery-powered (the unit mounts on a post) or solar powered. The last two are particularly useful if you have a power failure. But once horses get "bit" by electric fencing, they'll seldom test it a second time. Gina Cresse, who took most of the photos and drew the illustrations for this book, used to turn the power off to her fence in the afternoon when she came home from work. Her four horses didn't notice, but the coyotes did.

Don't try to ground electric fencing. If you do, it won't work anymore. The horse gets zapped because the electricity goes to ground *through* him. But you do want to make sure that the charging unit (electrical outlet, battery pack, or solar) is grounded.

Plastic wood: Wood completely covered by extruded white plastic is still popular, but it's also expensive. Unlike wood, it doesn't need painting, so it looks uniformly neat. But if your horse is a cribber, he'll crib on it and quite possibly pull the board out. In addition, the wood inside the plastic can rot.

All-plastic fencing—no wood involved—is popular with some owners. All-plastic means no cappers to protect the top of posts, no stains from rusting nail heads, and no rotten boards. In other words, fencing that's low maintenance but high dollar.

Overall Approval Rating

A horse who lives outside, especially in the company of other horses or a horse-substitute friend, will exercise himself. (You did buy your horse a friend, didn't you?) The big advantage of owning a pre-exercised horse is that you don't have to longe him half an hour every time you ride. Clean his feet, brush him, saddle and bridle him, and you're ready to ride.

Horses kept outside with other horses will get banged up, especially while they're establishing a pecking order. The

A high-tensile electric fence wrapped around wooden posts. (Drawing by Gina Cresse)

More white fencing. It looks like wood, but it's really extruded white plastic.

least dominant horse (usually the oldest one, or newest one to enter the herd) is likely to exhibit bite marks, the imprint of another horse's hoof on his rump, and other assorted scrapes and bruises. Keep an eye on him.

If adding a feeder doesn't solve the problem, consider taking the horse away from the herd during mealtimes and moving him to a separate enclosure. But make sure he can still see the other horses while he eats, otherwise he'll fret. If he still gets chased around and it's not during mealtime, watch to see which horses allow him to approach without chasing him away. Then move him and the horses willing to befriend him into their own pasture.

Rotate your pastures: If you have a lot of property, fence several one-acre pastures instead of one big pasture. Put your horse or horses (no more than three) in one of the pastures. Keep the flies and the parasites they carry under control by cleaning the manure out daily and releasing fly predators around the areas where the horses pass manure and where you spread their road apples. Since many parasites can remain in the soil a year or longer, tell your vet what you're doing and ask what changes in your worming program he would suggest.

- When the grass around the feeders or hay rack looks short or disappears entirely, move the horses to another pasture. By doing so you lower the risk of recontaminating your horses with parasites (fly larvae often cling to blades of grass), and your pasture grass will be healthier and last longer.

Drawbacks: Pastured horses tend to lose shoes, especially if it's raining (or the snow is melting) and they stand in mud for any length of time. As long as the shoe came off clean, without taking part of your horse's hoof with it, your horse will be fine until the farrier's next visit. It's the *other* horses you have to worry about—especially the one who finds the shoe, nail side up, of course, by stepping on it. If your horse comes to dinner minus a shoe, find it.

If you own a lot of property, another drawback is that your horse can get into trouble and you won't know about it because you can't see him. But if you work all day, you have the same problem even if your horse lives in a stall.

Another advantage: Pastured horses seldom get cast.

Historically, horses are foragers—on the move all day, finding edibles, arguing with their neighbors, then standing head to tail swatting flies off one another. Keeping your horse in a pasture with other horses is as close to his "wild" state as you can get. It's hard to improve on Mother Nature.

**Horse Owner's
Rule of Thumb:**

Always put up one
more feeder than you
have horses, so
everybody gets enough
to eat.

CHAPTER 5

WHERE TO KEEP YOUR HORSE:
THIS OLD BARN

If you build a barn or keep horses in a rural area, chances are most of your neighbors also own horses, so a few more won't be a big deal unless one of yours is really unusual—a zebra/Arabian cross, for example, or a pinto mule the size of a draft horse. But if you move to a residential area, be prepared for a lot of uninvited guests, primarily children.

Owners who don't want guests fence their property and post NO TRESPASSING—PRIVATE PROPERTY signs at fifteen-foot intervals.

Other owners welcome neighborhood kids and their families. They act as tour guides while they take visitors through the barn and into the pastures, educating them about horses and how to stay safe around them. Try to anticipate how children can get into trouble around horses; for example, explain that they don't crawl under a horse on their hands and knees.

Stress to the children and their parents that they're welcome to visit any time, *as long as you're home and they call first*. But if you're not home, they are *not* to visit.

Robert Frost's poem about good fences making good neighbors is only partially true. Working with your neighbors so that everybody understands the ground rules is a more tactful approach and will probably be more successful in the long run than a fence and KEEP OUT signs.

YOUR HORSE—AN "ATTRACTIVE NUISANCE"

But there's always the exception—the smart-alec kid who *has* to see how far he can bend the rules and sneaks into your pasture when he knows you're at work. But he forgets about the single strand of hot wire that you use to keep your horses away from the wooden fence. When he gets zapped, he runs home, bawling. According to him, it's your fault, even though you weren't there and he was trespassing. Can his parents sue you?

Here's another scenario. A trail cuts through one end of your property. You want to do the neighborly thing and allow other riders to use it—in part because you want to be able to use the trails on *their* property. One afternoon, a little girl's pony stumbles into a gopher hole you didn't know was there, and the pony bows a tendon. The little girl is heartbroken and her parents are upset. Can they sue you?

Suppose the pony fell with the little girl when he stumbled, and the girl *and* her pony got hurt? *Now* can her parents sue you?

Since I don't have a legal background, I can't advise you. I *can* tell you that liability laws vary widely. It's a good idea to find out what they are in the area where you live. In rural areas, where people still take other people literally at their word, one of the unspoken rules of horse ownership is that horses can get hurt and people who ride them can get hurt—and it doesn't matter whose property they're on. Nobody sues anybody.

The only repairs this barn needs are cosmetic. The owners have already started landscaping.

But other people think a lawsuit is the only solution to any problem. I strongly suggest that you familiarize yourself with the laws related to horse ownership, even if it means sitting down with an attorney. I also suggest an in-depth conversation with your home owners' insurance agent.

THIS OLD BARN

Suppose you're looking at property with a barn already on it. Do you like it enough to move your horse in as soon as the property is legally yours? Or does it need cleaning or renovating first? Or do you want to bulldoze it and start all over?

The Zoning Department, Revisited

Before you do anything, check with the zoning department. As I said in Chapter 1, just because the seller has horses on his property doesn't mean he legally *can*.

If the property is indeed zoned for horses, your next step is to check county records. Unless you find a building permit on file that matches the description of the barn, the seller may have built it without consulting the zoning board or paying for a permit. That omission usually means a fine and/or you have to bring the barn up to code before you move your horse in.

Check the water supply: Although some horse properties are close enough to civilization to have city water, many rural owners sink their own well. If that's your water source, ask the seller where the water comes from. An artesian well? Or does it come from an aquifer? Ask the seller where he dug the septic tank and leach field, and hire somebody (check the local newspaper or look in the yellow pages under Water and the subheading Well Drilling) to test the water for potability. Is the water safe to drink? Or is it contaminated because the seller raised cattle on the property for twenty years, or dug the septic tank too close to the well?

Also check county records to find out if other septic tanks have been dug on the property over the years, and where they're located.

When was the barn built? Ask the seller how old the barn is, although the seller is not necessarily the most reliable source of information. If the roof line sags, it's a pretty good indication that the barn has been here a while. Or it might indicate that the seller used inferior lumber, built it himself, and hasn't bothered with upkeep.

Some older barns are two stories: the horses lived at ground level and the owner used the second story for hay. (I've seen a few barns designed to store hay *underneath* the horses, so the entry to the stabling area is uphill.) Just because the barn was designed that way, store your hay elsewhere. Otherwise you have a fire waiting to happen. Two-story barns are now illegal in many fire-prone areas. So are any buildings with shake roofs (a roof with overlapping cedar shingles).

If the barn is a new-looking modular one, ask the seller if it's under warranty. Then contact the company and make sure the warranty will transfer to you as the new owner.

A roof over your horse's head: Ask the seller how recently he reroofed the barn. Is the roofing under warranty? Can he document it? If he "can't find" the warranty and your questions seem to irritate him, these are ▲ **Early Warning Signs**. ▼ In some states, undisclosed defects are grounds for a lawsuit. Better to find the defects yourself, *before* you buy the property.

A Walk-Through

Examine the barn—several times and preferably by yourself, without a realtor (or the seller) trailing you. This is a fact-finding expedition, so be prepared with a pen, notebook, camera, and a tape measure. Look the barn over as closely as you inspected the house.

Outside in: Sometimes owners keep horses in barns originally designed for a totally different purpose—to house goats or cattle, for example. In New Hampshire, where I lived for a while, a woman I knew boarded horses in a big field and fed them in an old goat barn. In sub-zero weather the horses were free to move deeper into the barn to stay warm, although most of them stayed outside, rump to the wind. The ceiling of a goat barn is much too low to use as permanent stabling for a horse. A cow barn is usually just a lean-to with a long feeding trough running the entire length, which is also not suitable for horses.

In both cases, rebuilding would be so extensive you're better off demolishing the structures and building a horse barn from scratch.

Manure Happens

If the structure is an actual horse barn, and actual horses live in it, find out where the seller has been disposing of the manure. If all he did was dump it in a big pile behind the barn, you have another fire waiting to happen. Spontaneous combustion occurs when manure mixed with straw or shavings is compacted instead of being spread out in six-inch layers to dry and decompose. The pile will look normal, but the inside is hot and getting hotter. Eventually the internal temperature will reach the flash point and the pile will ignite. If you buy the property, immediately call somebody with a tractor to move the manure elsewhere and till it into the soil.

Safety First

Has the seller taken care of the barn, fixing what broke without resorting to duct tape and orange nylon string that once held a bale of hay together? If you find a broken anything held together with baling wire, beware. In most areas of the country, wire hasn't been used to bale hay for twenty years.

Electricity: Does the barn have power? If everything else checks out and you buy the property, your second call (your first is to the guy with the tractor) should be to an electrician. First and foremost, make sure the barn is properly grounded and all the wiring is up to code. If you live in a mild climate, there's a good possibility that some of the original metal plumbing in the barn and adjacent outbuildings, including your house, has been replaced with PVC pipe, which could break the electrical system's ground.

■ In spite of a horse's size and weight, he's much more likely to be electrocuted than you are. But humans can get hurt too. When John ran a training stable in Rancho Santa Fe, he was almost electrocuted in the shower one morning because a space heater in one of the other houses had shorted out. Thanks to years of patch jobs by an unlicensed handyman who repaired broken iron plumbing with PVC pipe, the ground had been broken; the water itself was electrified. After a physician examined John, he congratulated him on still being alive. John spent the rest of the show season gamely fending off *Electric Horseman* jokes.

■ Make sure the electrician checks all the wiring and outlets. You don't want exposed wires anywhere in the barn except for temporary plug-ins (a coffeemaker, microwave, etc.) If the wiring must be exposed, make sure the electrician completely covers it in conduit.

Horse owners and their stuff: Horse people tend to be pack rats who hate to throw anything away. Who knows when a single rein might come in handy? Suppose the seller has nine horses in his twelve-stall barn. What do the other three stalls look like? Are they empty and more or less clean, or is the seller using them to store stuff?

In other words, how much cleanup will you have to do? Is it limited to moldy feed and old bedding, or does it include junk—manure-caked blankets, pitchforks with one bent tine—that needs to be hauled to the dump?

Look at the wood: As you jot down what needs to be repaired or trashed, examine each stall. Are the boards new-looking? Or are they scalloped because the previous tenant was a chewer? Or are the boards so rotten you can see rusty nails? If there are exposed nails in your horse's stall, he'll find them.

- The walls, or partitions, between stalls should be eight feet high, to keep your horse from going over the top if some intriguing, fresh-faced filly moves next door.
- Check the hardware. If the stall doors hang from metal tracks, do they slide easily, or are the tracks so rusted you can't move them? How about hinges—will you have to replace them? Sometimes, if you're lucky, all they need is a few drops of oil to restore them to working order.

Footing: Check the flooring, both in the barn aisle and the stalls. *Is* there any, or just hard-packed dirt? If it's wood, plan on removing it. Wood flooring is slippery and absorbs odors.

There is one exception: if the barn aisle and/or stalls are paved in wooden cobbles (six-inch square blocks of oak, end-grain up—the end-grain is the hardest surface of any block of wood), don't even *think* about replacing them. The cobbles are hundred-year-old antiques that are durable, provide excellent drainage, and resist odors. Before you move horses in, scrub the cobbles with soap and water, let them dry thoroughly, and bed each stall with shavings. For your horse's comfort you might want to add rubber pads, but if you bed your stalls deeply enough, that step isn't necessary. The cobbles will last another hundred years.

Feed: Check the feeders. In older barns these tend to be built right into the wall. Sometimes they're a round metal basin fitted into a wooden triangle. Sometimes the entire triangle is wood. The metal ones clean up very nicely with a stiff brush or scouring pad and a bucket of hot, soapy water. To disinfect while you clean, add household bleach to your bucket (four parts water to one part bleach), followed by a lot of rinse water. You'll have to evaluate the condition of wooden mangers yourself before you decide whether to leave them in or trash them. If you decide to keep them, clean and disinfect them the same way.

You Decide to Buy It

Suppose you love the barn just the way it is, even if it needs work. To be on the safe side, hire a building inspector to go over it completely before you make an offer to the seller.

Too big: You love the house, but the barn has to go. What to do next? Before you arrange to replace it with a brand new modular barn, go back to the zoning code one last time and read the fine print. Legally you may not be able to do that. But if the barn existed *before* the zoning laws that prevent you from building a new one took effect, you can usually renovate the existing barn under a grandfather clause. Depending on where you live, such a provision can give you enough latitude to gut the old barn, leaving just the roof and outer walls, and build a new one.

Find a reputable contractor who's built barns before. Before you talk to him, sketch out some plans. You don't have to be an architect. Just sketch out what you want. For example, you want all stall doors centered. Instead of a stall on one end, you want a washrack with a concrete floor and a drain. Since you plan to use the stall on the other side as a combination tackroom and storage room for pelleted feed (the contractor is also building you a hay shed), your tackroom must be rodent-proof and you must be able to lock it. Tell the contractor you want loosely-packed asphalt in the stalls.

Although you won't have your indoor arena—or your skylights—with a few more modifications, you just might have your dream barn after all.

SHELTER—A CHECKLIST

✓ Electricity. If you don't have power in your barn (you should), buy battery-powered lanterns at any discount store. A couple of these in your tackroom and feed shed will give you enough light to see what you're doing when you feed at night.

✓ A flashlight will help you find your feeder in the dark. Should your horse get out, it will help you find *him*.

✓ A phone—if you don't have electricity, keep a cell phone handy.

✓ A twelve-foot by twelve-foot stall if your horse lives indoors, preferably one that opens out into a twelve-foot by twelve-foot paddock.

✓ A twenty-four foot by twenty-four foot corral if your horse lives outdoors.

✓ Bedding for your horse's stall or corral.

✓ A knife to cut shavings bags open.

✓ A fenced area big enough to turn your horse out and let him play.

✓ A claw hammer.

✓ Assorted nails—you'll want to hang a calender on the wall and a cork bulletin board for easy display of emergency numbers, etc.

✓ Pliers. Useful for removing bent nails you can't reach with the claw end of your hammer.

✓ Two screwdrivers—a straight blade and a Phillips.

✓ Assorted screws.

A battery-driven hand drill—much quicker and more efficient than a screwdriver if you want to secure anything in your barn or tackroom with screws.

A saw.

A ladder.

✓ A feed bin (feeder, manger)—so your indoor horse can dine in comfort and your outdoor horse doesn't have to eat on bare ground.

✓ A lid for the feeder if your horse lives outdoors, so he won't get rained on while he eats.

✓ Solid rubber pads—lay two pads under the feeder for your outdoor horse so he won't eat dirt with his dinner.

✓ Solid rubber pads under the hitching rail so you can bathe your horse without making a mudhole.

✓ Fly bait traps.

✓ Two large, heavy-duty plastic buckets for watering your horse.

Or, half a fifty-gallon plastic barrel or drum.

Or, an automatic drinker.

✓ Two extra buckets—backup.

✓ A broom to sweep the aisleway and the tackroom floor occasionally.

✓ Cross-ties in the barn aisle—to groom and tack up your indoor horse.

Portable fans.

A coffeemaker.

A microwave oven.

A small refrigerator.

A radio or CD player.

✓ A hitching rail—to groom and tack up your outdoor horse.

✓ A rubber feed tub—so you can give your horse his pelleted grain substitutes while he's tied to the hitching rail.

A tine harrow that reverses to a drag.

An ATV, quad, golf cart, or pickup to pull the harrow.

✓ A pitchfork (or apple picker) to muck out your horse's living quarters.

✓ A wheelbarrow. Many of the colorful plastic ones hold too much for short or out-of-shape owners. I use an old-fashioned metal wheelbarrow with wooden handles. (Sand the handles or wear gloves to avoid splinters.)

A tine harrow makes arena maintenance easy.

Especially if you have a quad you can hitch it to.

You're not a serious backyard owner until you have your very own pitchfork. Gina shows off this century's version, sometimes called an apple picker.

Prop all gardening tools so the tines face the wall. If you don't, you'd be surprised how easy it is to brain yourself by stepping on one. . .

A muck bucket with handles. Some people would rather drag a muck bucket behind them than push a wheelbarrow.

✓ A rake with a bow head—to level the surface of your horse's corral. (He'll usually roll in the same spot every time.) If you're a small person, buy tools with a "D" handle that are especially designed for small people.

A round-point shovel—for moving dirt around.

A trenching shovel—for digging trenches.

A spade will come in handy when you strip your horse's stall or pipe corral. Since the bottom is flat instead of rounded, it's easier to dig out the area where your horse habitually urinates.

✓ A leaf rake—useful for general cleanup around the barn area.

✓ A hula hoe (also called a shuffle hoe)—useful for weeding around the barn area. Where we live, the fire department comes around periodically to check our "weed abatement program." Unlike conventional hoes, a hula hoe cuts off weeds at ground level if you pull the hoe towards you *or* away from you. (Other hoes are either/or.)

. . . as Brielle Jimmink just did.

Why you need a trenching shovel—to divert water out of your ring.

A weed whacker—the motor-driven version of a hula hoe.

✓ Hose bibs.

✓ Hoses—several heavy-duty ones that won't kink.

✓ Hose hangers—to coil your hoses and keep them off the ground.

✓ More double-ended snaps.

The usual suspects, left to right: a spading fork with a D handle—useful for digging up a stall with a packed dirt floor; a trenching shovel; a rake with a bow head—for leveling your horse's corral or a small turnout ring; a spade— for digging out layers of urine-soaked bedding; a leaf rake—for general yard and stable cleanup (in your spare time); a pitchfork.

CHAPTER 6

WHY YOUR HORSE NEEDS A VETERINARIAN AND HOW TO CHOOSE A GOOD ONE

I f you already own a horse, you should have a veterinarian. But if you're still in the wishful thinking stage—you have the property but you're waiting for the barn to go up or the pasture to be fenced before you buy a horse—it's a good idea to line up a veterinarian and a horse shoer as soon as possible. "Oh, I'm just looking" can very easily turn into, "Sweetie, come see what I just bought!"

Your horse needs a vet for the same reasons you need a doctor. The only difference is that you can communicate directly with your doctor to tell him where it hurts. Your horse can communicate pain only indirectly, by his behavior.

HOW TO FIND A VETERINARIAN

Since most horse people are animal people, you probably have a small-animal vet for your dogs and cats. Ask that person for a recommendation. That's how I found the horse vet I use, Dr. Mark Williams. In most communities the vets all know one another. Or, your small-animal vet may well be part of a larger practice that has two or three veterinarians. At least one should specialize in horses.

If that approach doesn't get you anywhere, ask at tack shops and feed stores—and pick a time of day when they're likely to be busy with customers. Horse owners love to swap vet stories, good and bad. (The bad ones usually make better stories, but take them for what they are—hearsay.)

Ask your horse-owning neighbors who *they* use.

Although more and more women are entering the field, most of the vets I've worked with over the years have been men. For the sake of simplicity, from this point on I'll refer to all veterinarians as "he."

Unless your vet specifically tells you otherwise, don't call him by his first name. He's a doctor: he earned that degree.

Watch Him in Action

If several owners suggest the same vet and the horse is already on your property, schedule a field call. Vets usually add a mileage surcharge when they come to you, particularly if you're out of their immediate area. If you're boarding your horse, ask the vet to come to the boarding stable, but check with the barn manager first. Most stables allow individual owners to choose their own vet. But a few have an arrangement with one particular veterinarian guaranteeing that he will do all the work for all the horses in the barn, no matter who they belong to.

While you're talking to the receptionist or the vet technician who's handling the scheduling that day, find out whether the vet has an actual, physical clinic—a horse hospital, in other words. Some vets work out of their truck or another vet's office and have an affiliation with a clinic sixty miles away in another town. If your horse needs emergency care and it's up to you to trailer him to the clinic, your horse might be beyond help by the time you get there.

Be at your barn when the vet arrives. Watch how he handles your horse. Vets love animals—that's why they became veterinarians—but a few don't act as if they do. Others are very horse-friendly but lack personality. And sometimes you and the vet just won't hit it off. A horse-owning neighbor may have told you there's a young vet trying to establish a practice in your area and described him as highly knowledgeable, a "thinking person's vet." *You* think the man's arrogant; he brushes off your questions and acts as though his next appointment is more important than the one he has with you. So you wrestle with your feelings: he comes highly recommended, but his attitude puts you off.

My recommendation: I'd follow my instincts on this one. If you don't like a particular veterinarian, do all three of you—your horse, your vet, and yourself—a favor. Choose a different vet. There might come a time when your horse's life depends on this man, and you have to be willing to trust him.

VACCINATIONS

Your veterinarian is your horse's only defense against an army of potentially deadly diseases. Even if you only call him once a year to immunize your horse against the most common ones, it's money well spent.

Your horse needs certain bacteria in his gut to help him digest food, but bad-guy bacteria can cause Lyme disease and infections like strangles. A lot of viruses can affect both of you—West Nile virus comes immediately to mind. Don't discount insects either, not only the

Prim doesn't like needles. On the other hand, she does like the horse cookies Dr. Williams carries in his pocket. Her ears indicate her indecision.

ones that transmit disease—such as ticks (Lyme disease) and mosquitos (West Nile virus)—but those that sting or bite. There's a wingless wasp with a sting so lethal its common name is "cow killer."

Your vet can't protect your horse from killer plant life—that's your job. (You'll find a detailed discussion of poisonous plants in Chapter 9.) Protecting your horse against parasites is your job too. But your vet *can* protect your horse from infectious diseases.

The good news: protection is usually available in a single shot, so your vet only has to stick your horse with a needle once. The bad news (for your horse): your vet *has* to stick him. Horses with a low pain threshold aren't fond of needles, and as a result they're not very fond of veterinarians. Other horses will nap through the entire procedure, even if it involves multiple sticks. Some vaccines (flu, strangles) can be "injected" by squirting the contents up the horse's nose.

The Usual Suspects

In the Southwest: The most common yearly vaccinations in this region are:

- Eastern and Western encephalomyelitis (inflammation of the spinal cord and brain; spread by mosquitos)
- Venezuelan encephalomyelitis
- West Nile virus (encephalitis that can cause inflammation of the brain; also spread by mosquitos)

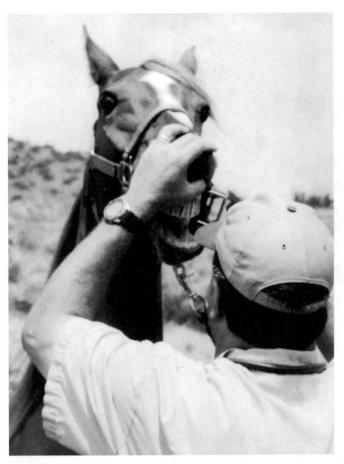

An uncooperative horse.

- Rhinopneumonitis (inflammation of the nasal membranes caused by an equine herpes virus; a sub-type of the virus can cause neurological damage; commonly called rhino or, more descriptively, snots)
- Influenza (acute respiratory infection caused by a virus; most people call it the flu)
- Tetanus (an infectious disease of the nervous system; also called lockjaw).

When your vet inoculates your horse, update your own protection. (A tetanus booster is good for ten years.)

In the Northeast: Owners in this region vaccinate their horses against all the usual suspects (see above) plus:

- Potomac fever (acute diarrhea, fever, and dehydration, usually accompanied by laminitis; a seasonal, summertime virus)
- Rabies (a viral attack on the central nervous system that leads to paralysis and death)

Strangles: Sometimes called distemper, strangles is a highly contagious bacterial infection that causes abscesses of the lymph nodes and upper respiratory tract. Since the disease is airborne, it spreads rapidly from pasture to pasture as the sick horses cough and sneeze. If there's an outbreak in your area, you may want to immunize your horse again, even if he's already been vaccinated *or* previously infected.

Proof of a negative Coggins: A Coggins test is a blood test administered by a veterinarian, who then signs a statement certifying that your horse has tested negative to equine infectious anemia, or EIA (also called swamp fever). If you show your horse, or before he crosses state lines (if you board him in Vermont, for example, while you build your dream barn in New Hampshire where taxes are lower), you may be asked to produce proof of a negative Coggins test. The disease is highly infectious and has no cure. In most states, a horse who tests positive must be quarantined until all the horses he potentially came in contact with have also been tested. Unfortunately some horses are carriers; they show few or no symptoms of the virus but can infect other horses. By law, these horses must either be permanently quarantined or euthanized.

Lyme disease: Unfortunately no vaccine has been approved to treat horses infected with this bacteria, which is transmitted by ticks and also infects humans, dogs, cats, and other domestic animals. (A vaccine for dogs is available.) The disease is very common in the New England area, New York, and New Jersey, but outbreaks have also been reported in Minnesota, Wisconsin, northern California, and elsewhere in the country.

Lyme disease affects the horse's joints, his musculoskeletal system, and his nervous system. An infected horse will suddenly pull up lame, with obviously swollen joints; the lameness can move from one joint to another. Occasionally a horse will develop laminitis, but behavioral changes are much more common. These include irritability, apathy, and a reluctance to move. Other symptoms include generalized soreness, loss of appetite, and swollen glands. The infection is treated with antibiotics.

If you ride in tick-infested areas, wear light-colored clothing (the ticks that carry Lyme disease are dark and the size of sesame seeds), tuck your shirt into your pants and your pant legs into your socks. Use permethrin-based insect repellent on your horse and clothes. As soon as you unsaddle your horse, check for ticks on his head, legs, beneath his tail, and under his belly. Ticks must feed on your horse for at least twelve hours in order to infect him. If you find a tick, remove it immediately. Use sharp-ended tweezers to grasp the tick as close to the horse's skin (and the tick's mouth parts) as possible, and pull straight back.

Preserve the tick in rubbing alcohol in a tightly-closed container labeled with your name, address, phone number, and the date, and give it to your vet or local health department. If you or your horse develops symptoms, a fast, accurate diagnosis is vital.

Your vet is your best source of information about other vaccinations common in your area.

A HEALTHY HORSE

The best way to tell if your horse is sick is to know what he looks like when he's healthy. A healthy horse *looks* healthy. His eyes are bright. His coat is shiny. His gums are pink, and so is the glistening inner lining of his nostrils; you see it when he snorts or breathes hard after exercise. He's interested in what goes on around him. This is one reason you feed him three times a day and check his water: to check on *him*.

All healthy horses present this appearance to some degree, although some horses don't care what goes on around them; it's too hot, they're too old, or enthusiasm just isn't part of their personality. But apathy—as opposed to lack of enthusiasm—is definitely an ▲ **Early Warning Sign.** ▼

Run your hands over your horse's body at least once a day to check for bumps, scratches, and hot spots, particularly on his neck, down his legs, and along both sides of his body. If you live in an area where Lyme disease is prevalent, examine your horse for ticks every time you ride. Even if you live in a tick-free environment, groom or inspect your horse when you feed. That heavy winter mane may be hiding a splinter he picked up rubbing his neck against a rail.

Clean your horse's feet daily, and if you wear gloves, take them off to do it. Notice the temperature of his feet. Body temperature is good. One foot (or both front feet) considerably hotter than the others is not good. Skip ahead to the section on laminitis in Chapter 7.

Dinner

By reputation, horses are gluttons. In reality, horses in the wild spent most of their day foraging for food. Unless you keep your horse on pasture twenty-four hours a day, you're forcing him to wait until you decide to feed him. His "gluttony" is instinct: if it's there, eat it. By tomorrow it might be under six feet of snow.

A healthy horse finishes his feed, although if you gave him more hay than he's accustomed to eating, he may scatter it on the floor of his stall and trample it into his bedding.

▲ **Early Warning Sign.** ▼ Most horses *are* gluttons. A horse who goes off his feed is giving you an important early warning sign. If he's not interested in eating, he's not feeling well.

Splish, Splash

Horses in the wild drank when water was available and they were thirsty. The average adult horse drinks approximately ten to twelve gallons of water a day. If the day is hot, he can drink considerably more, especially after exercise. Most horses drink very little at night.

▲ **Early Warning Sign.** ▼ When your horse doesn't drink, he's telling you he's not feeling well. If he's not eating *or* drinking, check his vital signs and prepare to call your vet. You may have an emergency on your hands.

VITAL SIGNS

When your horse is relaxed and in familiar surroundings—his own stall or corral—take his vital signs. If you've never gone through these procedures before, take his vital signs several times, writing down the results each time, until you don't feel nervous about inserting the thermometer and can unerringly locate the one spot under his jaw where you can feel his pulse. You already know how your horse looks and acts when he's healthy. Now you want a record of his "normal" vital signs so you know what to look for under abnormal conditions, when he may be too sick to tell you where it hurts.

A Quick Summary

A healthy horse, at rest, has a temperature range of 99.0°F to 101.5°F. Average is 100.5°F. His respiration rate—how often he breathes—is usually eight to sixteen times per minute. After strenuous work, especially during hot weather, his respiration rate can soar to one hundred twenty breaths per minute. The normal pulse rate of a relaxed horse is sixteen to thirty-six beats per minute. To find his capillary refill time—how long it takes blood to return to a particular part of his body—press your thumb into his gum, then withdraw it. A white spot will appear. In a healthy horse, the pink will come back within two seconds. Check for gut noises by putting your ear or a stethoscope directly behind your horse's girth area. You should hear a low, steady rumble.

How to Take His Temperature

If your horse is running a fever, you need to know about it. Most vets still use old-fashioned glass rectal thermometers with a column of mercury that rises with the horse's temperature. You need a similar one with a glass loop on the non-bulbous end; tack stores carry them. (The only differences between a horse thermometer and a human one is that little glass loop and the price.) Tie a string to the loop and tie the other end to a spring-operated clothespin. Clip the clothespin to your horse's tail, so if he accidentally expels the thermometer, it won't fall to the ground where he can step on it and break it. Although you might accidentally insert the thermometer too far, the horse can't suck it into his rectum. Those muscles work in only one direction.

Reading the thermometer: In order to see the mercury level, you have to hold the thermometer just so, at a certain angle, when the light is just right. A glass thermometer might be more accurate than other thermometers, but you won't know that if you can't read it. Consider buying a plastic digital model. Dr. Williams' advice: "Don't keep a glass thermometer in the barn—if the indoor temperature gets too warm, it explodes!"

■ If you want to attach a string to your digital thermometer, cut off a length of string, tie one end to a clothespin, hold the other end against the top of the thermometer, and add a drop of epoxy.

■ If you do use a glass thermometer, shake it down until the mercury level drops. Smear the silver bulb with a lubricant like Vaseline or K-Y Jelly, lift your horse's tail, and insert the thermometer *almost* all the way in. Clip the clothespin to his tail. Wait about two minutes, remove the thermometer, wipe it clean on his tail, read it, and record his temperature. When you're finished, shake the thermometer down again and wipe it clean with a paper towel dampened with rubbing alcohol. (Rubbing alcohol, available from your local supermarket, is a good general disinfectant to use for items like thermometers, combs, etc. to avoid spreading infection.)

How to Check His Respiration

Watch your horse breathe; his nostrils will dilate slightly. If you can't see it or aren't sure you see it, hold the back of your hand in front of one nostril to feel his breath each time he exhales. Using a watch with a second hand, count how many breaths he takes per minute. Or, count for thirty seconds and multiply by two.

How to Check His Pulse

Facing your horse's left side, where his heart is, place your finger on one of the following arteries: one lies directly behind his elbow; another can be found along the bottom of his jaw; another follows the inside of the cannon bone of his front leg, just below the knee on down. Some people feel a stronger pulse on the inside of the fetlock joint.

Observe the Whole Horse

In particular, observe your horse's bodily functions.

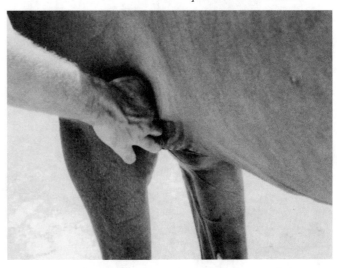

Dr. Williams checking for a pulse behind Prim's elbow.

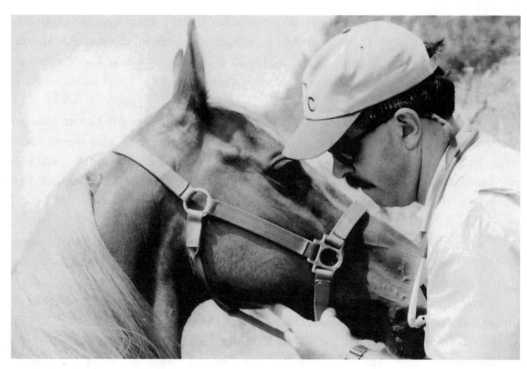

There's another pulse point under her jaw.

Dr. Williams' hand is in the shadow of Prim's raised foot; he's feeling for a pulse on the inside of her fetlock.

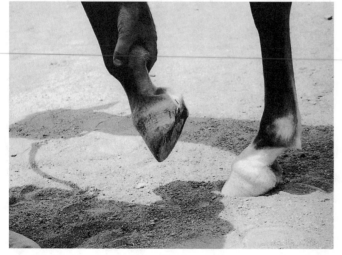

Urination: Have you seen him urinate recently? Horses assume a very specific stance when they urinate. Like dogs, a female's stance is different from a male's. A mare will usually rock forward until she's on the toes of her hind feet, squat slightly as she raises her tail, and urinate between her hind legs. Most geldings will walk forward a few steps with their front legs and spread their hind legs (you can often see creases in their haunches as they stretch). Some will extend their penis when they urinate, others will not. A gelding will usually urinate towards his front legs.

▲ **Early Warning Sign.** ▼ If your horse is straining to urinate and not succeeding, take his vital signs and call the vet.

Gut sounds: Have you listened to your horse's gut before, during, and after he eats? If you feed him three times a day you should hear continuous, low-level gut rumbles that sound like radio static. They indicate he's digesting his most recent meal.

Manure: Fresh horse manure is tan or tannish-green or green (depending on what you feed him), moist but not wet, and fibrous.

▲ **Early Warning Sign.** ▼ Diarrhea is never good. Neither is constipation.

Dehydration: Use the pinch test to see whether your horse is dehydrated. Gently pull on the skin of his cheek with your thumb and forefinger. His skin should be tight—you shouldn't be able to pull it out very far. As soon as you let go, the skin should slip right back. If you can pull his skin away easily and it stays "tented" longer than three seconds after you let go, he's dehydrated.

■ Another test for dehydration: raise the horse's upper lip and examine his gums. A healthy horse has moist gums. If they're not moist, he's definitely dehydrated—especially if he flunked the pinch test.

▲ **Early Warning Sign.** ▼ Your horse could be dehydrated because he's out of water. If he has water but isn't drinking it, he's probably not feeling well.

Behaviors That Only Look Alarming

Your horse's eyes roll back in his head. His ears flop. He draws his upper lip back from his teeth and his mouth gapes open. Before your conscious mind can overcome your panic long enough to run for the phone, the horse closes his mouth and licks his lips. One ear is still flopped but the other is pricked forward. His eyes are open and he looks relaxed and none the worse for wear.

What just happened? Your horse yawned.

Your horse suddenly assumes an odd position, one you've never seen before—both front legs outstretched, shoulders lowered, as though he were taking a bow. Is he straining to urinate? Colicking? Your dog looks like this when he wants to play—does your horse think he's a dog? Or your horse may extend one hind leg out behind him, full-length, then bring it back and extend the other leg.

What just happened? Your horse stretched.

Neither of these behaviors indicate a medical problem. But observe your horse's stretch stances. If they change or he does them more often and seems restless, they *can* indicate colic. Take his temperature.

A SICK HORSE

Know your horse. If he greets you with a nicker every morning but this particular morning he's mute as a fish, something's wrong. If he's usually active—moving around his corral or paddock, flicking his ears first one way and then another as he waits impatiently for his hay to hit the feeder—but today his ears are at half-mast or back (an indication of pain), and he stands apathetically in the same spot, something's wrong. Something's wrong if his tail hangs limply, he hasn't finished last night's dinner, or if the water level is exactly where it was last night when you filled his waterer.

Colic, the Number-One Horse Killer

Colic is every vet's most common emergency call. It's also the leading cause of horse deaths in the United States. Learn the symptoms so that when you call your vet, you can give him the information he needs right now. In an emergency, timing is everything.

A good yawn. Not a great yawn, but he's working on it.

What is it? Colic affects the passage of food through your horse's body, causing painful muscle spasms in the muscles surrounding his intestines that disrupt the normal flow of blood to the area. In the wild, horses spent most of the day foraging with their heads down, nibbling on what was edible, avoiding what wasn't. Their digestive tract was never designed to handle two pounds of grain at 7 A.M. every morning, hold the hay. The further you move from the "natural" horse—how he eats, what he eats, how much he eats—the more risks you take with his life.

The telltale signs: Because a horse can't burp or throw up—although he can cough—any digestive problem has to exit through his rectum, sometimes in the form of gas. An owner's first indication that something's amiss is often found in the horse's attitude: he acts listless and depressed. Other colicky horses will be agitated; they nip at their flanks, lie down, get up, and lie down again as they try to relieve the pressure in their gut. Take your horse's temperature. Is he running a fever? Check his skin for dehydration. A listless horse with a slight fever that otherwise looks and acts healthy and is not dehydrated can still be suffering from a mild case of colic—usually indigestion or gas.

Listen for gut sounds. A horse with gas will rumble like a freight train. Slip a halter and leadrope on him and walk him slowly for ten or fifteen minutes to see if whatever's bothering him clears up by itself. Sometimes it will.

If it doesn't, call your vet. An early diagnosis can be crucial.

▲ **The Early Warning Signs** ▼ of colic can be very subtle, especially if your horse *gradually* loses interest in eating or drinking and shows only vague signs of discomfort. Gradually means it might take you a day or two to pick up on the fact that he's not as alert as he usually is, and he isn't cleaning up his hay.

Take a closer look at him. Is he shifting from foot to foot when he normally doesn't? Does he nip at his sides, or raise a hind leg to kick at his stomach? Is he sweating for no reason (another indication of pain)? Can you hear any gut sounds? If you can't, call your vet. Your horse is colicking.

Sand colic: Sometimes colic is the result of a physical blockage in the horse's gut. Sand colic falls into this category.

■ If you suspect your horse is eating sand along with his hay, turn a sturdy, zippered plastic bag inside out and pick up two or three fresh road apples with the plastic between your hand and the droppings. Turn the bag rightside out and fill it half full of water. Park the bag on the toilet and wait twenty-four hours. Using a disposable plastic fork, hold the open bag over the toilet bowl and remove a road apple. It should be wet but intact. Slowly pour some of the water off. If your horse is passing sand in his manure, you can see it in the bottom of the bag. While this test is useful to see if your horse is passing sand, it won't tell you how much sand has already accumulated in his gut.

■ A horse fed on bare ground will pick up dirt with his hay, especially if the hay is alfalfa or one of the cereal grains (oat hay, barley, or wheat) because he can't resist going after the good parts—the tiny green leaves of the alfalfa or the grain in the hay. As you've just seen

This enterolith is one reason not to let a colicky horse roll.

for yourself, some of the sand will pass completely through his digestive system. But some will settle in his intestines and build up with each mouthful of sand-laden hay he eats. Eventually, so much sand builds up that the horse can't digest his feed and therefore can't pass manure. After you've taken his temperature (he'll have one) and checked for dehydration (he'll usually be dehydrated), lay your ear against his stomach and listen for gut sounds. If you can't hear any, the horse's digestive system has closed down. You'll hear the same silence through a stethoscope. Do not walk him. Do not let him roll. Call your vet immediately.

■ The bag test also won't tell you if your horse has any other kind of impaction. A gut impaction—a hard round "stone" that builds up around a foreign object like a tiny piece of wire—is called an enterolith. The one in the photograph weighs seventeen pounds, three ounces. The horse, unfortunately, did not survive the surgery.

My First Lesson in Responsibility

Bachelor, my handsome black Thoroughbred/Quarter Horse cross, "sanded" while he had the run of a big, fenced field with a pretty little Anglo-Arab mare named Daisy. Both the field and the mare belonged to my friend Anne, who threw alfalfa over the fence for the horses twice a day. No feeders. Neither of us had ever heard of sand colic.

One afternoon Bachelor was so listless he didn't want to walk over for a carrot, let alone go trail riding. When I realized that his half of breakfast was still on the ground, I called the vet.

The vet inserted a tube up Bachelor's nose and down his esophagus to his stomach and pumped mineral oil and water into him. (The same procedure is still used today, but the water contains electrolytes.) "Make sure he doesn't roll," the vet warned me as he left.

The only way I could do that was to stay with Bachelor, so I slept in my car that night, overlooking the field. Bachelor spent most of the night on his feet, his head hanging. Every couple of hours I woke up and checked on him. In the early morning, close to 3 A.M., I woke up to find Bachelor lying down, legs folded beneath him so he could hold his head up, but he wasn't rolling. After scrutinizing him a few minutes, I decided he was napping. I napped too.

Bachelor lived through the ordeal, and my education about sand colic—and how to feed a horse to prevent it—began. After the vet gave Bachelor a clean bill of health, he gave me some parting advice: "Sooner or later, any horse fed on bare ground will sand."

That's worth remembering, whether the bare ground is in Alabama, Maine, or Oregon. Ask your vet about the advisability of putting your horse on a maintenance level of psyllium, especially if the bag test I described earlier yielded sand.

Other types of colic: Colic can also be caused by a twisted intestine, which in turn can be caused if the horse rolls too vigorously. Horses can colic because of heavy parasite infestation (worms). Anything that causes abdominal distress, fever, and pain can cause colic. The warning signs are all very similar.

Colic—it can get worse: Colic can also lead to founder, although veterinarians aren't sure why. Since founder affects a horse's feet, I discuss it in the following chapter.

Responsible ownership. "Every horse will probably colic in his lifetime," observed Dr. Williams. "The critical difference is severity." Ride or exercise your horse at least every other day. Eliminate grain from his diet unless your vet tells you otherwise. Feed him good-quality hay for nutrition—to add roughage to his diet, and to keep him from getting bored. If you can, feed him three times a day to avoid overloading his digestive system. Make sure he has a plentiful supply of clean water. Keep a salt brick in his feeder—the salt encourages him to drink more water. In other words, if you follow the suggestions I outline in this book, your horse *shouldn't* develop a severe case of colic.

Know what's normal for your horse, both regarding behavior and his vital signs. When you call the vet because you think your horse is colicking, it will be helpful if your vet knows that your horse is running a temperature, for example, or that his heart rate has speeded up.

Lacerations

Minor cuts and major scrapes, which fall under the heading of lacerations, are a vet's second most common emergency call.

What are they? Your horse has wrapped a coil of rusty barbed wire around his front leg: that's a laceration. A pastured horse misjudges the distance from a branch to his face (at least I think that's what happened) and tears part of his eyelid off: that's a laceration. A horse rips his side up because the groom didn't slide his stall door all the way open, but the horse wanted out, shoved past the groom, hit the metal bolt but kept going: that's a laceration. Sinjun, my accident-prone Saddlebred trail horse, *did* rip part of his eyelid off, and *did* gouge a furrow in his side courtesy of a bolt. In fact that's how I came to own him—his owner was tired of paying vet bills and gave him to me.

The telltale signs: Because lacerations bleed so profusely they're easy to see. If your horse has hurt himself, you'll know it immediately. Your first step is to see what you're dealing with. Flush the wound with cool or cold water, which slows the blood flow. If the blood is from a superficial surface wound and doesn't involve your horse's eyes, tendons, or bones, you may be able to take care of it yourself. Most leg wounds fall into this category. Once the wound has stopped bleeding, cover it with a thin film of *water soluble* antibacterial ointment.

But if the blood spurts or doesn't stop after a few minutes, call the vet. Do not medicate the wound except to clean it. If your horse has seriously hurt himself—semi-amputated a body part or sliced a tendon—stay calm. Wrap a pressure bandage around the wound with anything that's handy and reasonably clean (don't wrap it *too* tightly—you don't want to cut off his circulation) to minimize the bleeding. If your horse can walk, move him someplace safe and quiet until the vet arrives and try to distract him from his pain.

Responsible ownership: If you can see bone or tendons (tight strings of shiny-white tissue) call the vet. Call the vet for any eye injury. If the wound is on the horse's leg, the vet will probably bandage it and give your horse antibiotics to fight off infection. Keeping the wound clean and reapplying the bandage will be up to you.

Horses usually injure themselves first on their legs, then their heads, then their bodies. And most horses don't even have to leave their corral to do it. If there's a loose board, they'll find it. The same goes for exposed nails. Metal feeders can take a beating if you keep your horse waiting for dinner too long. If a clamp pulls loose, leaving a sharp edge exposed, he'll find it. If something in the feeder breaks, he'll find it—usually before you do.

Punctures

If you feed your horse in the morning and find part of your split-rail fence sticking out of his shoulder, that's a puncture wound. The last time I boarded Prim (John and I were waiting for our house to be built) she was in a field with half a dozen other horses and *she* managed to poke a hole in her shoulder. Even though I walked the fence line inside and out—twice—I never did figure out how.

What is it? A puncture wound is deeper than it is wide. Because it's not as obvious as a laceration (most involve very little bleeding), you might not notice anything for a couple of days. As soon as you discover it, flush peroxide into it to thoroughly clean it. (Use a syringe; you can probably persuade your vet to give you one.) Puncture wounds can be hard to treat because they have to heal from the inside. If you don't discover them right away, they'll scab over and you won't notice anything until the wound abscesses and starts oozing pus.

Responsible ownership: Always call the vet for a puncture wound, whether it's recent or something you didn't notice until it abscessed. Your vet will flush it out and inject your horse with an antibiotic and a tetanus shot.

The smaller your horse's stall or corral is, the more likely he is to injure himself. He's bored because he doesn't have enough room to roam around in. Because of a horse's potential to hurt himself, vets prefer to see a horse in an indoor stall that measures at least twelve feet by twelve feet with an adjoining paddock, or a twenty-four foot by twenty-four foot outdoor corral.

Dr. Williams said it best: "Nothing will take the place of having sufficient room to move around in. Nothing will take the place of regular exercise. And nothing will take the place of attention."

Internal Parasites

Twenty-five years ago most horses were dead by the age of fifteen. Today horses frequently live well into their thirties, and veterinarians credit two factors. One is nutrition. We know a lot more about what horses eat and how they digest it than we did twenty-five years ago. The second is the development of safe, effective, over-the-counter paste wormers. To deworm a horse twenty-five years ago, a vet had to tube worm him—stick a tube down his nose and pump anthelmintic, or dewormer, directly into his gut. Many horses died because their intes-

A Horse Owner's Rule of Thumb:

Pus is more dangerous than blood. Any time you see pus, call your vet immediately.

tines were literally clogged with parasites. Others died because of the cumulative effects of poor nutrition and worm infestation.

Unless you religiously follow a worming program, early signs of parasite infestation include rough hair growth and/or failure to completely shed the winter coat, potbelly, tucked-up flanks, cough, lameness, depression, and conjunctivitis (an eye disease). Terminal signs include fever, diarrhea alternating with constipation, granular skin abrasions that are slow to heal, emaciation, and colic.

The most common worms (bots are not technically worms; they're the larval stage of certain flies) are as follows: ascarids (large roundworms), strongyles (large and small blood-worms—these pose the most serious threat to horses because they migrate to other organs, and because there are over forty different species), bots, pinworms, strongyloides (thread-worms), stomach worms, and tapeworms.

An ounce of prevention: Paste worm your horse on a regular basis—ask your vet if you're not sure how often to do it. If your horse mingles with other horses at shows or other competitions, your vet will probably recommend worming him every six weeks. Because Prim and Kyle live alone and Prim seldom comes into direct contact with other horses or their manure, Dr. Williams suggested that I worm her four times a year.

■ Paste wormers come in plastic containers that look like big syringes. Most have a rotating plunger on one end so you can adjust the amount of paste you deliver.

■ Since I don't worm Prim often enough for her to recognize a pattern, I can usually walk up to her, hold her nose with my left hand to steady her head, insert the syringe into the side of her mouth parallel to her gumline, and squirt the paste in before she has time to get suspicious. Paste wormers are aptly named; they're sticky, so the horse can't spit them out. If you don't insert the syringe far enough, you'll get dewormer all over your hands and your horse's face that's almost impossible to remove.

After you withdraw the syringe, feed your horse a carrot or other treat, so he'll chew it and swallow the dewormer along with it. But at this point your horse may want nothing more to do with you, carrot or no carrot. That's fine. He'll eventually swallow the dewormer, although you'll probably see him trying to get it off his tongue or licking it off the roof of his mouth for the next few minutes.

■ Make sure your horse doesn't eat directly off the ground. If his manure contains worm eggs, he can re-infect himself. Clean his corral or paddock every day.

■ If your horse lives outside in a field or pasture, clean the field or pasture daily too, particularly (if it's a big pasture) around the feeders. Rotate pastures whenever the grass is nibbled down and you see dust bowls forming by the gate and around the feeder.

■ Don't heap the manure in a pile. Even if all you have by way of farm or ranch equipment is you, a pitchfork, and a wheelbarrow, spread the manure in a thin layer as far from your horse as possible. You want to expose the worm eggs to direct sunlight and make sure the manure dries out.

■ Control the fly population by using fly predators and fly traps. Or use fly spray directly on your horse—whatever works best in your particular situation.

Bowed Tendons

Like most lamenesses, this injury doesn't involve blood. It does involve an emergency call to the vet, however.

Any horse can bow a tendon, although some are more susceptible than others because of their conformation. Horses with weak or over-long pasterns and big horses balanced on small feet are likely candidates for a bowed tendon. So are horses who overextend their front legs, particularly at a full gallop.

What are they? Most bowed tendons occur on the horse's forelegs between his knee and his fetlock. A bowed tendon has pulled away from neighboring bones and muscles, and you'll see the telltale swelling that resembles the "bow" of a bow and arrow. If your horse bows a tendon while you're riding, he'll probably pull up lame. If he bowed it by himself, while you weren't with him, the first thing you're likely to notice is that he favors one leg. Look at the leg—most bows are easily visible. Wrap both hands around it; if it's a bow, you'll feel heat. Since the inflammation causes tissue damage, it's important to call the vet as soon as possible so he can get the swelling down. Recovery time depends on how much damage was done to the tendon fiber bundles. If it wasn't too severe, you may be back in the saddle shortly—although any bowed tendon will never be as strong as it was originally.

A horse bows a tendon because he takes a wrong step or the footing is too hard. Bowed tendons are very common among race horses, particularly Thoroughbreds. Horses off the track with a history of bowed tendons—especially an old bow that bows again—are usually not suitable for anything more strenuous than light riding.

Responsible ownership: Call the vet immediately whenever your horse is lame. Although tendon boots have been around for a long time, the ones currently available really do protect your horse's tendons (they're marketed specifically as "tendon support boots") Play it safe; don't race your horse on hard or uneven ground or to the point of exhaustion.

Choke

An old problem with a new name, choke is what happens when a horse tries to swallow a piece of food that's too big. Pelleted feed that expands with moisture—such as your horse's saliva—can also cause choke. Signs include rapid head movements as the horse tries to dislodge the food item, snorting vehemently and often, and coughing, usually with his neck extended. If the food doesn't go down by itself, the horse will act restless and colicky, and you may see a foamy discharge from his nostrils that contains food particles. Call the vet immediately: your horse is in danger of choking to death.

Allergies

Most allergies appear as bumps or scabs that weren't there the last time you ran your hands over your horse. The culprit could be almost anything, since several different irritants can cause very similar symptoms, and not all horses react to them the same way.

First, see if you can pinpoint anything new or different in your horse's environment. When John ran the training stable in Rancho Santa Fe, a mare that belonged to one of his customers broke out in hives. After checking for new feed (no), new grooming products (no) or horse-cleaning products (no), John finally tracked down the culprit: a new brand of laundry detergent one of the grooms had bought to wash horse blankets. None of the other thirty-plus blanket-wearing horses had reacted to it.

Since the symptoms tend to pop up with mystifying speed—one day they're not there, the next day they are—don't spend a lot of time trying to isolate what's "different" about the horse's environment. Call the vet.

Other allergies cause mucus discharge from the horse's nose, intense itching (often an allergic reaction to the saliva of biting insects), or swollen legs. If your horse develops a hacking cough or swellings on other parts of his body *in addition* to swollen legs, call the vet immediately.

Scratches

Scratches don't happen when your horse plunges into a thicket of brambles. They happen when he stands in wet or even damp footing, particularly in cold weather. Your first clue is usually the presence of dry, hard scabs and/or oozing sores on his heels and pasterns. If you pull your horse's hair out when you remove the scabs, he probably has a related condition commonly called rainrot or scald. Horses with white on their lower legs seem to be more susceptible to scratches and scald than horses with solid-colored legs.

The treatment for both conditions is the same. Get your horse out of the wet, either by moving him indoors or by adding sand and shavings to his corral. Tie him up and fill a bucket with warm water. Using a washcloth and your fingernails, soak the scabs until they're soft enough to remove. With a clean towel, rub each foot until the hair is completely dry. Then spray the area with a horse product specifically designed to treat scratches, rainrot, and similar "crud." Follow the label directions.

You can also use fresh aloe. Snip an inch-wide piece of leaf from the plant, slit it open, and rub the "jelly" into your horse's skin over the scabby area. Repeat once a day for the next three to seven days.

Aloe, a useful plant. The jelly inside its thick, fleshy leaves soothes insect bites, sunburn, and other minor burns. It can also help skin conditions resulting from fungus, infection, and who knows what-all.

I've had success using both the fungicide and the aloe. Whichever method you choose, stick with it. Don't use a fungicide one day and aloe the next. If the condition doesn't improve within a week, try the alternative treatment. If *that* doesn't work, call your vet.

As an animal lover, I use cruelty-free horse products—developed without being tested on lab animals—whenever I can. If a product is cruelty-free, it will say so on the label.

Dandruff

Your best bet is Selsun Blue, a dandruff shampoo for humans. Follow the directions. For stubborn cases, rub the shampoo in with your fingers and let it set for five minutes before you add water and work it into a lather. Rinse clean with additional water. If the condition doesn't improve after two or three washings, call the vet. Your horse might have fungal dermatitis, which is more serious than dandruff.

Essential Information

Now that you know what a healthy horse looks like, here are some ways to identify a sick one. If something *is* wrong with your horse, you'll very likely be panicky when you call the vet. He'll ask questions, and you need the answers. By using this checklist, you'll have the information at your fingertips. Write everything down.

Take your horse's temperature. What is it?

Take his respiration and heart rate, or pulse. If your horse is sick, his pulse will usually be higher because he's in pain and/or fighting a fever.

When was the last time he passed manure?

Does he have diarrhea?

Is he eating?

Is he dehydrated?

Has his attitude or activity level changed?

ALTERNATIVE MEDICINE

Chiropractic and acupuncture have become extremely popular alternatives to conventional medicine in the past several years; some treatments are even covered by health insurance policies. Applying these alternative treatments to horses has also become extremely popular.

Chiropractic for Horses

In many states, chiropractors must have a prescription (oral or written) from a veterinarian before they can legally manipulate a horse. When you call a chiropractor, ask whether he has the appropriate training to work on horses, and if he's had experience working around them.

Many horses can benefit from chiropractic, but only if what's wrong with them is related to a dislocation in their spine. "I treat the vertebrae that are out of alignment," one chiropractor told me. (His patients included humans and horses, mostly racing Thoroughbreds.) "In a horse's body, every joint moves when [the horse] breathes. If one of those segments is fixated and can't move, that causes abnormal motion, and with that abnormal motion comes inflammation. Inflammation causes pressure. And that causes a nice, nasty little cycle. When it's broken, the body can heal itself. I can heal nothing. Nobody can. The horse can only heal itself. But it sometimes takes outside intervention to facilitate the process."

When a horse's vertebrae are out of alignment, they can block nerve impulses to other parts of his body. Chiropractic adjustment, or "cracking a horse's back," re-establishes normal alignment and relieves pressure on the nerves. Treatment is especially useful to relieve pain and the behavior problems caused by pain. Chiropractic can even heal certain internal disorders, for example, a blocked nerve impulse that causes a horse's kidneys to malfunction.

Chiropractic can't heal infectious diseases, bone fractures, colic, or abscesses—to mention a few of the more obvious exceptions. But one technique that can benefit nearly every horse is a brief series of flexion exercises, which are covered in Chapter 19. (Most of this information originally appeared in *Saddle & Bridle* magazine and has been reprinted with permission.)

Acupuncture for Horses

Much of what I said about chiropractic for horses is also true of acupuncture—certain injuries respond to it, others do not. Like chiropractors, some acupuncturists work primarily on humans and treat horses on the side. Other acupuncturists have a degree in veterinary medicine.

I've never consulted a chiropractor for my horses, but I did use the services of an acupuncturist once. Faced with a similar problem, I would do so again. (The following account also appeared in *Saddle & Bridle* and has been reprinted with permission.)

Late one afternoon while I longed Sinjun in the bull pen before riding, his hindquarters collapsed to the outside. He took two short strides forward, then lurched and almost fell.

Terrified, I ran to him, not knowing what had happened. Since he was clearly favoring his right hind leg, I led him slowly to the barn and called John, who was in the house. While I waited for John to pick up the phone, Sinjun stood next to me and drew his injured leg up under his belly like an egret until he was standing on three legs. After flexing it behind him as though he were stretching, he set the leg down and shifted his weight on it until he stood squarely. John didn't think it was anything serious, but suggested I turn Sinjun back out to pasture instead of riding him.

After turning him out again, I examined the bull ring board by board. Sinjun, my accident-prone Saddlebred, had done it again. One of the bottom boards had dry-rot; the only thing holding it together was paint. Of all the boards in the bull ring, Sinjun had managed to poke his hind foot through that one.

The following morning John looked him over and couldn't find anything wrong. But as soon as I rode him, I knew that something, somewhere, was definitely wrong. What followed was a frustrating, seven-year attempt to get an accurate diagnosis for a horse who was on-again, off-again lame.

The first vet said he'd pulled a muscle in his stifle and prescribed an internal blister (a technique no longer used) followed by six months of rest. The second vet gave him a full work-up of tests and X-rays. Diagnosis: bone spavin in the right hock and some calcification in the left. He put Sinjun on steroids and bute and suggested I shoe him with leather pads behind, to soften the concussion of hitting the ground.

By the time I contacted the acupuncturist, Sinjun and I hadn't cantered for three years, and he had stumbled and almost fallen with me twice, both times by knuckling over at the fetlock. Both times I remember feeling that the movement, the stumble, had started behind me but not necessarily from his hocks.

Although Sinjun never lost his playful disposition or his curiosity, there was an area on his croup he didn't like me to touch when I groomed him, and he was hesitant about going up or down hills. If he was in pain, I wanted to alleviate it. From the little I knew about acupuncture, I thought it might help.

I turned to a man who had wrenched his back so badly as a teenager that in spite of eight months of muscle relaxants, anti-inflammatory drugs, physical therapy, and chiropractic, he was still in so much pain he could hardly walk. When a friend suggested acupuncture, he went along with it since nothing else had worked. After three weeks of treatment, he was pain-free and knew what he wanted to do with the rest of his life: become an acupuncturist. An animal lover and horse owner, his first non-human patient was a friend's hunter. When he and I met, he was a board-certified acupuncturist with a thriving human practice in Boston and a license to practice equine acupuncture in Florida, Massachusetts, and California.

Acupuncture works by releasing endorphins, naturally produced pain-killers, into the body. "The whole nature of acupuncture therapy is to stimulate the body to function more efficiently," the acupuncturist told me. When I described Sinjun's problem, he said acupuncture would definitely make the horse more comfortable. But he stressed that when he healed a horse, even a horse in severe pain, he couldn't cure the underlying problem that was causing the pain. Acupuncture can relieve the pain of founder, for example, but it can't cure a rotated coffin bone (see Chapter 7).

The acupuncturist had three sessions with Sinjun, and each time he blanketed the horse's rump with needles. After the first treatment Sinjun was noticeably more relaxed; he also had less trouble walking uphill. By the end of the third treatment, the acupuncturist said he probably couldn't help Sinjun any more than he already had.

A horse doesn't know what a placebo is. Sinjun didn't know that getting stuck by dozens of tiny needles was supposed to make him feel better. But it did. He still tripped occasionally, but he moved more easily and with renewed confidence, and I watched his expression brighten as we resumed our trail rides.

A year later, he stumbled and almost went down with me for the third time. From the way he struggled to keep his footing, it felt as though he had crossed his hind legs—at the walk. After a new vet reviewed all Sinjun's X-rays, he diagnosed him as a wobbler and recommended that I put him down.

I was devastated. Wobbles, or wobbler syndrome, is a rare condition found mainly in young horses. When it shows up in an adult horse, it's usually the result of a spinal injury.

But the vet was right; it's not safe to ride a horse who doesn't know where his hind legs are. While part of my brain screamed *Don't do it!*, the rational part consented, even though I was crying so hard I could hardly force the words out.

Sinjun was my clown horse—my friend, my love. I still miss him. Then and now, my only consolation is that I gave him a good life, and before it ended, I kept him free of pain.

Thank you Bob Banever, wherever you are.

THE LONG GOODBYE

If you bought a mature horse, he'll probably stay sound and healthy well into his twenties. Others will come down with one or more of the debilitating conditions that affect old horses. Once that happens, there will come a time when you can't take care of your friend anymore. He's too far gone—too sick, too crippled, in too much pain—but maybe you can't see it. (Probably because you don't want to.) At this juncture, most vets recommend euthanasia.

This is why I said earlier that you *have to* trust your vet. If in his professional opinion it's time to put your horse down, it means that he's considered all the options. He's trying to do right by your horse and is unwilling to prolong his suffering. Most vets are very straightforward when it comes to life or death decisions. If yours suggests euthanasia, say yes—for the sake of your horse.

HORSE HEALTH—A CHECKLIST

What follows is a list of vet-necessary items that you should have on hand before a horse ever sets hoof on your property. Some will need replacing after a year or two, especially if your tackroom isn't insulated.

If you already own a horse and are boarding him at a nearby stable while your barn is being built, these items belong in your tack trunk. Must-have items are checked.

✓ A phone or cell phone. Keep a list of the following: your vet's phone number; his after-hours emergency number; numbers for fire, police, and local poison control.

✓ A pencil and a notepad. Use them to record your horse's vital signs.

✓ A wall calendar and/or a cork board. *The* most practical way to schedule your next vet or shoeing appointment.

A desk with a file drawer.

A chair.

✓ A thermometer. If it's glass, store it someplace that stays warmer than 32°F and cooler than 100°F.

Vaseline or K-Y Jelly—easier on your horse when you insert the thermometer.

✓ Rubbing alcohol. Use it to clean the thermometer, to pickle ticks, as a cold-weather rubdown in place of water (it evaporates faster), to remove tree sap from your horse or greasy, sticky substances (like neatsfoot oil) from your work area. It's a very good all-purpose disinfectant—your own doctor uses it to swipe your arm before giving you a shot—and is available at drugstores and most supermarkets. You can also use it as a brace on your horse's legs.

A stethoscope—some owners prefer using this gadget instead of straining to hear gut rumbles with their ear pressed to the horse's side. Tack stores and catalogs carry inexpensive ones.

✓ A watch with a second hand so you can check your horse's pulse and how fast he's breathing.

✓ Antibacterial ointment for horses.

✓ Hydrogen peroxide for cleaning wounds. It's especially useful for carrying air into deep puncture wounds, and air is what keeps the bad-guy bacteria from taking over.

✓ Leg wraps or absorbent padding—use them for bandages and/or to keep dirt and flies out of an open wound. They're also useful for hoof wounds, when you have to completely surround the foot to keep it out of the dirt.

✓ Self-stick bandages. Use them alone or to keep leg wraps in place.

✓ A horse blanket—optional for most horses under most weather conditions, but useful in emergencies. If it's way below freezing and you have a horse with a fever and the shakes and no barn, blanket him until the vet arrives.

✓ Scissors.

Paper towels.

✓ Rub rags—discards from the family towel closet are ideal.

✓ An aloe plant. The gel from a snipped-off leaf (use your scissors) soothes sunburns and friction burns on both you and your horse. It can also help oddball skin conditions like scratches. Since this plant is native to the tropics, it doesn't like cold weather, but it thrives in humid, semi-shaded areas. Keep it in an attractive pot by the entrance of your barn or tackroom. When frost threatens, move it inside your house and set it next to a window. When spring arrives, move it back to the barn. And remember—it needs water.

A FIRST-AID KIT OF YOUR OWN

✓ Peroxide—you can share your horse's.

✓ Band-Aids of varying sizes.

✓ Gauze—in case you have to make your own Band-Aids.

✓ Sticky tape (*not* adhesive tape) to secure the gauze.

✓ An antibacterial ointment for humans.

✓ An aloe plant—share your horse's.

✓ Baking powder—add water to make a soothing paste for insect bites and stings. Or, use aloe.

Snake Bite Kit

According to the rescue workers and medical personnel I know, the best first aid for venomous snake bites is your car, with enough gas to get you to the emergency room of the nearest hospital.

CHAPTER 7

WHY YOUR HORSE NEEDS A FARRIER AND HOW TO CHOOSE A GOOD ONE

No foot, no horse is a truism all horse owners live by. Unless you take care of your horse's feet, he may not stay sound enough for you to ride him.

In spite of the horse shoer's vital role in your horse's well-being, he doesn't need a college degree, although your vet does. Most horse shoers, or farriers, know their stuff; they wouldn't stay in business long if they didn't. But you'll only see your farrier every six or eight weeks, whenever your horse needs his feet trimmed. These facts shift the burden of daily hoof care to you. Learn as much as you can about your horse's feet and how to take care of them. That way, if your farrier suggests modifying your horse's front shoes, you can ask why—and actually understand what he tells you. Books on hoof care are available in bookstores, tack stores, and from the library. The best will give you the information you need in clear, nontechnical language that won't scare you to death—as in, "Oh, no! Is *that* what's wrong with my horse?" (See Appendix II.)

DEFINE YOUR TERMS

Horse-speak is not an international language. It's not even a national language. Depending on where you live and what kind of riding you do, your saddle either has a cinch or a girth. Most horse people know that if you ride Western, it's a cinch; if you ride English, it's a girth. Other terms are more obscure. If you tell a race-horse trainer you like the way his new two-year-old colt "wears his ears," the trainer—unless he's from the South or familiar with show horses—will look at you in bewilderment. (A horse with an alert, eager expression, both ears pricked forward in anticipation, is "wearing his ears.")

What follows is a brief discussion of some of the terminology peculiar to horseshoes and shoeing.

A Hoof in the Door

The words *hoof* and *foot* are often used interchangeably, but there is a difference. A horse's hoof is the part you can see—the wall, sole, and frog. The hoof and everything inside it—all the bones, tendons, tissue, veins, arteries, nerves, and so on are the horse's foot. Most owners say they clean their horse's *feet*, although hooves would be more accurate.

A horse grows new hoof from the coronary band down, similar to the way your fingernails grow. When a shoer trims a horse's feet, he's removing excess growth from the oldest portion of the hoof.

When a shoer talks about the *bearing surface* of the hoof, he means the part that comes into direct, physical contact with the ground.

When a horse *breaks over*, he rocks forward on his hoof until the front rim leaves the ground.

A *barefoot* horse doesn't wear shoes.

Sometimes a shoer will *re-set* shoes if they haven't worn down very much: he'll remove them, trim the horse's feet, and nail them back on. Mark Stallings, my shoer—who came rec-

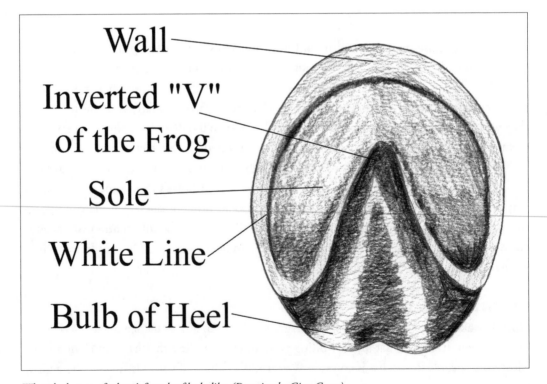

What the bottom of a horse's front hoof looks like. (Drawing by Gina Cresse)

ommended from Dr. Williams, my vet—doesn't do re-sets. Although some shoers will charge less for re-sets, it takes almost as much time to re-set a horse's shoes as it does to fit him with new ones.

Farrier, Shoer, or Smith?

I have two horseshoes on my desk that I use as paperweights. I've carried them around with me for more years than I care to count; they come from New Jersey, where I grew up, and belonged to Playboy, my first backyard horse. But Playboy didn't really belong to me. He belonged to my next-door neighbors, who both worked and didn't have time to feed at night, especially in the winter, or to ride. So they paid me to do what I would gladly have done for free: clean Playboy's stall, fill his water buckets, feed him dinner, and ride him whenever I wanted to.

I remember watching once, in fascination, while a farrier shod him. First the farrier heated a length of bar iron in his forge until it turned rose-gold. Then he pounded the molten iron into shape on the anvil, punched in nail holes, drew out toe clips with his hammer (toe clips prevent a shoe from sliding back on the horse's hoof and loosening the nails), briefly held the still-glowing shoe against the bottom of Playboy's hoof to see if he'd sized it correctly (a lot of smoke and sizzle, but the hoof wall doesn't conduct heat and Playboy didn't even flick an ear back), doused the shoe into a bucket of water to cool it down (more sizzle and clouds of steam), and nailed it on.

Farriers, often called shoers, are iron workers and horsemen (very few farriers are women). The Latin word for iron is *ferrum*; a farrier works with iron. A blacksmith also works with iron, the so-called "black" metal. But many blacksmiths make a living by forging garden gates, book ends, fireplace tools, plant stands and other items out of wrought iron and don't know a thing about horses.

No matter what you call them, today's farriers rarely shoe a horse the way my neighbors' New Jersey farrier did. Instead of hand-shaping each horseshoe, they buy keg shoes, which are premade shoes that come in assorted sizes. Some farriers do only cold-shoeing—no forge. Others still use a forge, but only if they have to modify the shoe. For example, they might add a bar across the heel area to encourage the horse to transfer his weight from the toe of his foot to the heel.

Corrective Shoeing

Corrective shoeing can "correct," or improve, the horse's way of going—how he moves or travels. Some horses who are lazy in front and shuffle and stumble from one stride to the next can often be helped by rolling, or rocking, the toes of their front shoes upward to stimulate breakover—that is, to pick their feet up sooner.

Corrective shoeing can also help a horse with faulty conformation, especially one who interferes with himself. For example, if a horse has one splayed front hoof, corrective shoeing can stop him from hitting his other front leg. If a horse forges—hits the sole of his front foot with a hind foot—the shoer may change the angle of the horse's hoof (cut more heel away so the horse has more toe than usual, or cut more toe away to leave the heel higher). Or he might roll the toes of the horse's front shoes to encourage faster breakover and/or add heel caulks to the horse's back shoes to shorten his stride behind.

If you have a horse who forges or scalps himself—hits his coronet or the bulbs of his heels with a hind hoof—you have to do your part too. When you turn him out, put bell boots on him. Horses usually step on themselves when they change direction suddenly at speed. On the trail, your horse will probably not interfere with himself as long as you keep him at the walk with an occasional jog or lope thrown in for variety's sake. But if he does interfere with himself, put bell boots on him before you set out.

A horse who continues to scalp himself risks a more serious problem: scar tissue may form on the coronary band. Since a horse's hoof grows from the coronet down, scar tissue can alter the natural growth of his hoof. In a worst-case scenario, your horse could develop a condition called quittor, an inflammation of the cartilage that involves not only the coronary band but also, if left untreated, nearby joints and tendons.

HOOFING IT
Here are two important rules of horse ownership. *Rule #1:* Clean your horse's feet every day. Otherwise manure and dirt collect in the sole and along the grooves on each side of the frog—that part of your horse's hoof that resembles the letter V.

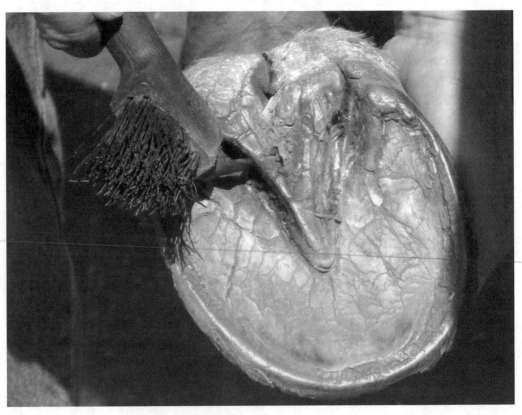

Cleaning the grooves on either side of the frog with a hoof pick. (Photo by Gina Cresse)

Rule #2: Use a good hoof pick. The kind I like has a plastic handle with a pointed metal digging device on the end. Reverse the handle and you now have a brush with short, very stiff bristles on the end. Use the pick first, to dig out anything lodged in the sole of the horse's hoof. If your horse is shod, that area is between the bearing surface of the horseshoe—where it contacts the ground—and the actual sole of your horse's foot. Because the sole is slightly concave, manure, shavings, dirt, and even small stones can pack so tightly they form a literal dirtball that's hard to dig out, even with the business end of the pick. Then go to work on the grooves alongside the frog, and the cleft of the frog itself. Use the brush to whisk away the dirt your hoof pick has

This is the kind of hoof pick I like—with a brush on one end. (Photo by Gina Cresse)

loosened. You can buy inexpensive hoof picks made entirely of metal, but they lack a brush. Cleaning debris out of the hoof is the only way to tell whether you've done your job.

Smelly, Crumbly Stuff

When you dig out your horse's frog, you may encounter a crumbly, black and white substance with an unpleasant smell. It indicates the beginning stage of thrush. Consider these crumbles as an ▲ **Early Warning Sign** ▼ that you need to clean your horse's feet *and* his living quarters more often. Treat the crumbly stuff by squirting the frog—in particular the grooves on either side of it—with a product specifically formulated for thrush. In advanced cases of thrush, an infection is present. At this early stage, you don't need an antibiotic because you're not dealing with an infection. You need an antiseptic drying agent.

The most effective thrush-busters come in two colors. One is purple, the other is traffic-light green. Both are guaranteed to dribble off your horse's hoof and bleed all over your hands and his lower leg, especially if his leg is white. Unless you *want* a horse with purple/green stockings, get rid of the stuff while it's wet, or he'll still be wearing it next week. To get it off, work fast; wet a small, stiff brush like a nail brush for humans and scrub against the hair of his leg. (Use the undyed hand or you'll just add to the problem.) Wet it again and scrub some more. Repeat. Repeat. Then scrub his hoof. Repeat. You won't remove all of it, but by tomorrow only a pale, Easter-egg pastel will remain.

Dr. Williams, who put himself through vet school by shoeing horses, added this tip: "With cases of significant thrush, make sure the farrier is trimming out questionable frog or sole *every time.*"

Frogs

A healthy frog has some give to it. While the horse's frog, the sole of his foot, and the walls of his hoof are all composed of keratin, which is what your own hair and nails are composed of, the frog contains the most moisture and thus has the most give. (Contrary to what old-time horsemen may tell you, a white hoof is not necessarily a weak hoof. Keratin is keratin is keratin.)

Hold your thumb against the frog, close your eyes, and press hard. You should be able to feel the frog yield slightly. A water hose in cold weather has about the same amount of give. (The bulbs of your horse's heel and the coronary band just above them yield more easily, if you want to compare them.) The frog is the hoof's shock absorber. Since the bearing surface of a horse's hoof is smooth and potentially slippery (shoes give him additional traction), the frog also helps the horse keep his footing when he shifts his weight to turn or stop. To keep the frog working the way it was designed to, keep it moisturized by applying hoof dressing once a week, or whenever the frog looks and feels dry. Your tack store stocks a multitude of products to help you do that.

Do not apply a drying agent on the smelly, crumbly stuff the same day you use hoof dressing. Apply the green stuff one day and the moisturizer the next day. If you clean your horse's hooves daily but only check for thrush once a week and don't see any crumbles, *don't* apply the purple/green stuff. By the same token, as long as his frog yields slightly to pressure, your horse doesn't need hoof dressing.

Why Your Horse Needs Shoes

Your horse might *not* need shoes, but he definitely needs his hooves trimmed every six to eight weeks. A horse's hooves grow one-quarter to one-half inch per month. His hooves grow even if he's shod. Before he can be re-shod, the farrier has to pull off his old shoes and trim off excess hoof.

The ideal: With every step a horse takes, one or more of his feet leaves the ground, and one or more lands on the ground. If you watch him, you'd probably conclude that each hoof lands flat. In reality (you can see this if you watch a horse in slow-motion), horses move almost the way humans do. As he strides forward with one front leg extended, that foot will land heel first. As soon as the horse's heel—frog first, with the pastern extended—touches the ground, the horse rocks forward and digs in with his toe to "grab" the ground for his next stride. Even if the horse is shod, his frog and the bulbs of his heel expand upon impact to absorb the concussion, then contract (return to their normal shape) once the leg is in the air. The faster the horse is moving, the more obvious the flexion of the pastern and the rocking movement will be.

To see how much weight a galloping horse's front feet absorb when he lands and how far the pastern can extend, watch a Grand Prix jumper in slow motion. According to course designer and hunter/jumper judge Jamie Alder, a horse coming down from a very high jump or one wider than it is high—a water jump is a good example—can extend his front pasterns so far that his fetlocks touch the ground. But, keep in mind that show ring footing—especially for fast, tricky grand prix courses—is deeper and "bouncier" than anything you'll have in your backyard.

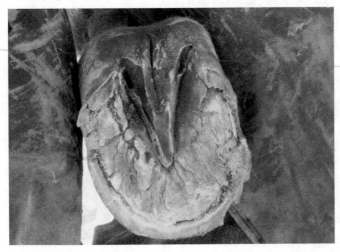

Mark Stallings, my farrier, has trimmed away part of Prim's sole and frog.

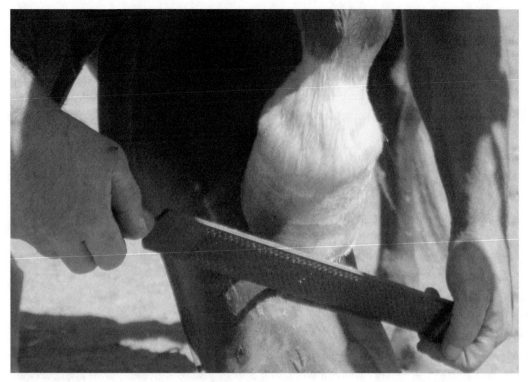

Now he's rasping the outside edge of the wall. (A rasp is a horse-sized nail file.)

If you want to see a horse who can travel at any speed without interfering with himself and wear his hooves down so evenly he doesn't need trimming, look at a mustang. These horses are walking examples of survival of the fittest—evolution on foot. As Dr. Williams remarked, "The ones that make it don't colic, never need their teeth floated, and keep their own feet trimmed."

Think about it.

The real thing: You want a horse with long, sloping pasterns not only because they're attractive, but because they act as shock absorbers for the horse's entire body. A horse with long, sloping shoulders that parallel his long, sloping pasterns will probably give you a very comfortable ride. A horse with short, stumpy, upright pasterns will give you a very bumpy one.

For most breeders, speed is a priority, or the ability to jump is a priority, or high knee and hock action is a priority—performance, in other words. They don't breed for good feet. As a result, a lot of horses, many of them registered, don't *have* long, sloping pasterns or good feet. Instead, they have weak, poorly-shaped feet that must be protected by shoes, and are susceptible to navicular and other physical problems.

■ A horse's feet should be in proportion to his body. If he's a big-bodied warmblood, he should have soup bowl-sized feet. In the real world, far too many 1,200-pound horses are walking around on feet so small and dainty they wouldn't look natural on a 900-pound horse. These 1,200-pounders aren't even good for trail riding; their feet can barely support them.

■ Because horses carry most of their weight on their front feet, their front hooves are rounder and have a broader heel than their hind feet, which are oval-shaped with less space between the bulbs. The shape of the front feet makes it easier for the horse to break over. Because the soles of a horse's hind feet are more concave than the soles of his front feet, he's able to "grab" more dirt and keep his hindquarters underneath him long enough to thrust his body forward. At all gaits, the stride originates with the placement of the horse's *hind* feet.

Barefoot

These days, few horses have feet sturdy enough for them to go unshod. Of all the horses I've owned, leased, or otherwise ridden, only Prim and Sinjun went barefoot. Horses with shelly feet—meaning that the walls chip and crumble easily—need shoes. Horses who don't grow any heel—meaning that most of the growth is in the toe area—need shoes. Most horses need shoes, even for trail riding. But if the footing is decent and you don't do a lot of off-roading in rough terrain, you may be able to shoe your horse in front instead of shoeing all four feet. Ask your farrier.

Your Shoe Budget

According to the Arabian Horse Association brochure that I mentioned in Chapter 1, keeping your horse's feet healthy will run you about $300 a year. But because Prim goes barefoot and I don't show or ride competitively, I don't spend money on shoes—not for her, anyway. When I bought her as a three-year-old, I asked the farrier to pull her shoes. Since then I've only had her shod once, in front, when she developed a sand crack (more about sand cracks later in this chapter). The farrier continued to shoe her until the crack grew out. She's gone barefoot ever since.

HOW TO FIND A FARRIER

Ask your vet. He sees a lot of horses in the course of a year and is in a position to evaluate the work of every shoer in your area. When he gives you some names, jot them down. After dinner, because most shoers will have finished work by then, call a few. Ask about the shoer's background. Has he gone to a farrier school? Or did he apprentice himself to an older, more experienced shoer? Does it matter? When I asked Dr. Williams that question, he replied, "It depends on where they went to school—some schools do a very good job but others don't—and who they learned from."

Mark Stallings learned to shoe horses by attending a hands-on, labor-intensive farrier's school in northern California. I like Mark not only because he's good at what he does, but because he works so quietly—no loud laughter or sudden moves. Horses relax around a shoer like that.

Most successful horse people I know, from Olympic-caliber amateurs to professional trainers, are quiet around horses and very quiet in the saddle.

I also like Mark because he does Prim's feet even though I'm just a one-horse account. When he was laid up following carpel tunnel surgery, I called five different shoers about trimming Prim's feet. Only one returned my call. A one-horse account for a horse who doesn't wear shoes does not appeal to many farriers.

If you own only one horse, be prepared to make a lot of phone calls.

Lameness

A lame horse limps, although you'll never hear horse people say that. You'll hear them say things like, "That mare's a little off behind," which means the mare is gimping slightly; one hind leg takes a shorter stride than the other. The short-striding leg is the lame one. Or you'll hear, while the speaker watches the horse trot, "That horse isn't traveling square."

Unfortunately, a horse that is slightly or sporadically "off" is quite common and a source of frustration for everyone involved—you, the vet who's trying to figure out why he's lame, and the farrier who's trying to help him with corrective shoeing.

There are any number of reasons your horse might pull up lame.

Sore feet: If your horse goes barefoot and the shoer just trimmed his feet, your horse might have sore feet, especially if the shoer nipped off too much wall. As a result, the sole of your horse's foot comes directly in contact with the ground. It shouldn't. The bearing surface of the hoof is the wall, not the sole.

Other possibilities: If your shod horse pulls up lame, he might have a stone bruise, the beginning of an abscess, contracted heels, a bowed tendon, or a mild case of laminitis—or the farrier might have driven a nail too close to the white line.

As a rider, your first clue that you have a lame horse is usually that he *feels* off, particularly at the trot. The steady, two-beat rhythm of the trot is no longer steady or rhythmic. Call the vet.

Thrush

The most common complaint of most owners is thrush. In advanced stages, it can cripple your horse. As I said earlier, it's easy to identify and very easy to treat in its early stages.

What is it? I've already discussed the crumbly, black and white substance with a bad smell that indicates the early stages of thrush. Horses get thrush from standing in muck—manure and dirt, especially mud. Occasionally a fungus or contracted heels causes it. Unless you want the expense of treating an advanced stage of thrush, clean your horse's feet daily, as well as his stall or corral.

If he's in a field hock-deep in mud, move him somewhere else (an indoor stall bedded with shavings is ideal) until the mud dries. If your horse must live outside because you don't *have* stalls, fence off a small area for him on high ground, or at least someplace where the water will drain away from where he's standing, and add four or five bags of shavings. Then call the vet and hope thrush is all that's wrong with your horse.

Left untreated, thrush rots your horse's frog and sole and can penetrate into the sensitive inner tissues of his hoof, causing serious lameness and a whopping big vet bill. If you catch it before it damages the interior of your horse's foot, the condition is reversible. Once your vet is satisfied that the horse is growing healthy new tissue, he'll probably recommend corrective shoeing to protect the new frog while it grows.

Responsible ownership: Clean the manure out of your horse's stall or corral daily. Buy a bottle of the green stuff and keep it in your grooming box along with your hoof pick. Pick out your horse's feet every day.

Contracted Heels

A horse with contracted heels develops a very narrow foot, especially in the frog and heel area. For that reason your farrier might be the first person to notice something's wrong.

What is it? Most cases of contracted heels are caused by lack of moisture in the hoof, or because the frog doesn't come into direct contact with the ground. Usually a horse will only have contracted heels in his front feet, and sometimes only one foot is involved. If the horse is lame (and that's not always the case), he'll usually work out of it—in other words, the lameness disappears with exercise.

If lack of frog pressure is the cause, contracted heels can indicate an underlying problem, such as poor conformation (one crooked front leg, i.e., a club foot), an abscess in the horse's sole or frog, or navicular disease.

Responsible ownership: If there's no underlying problem, you can treat contracted heels by applying a moisturizer to your horse's hoof and making sure he's trimmed and shod correctly (more corrective shoeing) so that the frog physically contacts the ground. Be sure to have your horse's feet trimmed every four to six weeks. If the farrier comments on how narrow his front feet are getting, call your vet.

Sand Cracks

Sand cracks is a catch-all term for cracks, usually perpendicular, in the wall of your horse's foot. Generally cracks start at ground level—the bearing surface of the hoof—and work their way up. The dangerous ones start at the coronet, usually because of injury (the horse keeps interfering with himself, or wraps barbed wire around his foot), and grow down. They're dangerous because they can split the wall of the horse's hoof apart.

What are they? Cracks can occur in the toe area, the quarter (the back quarter of his hoof), or the heel (the area closest to his frog). Quarter cracks and heel cracks are more serious than toe cracks because the hoof wall thins towards the back, and there's not much space between your horse's coronary band and his heels.

If your horse goes barefoot and develops cracks, this is an ▲ **Early Warning Sign.** ▼ Your farrier may need to evaluate your horse's balance, or your horse may need shoes.

Responsible ownership: Call your vet. He'll determine whether the sensitive tissues of the horse's foot are involved, and what kind of corrective shoeing your horse needs. Toe cracks that originate from the bearing surface, for

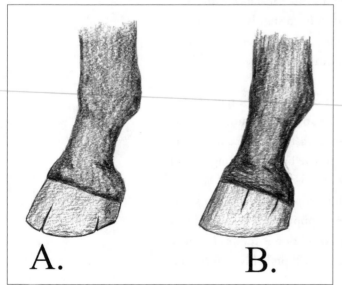

Sand cracks. Those on the bearing surface, where the bottom of the horse's hoof contacts the ground (Drawing A), are the most common and least serious. (Drawings by Gina Cresse)

A. B.

Prim had a very small quarter crack (located in the back quarter of her hoof). After Mark trimmed her feet, it was gone.

Two newly-trimmed front feet. Note that the leg on the left, with the white sock, has a white hoof while the other hoof is dark.

example, usually heal nicely if the horse is shod with side clips and the crack is held together by a metal plate or tough, quick-drying acrylic to prevent the crack from splitting farther.

Navicular

Navicular disease is more serious than thrush or sand cracks because it involves the navicular bone (buried deep inside the sensitive tissue of the horse's foot) and the deep flexor tendon.

What is it? Poor conformation—for example, small feet and straight stubby pasterns—and too much work on hard surfaces are the most probable causes. It's also possible to inherit a predisposition for navicular disease. Poor shoeing and poor nutrition can also contribute to the disease, which progresses very slowly.

As a rider, your first clue will probably be that your horse is lame. He can be lame when you first longe him, for example, but work out of it. Or he can start sound but then pull up lame because he favors one foot, usually in front. Tripping can be another early sign.

Eventually, the navicular bone erodes or develops spurs, and wears away the surface of the deep flexor tendon. When that happens, you'll notice that your horse has suddenly developed some odd behaviors—such as shuffling when he walks and trying to land on his toes instead of his heels. When a navicular horse stands still, he usually holds one foot, the one causing him the most pain, in front of him to avoid putting weight on it—the so-called navicular point.

Responsible ownership: If your horse does develop navicular disease, he'll get progressively more lame. The condition is irreversible. But if you catch it early enough, corrective shoeing plus supplements that contain glucosamine and chondroitin sulfate can make your horse more comfortable and allow you to ride him without hurting him—although not very hard or for very long. Your vet may also put your horse on a maintenance level of bute to relieve his pain, and/or recommend other drug therapies. Nerving a navicular horse used to be common practice. Today, few vets perform the surgery because the horse doesn't feel pain in the nerved foot and can further injure himself without knowing it.

Laminitis and Founder

Although both laminitis and founder affect your horse's feet, the condition usually originates in another part of his body. Many veterinarians use the word *founder* interchangeably with the word *laminitis*. Others think laminitis *causes* founder.

What is it? The layers of soft tissues inside the horse's hoof, called the laminae, become inflamed and extremely painful because the tissue can't expand past the wall of the hoof.

■ Any horse that colics can develop laminitis. Your horse can colic (and it can turn into laminitis) if you change his diet too quickly. If you turned him out to pasture for the summer this morning, but yesterday he ate two square meals of alfalfa hay and crimped oats, you changed his diet too quickly. Your horse can colic if the pasture is too rich—it contains too much high-protein clover and alfalfa. He can colic if he eats too much grain at one time.

■ But not all horses colic first. Some just come down with laminitis. As I said earlier, a horse forced to stand in mud for any length of time is a likely candidate for both thrush and laminitis.

■ In addition, there's acute laminitis and chronic laminitis. Acute means the inflammation is sudden and severe enough that it can cause a ridge on the horse's hoof parallel to the coronet, commonly called a founder ring (or fever ring or stress line). A horse that has had several attacks of acute laminitis usually develops chronic laminitis. Acute laminitis lasts from twenty-four to seventy-two hours; chronic laminitis is ongoing and long-term. According to Dr. Williams, "Any source of stress (changes in your horse's environment, food, internal functions, etc.) can potentially induce laminitis."

■ As an owner, you may discover that your horse has laminitis when you clean his feet. One hoof feels hotter than usual—not only the wall, but the sole and coronary band. If your horse has acute laminitis, he's in a lot of pain and may not *let* you pick up his feet—especially if the foot you want is the one he's standing on to relieve the pain in his other foot. Take his temperature. Most horses with laminitis run a fever of 103–106 degrees (normal is 100.5 degrees). Then take his pulse on the inside of his fetlock joint; his heart will be pounding so hard you won't have any trouble finding the artery. If your horse is also sweating, breathing rapidly, and/or trembling, he's in pain. Call the vet. This is acute laminitis and it's an emergency.

While you wait, pack your horse's feet in ice to bring the inflammation down, or run cold water over his lower legs until he's standing in a puddle. (Skip this step if he's been standing in mud. Run enough water over his feet to clean them off, so the vet can see what he's dealing with, and move him to dry ground.)

Responsible ownership: Once your vet arrives and has confirmed that your horse has laminitis, he'll recommend changes you can make to help your horse. From then on it's up to you. *You* have to cut back on the grain (or stop feeding it entirely), or turn him out on lush pasture only a few hours a day. Your vet will probably suggest corrective shoeing. Ask him to tell you *specifically* what he wants the farrier to do. (Some farriers can be very opinionated.) If you identify laminitis in time, even an acute attack will usually respond well to treatment, and you'll soon be back in the saddle.

With proper care, your horse shouldn't develop acute laminitis more than once. But if he does, the condition will likely turn chronic—in other words, your horse will founder, and the founder rings on the wall of his hoof will tell you exactly how many times. Even at this advanced stage you can keep your horse relatively sound with bute, proper feeding, and corrective shoeing.

As I said earlier, a horse's weight is supported by an intricate network of muscles, bones, and tendons, some deep inside the foot itself. Externally, the wall of his hoof, the frog, and the sole support his weight. Internally, support is provided by the coffin bone (one of three small bones in his foot), and the surrounding tissues that attach the coffin bone to the interior wall of the hoof. If a horse founders badly enough to destroy the connective tissues, the coffin bone will rotate, and the weight of the horse's body will push it deep into the hoof. In the most severe cases, the bone can push completely through the sole of the horse's foot. A horse this badly foundered is in excruciating pain, and most vets will recommend euthanasia.

Always call your vet if you think your horse is lame. He may not be able to identify the problem immediately, but he can figure out what *hasn't* caused the lameness by ruling out other possibilities. As I've said earlier, most foot problems are treatable if you notice them in time. Don't wait until your horse is standing on three legs to call your vet.

HOW TO KEEP A FARRIER

In addition to cleaning and caring for your horse's feet daily—and making sure his living quarters are clean and dry—you can help your shoer in some very specific ways.

Teach Your Horse How to Stand

Asking your horse to stand still while the farrier works on him sounds very basic. It *is* very basic—except some horses won't do it. Unfortunately if you just bought the horse, you have no way of knowing whether he'll stand while being shod until the farrier arrives.

Before you call the farrier: Watch your horse's behavior when you clean his feet. Does he give them to you reluctantly? If so, he may be in pain—an arthritic knee, a bowed tendon, or a mild case of laminitis. Check his feet; is one of them hot? Run your hands over his legs; does he flinch? Take his vital signs. If you feel or see *any* of these ▲**Early Warning Signs,**▼ call the vet. But since you had this horse vetted before you bought him (you did, didn't you?), he shouldn't be in pain. He may simply be testing you to see which of you will dominate your relationship.

If your horse is not in pain and raises his foot when you ask him to, reward him.

Brielle holding Prim's foot with one hand. Your horse ought to hold his feet up himself when you clean them—don't let him lean on you. Horses at rest stand on three legs all the time.

Young or inexperienced horses can be skittish about having their legs handled, especially their hind legs. Move slowly and work quietly. After an uneventful couple of weeks the horse will accept having his hind legs brushed and his feet cleaned as part of life and will relax.

If your horse steadfastly refuses to pick his feet up, follow this procedure. Follow it every time you clean his feet.

■ Face his tail so you're in position to pick up his near, or left, foreleg. Run your hand down the back of his cannonbone. If he doesn't raise his foot, use a little persuasion: pinch his fetlock with your fingers, your thumb on one side and two or three fingers on the other side, and add a voice command. It can be as simple as "Foot." If that doesn't work, use your fingernails and the voice command. If *that* doesn't work, rub your nails up and down the tendon area. (You might want to change your voice command to something like, "Gimme your damn foot.")

■ If your horse still refuses, lean against his shoulder. Because your horse doesn't want to fall over, he'll shift his weight to the right. Repeat your voice command and pinch his fetlock.

■ If he continues to refuse, pick his foot up yourself. While your horse is off-balance (because you're leaning against his shoulder), use your left hand behind his knee to bring it up and forward, and slide your other hand along the front of his fetlock to his hoof. Once he yields his foot, tell him he's a "Good boy," even if you have to say it through gritted teeth.

Rest his foot in your left hand while you use the hoof pick in your right hand to clean it. When you're finished, guide his foot back down. Always guide your horse's foot down with your hands. He has no way of knowing when you'll let go, and if you just drop it, he won't have time to make sure it lands flat.

■ Move to his off-hind leg and follow exactly the same procedure you did with his front leg. Slide your hand down his cannon bone and squeeze his fetlock. If he doesn't respond, you know what to do. It's a little harder to displace his weight from this position, but it's possible. Once he gives you his foot, hold it with your left hand, clean it with your right, and give it back to him.

■ Many right-handed people find cleaning the horse's off, or right, hind leg difficult, because they have to hold his foot with their right hand and clean it with their left. Although it's awkward, it is possible. Other people use the same method your farrier will, but don't try

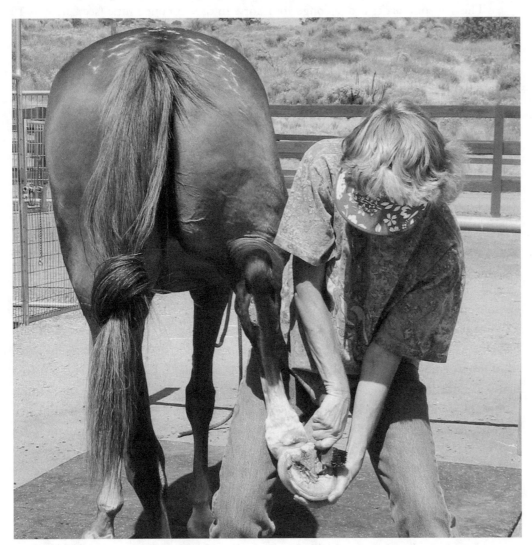

To clean Prim's left hind leg more easily (I'm right-handed), I rest her fetlock on my thigh. I tied a loop in her tail because it was blowing in my face. (Photo by Gina Cresse)

it until your horse has settled down and accepted the fact that you won't hurt him. As soon as the horse raises his foot, crouch slightly and *slowly* move your right leg underneath his foot so his hind leg rests on your right thigh. (As the horse raised his leg, you slid your right hand to the front of his cannonbone and then transferred the hoof to your left hand.) Now you're supporting his foot entirely with your thigh and left hand, which leaves your right hand free to clean his foot. When you're finished, lay down your hoof pick. When you know your horse better you can toss it aside, but inexperienced horses may startle at the noise and pull back. Hold his hoof with both hands while you slide your right leg out from under him. Guide his hoof to the ground.

Repeat this procedure every day, without any changes. Pretty soon your horse will pick his foot up as soon as you run your hand down his cannon bone.

The day your farrier is due, longe your horse to tire him out a little (see Chapters 15 and 16). By the time the shoer arrives, your horse will not only stand still, he'll pick up his feet on command.

Nine Helpful Hints

First, here's how *not* to help your farrier. People may tell you that feeding is a good way to get your horse to stand quietly without jigging or fussing. But *do not feed your horse*, particularly grain or a grain supplement out of a bucket, while the farrier works on him, and then withdraw the feed as soon as the farrier is done. Feeding your horse will make the farrier suspicious. "Is this horse such an outlaw he has to be bribed because otherwise he'll kick me into the middle of next week? What if the owner runs out of feed?"

Feeding your horse won't help if your horse is afraid of shoers. I once watched a farrier work a horse over by whacking him in the belly with the end of a rasp because the horse was jigging and refused to stand still. (No, it wasn't my horse, and the owner was nowhere around.) If that's been your horse's experience, you may be faced with a suspicious farrier *and* a suspicious horse.

Stand still with your horse: Instead of feeding your horse, practice standing still with him. Every day after you groom him, put your grooming box away and stand by his head. Most horses enjoy being groomed and are usually in zombie land by this time. Don't feed him—just stand there. You can tickle his whiskers if you want to, or blow in his nose, wrinkle his lips, play with his forelock, or stroke his neck. But don't feed him grain out of a bucket. After he's stood two or three minutes, reward him with a single carrot and return him to his stall. Gradually build up to five minutes.

Then pick up his feet one by one. After holding each about thirty seconds, put it down. If he doesn't object to having his feet held, lightly slap your open palm against the sole of his hoof or shoe. (Trainers use this method on weanlings headed for halter classes, so the farrier doesn't have to wrestle a frightened, uncooperative foal in order to shoe him.)

Should your horse try to yank his foot back, don't slap his hoof again. Just hold his foot in your hand until he relaxes. Then move in front of him and stretch his foreleg out, following the directions in Chapter 19. If he lets you stretch his leg, give him a carrot. The next time he lets you, cup your hand and *gently* slap the bottom of his hoof. If he doesn't try to snatch it away again, give him a carrot. Give him a carrot every time you slap the bottom of his hoof and he ignores it.

The next time the farrier comes, stand by your horse's head the entire time, but don't feed him anything—not even carrots. If the shoer works quietly and doesn't do anything to scare or hurt your horse, your horse will put it together; he has nothing to be afraid of. On the contrary, he has something to look forward to: if he stands still while the shoer works on him, you'll reward him with a carrot when the shoer is finished.

HOW TO HELP YOUR FARRIER:

1. Be with your horse when the farrier arrives. Shoers are usually prompt—more so than vets, who may have responded to a couple of emergency calls before arriving at your place. If possible, ask the shoer to phone you when he's about ten minutes away.

2. Have a level workplace where your horse and the farrier can stand. If you've put down rubber mats by the hitching rail, that's the perfect spot—unless it's raining. Whenever possible, have a covered area where your shoer can work regardless of the weather.

3. When the farrier works on your horse's front feet, don't let your horse lip his shirt, especially if your horse has just eaten a hearty alfalfa breakfast. The shoer won't find green slime on the back of his shirt as funny as you do. He'll also worry about being nipped.

4. When the farrier works on your horse's left legs, stand on the left side of your horse. If anything happens, pull the horse towards you so his hindquarters swing away from the shoer. You don't want your horse to kick your shoer. He might not come back.

5. Keep your horse's head still. If something catches his attention and he jerks his head around to look at it, the farrier will feel the aftermath. Stand close to your horse's head and rub his nose, tickle his whiskers, or otherwise keep him occupied to prevent him from looking around. As an alternative, tie him to the hitching rail with very little slack in the leadrope. Since it's where you saddle and bridle him, he already associates the hitching rail with standing still.

6. Keep a bottle of fly spray handy.

7. Some farriers like to talk and gossip; if so, feel free to join the conversation. Others prefer to work in silence. Respect your shoer's preference.

8. It's always a good idea to be there when your shoer comes. But if the shoer gets along with your horse, he'll probably be willing to tie him to the hitching rail and do his job without you, especially if you have to leave work in order to be there.

9. Make sure you have cash or your checkbook with you. Not many shoers take credit cards.

HOOF HEALTH—A CHECKLIST

✓ A hoof pick.

✓ Thrush medication.

✓ Hoof dressing (moisturizer).

✓ Bell boots for your horse's front legs, so he won't scalp himself when you turn him out.

CHAPTER 8

BASIC FOOD FACTS: FEEDING AND WATERING YOUR HORSE

All animals need food to live.

Some birds seek out only one kind of food—the African honeyguide, for example, prefers to dine on beeswax from wild honeycombs.

Other animals, such as coyotes and humans, will eat almost anything. But what the modern coyote now considers "food" has changed so quickly that we humans can only marvel. Our taste buds took thousands of years to evolve. But it took coyotes only a few generations to switch from elk carcasses and mesquite pods to campsite leftovers, fast food, garbage, pet food left outside, even pets left outside—collars included.

Horses have more in common with honeyguides than coyotes, although what they consider food covers a slightly broader spectrum. This chapter will examine a horse's basic dietary requirements—what, how much, and how often. Chapter 9 will cover the place of supplements in your horse's diet, the special needs of older horses, and various toxic trees and plants you need to watch out for when feeding horses of any age.

WHEN HORSES WERE WILD

Horses can live without food much longer than they can live without water—not a surprising statement when you consider that sixty to seventy percent of your horse's body weight is water. Before automatic drinkers and space-age stainless steel waterers, horses depended on streams, rivers, and natural springs for their water. If you're lucky enough to own pasture with a river running through it, your horse will drink when he's thirsty, usually before or right after he eats.

Make sure your horse has water available to him at all times. Thanks to modern plumbing, most horses drink the same water you do—whatever comes out of your kitchen faucet. The city or municipality provides it, or you have your own well. Or, if you really live in the backcountry, you have it trucked in. Water for agricultural purposes is available in some areas at a lower rate than water designated for human use. Agricultural water costs less because it hasn't been chlorinated, and it contains larger particles of minerals, ground-up snail shells, etc. than your tap water. This doesn't mean the water is contaminated. It does mean you might want to think twice before drinking out of the hose.

The average horse drinks approximately ten to twelve gallons a day. Your horse's water intake depends on how often and how hard you ride him, how much he weighs, whether he lives inside or outside, and the temperature and weather conditions. Stalled horses usually drink less than horses kept outside, especially if the barn has poor ventilation, since water in a

Timothy. (Drawing by Gina Cresse)

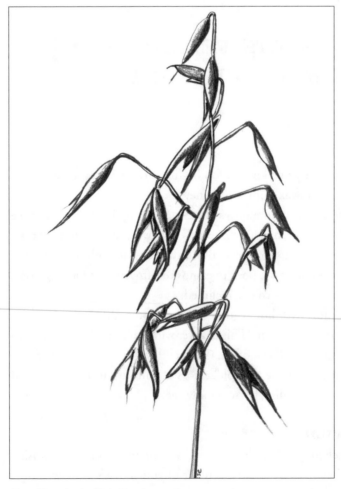

Oats. (Drawing by Gina Cresse)

Wheat. (Drawing by Gina Cresse)

tub or bucket picks up odors very quickly. All horses drink more during the day and in hot weather than they do at night and in cold weather.

Eating and Running

In the wild horses spend most of their day on the move, grazing (the technical term is *foraging*) on grasses and other plant life. For ease of discussion, nutritionists talk about forage by breaking it down into categories. Probably the easiest way to categorize forage is to divide it into simple grasses, cereal grasses, and legumes.

Grasses: The most common simple grasses include orchard grass, Kentucky bluegrass, coastal Bermuda grass, and timothy. The so-called cereal grasses include oat hay, wheat hay, and barley hay. These pack a higher nutritional wallop (more energy) than simple grasses because they contain kernels of grain. You can feed both types as pasture grass—in other words, you can grow these grasses in a pasture so your horse can graze on them—or you can buy them dried and baled as hay.

Don't confuse hay with straw: Straw is what's left of cereal grasses after the last cutting (or threshing, if it's grown for grain) of the season, and consists of coarse, dried stems that have little if any nutritional value. Horses usually won't snack on wood shavings, but some will eat straw if they're bored enough. (Some horses will eat almost anything if they're bored enough.) Bed your horse on straw if you want to. But unless your horse is so fat that your vet has put him on a diet, don't *feed* it to him.

Alfalfa: One of the most popular forage plants, alfalfa is not a grass at all. Like clover, a popular pasture forage, it's a

Barley. (Drawing by Gina Cresse)

Alfalfa. (Drawing by Gina Cresse)

legume. Alfalfa contains more protein than simple grasses and cereal grasses, which is why many owners are reluctant to feed it. Most hay is a blend of alfalfa and various grass and cereal hays. Dried clover is never baled alone, the way alfalfa is, and can be bought only in mixed hay.

What We Learned about Grain from the Greeks

The Art of Horsemanship, the earliest known guide to riding horses, was written about 400 BC by the Greek horseman Xenophon. Although horses may have been domesticated in isolated regions and used for hunting and transportation as early as 4500 BC, by 2000 BC they were being used for warfare throughout central Asia, Mesopotamia, Egypt, and Greece—usually pulling chariots. The Greeks, superb horsemen who both drove and rode their horses, observed that if they fed their war horses only forage, the horses tended to develop hay bellies and get winded easily. But if they grained their horses, the hay bellies disappeared and the horses grew sleek and fit. They ran faster and had more stamina—and they foundered.

Many of today's owners still feed according to that time-honored but erroneous principle: grass (either as pasture grass or dried and baled as hay) for maintenance, and grain for that extra edge. But your horse doesn't *need* an extra edge. He's not a war horse, he's a trail horse.

In spite of approximately four thousand years of domestication, the horse's digestive system hasn't changed much. It still allows him to get the energy he needs from low-calorie, low-fat vegetation—forage, in other words—as long as he eats enough of it. A horse's hooves, teeth, and every last bulge and turn of his 100-foot gut evolved to maximize the feed he ate as he roamed and foraged, fled from predators (or what he thought were predators), and foraged some more. The modern horse, who spends most of his day standing in a stall getting progressively more bored, still digests feed as if he foraged for it.

My point: Your horse's digestive tract isn't designed to process two big meals a day, especially meals heavy with grain. His stomach is too small, and the grain doesn't stay there long enough for him to digest it. Colic is one likely result; founder is another. Feeding your horse "lunch" makes you sound like a horse-crazy teenager with not enough homework and too much free time. But if you feed your horse three times a day, you're doing his digestion *and* his outlook on life a huge favor. When horse people talk about feeding smaller portions of hay three times a day instead of twice a day for "the boredom factor," they mean it takes time to chew hay, and chewing gives your horse something to do—especially if he lives by himself in a stall.

After the ancient Greeks discovered the benefits (but ignored the consequences) of graining their horses, somebody discovered that horses thrive on alfalfa. Shortly after that, somebody else discovered there was a relationship between a horse's need for calcium and his need for phosphorous. Since then, nothing about feeding horses has been easy.

PROTEIN, FAT, AND FIBER—THE SAME OLD SONG

Another way nutritionists classify feed is by evaluating how hard your horse works.

Maintenance: A horse you trail ride once a week is considered to be working at maintenance level, which means he shouldn't need additional feed to meet his nutritional requirements. A horse who's maintaining will not gain or lose weight.

A spokesperson for Purina Mills Equine Research defined the next category, called light work, as two or three trail rides a week that don't last longer than an hour. A horse doing a moderate amount of work is probably in training with a professional to learn barrel racing, jumping, how to be a fine harness show horse, etc. Heavy work describes horses who race, compete in endurance rides, or are involved in other high-performance sports.

Other variables: These include your horse's age and physical health, how hard you ride him, whether or not he's an easy keeper (hard keepers have to eat more to maintain their weight), and your environment (if the temperature is below freezing and the air is very dry; or if the humidity is ninety-eight percent and so is the temperature; or if a First Stage Smog Alert has been declared).

But the main way nutritionists and veterinarians talk about feed is by classifying it according to its nutritional components.

P Is for Protein

Protein: Protein is important because it's used to build and replace body tissues. Most nutritionists agree that a mature horse at maintenance doesn't need more than twelve percent protein in his diet.

Alfalfa: Alfalfa is approximately fifteen to eighteen percent protein (see the "Nutrients in Common Horse Feeds" chart on page 143). But depending on the weather, the composition of the soil, how the soil was fertilized, and the cut (was this hay cut early or late in its growth stage?), the protein content can go up or down several percentage points. Hay cut early has no mature seeds or flowers. Bermuda grass, which normally contains about seven percent protein, can, under ideal growing conditions, contain sixteen percent. Oats fed as grain, not hay, can vary from nine to thirteen percent protein.

Regional preferences: Your region also plays a role. Traditionally, West Coast owners feed alfalfa hay because it grows so well here, and add grain or another supplement to balance their horse's diet. But on the East Coast, many owners are suspicious of alfalfa—it's not native to the region and has a reputation (deserved, in some cases) for giving horses too much energy. These owners prefer to feed timothy hay plus a grain supplement, usually oats. Throughout New England and the Midwest, owners pasture their horses over the summer but also feed them hay that can contain clover, alfalfa, Kentucky bluegrass, orchard grass, and other native grasses. In the South, many owners think alfalfa is too "hot" for their tropical climate and prefer to feed a baled mixture of hays. Horse owners in the deep South usually feed locally grown grass hay. Some grasses are good, but others are so low in nutrients that feed stores refuse to carry them. In Arkansas, horse owners mainly feed Bermuda grass. Half the state's owners grow their own; the other half buy it at a farm store.

Throughout the country: The most recent trend is to blend. You don't have to choose between alfalfa and timothy. You can have both—two-way hay, which is usually alfalfa planted, cut, and baled with timothy. Or you can have three-way hay—alfalfa plus two grass hays. Some three-way hay contains no alfalfa and consists of oat, barley, and wheat hay in a single bale.

The Other *F* Word—Fat

Grains also contain fat. But for horses, that's a good thing—fat provides energy. The war horses of ancient Greece probably developed their edge from the fat in the grain as well as from the grain itself. Keep in mind that modern grains are light-years away from the crude cereal grasses that the ancient Greeks planted and harvested for their war horses. With few exceptions, today's horse grains are hybrids, so refined they're hardly comparable to the cereal grasses that grew over two thousand years ago on another continent. Modern-day grains contain mainly starch. In fact oats, corn, and barley are fifty to seventy percent starch.

Fat is beneficial for horses: Horse feed labels reflect the recent shift from feeds with two to three percent fat to those with five to six percent fat. Some feeds contain even more. Horse nutritionist Judith A. Reynolds, PhD, PAS (the initials stand for Professional Animal Scientist) points out that "horses require fatty acids to build fatty tissues. However, we don't know much about fatty acid requirements now. It is one of the areas of horse nutrition currently being studied." But she and other nutritionists have come to the near-unanimous conclusion that fat is a safer way of adding energy to a horse's diet than feeding him grain. It also puts a shine on his coat.

To provide your horse with fat, Dr. Reynolds—who has owned horses for over thirty-five years and is also a breeder, trainer, and judge—recommends feeding him half a pound to two pounds of stabilized rice bran a day; it's available in bags from your feed store. According to her studies and the current literature, "rice bran is loaded with antioxidants, essential amino acids, etc., and has virtually 100 percent digestibility."

Alternatively, Dr. Williams suggests adding one-quarter cup of corn oil (less expensive) to your horse's feed once a day for several days, then raising the amount to half a cup. While I've heard of owners feeding other types of fat, including bone meal, which contains rendered animal fat and fish oil, I don't recommend it. Horses aren't carnivores; why feed them something they would never eat in the wild?

While Dr. Reynolds has mostly praise for stabilized rice bran, she doesn't have much good to say about wheat bran, except that it provides about as much energy as oats (see the chart on nutrients on page 143). Bran is the outer covering of cereal grains stripped away during the milling process. Some owners feed wheat bran dry, for its nutritional value; other owners mix it with hot water (a bran mash) and use it to relieve constipation or colic in their horses. "Bran alone is not a balanced feed, and it is not a laxative in horses as it is in people. Horses digest it," says Dr. Reynolds. "Owners can achieve the same warm, fuzzy feelings by adding warm water to their horse's normal feed or adding apples or other treats. That way they are not changing the nutrient supply to their horse's enzymes and bacteria with a weekly bran mash."

Add a few more categories to the protein and fat and your horse's diet starts to look a lot like yours. (Check the nutritional information on the back of a loaf of bread. Then compare it to the nutritional information on a bag of horse feed.) We omnivores, Latin for "they'll eat anything," get most of our protein from poultry, meat, and fish. Horses get, or should get, theirs entirely from vegetation.

Carbs and Fiber

Another source of energy for horses is carbohydrates, but you won't find them on horse feed labels. Carbohydrates can be sugars, starches, or fibers, which are further divided into digestible fibers and indigestible fibers, the latter popularly called roughage. (Humans can't digest either kind, so to us it's all roughage.) Soybean hulls and beet pulp are good sources of digestible fiber for horses, which accounts for their current popularity as energy sources. They also contain very little indigestible fiber.

Horses get "high" on sugar just as kids do, and they behave much the same way. While a horse doesn't need sugar nutritionally, the way he needs salt, once he tastes that first molasses horse treat, he's hooked.

The Digestive Process: A Brief Digression

After the horse swallows his feed, it passes through six feet of esophagus and goes to his stomach. The stomach starts digesting small amounts of feed before passing them along to the small intestine, where most of the sugars, starches, fats, and proteins should be digested so they can be absorbed into the blood. Vets and nutritionists call the stomach and small intestine the foregut.

Feed particles not absorbed from the small intestine proceed to the hindgut for additional digestion. The hindgut includes the cecum, large colon, and the small colon. In the hindgut, billions of bacteria and other microbes work twenty-four hours a day to digest fiber.

If your horse is eating sand along with his hay, it will usually settle in the cecum or large colon. Impaction colic tends to occur wherever the gut diameter narrows suddenly. Enteroliths—stones made up of calcium, magnesium, and other minerals—can form around a foreign object in the hindgut and also result in impaction colic.

Back to Starch

Fat is safer than starch because horses can't digest starch very easily in the foregut, and if you grain your horse, that's what you're feeding him—starch. "From whole oats, which contain fifty-three percent starch," says Dr. Reynolds, "eighty-five percent of the starch is absorbed from the foregut. From whole or cracked corn (seventy-one percent starch), only twenty-eight to twenty-nine percent is absorbed, and the rest goes to wreak havoc in the hindgut. Barley (sixty-five percent starch) has only twenty-one percent foregut digestibility. I recommend feeding oats, but corn must be processed, preferably ground, and included as twenty percent or less of a pelleted feed. I don't feed barley."

Undigested starch also moves through the horse's intestinal tract too fast, which can cause intestinal upsets like colic. Feeds that contain molasses as a binding agent, to hold the feed particles together, add to the problem.

Good-Guy Bugs

Roughage is digested in the horse's hindgut while nondigestible fiber passes completely out of the horse's system as manure. Although horses need both types of fiber to stay healthy, they need more digestible fiber because that's their primary source of energy. An overload of indigestible fiber can give your horse a hay belly, make him lose weight, and cause impaction colic. Hay that's cut early contains much more digestible fiber than hay cut later in its growth stage. Dr. Reynolds compared indigestible fiber to tree bark. "Nothing except termites and fire can break it down."

What breaks down the *digestible* fiber are the friendly bacteria I discussed earlier, and they're another reason to feed three smaller meals a day instead of two big ones. With smaller meals, your horse's digestive tract spends less time "full" or "empty," thereby giving your horse and the bacteria something to do. If the friendly bacteria don't thrive, neither will your horse. Among other things, an unthrifty horse is susceptible to anxiety. A horse not fed within eight hours of his usual feeding time can develop ulcers, diarrhea, and colic.

Once a Day

Vitamins: Hay also provides fat-soluble vitamins (A, D, E, and K) that your horse can store in his body fat and draw on as he needs them—the same way you do—as well as water-soluble B vitamins he can't store. If your horse lives inside, and you keep him blanketed even when you turn him out, he may not be getting enough vitamin D, sometimes called the sunshine vitamin. It's up to you to supply those vitamins that your horse can't store, especially if you take away the grain or fortified grain supplements that ordinarily provide them.

Salt of the Earth and Other Minerals

In the wild, horses and other animals seek out naturally occurring salt licks to feed their need for salt. Charles Hood, a colleague of mine at Antelope Valley College, is a poet and ornithologist who has been to parts of the world I can't even pronounce. He's also the only person I know who has tasted a salt lick in the wild. "I have seen them in Africa and the Amazon—they occur all over the world. Good places to watch for wild game. A salt lick is just dirt with a high mineral content. It looks like a mud wallow. In clearings in the African forest, river hogs root with their tusks to gouge up mineral-rich soil. In South America, tapirs seek out caves that contain natural salt deposits. Parrots use exposed cliff-faces, hovering en masse to scrape out bites of dirt with their bills."

Supplying salt: Since you probably don't have a cave or a natural salt lick in your backyard, it's up to you to provide salt for your horse, since it's vital to his overall health. Horses who don't get enough salt don't drink enough water. As a result, they're chronically dehydrated and walking candidates for impaction colic. Salt is most commonly sold in two or five-pound bricks as plain salt (white) or with trace minerals (reddish-brown). Since your horse has a feeder, put a salt brick in the bottom so he can eat it whenever he wants to. Virtually all commercial horse feeds contain salt; the brick lets your *horse* decide if he wants more. Salt is also available in fifty-pound blocks, but you don't need that much for one horse. If he lives outside, keep the salt block sheltered—salt dissolves in the rain.

Some nutritionists, Dr. Reynolds among them, prefer to offer horses loose salt, the kind you put in your salt shaker, in a separate, non-rust container. In her opinion, a vitamin/mineral supplement containing salt is even better, because a trace mineral block does not supply the horse with what he needs in the amounts he needs. Other necessary minerals include calcium, phosphorus, magnesium, selenium, copper, zinc, iodine, iron, manganese, and cobalt.

A BALANCING ACT

In the "Nutrients in Common Horse Feeds" chart, Dr. Reynolds uses crude protein, fiber, calcium, phosphorus, ash (mineral content) etc., because these are the same categories used by feed companies—as you discovered for yourself when you looked at the label of a bagged horse feed. She also added columns for energy and starch to emphasize the difference between feeds.

A well-used plain white salt lick, pasture-size.

Calories: A "calorie" in horse feed means the same thing it does when you talk about your own diet. It measures the amount of energy released when you digest food. The only difference is that horses, being bigger, need more calories than you do.

According to Dr. Reynolds, a mature, 1,100-pound horse at maintenance requires 16,000-plus calories a day, compared to about 2,000 for a person. The more researchers learn about feeds and how horses digest them, the more convinced they are that salt and forage—or hay, its domestic equivalent—are, nutritionally, the only feed your horse needs to meet maintenance requirements. (Elderly horses are an exception, as are horses who have difficulty chewing.) A backyard horse given his fill of fresh, clean water and fed large quantities of high-quality mixed hay several times a day, with a vitamin/mineral supplement to fill in any nutritional gaps, should stay sound and healthy and enjoy a good long life.

Nutrients in Common Horse Feeds*,**,***

Feed	Crude Protein, %	Crude Fat, %	DE°, Mcal/lb	Crude Fiber, %	NSC†, %	Calcium, %	Phosphorus, %	Ash, %
Alfalfa hay	15.5–18	1.8–2.6	0.89–1.0	20.8–27.3	24	1.08–1.28	0.19–0.22	7.1–8.4
Barley hay	7.8	1.9	0.81	23.6	17	0.21	0.25	6.6
Bermuda hay	7.3–10.6	2.4–2.5	0.79–0.89	26.7–30.4	14	1.24–0.35	0.17–0.24	6.7–7.5
Oat hay	8.6	2.2	0.79	29.1	17	0.29	0.23	7.2
Timothy hay	6.9–9.6	2.4–2.5	0.72–0.83	30.0–31.5	18	1.34–0.45	0.13–0.25	4.8–5.1
Wheat hay	7.7	2	0.76	25.7	21	0.13	0.18	7
Barley grain	11.7	1.8	0.81	4.9	65	0.05	0.34	2.4
Corn grain	9.1	3.6	1.3–1.54	2.2	71	0.05	0.27	1.3
Whole oats	9.1–12.5	4.6–5.1	1.30	10.7–11.2	53	0.05–0.10	0.31–0.34	3.0–3.8
Wheat grain	11.4–13.0	1.6	1.55	2.4–2.5	65	0.03–0.04	0.36–0.38	1.7–2.1
Wheat bran	15.4	3.8	1.33	10	33	0.13	1.13	5.9
Stabilized rice bran	13.0	20	2.4	8.0	19	0.10	1.60	8.0

*Average values from analysis or estimated values. Large variations in nutrient content occur between individual feed samples.
**As fed basis, dry matter values are usually about 10% higher.
***Modified from *Nutrient Requirements of Horses,* 5th Edition, 1989, and other sources.
°Digestible Energy in mega-calories per pound or feed.
†NSC, Nonstructural carbohydrate consists mostly of sugars and starches. It is calculated from values from analysis.
Table courtesy of Judith A. Reynolds, PhD, PAS, and ADM Alliance Nutrition.

Hay and grain: The belief that hay and grain are the ideal horse feed dies hard, and many owners feel guilty if they don't grain their horse. If you truly feel that you're failing to do right by your horse by not graining him, Dr. Reynolds won't yell at you if you scatter a handful or two of oats or a pelleted grain-based supplement that your horse likes on his hay as a top dressing.

If you're working your horse harder than maintenance, consider adding a supplement rather than straight grain. Pelleted grain-based supplements, fortified with essential vitamins and minerals, are becoming increasingly popular. Pelleting ensures uniformity, so the percentages of protein, fiber, etc. remain consistent.

The one undeniable benefit of grain or grain supplements is that horses like them much better than they like hay. They especially like sweetened supplements that are easy to carry in your pocket and dole out to your horse to reward good behavior.

The Twinkie defense: As I said earlier, horses can react to sugar exactly the way children do. If you already own a horse, one who spooks at butterflies, would rather jig than walk, and has to buck before loping, you may not be seeing "your horse." You may be seeing "a horse" high on sugar. To find out which, Dr. Reynolds suggests that you remove all sweet feed and grain from your horse's diet and replace it with additional hay over a week's time. Make sure he has salt and a vitamin/mineral supplement in front of him at all times. Within two weeks your horse will reveal his true personality. (Some owners find they liked their "first" horse better!)

THE SECOND GREAT DEBATE: CALCIUM VERSUS PHOSPHORUS

Want to go crazy? Talk to two different nutritionist about the ideal calcium-to-phosphorus ratio. Calcium and phosphorus, both minerals, are vital to your horse's health. But one nutritionist thinks a mature horse needs 1.1 parts calcium to 1 part phosphorus—a figure that Dr. Williams and Dr. Reynolds both disagree with. They want to see owners feeding more calcium than phosphorus, and for mature horses they want to see a ratio closer to 2 parts calcium to 1 part phosphorus.

If your horse is on pasture or eating grass hay, he may need additional calcium. If he's eating alfalfa, which can be too high in protein for a mature horse, he may need additional phosphorus. Too much or too little of either can hurt a horse, especially a young horse that's still growing, a category that includes three-year-olds. When I bought Prim, a cob-sized halter fit her perfectly. The following year I had to buy her a horse-sized halter. Feed a young horse too much phosphorus and not enough calcium and his bones won't develop properly; he'll be prone to shin splints and intermittent lameness. Too much phosphorus can affect muscle development. As Dr. Reynolds observed, "The big mystery about the calcium-to-phosphorus ratio is that we really don't know how to prevent all growth-related bone disorders yet. This is a frustrating issue veterinarians and nutritionists face on a daily basis."

When you're not sure which feed contains how much of what, check Dr. Reynolds' "Nutrients in Common Horse Feeds" chart (page 143). That's why I asked her to draw it up—so you can see for yourself approximately how much calcium, phosphorus, protein, etc. is contained in alfalfa, grass hay, oats, and other common feeds.

My Recommendation

I second a suggestion Dr. Reynolds made: consider your veterinarian, your nutritionist, and your shoer as your teammates. When you find the horse you want, consult with the first one before you write the check. After your horse arrives on your property, consult with all three.

Finding a nutritionist: You can't find nutritionists in the yellow pages. But you can find them at universities, especially those with agriculture or equine departments. Ask your vet, shoer, or your local state extension service agent for referrals. Look on the label on any bag of horse feed. Check the feed ads in magazines. Do a web search. They're out there.

HAY: WHERE TO BUY IT AND WHAT TO LOOK FOR

Most horse owners buy hay at feed stores. In rural areas they're easy to find by looking under Horse in the yellow pages. If you don't see anything listed under Horse Feed, call one of the boarding facilities. Horse people are usually willing to help each other out. In suburban areas, some pet stores carry horse feed.

Feed stores sell all types of hay, shavings, straw, salt blocks, and bag after bag of cereal grains, pelleted grains, shaved alfalfa or crumbled or cubed alfalfa. Most also carry feed for cattle, chickens, goats, sheep, swine, and other farm animals. They all deliver directly to your barn, but some give you a better deal if you buck your hay bales into your pickup and drive them home yourself.

Buying Local

As a one-horse owner you usually can't buy hay directly from the grower, unless the grower is a small farmer who plants enough for his own use plus a little extra. But be careful—sometimes the reason he has "extra" is because it's not hay anymore. It's too far gone.

When I was very new at backyard horsekeeping, I kept Bachelor and Anne's mare Daisy while Anne fenced a pasture on her property. Once it was finished, we took turns. Both horses would stay at my house for a while—all I had was a big corral, but I also had easy access to unlimited back-country trails. Then we'd ride to Anne's and turn the horses out for a couple of months where they had room to roam. Another attraction: her house was twenty minutes away from the Pacific Ocean.

When I noticed a HAY FOR SALE sign on my way home one day, I stopped to investigate. I don't remember if it was wheat or barley hay. I do know Anne and I were feeding alfalfa, so we were careful about introducing the new feed and phasing out the old. When the horses were three or four days into the transition, we decided to go riding. Anne slid the bit into Daisy's mouth and gasped. Quickly she scooped a handful of soggy foxtails that had wadded up like chewing tobacco between Daisy's lower lip and her teeth. The mare even had foxtails under her tongue. I checked Bachelor—same thing. Anne and I hadn't noticed that the grain heads were so dry they had little hooks all over them. Most horses who get a foxtail or other prickly plant particle lodged in their mouth will drool long strings of saliva. But not these horses.

Of course Anne and I immediately discontinued feeding the hay. Since I wanted to be a good neighbor, I didn't call the farmer to complain. But when I saw his HAY FOR SALE sign the following year, I drove on by.

What, How Much, and How Often Should You Feed Your Horse?

The average trail horse should eat approximately twenty pounds of hay per day. How can you tell whether he's maintaining on this diet? The best way to determine that is to weigh him, an option not open to most backyard owners. But the eyeball test can be just as reliable. What does your horse *look* like?

THE HORSE CONDITION SCORECARD

You may want to photograph your horse before looking at the photos in this section and reading the information that follows.

Popularly called the "The Horse Condition Scorecard" (or simply "the scorecard"), the information allows you to evaluate the amount of visible fat on a horse's body. Developed by Don R. Henneke and his colleagues G. D. Potter, J. L. Kreider, and B. F. Yeates at Texas A & M University over twenty years ago, the scorecard is used by feed companies and nutritionists nationwide. The version I discuss here appeared in a study by D. R. Henneke et al., "A

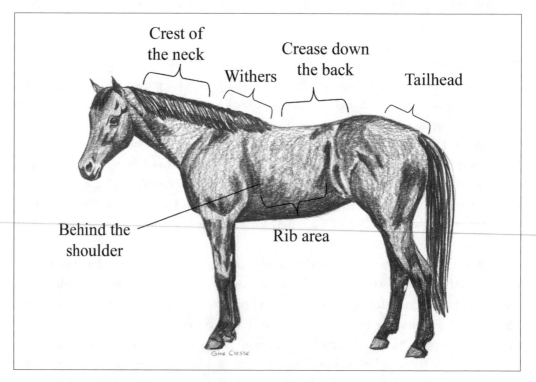

Areas on the horse's body where fat accumulates. Ordinarily a horse's backbone is lower than the surrounding flesh (so is a human's); the "crease down the back" refers to that lowered area. (Drawing by Gina Cresse)

Scoring System for Comparing Body Condition in Horses," *Equine Veterinary Journal* 15:371, 1983, and is used with the permission of Dr. Henneke. (The photographs that accompany the scorecard were taken by Dr. Reynolds and did not appear in the original study.)

Like humans with love handles, horses tend to accumulate fat on certain parts of their bodies, specifically the crest, withers, spine, tailhead, behind their shoulders, and over their ribs. Normally a horse's spine is slightly indented, or creased, like a human's. A horse who gains fat over his back will lose that indentation.

The scorecard ranks the horses from #1 to #9 according to how much body fat they're carrying. The horse in category #1 has no visible fat anywhere on his body. The horse in category #9 is so obese her bulges dimple. You want your horse to score between #5 and #6.

In these photographs, horses #1, #2, #4, #5 and #7 are geldings. The rest are mares. The #1 photo and the #2 photo show the same horse, a six-year-old Thoroughbred gelding. Photos #3 and #6 are of the same twenty-eight-year-old Quarter Horse mare.

Horse #1 is a walking skeleton; the next stage is death.

Horse #2 shows less of his skeletal structure, especially along his back, rump, and ribs.

Horse #3 has filled out more. Although her ribs are easily visible, her hip bone is not.

Horse #4 is still too thin, you can see the outline of his ribs, but fat is visible along his shoulders and back.

Horse #5 has enough fat covering him that his ribs don't show. His neck blends smoothly into his shoulder, and his shoulder blends into his body. His hindquarters have filled out and fat is visible on his tailhead.

> **A Veterinarian-Approved Horseman's Rule of Thumb:**
>
> The scorecard is a refinement of a very basic rule: you should be able to feel your horse's ribs but not see them.

Horse #1.

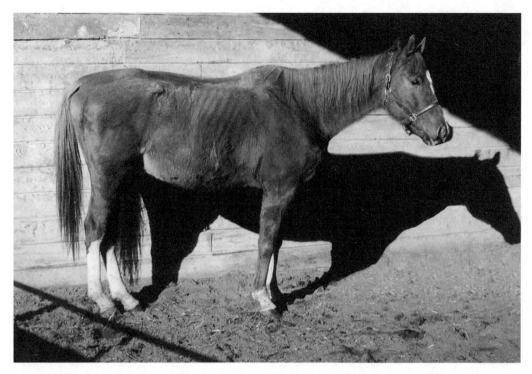

Horse #2.

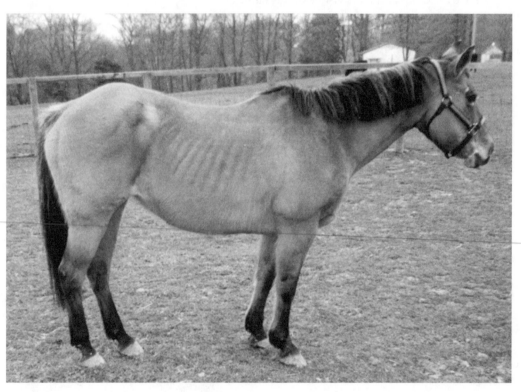

Horse #3.

Horse #4.

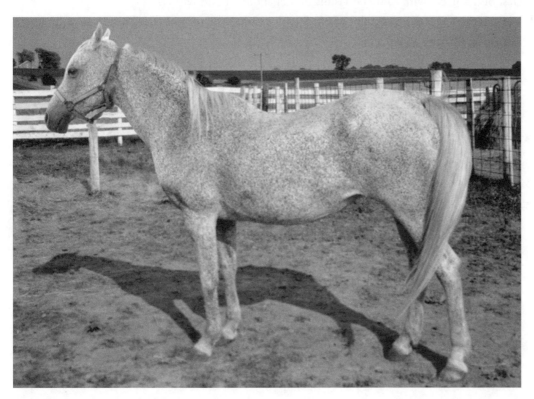

Horse #5.

Horse #6.

Horse #6 is carrying a little more weight than the previous horse. (Remember—you want your horse to fall between categories #5 and #6.) You can see a slight fat deposit on the crest of her neck, with more fat visible on her shoulder and withers.

Horse #7 is carrying a lot of fat. His ribs cannot be seen or felt. The crease of his spine is completely filled in with fat.

Horse #7.

Horse #8.

Horse #8 is obese. Her body looks bloated and she carries a noticeable fat deposit on her crest. I've seen some "cresty" horses carrying so much fat that the crest has collapsed to one side.

Horse #9 would be morbidly obese if she were human. Her body is mottled with fat.

Horse #9.

Changing Your Horse's Feed

Suppose you already have a horse and are feeding him sweet feed and alfalfa cubes. But after looking at the scorecard photos and reading the nutrients chart, you realize that maybe you can correct your horse's little bucking fits by using diet, not discipline.

How do you do that?

Very gradually.

The same advice holds true if you buy a horse, and I'll go over the process in depth in Chapter 10.

After you use Dr. Reynolds' chart to figure out which hay you want to feed, visit your feed store. Ask the manager if she (or he) minds if you check out her hay.

Look it over: Hay bales can be sun-bleached on the outside from standing in the field. But if you examine one closely by separating the flakes—don't open a bale and take it apart unless you buy it—the interior of the bale should be green.

Pull a few flakes apart. All baled hay will divide more or less naturally into sections, or flakes. A flake of alfalfa may be bigger and weigh more than a flake of oat hay. And a flake of alfalfa from one bale may be larger or smaller than a flake from another bale.

Cereal grass hays should be cut before they're mature enough to have fully-formed seed heads. The stalks should be fine and round, not broad and flat or "stemmy."

Examine individual flakes—what do you see? You shouldn't see anything, but I've found any number of dead, flattened birds and rodents in hay, along with moldy patches, unidentifiable bristly weeds, tractor parts, and even cow pies—courtesy of a local rancher who turns his cows out on his alfalfa fields after each cutting. At a stable where I once boarded, the hay was so heavy with fine, red-clay dirt that Tim, a horse I owned at the time, had at least a pound of it in the bottom of his feeder by the time he finished pulling the hay out.

A serious hay barn for multiple horses. Note the arrangement of the bales; they're stacked like this so they won't topple over.

Smell it: Good hay should *smell* good, like dried grass. It shouldn't smell dusty or moldy. If you release a cloud of fine, gray powder when you pull a flake out and the hay itself is mottled with black spots, the hay is moldy. Horses usually avoid moldy hay, but if that's all there is, they might be hungry enough to eat it. The usual result is colic. If you already have the hay, cut open another bale or two. If they all look moldy, call the feed store and explain the problem. Better yet, go there in person, holding a flake as Exhibit A. Most stores will give you an even exchange.

Make your purchase: If it's good hay and you bought it at a fair price, and you have a big, rainproof hay barn, buy as much hay that will fit in it. But use your common sense. If you just have one horse, it's going to take him forever to eat a hundred bales of hay, and hay loses nutrients the longer it's stored. For another thing, hay bales are like apples—one wet, mildewed bale can spoil the bales above and below it, especially if they're wedged in tight without air circulation.

I buy eight to ten bales at a time because that's all my hay shed will hold. Each bale weighs over 100 pounds. As a safety precaution, since I live on a dirt road that washes out with every hard rain, I always reorder hay when I'm down to two bales—about ten days' worth.

It's in the Bag

All hay, including alfalfa, is sold in bales. Alfalfa also comes bagged in cubes. Sometimes alfalfa and timothy are added together after harvest and compressed and sold as cubes. Many people prefer cubes to baled hay—less dust, and the product is more consistent. Bags of alfalfa are also available as pellets, crumbles (both are usually bound with molasses—horse people call the mixture alfalfa and molasses, or A & M for short), and shaved. Most vets consider the last three categories to be little better than floor sweepings and usually restrict them to carrier-only status. In other words, they're something sweet you add in very limited quantities to whatever bad-tasting supplement your horse needs, so he'll eat it. Like many owners, I have never fed cubes: unless I can see and smell the original hay, there's no way I can evaluate the quality of the end product. Some owners have found that cubes cause a (self-explanatory) condition called choke, which can be life threatening.

Feed more hay than you do grain or fortified grain-based supplements. Most backyard owners feed hay by the flake (one flake in the morning, half a flake at noon, a flake at night) and grain by the coffee can, the thirty-six-ounce size. All trainers, amateur owners, and serious breeders feed by weight. It's not a bad idea for you to feed by weight too, especially supplements, since manufacturers normally base their feeding instructions on the feed's weight. Buy an inexpensive postage scale from an office supply store that will weigh anything up to five pounds. Pour the amount of grain you normally feed your horse into an empty, lightweight metal pie tin (most only weigh two or three ounces), and find out how much the grain weighs. Weighing hay by using this method isn't practical. Give your horse enough hay so he's not hungry, but don't overfeed him to the extent that he leaves half of it scattered around his stall or corral.

Round bales of hay for horses and cattle, usually seen only in snow country. The animals eat the hay on the outside first. Once it's wet and rots, horses will ignore the inedible sections and use their teeth to pull out the good hay inside.

Free-Feeding

Never allow your horse free access to any kind of feed: he's likely to colic and/or founder. If you have pasture, don't just turn your horse out on the first warm spring day of the year and leave him there. He too is a candidate for laminitis.

KYLE THE GOAT: A SURVIVOR'S STORY

I'm not a nutritionist, and my college major was English, not animal husbandry. But anybody who knows animals can tell when one is sick.

Kyle was sick.

Like all goats, Kyle is an outstanding gymnast. He can bounce, stiff-legged, so high off the ground I'd swear he has a spring on each foot. The first time I saw him do a back flip I thought he was going to break his neck. (He didn't. He did another back flip.) When he was glad to see me, which was any time I had food, he wagged his tail. Goats love to climb—boxes, lumber, cars—and will try to climb you if you're not careful. Kyle had been bottle-raised by a teenage girl and loved to climb on me, one front hoof on each shoulder. This behavior was cute when I first bought him. The last time he tried it, he knocked me flat. I weigh 120 pounds. Kyle, now fully mature, weighs about 160 pounds.

But on this particular day, instead of running to greet me, Kyle lay quietly in a forlorn tri-colored heap next to the fence. (Nubians are usually black, buff, and white.) I knelt in front of him and offered him some raisins, his favorite treat. Raising his slitted amber goat-eyes he *baa-a-a-*ed at me, then reluctantly ate a few raisins.

Kyle is castrated. Since Nubians are dairy goats, a neutered male has only one future—and it leads straight to somebody's freezer. Most of what I know about goat-keeping came from his former owner, pamphlets in the feed store, and library books. His former owner fed her goats alfalfa. Perfect, I thought. I won't have to change Prim's diet. All I have to do is physically remove her from the corral so I can feed her psyllium twice a week without Kyle eating most of it. (He chews faster than she does.)

Still on my knees, I grabbed a handful of alfalfa and held it under Kyle's muzzle so I would know what to tell Dr. Williams when he asked me whether Kyle was eating. After sniffing the hay, Kyle hauled himself to his feet, walked to the waterer, and drank deeply. Then he stood perfectly still for about thirty seconds, looking as though he had a hangover. His apathy was so far out of the ordinary it scared me, and I ran to the house and called Dr. Williams.

When he arrived, we watched Kyle for a few minutes. Kyle looked, if anything, even more listless than he had earlier. Dr. Williams had a technician with him. (The people who work in his clinic accompany him on ranch calls because what he does sometimes requires two people, and sometimes the owner isn't home). While all three of us watched, Kyle struggled to his feet to investigate us, then headed for the waterer again. Dr. Williams asked whether I'd seen any fresh goat droppings that morning. I told him I had. Then he asked if I'd seen Kyle urinate recently. I told him that was a trick question, because goats, unlike dogs, cats, and horses, do not assume any specific stance when they urinate.

As I knew he would, Dr. Williams asked me about Kyle's appetite. But then our conversation shifted to the West Nile virus, which in turn sparked a conversation about the last mosquito sighting in the Antelope Valley.

Suddenly the technician pointed at Kyle. He was standing perfectly still in the same position I had seen him assume earlier after he drank, but this time he was clearly straining.

"I wouldn't worry about West Nile virus if I were you," said Dr. Williams. "I'd worry about my goat."

So off Kyle went to the vet clinic. When I called later that afternoon, Dr. Williams told me Kyle had a bladder infection. I laughed. Women get bladder infections, not goats. "And how did he get one of those?" I asked.

"Alfalfa," said Dr. Williams. He explained that castrated male goats and sheep (both technically called wethers) often collect a sludge of calcium in their bladder that doesn't move out with the urine. Female and uncastrated male goats and sheep don't have that problem.

I related this little story for two reasons. One: to illustrate how dramatically feed can affect an animal. If I had waited much longer to call Dr. Williams, Kyle would be long gone—a small stone marker in the field behind the corral. Two: if you plan to buy your horse a buddy and you feed your horse alfalfa, buy a *female* goat.

Sweet Treats

There's another feed that's not essential to your horse's health, but you can't call it a supplement. I'm talking about those little treats we use to coerce our horse into good behavior. Is that okay? And what kind of treats?

For most horses, most of the time, food treats are okay. A lot of movie horse trainers rely on food rewards to get the action they want. I was at a Grand Prix jumping event recently where I saw two Olympic-level contenders feed their horses a treat after completing a successful round. The horses clearly expected the treat. As each rider leaned forward holding the treat, the horse swung his head around to accept it without even breaking stride. But what really surprised me was that both riders were men.

The classic horse treats are sugar cubes, carrots, and apples. A lot of European trainers relied on sugar cubes, and by trainers I mean military men, circus trainers, and dressage trainers. But these days sugar has such a bad reputation that most supermarkets don't even stock sugar cubes. They're fine for horses because a horse's teeth continue to grow throughout his life, and horses rarely develop cavities. Carrots and apples are still okay. But don't be tempted to feed your horse full-sized carrots—he might try to swallow one whole. The result? The carrot gets stuck in his throat and causes choke. Even though packaged mini-carrots are more expensive, they're less work (I don't have to cut them into pieces), and I can snack on some myself while I walk to the corral. Cucumbers make a good summer treat—cut them in half and quarter each half. (Since the ones from the supermarket usually have waxed skins, I peel them first.) Most horses also enjoy watermelon rinds cut into cubes. Their mouths will probably get frothy, but don't worry about it.

I feed Prim carrots as part of her lunch, and occasionally raisins, because Kyle likes them and wants his share of treats too. I stay away from packaged horse treats, but that's personal preference. Dr. Williams rewards all his patients with horse cookies. Since most are heavily laced with molasses, horses love them.

Some horses should never be hand-fed any kind of treat because they get nippy. Instead of nudging you and sniffing your pocket, they'll bite.

Sinjun was a born clown and the mouthiest horse I've ever owned. I've never had a two-year-old kid, but I've watched plenty, and everything they can get their hands on immediately goes in the mouth. Sinjun was the same way. One of the few times I showed him, he got bored in the lineup, swung his head around, and grabbed the toe of my boot. He didn't bite down, he just held my boot in his mouth until he got bored with that. Then he let go.

After he injured himself, I moved him to a layup ranch to give him some time off. Because he had so much personality, the couple who ran it spoiled him rotten by hand-feeding him. When Sinjun came back home I had to stop giving him any treats except carrots; I was worried about losing body parts.

But if your horse doesn't get obnoxious about it, feed him treats whenever you want to, whether to reward him for good behavior or just because you l-o-v-e him.

FEED—A CHECKLIST

✓ Hay—you know what the previous owner fed your horse and what *you* plan to feed.
   A local feed store has delivered everything you need to make the transition.

✓ Pruning shears or wire cutters to cut the string that holds the hay bales together.
   Most scissors are too flimsy and belong in your grooming box, not you hay shed.

✓ Heavy metal garbage cans (new)—to store your grain or grain supplements. Any rodent worth his incisors can gnaw through plastic.

✓ Salt or a vitamin/mineral supplement that contains salt.
   Hay hooks. Even if you don't buck your own hay they're handy to have around in
   case you have to move a bale or two.
   An empty thirty-six-ounce coffee can.
   A postal scale.

CHAPTER 9

ADVANCED FOOD FACTS: SUPPLEMENTS AND SENIOR HORSE CARE

Fads come and go in the horse world just as they do in fashion. Some fads, unfortunately, have to do with feed and aren't as silly as how high women will wear their hemlines this season.

To most trainers, nutritionists, and veterinarians, "feed" means "hay." Anything else—grain alone or in combination with other grains—is a supplement. Pelleted grain-based feeds, often fortified with vitamins and minerals, deliver genuine nutritional value. The majority are formulated to be fed with hay. Several are formulated to *replace* hay and are sold specifically for elderly horses whose teeth aren't as good as they used to be. Corn oil and stabilized rice bran both have nutritional value and are also considered supplements.

OTHER SUPPLEMENTS

Many supplements don't have any nutritional value whatsoever and don't pretend to. If you don't know what I'm talking about, pick up a horse magazine and look at the ads. Better yet, pay your local feed store a visit. What you'll find are products that claim to strengthen your horse's hooves, increase his circulation, fuel his muscles (I thought hay and grain did that), "help" his nervous system (help it do what?), de-stress him, and improve his behavior. Most of these products have appeared within the last ten years. A few actually do what their labels claim they do. As for the rest of them, the skeptic in me keeps wondering if they're so necessary, how have horses managed to get along without them all these thousands of years?

Before you part with your money to medicate your horse, consult with your vet and your nutritionist—and your shoer, if the supplement claims it can fix his feet. You can ask your feed store manager, but he probably won't commit himself. He doesn't want to be quoted—or sued. "But Joe at the feed store *recommended* it!"

Before you even pick up the phone, ask yourself this question: "Does my horse really *need* a supplement?"

You can usually answer the question yourself: "No."

One vet told me she'd gone to examine a horse because his owner thought he wasn't quite "right," although the owner couldn't pinpoint anything. The vet asked what he was feeding his horse. When the owner came back with a bucket filled with twelve different supplements, the vet told him to trash all of them.

Veterinarians aren't the only people upset about the increase in supplements. "Nutritionists are concerned because many products contain the same nutrients," says Dr. Judith Reynolds. "When fed together, they might result in nutrient overdoses and medical problems. Also, supplementing only one or two nutrients at a time can upset important ratios such as the calcium/phosphorus ratio."

All Natural Ingredients

Some supplements, especially those that claim to be "natural" (oleander is a beautiful flowering shrub that can kill a Clydesdale in twenty minutes, but it's completely "natural"), have not been studied long enough to know whether they're effective or even safe. Overall, supplements can be dangerous because it's very easy to over-supplement your horse (a little bit of this, a little bit of that). By the time you notice there's a problem, it may be too late to fix it.

The problem is one that horse owners themselves have contributed to. "Modern horses are bred to grow faster and larger, run faster, turn harder, produce a foal every year by February 1st and live to be thirty-five years old," Dr. Reynolds observed. "Compared to the way wild horses ate, modern feeding is required to do all those things. I agree that a lot of supplementation is unnecessary. But I wouldn't close the door on all of it."

If you read horse magazines, you know what the horses in those ads look like—especially ads for the so-called broad-band supplements that claim to treat more than one condition. The horses are drop-dead gorgeous. Each hair glistens with good health (and probably a show-ring product to enhance shine), and the horses themselves are muscular and very, very fit. They are, in fact, models. But the clear implication is that your horse will look just as gorgeous, muscular, and fit if you use these products.

Do I use a broad-band supplement on Prim? No. Have I ever been *tempted* to? No—because Prim isn't a performance horse in danger of stressing her joints or her mind or her kidneys. She's not an equine athlete. She's a trail horse, just like yours.

Good-Guy Supplements

But some supplements are not only good for your horse, they're essential to his health.

Sand colic: This condition is common throughout the Southwest and is usually fatal. If your horse has sand in his gut, even if he's never colicked, your vet will probably suggest feeding him psyllium on a maintenance basis to make sure the sand moves through his digestive tract and is expelled in his manure. Psyllium—more accurately the psyllium's husk—is classified as a soluble fiber; it's the main ingredient in for-human-consumption products like Metamucil. Since psyllium doesn't taste good to horses (does it taste good to you?) most vets recommend that you feed it with a carrier like A & M (alfalfa and molasses). Some horses get very adept at eating the carrier while carefully nibbling around the psyllium, even when the psyllium is fed in pelleted form. (Horses like the powder even less.) Other horses will sniff the whole mixture once and walk away. To make it more palatable, many owners resort to the cheapest bulk syrup and vegetable oil they can find, and pour them over the psyllium *and* the carrier until the horse decides the mixture's edible. Some brands of psyllium, as well as some of the bagged feed supplements, contain anise seed oil. It smells and probably tastes like licorice, and Prim finds it so irresistible that I've thrown out the syrup.

Joint problems: Arthritis, bone spurs, and other age- and stress-related joint problems afflict elderly horses just as they do elderly people. Supplements that help horses with joint problems contain glucosamine and chondroitin sulfate, the same two ingredients medical doctors now recommend to their human patients. (They're available over the counter as a liquid or in pill form, but they're for *you*. Buy your horse a supplement specifically formulated for horses.) While this supplement can't "heal" his arthritis, it does strengthen and regenerate cartilage.

Vitamins and minerals: These are the only other exception to my "Just Say No to Supplements" policy, *unless* you feed a fortified grain-based supplement and follow the directions. It already contains vitamins and minerals, and if you add yet another supplement, you're doing what Dr. Reynolds warned you against. An additional supplement can throw the balance of certain essential vitamins and minerals out of whack.

Electrolytes: This salt and mineral supplement, mixed with additives to make it taste good, was specifically formulated for sweaty, overworked horses. Under most circumstances you won't ride a trail horse so hard that he needs electrolytes—he usually just needs water. (I'll discuss electrolytes in greater detail in Chapter 13.)

EDUCATE YOURSELF

After Bachelor sanded, Anne and I moved our horses back to the big fenced corral in my backyard, because I had feeders. Even though the horses pulled out some of the hay in order to eat it at ground level, where horses have foraged for their food for thousands of years, I was so determined to do right by Bachelor that I spent hours at feed stores, reading the fine print on feed bags.

I learned a lot. But the pelleted grain supplements we have today didn't exist then, and what I mainly learned was what *not* to feed.

The first supplement I tried and discarded was sweet feed. Corn provides a lot of energy. Mix it with molasses and you get a horse so high he's ready to jump out of his skin. Bachelor bucked me off several times—once when I sneezed—because he felt so good he couldn't resist throwing in a buck and wing every so often. I stopped giving him sweet feed.

After several more experiments, I decided on crimped oats to round out his alfalfa diet, along with a vitamin/mineral supplement. In those days I rode three or four times a week, nothing strenuous, mostly long, relaxing trail rides in the back country.

A few years after Bachelor and I moved to New Hampshire, I got interested enough in dressage to coauthor a book about it called *The Beginning Dressage Book*. (Originally published by Arco in 1981, the book was republished in 2004 by The Lyons Press.) When it was time to return to California, I sold Bachelor as a dressage prospect to a girl whose parents had given her an ultimatum. She was engaged to be married but had fallen in love with Bachelor. The ultimatum was this: "We'll pay for the wedding or the horse, but not both." She chose Bachelor, and he lived a long and healthy life.

SENIOR CARE

If you bought a mature horse for yourself or one of your children, after a few years he won't be mature any more. He'll be old, and his needs will change accordingly.

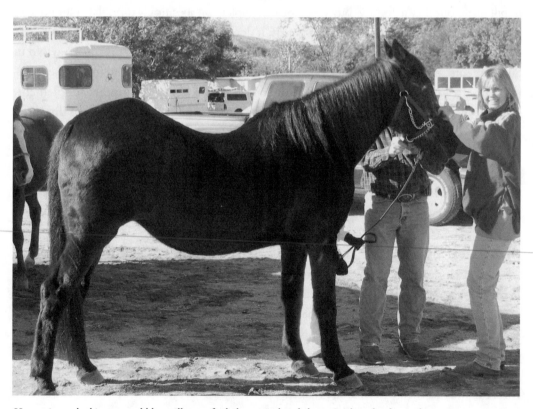

Hopper is nearly thirty years old but still game for halter or in-hand classes. Look at the gloss on her coat.

Prim at sixteen.

Today, researchers know much more about the nutritional needs of elderly horses than they did when I owned Bachelor. As a result, most horses *are* living longer, healthier lives than they used to. According to one estimate, twenty percent of America's horse population is over twenty years old. I know of a three-day-event horse sound enough to compete at eighteen, yet according to books published in the 1950s, horses rarely lived past the age of fifteen. Prim is now sixteen and shows no sign of slowing down.

Recognize There's a Problem

Once I knew Kyle was going to recover from his calcium-induced bladder infection, I went through a similar *now*-what-do-I-feed crisis. Alfalfa was clearly out. Because Dr. Williams floats Prim's teeth every eighteen months, her teeth are in pretty good shape, and Dr. Williams suggested a diet of mixed hay plus a pelleted senior feed for Prim.

I was appalled. Prim? A *senior*? If she was a senior, what did that make *me*?

Dr. Williams saw my look of consternation but misread it—or chose to. "Feed companies hire nutritionists to figure this out," he said, referring to the nutritional requirements of elderly horses. "They know more than we do. They're the specialists—let *them* do the work."

This time there wasn't much trial and error involved. I followed his suggestions and fed Prim a senior feed along with three-way hay—oats, barley, and wheat. Prim won't defend her hay from Kyle, but she will defend her senior feed. So far, everybody's doing fine.

Dental Care

Keeping your horse's teeth healthy is one of the biggest favors you can do for him no matter how old he is. Since most breeders want to reproduce the desirable traits of their particular breed, they don't breed for horses with good feet *or* a good bite. As a result, by the time most horses turn five, they've already had their teeth floated. Some breed registries insist that parrot-mouthed horses, i.e., those with an overbite, must be identified as such on their registration papers, but these horses *can* be registered as breeding stock. (Does this make sense?)

Because horses grind their food by moving their jaws from side to side, bite misalignments and the shape of their heads and mouths can cause their teeth to wear unevenly, leaving such sharp edges that the horse is reluctant to eat. One result is that the horse resists the bit. Another result: he doesn't chew his feed thoroughly before he swallows it, which can lead to digestive upsets. If you notice feed spilling out of his mouth as he chews, your horse probably needs his teeth floated. Another sign to watch for is decreased appetite.

It's not unusual for a senior horse to lose a tooth. Let's say it's one of his incisors, the teeth in front of his bars (the teeth behind his bars are his molars). Unless your vet checks your horse's mouth regularly, the horse's matching *upper* tooth will grow into the vacant space. But because the bottom tooth isn't there, it can't grind against the upper tooth to keep it level. The upper tooth can grow so long it digs into your horse's jaw.

Mares have twelve incisors and twenty-four molars, or grinding teeth; male horses have the same number but can also have four nonfunctional canine teeth behind their incisors.

Medical Care

In addition to bad teeth, elderly horses are prone to tumors, anemia, and liver, kidney, and thyroid problems. Horses also have trouble with their pituitary gland (both horses and humans can develop Cushings disease). Many horses grow lame because of arthritis. Since any kind of pain can cause a horse to go off his feed, elderly horses tend to lose weight. They also tend to salivate less, which makes them susceptible to choke. If your horse bolts his feed or has choked in the past, wet his pelleted feed supplement. Occasionally horses will wet their own hay by carrying a mouthful to the waterer and dunking it. You have so many good feed supplements on the market today to choose from that there's no excuse for having a thin horse, no matter how old he is, even if he suffers from a variety of medical ailments.

But don't go to the opposite extreme and feed your horse so much he gets fat. Obese horses have the same problems obese people do. The excess poundage adds stress to inflamed, arthritic joints, causes hoof problems, and overtaxes your horse's heart.

Since you see your horse two or three times a day, you might not notice whether he's losing or gaining weight. Consider photographing him at the beginning of every month and giving him a body condition score (see Chapter 8). Summer or winter, indoors or pastured, your senior should maintain a body score of five or six.

Behavioral Changes

As your horse's health changes, his behavior might too, especially if you have more than one horse and keep them outside. If your horse is the oldest or lamest, his mojo will probably diminish, and the other horses may drive him away from his feed. If that happens, many owners separate the horses so the old-timer can eat by himself, preferably someplace where he can still see the other horses. When he's finished, they turn him back out with the gang.

Special Diets

For seniors with bad teeth or who have trouble salivating, a complete feed, one that completely replaces hay *and* grain, is your smartest choice. All complete feeds can be fed moist, like a mash. When alfalfa pellets are wet, they expand up to three times their size. Pelleted alfalfa and beet pulp are excellent feed for elderly horses in limited amounts (both are high in calcium). But as long as your horse can still chew, feed him hay, especially if he's indoors. He needs *something* to occupy his mind, and the extra roughage won't hurt either.

Suppose your old friend is on pasture. If you supplement his hay with a pelleted senior-horse feed, is that enough? Yes, provided that you're diligent about worming him and having his teeth floated. Otherwise he'll have too much trouble chewing to get the nutrients he needs, even on lush pasture.

Your Reward

If you take care of your horse, feed him what's good for him, and see to his shoeing, dental, and medical health, you can ride him a long time. Gayle Lampe owns an American Saddlebred gelding she calls Fred. She uses Fred as a lesson horse at William Woods University, where she teaches. Five days a week, Fred teaches novice riders how to walk, trot, canter, slow-gait, and rack. Fred is twenty-eight years old.

STILL SKEPTICAL

Even though Prim's senior-citizen pelleted feed seems to be doing what it's supposed to, I've started looking at the competition. I want to know what's in these feeds and in what percentages. I shop for my own food the same way, because I'm old enough to remember when butter was bad for you, but margarine—or so the manufacturers claimed—was not only heart-smart but could save your life. Now we know that eating margarine, especially the kind that won't melt, isn't smart at all. As a result, I'm not convinced that manufacturers always have the consumers' best interests at heart. Why should horse feed manufacturers be any different?

Feed companies are required by law to list all the ingredient categories of their product (wheat middlings, dehydrated alfalfa meal, grain products, forage products, etc.) and to state how much crude protein, crude fat, crude fiber, etc. each feed provides. But labels don't always give consumers all the information we need to make an informed choice. Here's an example. One line of complete feed for elder horses lists its *minimum* protein content as fourteen percent; no maximum given. Its close competitor lists the feed's *maximum* protein content as fourteen percent; no minimum given. For the consumer, this information is like comparing oranges to peanut butter. If the feed contains no less than fourteen percent protein, what's the maximum? And if the feed contains no more than fourteen percent protein, what's the minimum? And why isn't the company telling us?

A Conflict of Interests

Many nutritionists work for feed companies, where they conduct studies and sift through the results to formulate new feeds and improve existing ones. Dr. Reynolds, for example, works for ADM Alliance Nutrition, Inc., the third largest animal feed manufacturer in the United States. She knows more about what horses eat and how it affects them than anybody I know, and without her help, Chapters 7 and 8 of this book would be considerably shorter and much less informative. When I asked her about a potential conflict of interest when horse owners consult nutritionists who work for feed companies, she didn't duck the issue. "Representatives of a reputable company will answer your questions about their feeds," she replied. "Ideally they will also help you with total rations [your horse's complete diet]. However, they are trying to sell feed. I hope nutritionists have the best interest of your horse in mind, but they might not. If they don't, shame on them."

My recommendation: Although I did receive the Betty Crocker Homemaker of the Year Award when I was in high school, I don't know a wheat middling from a muffin. When it comes to horse feed supplements, I question my veterinarian and my nutritionist, evaluate their answers, and let my common sense be my guide. My advice to you is to do the same.

Privet Hedge. (Drawing by Gina Cresse)

DON'T EAT THAT—IT'S POISON!

Bad-guy plants grow everywhere, and you still have to worry about them even if your horse lives in an indoor stall and you bed him on the wrong kind of shavings. Some plants, like privet hedge, are often grown as ornamentals by horse people who don't know how poisonous they are. I used to live on a ranch that had a long, straight driveway. A previous owner, who also owned horses, had planted a beautiful flowering shrub the entire length of the driveway. His shrub of choice? Oleander. Anybody who's read Janet Fitch's best-selling novel *White Oleander* can tell you that it kills humans. It also kills horses.

Before Sinjun hurt himself, we were trail riding when I saw a big, healthy bush with glossy red-green leaves that looked familiar. I grew up in New Jersey, where I almost didn't attend my own high school graduation because I had an allergic reaction to poison ivy; but we don't *have* poison ivy in California. Sinjun swiped a mouthful of leaves. Ten seconds too late I recognized the bush for what it was—poison ivy's California cousin, poison oak.

I was so scared I did something I never do. I galloped back to the barn.

"John!" I screamed, sliding off. "Help! Sinjun just ate poison oak!" I yanked off Sinjun's bridle to check his mouth, envisioning blisters forming on his tongue and gums, in his throat, inside his stomach. Should I call the vet? Would hosing his mouth out with water help? Or was it already too late?

John gave him a cursory glance. "Horses eat it all the time. Don't worry about it."

I stared at him. "But if I even *touch* it I break out in—"

"Horses don't," said John. "He'll be fine. But if it makes you feel better, call the vet." With those encouraging words, he sauntered off. I didn't call the vet, although I would have if John hadn't been there. But he was right. Sinjun *was* fine.

Oleander. (Drawing by Gina Cresse)

In addition to privet and oleander, many bushes, flowers, shrubs, and even trees are poisonous to horses. While the chances of your horse encountering any are remote, take a few minutes to acquaint yourself with the most common ones. Horse-owning neighbors, feed store managers, your state extension specialist, and your vet can tell you about others in your area. In most cases, if your outdoor horse has enough pasture and hay to eat, he won't be tempted to snack on unfamiliar life-forms.

Toxic Trees

Some trees can poison your horse. Is your driveway lined with red maples? In autumn they're spectacular, but don't let your horse near the leaves. They're especially dangerous when they turn color and fall off, or if a branch breaks and the leaves wilt. What if you discover that the trees in your pasture that your horse depends on for summer shade are red maples (also called scarlet maples, swamp maples, water maples, and Carolina maples)? Trim the lower branches so the horse can't reach them, and remove any fallen leaves as soon as possible. Fencing the trees is another possibility, so your horse can't get close enough to them to nibble.

Is your driveway lined with stately oak trees—the deciduous kind that shed their leaves each fall? (Live oaks stay green all year round, have much smaller, tougher leaves, and pose very little threat to your horse unless he doesn't have anything else to eat.) The leaves of deciduous oaks are toxic, particularly in spring, just after they've sprouted. Even the cute little acorns are toxic. Both affect the horse's urinary system. Because oaks are tall with spreading branches, they're often planted in pastures as shade trees.

In addition to being poisonous, oak trees attract lightning. They have an elaborate root system that lies close to the surface of the soil. Although it rarely happens, if the ground is wet

Black Walnut. (Drawing by Gina Cresse)

and the tree is struck by lightning, electricity can travel along the roots and electrocute any horse standing under the tree to keep dry.

All yew trees (Japanese yew, American yew, English yew, and Western yew) are poisonous. Horse chestnuts, also called buckeyes, come from horse chestnut trees. The leaves are poisonous. Despite its name, the nut itself—the horse chestnut—is also poisonous.

Black walnut trees can poison a stabled horse who never goes outside—the shavings are the culprit, even if they're only twenty percent of your horse's bedding. Nobody's exactly sure what the toxin is or how it enters the horse's body—the horse might have nibbled on the shavings or even inhaled dust from them—but within twelve hours the horse can colic or develop laminitis. The shavings are so toxic that contact with the horse's hooves may be enough to poison him. As an owner, your safest policy is to buy prepackaged shavings from a reputable feed store. Keep buying the same brand of shavings from the same store to make sure you get a consistent product. (Black walnut shavings tend to be darker than most shavings.) If you pasture your horses, don't plant black walnut trees or English (or Persian) walnuts that have been grafted onto black walnut rootstock.

Fatal Flowers

All azaleas, including wild azaleas, are poisonous to horses. So are the rhododendrons that often grow next to them in the woods throughout the East and Midwest. Other deadly Eastern flowers include tansy and buttercups. In the South, watch out for day jasmine. On the West Coast, certain kinds of lupine—those beautiful blue flowers that grow wild in fields and meadows—are lethal to horses. Beware of yellow star thistles in California—they also kill horses. These tough, spiny plants, which can reach a height of six feet, are a major threat to rangeland because they're spreading so fast. Also watch for wild onions with their attractive blue flowers; their smell makes them easy to identify. Bracken fern (or brake fern or hog-break), which affects the horse's central nervous system, is found throughout North America.

The effects of some poisons are mild and temporary. Dutchman's breeches, a pretty little wild flower that grows in wooded areas, will cause a horse to salivate, tremble, and show extreme nervousness, although the symptoms don't last and the toxin has no long-term effect. But the dried seeds of wild sweet peas—a showy, bright pink wildflower that grows throughout the continental United States—attack the horse's nervous system and commonly affect his hindquarters, lymph nodes, and liver. Full recovery can take up to two years. The effects of a few poisonous plants are irreversible and lethal. Jimsonweed can kill a horse in a matter of minutes. Japanese yew trees and rhododendrons attack the horse's cardiovascular system and are invariably fatal.

Pretty Poisons

Some toxic plants are very attractive. All milkweeds, with their bursts of small white flowers, are poisonous to horses to some degree. Foxglove, a showy garden plant that also grows wild, is toxic to horses. Other attractive but poisonous plants include ragwort, hounds tongue, white snakeroot, and hoary alyssum. Poison hemlock and water hemlock (also called wild parsley or cowbane) are lethal to humans as well as horses. The Greek philosopher Socrates was given poison hemlock to drink as a death sentence.

Horses can become addicted to locoweed (also called crazy weed, poison vetch, milk vetch, and timber vetch), which causes irreversible brain damage. Pastured horses with plenty to eat usually leave locoweed alone.

Since these culprits can pop up in places where they shouldn't—your pasture, for instance—check for invaders at least once a week. Seeds that sprout from bird droppings are the usual reason poisonous plants grow outside their normal range.

In a Class by Themselves

Blister beetles, or their remains, are occasionally found in alfalfa hay. Even dead beetles baled in hay contain a toxin so strong it can be fatal to horses and remain fatal for up to a year. Cases have been reported in the cold country of New England and upstate New York, Michigan, Wisconsin, and North Dakota as well as in the Southwest. The toxin has also been found in cereal grasses that contain flowering plants such as goldenrod. There is no known antidote. As an owner, you can protect your horse by buying hay from areas free of blister-beetle infestation, or hay harvested before or after the beetles' mating season, which is roughly May through September.

What to Do

How can you tell whether your horse has eaten a toxic plant? If anything about his behavior seems out of the ordinary—quick, shallow breathing, trembling, he drools, his muscles suddenly go rigid, he adopts an odd stance and seems reluctant to move, he's running a fever, his heart rate has accelerated—contact your vet. You have an emergency. Then contact a poison control center. The 24/7 hotline of the national ASPCA is (888) 426-4435.

If you follow the feeding guidelines in these chapters, and your horse has enough good forage or pasture to keep him occupied, the odds of him poisoning himself are slim. The best way to protect your horse is by knowing what wild plants grow in your area of the country and which are toxic.

CHAPTER 10

HOW TO BUY A HORSE (FINALLY!)

Y ou've bought (or built) your dream barn on your dream property, and have fenced an arena. You have a veterinarian, a shoer, and a nutritionist lined up. You know what feed stores carry the best hay at the best price. You plan to ride English, although you want a Western saddle too because camping on horseback sounds like fun (it is). You'll consider most breeds. If the price is right, you'd buy a registered horse; if not, you'll buy a grade horse, a gelding, if possible. You'd like a horse who's young but not silly.

Where do you *find* backyard horses? And what questions should you ask the owner/ seller to find out if this horse is your dream horse?

DO HORSES READ?

No, but you do. And so do owners who want to sell a horse.

The first place most horse shoppers look is the classified section of their local newspaper, or for-sale notices at tack and feed stores. Some shoppers buy from local breeders, who also advertise in the paper or at feed stores. Others find out about a horse through word of mouth. Still others want a horse that a professional trainer has bred, trained, or recommended. A few buy over the Internet or at auction.

Newspapers

Check your local newspapers first. Most owners/sellers will advertise there instead of a big-city paper. Even though the city paper lists more horses and reaches more readers, it can take you three hours of driving time just to look at a horse you *might* be interested in.

Nearly all feed and tack stores carry free penny saver-type newspapers that list horses for sale. Check them out—some even run color photos. They usually list horses alphabetically, by breed, so you'll have to hunt (by area code) for which horses are in your area. Since these papers also run want ads from people like you—people looking for a specific breed or quality (a gelding who "can go English or Western")—that's another possibility. After you've searched a few weeks but still haven't found anything you like, it might be worth the money to place a want ad of your own.

Bulletin Boards

Before you leave the tack or feed store, check their bulletin board. Many local owners prefer to sell their horses this way because the store doesn't charge them, yet their ad will be seen by dozens of potential buyers. Nearly all ads feature a color photograph of the horse and include a few essential facts about him, such as his breed, sex, age, and the seller's name and phone number or e-mail address. If there's no information about the horse's breeding, the horse is probably not registered. If he were, the owner would want you to know that because a horse with papers is worth more than a grade horse. Some ads give specific information about the horse's temperament and strong points. For example, "Kind and gentle, great with kids." Or, "Can ride or drive." Or, "Good trail horse, guaranteed sound." Or, "Experienced riders only." This last horse is not for you; don't even write down the phone number.

Suppose you see an ad for a "green-broke AQHA filly." The phrase green-broke usually, although not always, indicates a three-year-old. AQHA stands for American Quarter Horse Association, so the filly is a registered Quarter Horse. As I said earlier, you might enjoy a young horse, provided you ride well enough and are confident of your ability.

Small Breeders

Small breeders often advertise using the bulletin-board method. If the breeder is local, it shouldn't be hard to find out about her (or him). Ask people at the feed store. Ask your veterinarian, but don't be surprised if he says he's never had any dealings with her and can't comment. He's simply being prudent. Ask how long the breeder has been doing business. Does she have a good reputation? Does anybody own one of her horses? If you're lucky enough to get names and phone numbers, call these people and ask if dealing with this breeder was a pleasurable experience. Are they happy with the horse? Would they buy another one from her?

You can also find small breeders in the yellow pages; look under Horse Breeders.

After a couple of bad experiences with older horses, both of them as a consequence of my poor judgement (don't buy a dull horse who really doesn't want to do anything except eat and sleep, and don't ever buy a horse named Spook), I went to see a four-year-old chestnut gelding advertised in the paper. The owner was a woman who lived out of my area, so I had no way to check her reliability. Since I wasn't taking lessons at the time, I *should* have shopped around for a good trainer and asked him (or her) to come with me. But I didn't.

The gelding was well built but on the small side. The owner said she had bred the horse and named him Tim because his sire was a running Quarter Horse with Tim Tam breeding. (Tim Tam won the Kentucky Derby in 1958.) She said Tim's dam was a grade mare, "mostly" Quarter Horse. The sire was not on the premises. Neither was the dam; the woman said she'd sold her. When I asked to see the sire's papers, she told me they were in her house and she would have to look for them.

I didn't find this story particularly believable. She had a horse for sale she claimed was half Quarter Horse, but she couldn't produce the sire's papers? After test-riding Tim, I thanked the owner and left. I liked the gelding, but not enough to buy him without trying a few more horses.

Two weeks later, when I decided I *did* want to buy him, the owner raised the price. (If I'd brought a trainer along, I doubt that would have happened.) I almost walked away, but I had spent a lot of time eliminating possibilities. For the money, Tim was as good as I was likely to get. After having him vet-checked, I bought him.

Over the years I've heard about other owners who do business that way—by manipulating prospective buyers, especially ones who live out of the area. Having a professional trainer with you can help you deal with owners as well as evaluate their horses.

But most breeders run their business *like* a business, which means they treat potential customers with courtesy and respect. If such a breeder has advertised the horse as a registered Quarter Horse, she'll have the papers out before you ask for them. If you buy a horse from her only to realize you misjudged your ability to handle him, most breeders, particularly local ones, will work with you. Some will even agree to take the horse back and refund every penny, so that whenever somebody asks *you* about their reliability, you can give them two thumbs way, way up.

Word of Mouth

I once told a bank teller I wanted to shift money from my savings account to my checking account because I planned to buy a horse. She said, "Are you *serious*? Jennie [not her real name] at the next window has a horse for sale! Do you want me to give her your phone number?"

But the usual way you hear about horses for sale—as opposed to reading about them—is by hanging around boarding stables. If the barn has a trainer, he (or she) often has horses for sale. Sometimes the horse belongs to a customer, sometimes the horse belongs to the trainer himself. Such horses are usually very reliable because they're so well trained. On the other hand, they usually cost more.

There might also be another owner at the barn/farm/ranch who breaks and trains young horses as a sideline. I bought Bachelor from a cowboy whose day job was shoeing horses, but he made a little extra money every year by breaking a couple of young horses. When I met him, I was leasing one of the ranch horses. The cowboy was training Bachelor at the same ranch. I fell in love with Bachelor on the spot and bought him, even though I didn't know much about green-broke horses. Although the cowboy wasn't a trainer (the barn didn't have a trainer, only a manager), he patiently watched me ride Bachelor three or four times a week, offering help and advice, until I was ready to ride on my own.

Rental or Lesson Horses

It's hard to find a stable these days where you can rent a horse for an hour or two and go trail riding. When I was a kid, rent strings were very common. In fact I grew up riding rental horses. Two of my father's coworkers ran a string of about twenty horses and let me ride free. When I started riding there I was about six. After that first ride, I spent every Saturday at the ranch pretending to be a cowboy until the owners sold it. Rental horses have to have good feet, sturdy bodies, and a good attitude. Their owners keep the ones who stay sound and don't buck their riders off.

The summer I was eighteen I taught horseback riding at a summer camp in Pennsylvania. When camp was over, I considered—not very seriously, because I didn't have the money—buying one of the mares in our string. (Camp horses are often supplied by dealers who *want* to sell their horses before the end of the season so they don't have to feed them over the winter. The following spring they'll go to auctions and buy a new string.) The mare's name was Heidi, and even though we taught Western riding, she was the only horse who didn't know how to neck rein. She was a young mare, and after six weeks of being ridden five and six hours a day was still sound and good-natured. But I was on my way to my first year of college at the University of Michigan, and I knew I couldn't smuggle Heidi into my dorm. More realistically, I couldn't afford to pay a monthly board bill.

If you're taking riding lessons, be sure to tell your instructor you're looking for a horse. Occasionally the horse you ride—your lesson horse—will be for sale, although not if the horse belongs to your instructor personally. A sound, good-tempered lesson horse is irreplaceable because he's the perfect baby-sitter. That's why Gayle Lampe will never sell Fred.

But if an *owner* has a horse for sale, the owner will sometimes allow an instructor to use the horse as a lesson horse for riders at a certain level of ability. For example, the horse might not be suitable for a novice rider (somebody who knows more and rides better than a beginner) but would be a good match with a more advanced rider. The owner hopes somebody will ride the horse, fall in love with him, and want to buy him.

Horse Dealers

You can find dealers in the yellow pages (look under Horse Dealers). Most buy their horses at auctions, although a few specialize in buying racehorses off the track, either Thoroughbreds or racing Quarter Horses, and retraining them as riding horses. (A racing Quarter Horse, also called an Appendix-registered Quarter Horse or a running Quarter Horse, is part Thoroughbred. Bachelor's height and conformation came from a Thoroughbred grandsire.)

Wherever the horses come from, dealers choose the ones with good temperaments and a future as trail horses, show horses, or—if the horse is sound enough—a hunter/jumper prospect. If you'd like to visit a dealer and see what he (or she) has to offer, ask your riding instructor or some other experienced horse person to go with you.

Auctions and the Internet

I strongly advise you not to buy a horse at auction, even if your instructor is sitting right next to you. Since most of these horses will be bought by "killers"—dealers who sell them for slaughter—it's too easy to be swayed by your emotions.

The only exception is mustangs sold at auction. But if this is your first horse, stay home and read the classifieds for something more suitable. Most mustangs are beyond the age they can be trained to ride. A younger one will cost more, and you'll have to put him in training. Not all trainers are willing to work with a three-year-old who's never even been haltered.

Buying a horse over the Internet can be as safe as you want it to be, with one disadvantage: unless the horse lives in the same general area that you do, you can't ride him before you buy him. While horse trainers often buy a horse sight unseen on the recommendation of another trainer, you're not a horse trainer. Leave the wheeling and dealing to them.

Q-AND-A

Once you've assembled enough ads and phone numbers and e-mail addresses, sit down at the table and spread them out. Then rank them using the time-honored three-pile method: #1 pile is "yes," #2 is "no," and #3 is "maybe." As you sort through your notes, review your priorities. How committed are you to riding English? If it turns out that you can afford a registered horse, what kind would you like—color-specific or breed specific? Does the horse *have* to be a gelding? If you see an ad for a buckskin mare in your price range that appeals to you, put her in your "maybe" pile. You'd be surprised at how eye-catching a buckskin looks in English tack. Even if price is your bottom line, your decision to buy a specific horse will probably be based on more than one consideration.

Once you have your three piles, jot down a list of questions you want to ask the owner.

When you finish your list, pick up the phone. If nobody answers, leave a brief message stating that you saw the ad and would like to look at the horse. Be sure to leave your name—your first name is fine—and phone number. Most owners with a horse for sale check their messages several times a day. If nobody calls you back, it usually means the horse has been sold.

Important Questions

If you do reach the owner, the first thing to do is verify the information you saw in the ad. If it described the buckskin as a five-year-old gelding, make sure that's the horse you and the owner are both talking about. Ask all the questions on your list. One of the most important is, "Why are you selling this horse?"

This question is particularly pertinent if you know the owner is a small breeder, because most breeders want their horses off their account books and out of their paddocks as soon as possible. Realistically, that means by the time the horse is three. Why has this gelding been hanging around for two additional years? Listen closely to the answer—is it believable? To me, an answer like "My daughter rode this horse but she's getting married and moving out of state," sounds believable. An answer like, "He did a lot of winning for us but now it's time for him to move on," does not. *Why* is it time to move on? Did the horse hurt himself? Did the horse hurt his rider? Some shoppers like to ask this question twice: once on the phone, and a second time when they ride the horse and their riding instructor or trainer is standing there listening.

Ask if the buckskin has ever been ridden in English tack. If you think you'd like to do some jumping—that's why you want to ride English—ask if the horse has ever been jumped. If all you want to do is trail ride in your hunt-seat saddle, ask how he behaves on the trail. Does he like company? Or does he like to be alone? (As a rider, what's *your* preference?)

If the buckskin was described as "registered," that's your second important question. Ask the owner, even if that information appeared in the ad. Ask what the buckskin is registered *as*. Buckskin is both a color and a color registry, and there are two of them. One is open to all breeds, while the other accepts horses of mixed breeding as long as they don't look like ponies or draft horses. If the owner tells you the horse is a registered Quarter Horse, be suspicious. Because that information is such a strong selling point, it should have appeared in the ad. The horse may legitimately *be* double-registered as a Buckskin and a Quarter Horse, but the ad should have said so. Ask the owner if she has the buckskin's AQHA registration papers. If she says anything except "Yes," either break off negotiations or tell her you can't meet her asking price unless she produces the horse's papers.

Once you learn some basic facts about this registered buckskin and are still interested, make an appointment to ride him. Then phone all the other prospects in your "yes" and "maybe" lists. Keep making phone calls until you've narrowed your choices down to three or four horses.

Don't Decide Alone

If you've been taking riding lessons, or plan to put your new horse in training a couple of months before you take him home, ask your riding instructor or the trainer to come with you. They will expect a commission—they want to be paid for their time. That's fair. Just make sure you know in advance how much they want. Ten percent of the horse's asking price is standard, and since the trainer is acting as your agent, you're expected to pay the percentage, not the owner/seller. In round numbers, if the owner/seller is asking $1,500 for the horse and the trainer's commission is ten percent, you'll pay a total of $1,650 for the horse—$1,500 to the owner and $150 to the trainer. If you don't want to pay a commission, ask a knowledgeable horse-owning friend to accompany you. Just make sure *that* person doesn't expect a commission.

If you already have your hunt-seat saddle, by all means bring it with you. You should ride a horse at least once (twice is even better) before you make an offer.

What to Look for—Conformation

When you arrive at the owner's barn, try to get there early so you can see the horse at liberty, in an arena or a field. Let's say you decided to see the buckskin first. If he's stalled, ask the owner to turn him out for you. You want to evaluate how the horse moves and balances himself without a rider on his back.

That may not be possible if the owner has already cross-tied him in the barn aisle, and the gelding is freshly washed, brushed, and ready to ride. Count that as a big plus—it means the owner cares enough about presenting her horse that she put in extra work to create a favorable first impression.

While the owner saddles the horse, ask to see his papers. The owner/seller's name should be listed as the *current* owner. If the horse's papers are in order, look at how the horse is built—his conformation. Even though your trainer's with you, you'll want to discuss the horse with him before you buy him. No professional is likely to buy a horse just because he "has a pretty head."

Having said that, I'll also say a pretty head can be a major selling point. Most people want a refined head in any breed of horse—short, with a small muzzle and big eyes set at the edges of his face (he can see more if his eyes are closer to the side than the front). The horse's nostrils should be thin, not thick and fleshy. His lower lip shouldn't hang or droop, especially if he's young. Small ears, set fairly close together are attractive, and alert ears (they're pointed at something, probably you, since the horse has never seen you before) usually indicate an alert mind. You should be able to see a very definite transition between the horse's head and his neck—his throatlatch, in other words. A horse with a thickened throatlatch will find it difficult to bend his head (to flex at the poll) and may not be as responsive to your rein aids as a horse with a clean throatlatch.

If possible, watch the horse without a rider. You can tell a lot about how he moves and his attitude when he's just "being a horse." (Photo by owner Jean Johnson)

Who could resist this face? (Photo courtesy of the American Morgan Horse Association)

Long necks are usually good. A horse who can raise his neck until it's nearly vertical and then lower it effortlessly in order to graze usually has good shoulder action and is a good candidate for a trail horse. Long legs can sometimes accompany a long back, which can be a weakness—such a horse can become swaybacked as he ages. But long-backed horses often give their rider a smoother ride than horses with short backs.

Long legs usually indicate athletic ability, especially if they're combined with short, strong cannon bones and long, sloping pasterns. Look for a horse who uses his hocks, especially if you think you might want to jump him someday.

The horse's hind legs should be set well under him, because the "push" for every stride he takes starts from behind. A Quarter Horse's muscular hindquarters are the reason he can stop on a dime (and give you back a nickel in change), sprint down the home stretch, and change direction faster than most people can blink. Old-time cowboys used to say they wanted a Quarter Horse "with a lady's dainty face and the behind of a cook."

My recommendation: If your funds are limited, you probably can't afford a perfectly conformed horse of any breed—and sometimes that's a good thing. How a horse moves is more important than how he looks, although there's usually a correlation. A horse with an old injury who is otherwise sound—an old, slightly bowed tendon, for example—might be an excellent buy. In fact your trainer would probably recommend that horse over a blue-ribbon conformation winner (he won halter classes, in other words) who may be perfectly conformed but has feet tinier than Cinderella's. You're better off buying a horse with a kind eye, a willing temperament, and four straight legs, even if one of them is slightly bowed.

Ground Manners

Observe the buckskin's behavior before the owner rides him. Does he seem to enjoy being handled and groomed? (If the answer is yes, give the horse another plus. You don't want a horse who fights you every time you pick up a curry comb.)

When the owner cleans his feet, does the horse try to yank his foot back? (Count this one as a minus. A five-year-old should pick up his feet willingly and even anticipate which one to pick up next.)

Does the horse accept the bit willingly (another plus), or does the owner have to fight with him to lower his head? (Another minus.)

Take me home with you?

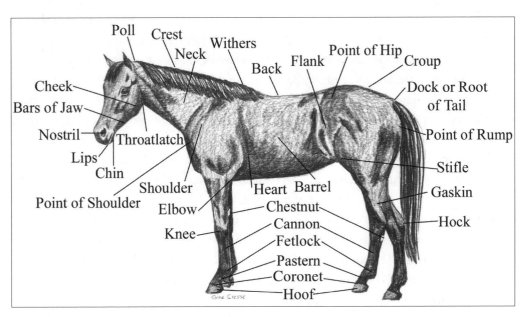

The horse's conformation. Since you already know where his eyes, ears, forelock, mane, and tail are, they're not identified. (Drawing by Gina Cresse)

Like most horse-shoppers, you'd probably fall for a horse who rests his head on your shoulder. This is why you brought a trainer along. Sinjun, looking for—and getting—lots of attention from Kim Bassett.

When the owner cinches the horse up, does the buckskin pin his ears and toss his head? (A *big* minus.) A horse who lays his ears back and threatens to bite is unhappy about something—the saddle, the rider, or the prospect of being ridden. Why buy a horse who isn't happy about being ridden?

The owner should ride the horse before you do, so you can watch. When she swings into the saddle, does the horse stand still (another plus), or does he move off before the owner slides her feet in the stirrups? (Another minus. A horse should stand while being mounted until the rider tells him otherwise.)

Manners in General

Watch the owner work the buckskin in the ring. How does he look? He ought to look alert and cooperative, with both ears pricked forward, or, better yet, one ear pricked forward and the other back towards the rider. That means he's interested in what's ahead of him but is still paying attention to the person on his back (a big plus).

Most riders walk, trot, and lope a horse going one direction and then reverse. Watch how the horse moves. He should step underneath his body with his hind legs—another indication of his pushing power. A horse can't push off with his hind legs if they're behind him instead of beneath him. (Such a horse is said to be *trailing his hocks*, which is a big minus.)

At the walk, the horse should have a distinct over-stride—in other words, you should be able to look at his hoofprints and see that the horse's hind feet hit the ground *in front of* his front feet. As the horse passes you, watch for sideways motion. A horse with four straight legs will usually travel straight and stay sound because he's bearing his weight equally on all four legs. A splay-footed horse, one whose front feet turn out to the side, tends to interfere with himself—in this case, kick himself in the shins or cannon bones with the opposite foot. Such horses usually break down prematurely. A pigeon-toed horse, who toes in, will paddle or wing with each stride—in other words, his feet swing out. Although a pigeon-toed horse isn't as desirable as a straight-legged one, at least he won't hurt himself when he travels.

If you're buying a horse that walks, trots, and canters (as opposed to a gaited horse), listen to his footfalls. At the walk, you should hear an even one-two-three-four rhythm. At the trot, you should hear a steady one-two, one-two rhythm. The canter should be a consistent three beats, although the beats are uneven: ta-ta-DUM, ta-ta-DUM. A four-beat canter usually indicates the horse is lazy behind and doesn't pick his feet up (a minus).

As the owner swings out of the saddle in preparation for you to ride, ask yourself how the buckskin behaved in general. Was he alert and willing, and did he respond correctly every time the owner asked him to do something? (Another big plus.) Or did you see a horse with sour ears (his ears were back, indicating a bad temper or pain) who prefers to jig sideways rather than walk? (Another big minus.)

Your Turn

Switch to your English saddle. Most owners will stand by the rail to offer suggestions and advice, although they will usually defer to a trainer. Take this opportunity to ask the owner about what size and type of bit the horse is wearing. Once you're in the saddle, ask the buckskin for the same three gaits the owner did. How much rein contact does the horse like? Since you want to ride English, if you shorten your reins and tighten your legs on him, is he willing to move forward (a plus), or does he lower his head or toss it to get away from the pressure of the bit? Are his gaits comfortable? They better be—you're going to spend a lot of time on this horse.

When you ask him to lope, does he move off immediately or does he simply jog faster? Since no two people train horses the same way, he may be waiting for a different cue than the one you gave him. Here's where the owner can offer advice.

Once you've successfully loped the horse, slow to a jog, then a walk. Does he resist you in any way—fuss and toss his head? (Another minus.) Stop him completely. Will he stand still for a few seconds? (Another plus.) If the owner backed the buckskin, ask him to back using the same cues she did. If the owner *didn't* back him, ask her what cues she uses. Does the horse back willingly? He's five years old—he should.

Turn him around and ride him at all three gaits again. Horses, like people, are either right-handed (or -footed) or left-handed. In other words they will lope using the "foot," or lead, they prefer because it's easier for them.

After thanking the owner for her time, move on to the next horse.

Once you and the trainer have left, find out what he liked or disliked about the buckskin and why. If you had a different reaction, tell the trainer. If the horse looked thin to you, ask the trainer about that too. Owners with a flighty horse will often underfeed him deliberately, so he behaves himself when a prospective buyer comes to ride.

At the second barn, follow the same procedure you did when you rode the buckskin. By the time you've ridden all the horses in your yes and maybe categories, you should know which horse you want—the buckskin. But don't make an offer just yet.

Second Time Around

Call the owner and ask to ride the buckskin again. This time, come alone. Your trainer will probably be reluctant to come out a second time, and you already know his opinion of the horse. Now that the owner knows you're seriously interested, she'll probably try to persuade you to buy the horse as soon as you step out of your car. Be polite, but don't commit yourself.

First, ask her if the horse knows how to longe. If she says yes, ask if *you* can longe him. Watch his reaction to the longe whip. He should respect it but not fear it—and he definitely shouldn't pin his ears and kick at it.

If your second ride is as enjoyable as your first, tell the owner you'll buy the buckskin *if* he passes a prepurchase vet exam. Also discuss feed with her—what the buckskin eats and how much of it, and tell her you want to buy a week to ten days' worth of feed.

Most owners will be happy to oblige when you ask for a vet check. Ask her which veterinarian she uses, and hope it's not the same one you plan to use. There's too much potential for a conflict of interest; find another vet. The owner's vet might know, for example, that the horse has foundered a couple of times, but he doesn't disclose that fact to you because the owner is a good client of his. (If the horse foundered badly enough, your trainer would have noticed the founder rings in his hooves the first time around, and you wouldn't be here.) If the owner tries to tell you that you don't need a vet check, they're a waste of money and those overeducated college boys don't know beans about horses—beware. This owner knows something about this horse she doesn't want you to find out about.

For the same reason, many prospective buyers will drop in to see the horse unannounced—the owner doesn't know you're coming until you show up. The world is full of unethical people. Unfortunately, some even have horses for sale.

The Vet Check

When you schedule an appointment, make sure you're there when the vet arrives. Carry your cell phone with you. If the horse you're having vetted is the thin buckskin, discuss his weight with the vet. You want to be sure there's no underlying medical problem.

A good vet will ask you questions while he evaluates the horse. Before I bought Prim, I looked at a gray Thoroughbred mare. She had been raced, and one knee was bigger than the other. The owner assured me that the mare had never taken an unsound step in her life. I called a vet anyway.

As he examined her, he asked what I planned to use her for. I told him I wanted a trail horse, preferably one I could do a little dressage with. The vet asked me to trot the mare straight ahead, away from him. Next he asked me to trot the mare straight back towards him. I had her on a lead shank and I led her—I didn't ride her. (A vet can see physical weakness or pain much more accurately that way.) Next he flexed the mare's right front leg at the knee and fetlock and held the position for sixty seconds. Then he put her foot down and asked me to trot her away from him. Then he flexed her left leg, the one with the big knee. As far as I could see she didn't favor the leg, but he repeated the test. Then he asked how long I planned to keep her. When I told him it would be a lifelong commitment, he advised me not to buy her. The mare's big knee bothered him; he wasn't sure how long she would stay sound. Did I really want to buy a horse guaranteed to break down sooner instead of later?

I took his advice and called the owner to decline. She started to argue. "Why," I asked her, "would I call a vet in for his expert opinion and then ignore what he tells me?"

The owner wasn't happy, but she accepted my explanation. It's a good one. Feel free to use it if you find yourself in a similar situation.

Vet Checks and Commissions—Yes or No?

Suppose the horse you like the best is one a trainer has for sale. Do you still need a vet check? The answer is yes.

Suppose the trainer doesn't own any sale horses but knows somebody who does. If you decide to test-ride this horse, the trainer will want to come with you. In fact he'll probably offer to drive. If you buy this horse, are you still obligated to pay him a commission?

Yes. He acted as your representative. As soon as he mentions knowing about a horse for sale, ask what his commission is. You don't want any last-minute surprises.

Do you still vet check the horse? Yes.

Suppose *you* find a horse you want to buy—the buckskin—but you'd like a trainer or riding instructor to look at him before you make an offer. Since you found the horse yourself and negotiated your own price, do you still pay the trainer or instructor a commission?

No. But you're asking for the trainer's time and expertise—you should pay him *something*. Explain the situation, offer him a flat fee, and ask him if he'd be willing to look at the horse. If you take lessons from him or know how much he charges per lesson, base the fee on what he charges for an hour-long lesson. If it takes twenty minutes to get to the horse, you ride the horse for twenty minutes, and then you and the trainer drive back to the barn, offer to pay him the same amount he would make if you took an hour-long lesson from him, plus a little extra for gas and incentive. He could just stay at the barn and give somebody else a riding lesson. Or, if you trust your veterinarian, skip the trainer and go directly to the vet check.

Buying a Horse from a Friend—Yes or No?

This question is a little like asking your father to teach you how to drive a car. You both mean well, and sometimes you *do* learn to drive and both of you are still on speaking terms afterwards. Sometimes.

I've never actually bought a horse from a friend. But I did sell one. The mare was another Quarter Horse cross who lived in my backyard—except the "yard" was a public stable where John trained American Saddlebreds. Cassie had a twelve-foot by twelve-foot indoor stall, and the grooms mucked out and fed her daily. Since I was at the barn almost every day to ride, I made friends with Kelly, one of the grooms. Kelly seemed impressed with Cassie and the basic dressage work I was doing with her, although her real interest was jumping.

Then one of John's Kentucky customers, who had shipped some horses to John for training, gave me Sinjun. He was 16.2 and a typical Saddlebred—long swan neck, long legs, and an easy, comfortable trot. Since I felt bad about asking John's grooms to feed and clean up after *two* horses, I decided to sell one. But which one? Cassie was more reliable on the trail, but Sinjun had a more engaging personality. I decided to keep him.

I had been discussing my horse dilemma with Kelly, and when I told her which horse I'd decided to keep, she immediately asked how much I wanted for Cass. I told her, and just like that, Cass had a new owner.

I think Kelly was too shy to tell me she wanted to have Cass vet checked. Instead, she waited until the sale was completed. *Then* she called a vet. To my horror, Cass had a bowed tendon. A very slight one; she wasn't lame, and the bow wasn't even noticeable unless you were looking for it. Since the mare wasn't under John's direct supervision—he wasn't training her, and I was the only person who rode her—he hadn't noticed either. But it was there, nevertheless. And I hadn't seen it.

I braced myself for a string of (justifiable) accusations, but they never came, at least not from Kelly. I ended up accusing *myself* of negligence and stupidity. I had sold a friend a defective horse. I was sure our friendship was over.

Luckily Kelly didn't see it that way. John agreed to let Cass stay in the barn rent-free until she was sound, and Kelly and I took turns wrapping her foreleg and discussing The Things We Learn from Horses. Are we still friends? Yes. Sinjun, my beautiful, accident-prone Saddlebred, has been dead for many years. Cass, now thirty, lives peacefully in Kelly's backyard in Riverside, California.

THE THINGS WE LEARN FROM HORSES

Here are some very basic horse-buying tips.

#1: Follow your heart.

If you're horse shopping and stumble across one that looks sickly, abused, abandoned, or starving, call the nearest ASPCA or Humane Society representative, your local animal shelter, or a horse rescue group. I've heard stories about people who rescued a horse only to find—after spending a small fortune rehabilitating him—that he was an outlaw. But to balance the equation, I've also heard stories about owners rescuing horses and everybody lived happily ever after. The owner did a good deed and ended up with a wonderful horse.

Whether you call the ASPCA or buy the horse yourself, do *something*.

#2: Have the horse vetted before you buy him.

I bought Prim as a three-year-old from a small breeder. Because I knew the breeder, and because Prim had no obvious physical or psychological defects, I didn't call a vet. But that was almost fifteen years ago. These days, when people sue one another over the temperature of a cup of coffee, I'd get a prepurchase vet check. They're cheap insurance.

#3: Should you buy a horse from a rent string?

Yes, if you've ridden the horse long enough to evaluate his personality and abilities and whether you like him. Have him vet checked.

#4: Should you buy a horse at auction?

Not unless you're a pro, know exactly what you want, and have bought a horse at auction before. (If you're reading this book, you most likely are not a pro.)

#5: If you're only buying one horse, should you buy him a buddy?

Yes. (see Chapter 12).

WHAT BELONGS IN YOUR GROOMING BOX—A CHECKLIST

Once you're sure you actually own this horse—and can take your first-ever trail ride on your own property in a few more days—go shopping. Although I mentioned a few necessary grooming items in earlier chapters, it's the one category of "stuff" I haven't discussed in detail.

In addition to hoof-care tools and products, you'll need:

✓ A heavy-duty plastic grooming box for all your tools.

✓ A soft rubber curry mitt that fits over your hand like a mitten. Especially good for removing winter hair from your horse's face and the bony areas of his legs.

✓ A hard, oval-shaped rubber curry comb. Don't buy plastic; the teeth are sharp and thin-skinned horses dislike them.

A soft brush to use on your horse's face. Some horses don't care for coarse bristles. Other horses prefer them. Be prepared.

✓ A stiff body brush to wipe dirt and dander off your horse's coat.

✓ A hairbrush for humans with stiff nylon bristles. Use it on your horse's mane and tail along with a detangling product.

✓ A detangling product that comes in spray form. Some also promise to add shine to your horse's coat, but save the shine for the show ring. **WARNING:** Most spray bottles have a moveable square tip that gives you options, in some cases very simple ones: do you want the sprayer "on" or "off"? Be sure to turn it off when you're finished—some products leak. The next time you reach for the spray bottle, it will be empty.

You need a grooming box to hold your brushes, hoof pick, sweat scraper, etc.

A curry mitt is especially useful for grooming the bony parts of your horse. Some owners like to use it on all the parts of their horse.

✓ Two extra spray bottles, because the pump on your detangler or fly spray will inevitably fail. Buy them at a tack store; the ones at supermarkets aren't sturdy enough.

✓ A metal sweat scraper that reverses to a shedding blade (with teeth).

✓ Vinegar. Add some to the rinse water when you bathe your horse; it removes soap scum.

✓ A cactus cloth mitt. Most horses love this stiff, scratchy fabric, especially on their heads. I use it as the last step of a full-body grooming.

✓ Human hair conditioner, to make your horse's newly-washed mane and tail behave.

A hair dryer to quick-dry your horse's tail. It will even dry the whole horse in cold weather.

✓ A clipper to keep your horse's bridle path and fetlocks trimmed.

✓ Clipper oil, to clean your clipper and keep it humming.

✓ Kerosene. Keep a little in a coffee can. While your clipper is running, dip the blade in to flush out hair and dirt.

✓ Some way to heat water. If the barn is plumbed for cold water only, buy a plug-in heating gadget so you can heat a bucket of water.

Spider spray. Optional unless you live in black widow spider country.

Kleenex. Optional unless you have allergies.

See-through plastic storage boxes with lids. A good way to organize seasonal stuff and spares—an extra pair of reins, extra halters, bell boots, etc.

✓ Rub rags. Although many people prefer sponges, I find cloth rags last longer and are more versatile—you can use one to clean a scraped hock, for example, and then apply peroxide to it by pouring the peroxide on a different part of the same cloth. Rub rags are unbeatable for putting a show-ring shine on a horse's coat.

CHAPTER 11

DELIVERY DAY: HOW TO PREPARE
AND WHAT TO EXPECT

Arrange to have your horse delivered on the weekend, when you're home. You want your horse to associate his new home with you, and you want those associations to be as pleasant as possible. Horses have very good memories.

When you bought him, you discussed his diet with his previous owner and arranged to buy from her a week's worth of whatever feed he's been eating, which is now stored in your hay shed. Suppose she fed the horse sweet feed and alfalfa cubes twice a day. But after reading the "Nutrients in Common Horse Feeds" chart on p. 143, you decided to eliminate the sweet feed entirely and replace the cubed alfalfa with timothy/alfalfa hay. Since his coat looks a little dull, you plan to add stabilized rice bran and a vitamin/mineral supplement, and feed him three times a day instead of two. In addition to his old feed, your hay shed also contains eight to twelve bales of timothy/alfalfa hay. The stabilized rice bran and the vitamin/mineral supplement are in there too, inside their original packaging in metal garbage cans.

You are, in other words, prepared.

If you own a horse trailer, you can go get your buckskin and drive him home by yourself. But not all backyard owners know how to haul horses and prefer to pay somebody else to do it. (For do-it-yourself horse hauling, see Chapter 18.)

It's the hauler's obligation to make sure your horse's journey is safe and uneventful. Whether she (or he) is part of a nationwide fleet, a local person recommended by a friend, or the horse's previous owner, the hauler will lead your horse out of the trailer and hand you the leadrope. If the hauler is your horse's previous owner, she may prefer to deliver the horse *and* the feed at the same time. Ask her to unload the feed first—you want some of that sweet feed and alfalfa cubes in your horse's feed bin when he enters "his" corral for the first time.

Once the hauler hands you the leadrope, her part of the bargain ends. She drives away, leaving you and your horse, near-strangers, connected to one another by a single piece of rope. Both of you are a little jittery and very excited. Now what?

DAY 1

Don't ride your horse for the first few days. He's in unfamiliar territory; one reason why he's jittery. Is that a saber-toothed tiger crouched behind the tackroom (your horse can see its shadow) or your ATV? Let your horse get acquainted with his new home before you ride him away from it.

Since you've read Chapter 2, you know what kind of tack you want. If you already have tack and want to know whether it fits your new horse, wait a few days to do that, too, until he's more relaxed. All you're going to do today is lead your horse into his new living quarters and then leave him alone.

Let's say you have a twenty-four-foot by twenty-four-foot pipe corral, ready and waiting for its new occupant. You've bedded it with shavings. You've filled the half barrel in the far end of the corral with clean, cool water. Your horse's feed bin (in the other end of the corral) contains a salt brick, sweet feed, and alfalfa cubes, just like home. For the first *full* day your horse spends with you, give him his usual feed in the usual amounts. He's already experienced changes—a new person handling him, new surroundings—and he feels tense. As Dr. Williams pointed out, any horse in this situation is vulnerable to medical upsets, including colic and/or laminitis. Don't underestimate how much a change of environment can affect a horse. And don't add to his stress level by feeding him unfamiliar food.

So your first step is this: lead your horse to his new living quarters.

Who's Leading?

Do you both agree on what leading means? There's a right way to lead a horse and several wrong ways, and in this case "right" means the safest position for *you*. Your horse's head should be in front of you, and you should walk next to his shoulder on his near (left) side— the same side you mount on. Hold the leadrope a few inches under his chin with your right hand. The rest of the leadrope is in your left hand, looped or folded twice (not coiled—you don't want your hand caught should your horse decide to bolt) so the very end of the rope is closest to your body.

As long as you walk shoulder to shoulder with your horse, you can usually predict what he'll do next. If he shies at the ATV, it's easy to nudge him in the ribs with your elbow to remind him that you live on this planet too, and it's not smart to step on his new owner. But don't *punish* him for shying. He shied because he's scared, and if you yell at him as you jab him with your elbow, he may conclude your ATV really *is* a saber-tooth tiger and refuse to go anywhere near it.

If you let your horse lag behind you, you can't see him. He could be doing any number of things, such as stopping dead in his tracks to grab a mouthful of grass. Or he may see something scary ahead of him, such as your dog running around the corner of the tackroom, and spin around so he can run the other way, yanking the leadrope out of your unsuspecting hands. (*You* didn't see anything scary.) Or he may hear something behind him and jump forward, attempting to join you in your space because he's a herd animal who knows there's safety in numbers.

If you allow your horse to walk ahead of you, you're inviting him to step on your foot. If you don't *feel* him step on you (because you're wearing steel-toed boots), you'll try to take another step forward. But because your foot is pinned under his, you'll fall flat on your face.

Most horses are accustomed to being led by a person who stands next to their shoulder. Make sure to keep your right hand near the snap of the leadrope because if he panics, you can let go of the rope with your right hand. If he hits the end of the rope and swings to face you, backing up because he's frightened, you can release the second "fold" without letting go of the entire rope. Most leadropes are twelve to thirteen feet long, and giving your horse that amount of slack will usually reassure him that he *can* escape if he still thinks he has to. Most horses will feel reassured enough to stop backing.

But what if yours doesn't?

Let him keep backing up. You can't stop him by pulling on the leadrope—he weighs more than you do. Instead, follow him without facing him. (He thinks facing him means you're confronting and possibly chasing him, and he'll continue to back away.) In other words, follow your horse by moving sideways until he backs into something— the door of a stall, a fence—and stops. Or you can back him into something deliberately. Once he stops, move to his shoulder so you're both facing forward and cluck to get him moving again.

Gates and How to Go through Them

When you arrive at your horse's pipe corral, open the gate by pushing it to the *inside*. Horse gates (including stalls with Dutch doors) usually swing out, but the gate of a pipe corral swings both ways. Move a little closer to your horse's head than you normally would so you walk into the corral ahead of him, still holding the leadrope with your right hand just below his halter.

I know Prim too well. For safety's sake, I should be holding the leadrope closer to her chin (compare this photo with the one of Prim and Dr. Williams on p. 97), and I should be walking shoulder to shoulder with her. Note the folded leadrope in my left hand. (Photo by Gina Cresse)

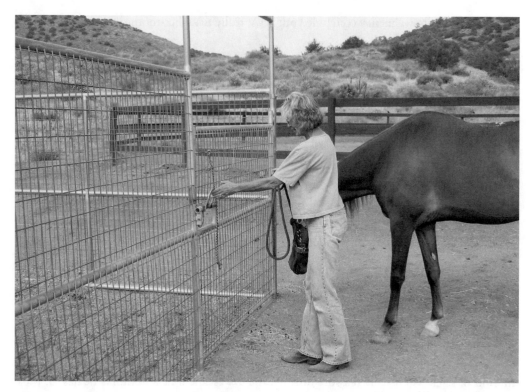

Whenever you and your horse enter a corral or stall, walk ahead of him to open the gate (or stall door). (Photo by Gina Cresse)

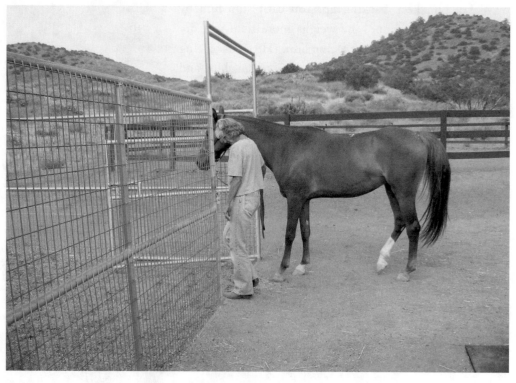

Push the gate open and enter the corral by walking ahead of your horse. (Photo by Gina Cresse)

Step immediately to your left, your back to the fence; if something startles your horse, he won't run over you. (Photo by Gina Cresse)

Walk your horse around you in a semicircle, still with your back to the fence, until he faces you. Then you can transfer the leadrope to your left hand and close the gate. (Photo by Gina Cresse)

Step *immediately* to your left, so the fence is behind you, and let the horse walk past you through the gate. Because you're still holding the leadrope, he'll start to circle you going left. Turn him completely around to face you and switch hands, so you can use your right hand to swing the gate closed. When you and your horse are both inside the closed corral, walk up to him and unbuckle his halter.

You follow this procedure to prevent your horse from rushing into his corral—because he's over-anticipating mealtime, for example—and running over the top of you. If you open the gate by pulling it towards you, so it opens outwards, it's harder to close once you're inside. And since your horse doesn't know that this is "home" yet, he may try to run out the gate while you're still struggling to close it.

Pat him on the neck and tell him he's a good boy. He knows how to lead and he didn't run into you—he *is* a good boy. Exit the corral, this time by opening the gate *towards* you. If you push it out, away from you—especially on your horse's first day—your horse may view that as an invitation to run past you or over you as he gallops out the gate.

Resist any temptation to stay in his corral and bond with him while he eats. Some horses are so protective of their feed they'll flatten their ears and bare their teeth to make sure you don't steal it. Play it safe and just walk on by with a promise that you'll be back later on, with dinner.

If other horses live in the neighborhood, especially ones your horse can see, you're likely to have horse conversations going on for the next few hours as they whinny back and forth swapping "cats with fangs" and "stupid owner" stories. Go do something else until his dinner time.

DAY 2

Many people's first reaction is to turn their horse out as soon as he arrives. Leaving him in his corral with plenty of food is a much smarter way to introduce him to his surroundings than turning him out. Why? Because you might not be able to catch him again.

On day 2, walk into your horse's pipe corral, fasten his halter, and walk him out the corral gate. Now that you're exiting with your horse, walk a little in front of him so you go through the gate before he does, and this time *do* swing the gate out. If the horse thinks he wants to escape for some reason, it's easy to push the gate open wider and flatten yourself against it while he runs past you.

Walk him to the arena. If you're sure you can catch him, take his halter off. If you're not sure, replace the one he's wearing (usually an old one the previous owner wanted to get rid of) with a leather or breakaway halter. Don't keep a halter on your horse all the time. If he catches it on something—the metal edge of the feed bin, the fence, a tree branch—he'll fight to free himself. A leather halter will break, and that's exactly why you want one. Your horse can't free himself if he's wearing an unbreakable nylon halter. You don't need a frantic horse *and* an emergency visit from your vet the first week your horse is in your backyard.

As soon as you turn him loose, he'll probably run and buck to let off steam because he didn't get any exercise yesterday.

Gina demonstrating the correct way to leave a corral or stall. She opened the gate by pushing it out, away from her—the only way this gate can be opened. As she walks out ahead of Prim, she keeps Prim to the side to make sure Prim doesn't step on her.

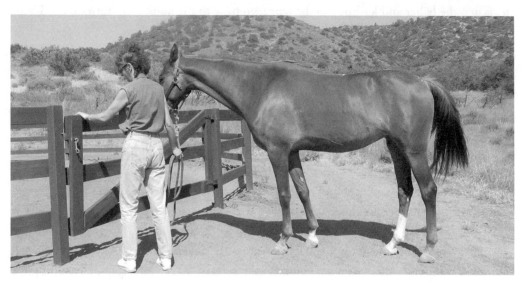

Gina has turned Prim around so they both face the gate while Gina swings it shut.

Catch Me If You Can

After your horse has spent a few hours in the arena, it's time to put him back in his corral. (If you know how, longe him first.) Latching the gate behind you, walk towards your horse holding his leadrope and halter. But to your astonishment, your horse—instead of running over to you like a happy puppy—snorts at you, wide-eyed, and races to the far end of the arena. Then he wheels around and snorts again.

What's this? "This" is a spoiled horse, and since the previous owner didn't tell you he was hard to catch (did you ask?), he's not wearing a halter. One of his previous owners taught him this fun little game of tag, possibly without intending to. At least the horse thinks it's fun.

Since you now carry baby carrots, horse treats, or handfuls of feed in your pocket at all times, try to bribe your horse by walking slowly towards him, food in your outstretched hand, the leadrope (snapped to his halter) at your side. But your horse knows all about this game. He knows what a halter is, and he'll let you come only so close before racing off again, snorting and bucking.

Give him one more chance. Still no go? You have three options.

Option #1: Call for help. It's much easier for two people to corner and catch a horse than it is for one person. But have you taught the horse anything by using this method? No. By the time you catch him, he's probably tired of the game anyway and most likely hungry. If you're satisfied with—make that resigned to—calling for help every time you want to catch your horse, fine. End of problem.

You *are* smart enough not to yell at him once you catch him, right? Or whack him on the rump with your leadrope a couple of times to "teach him a lesson"? If this is how you solve problems, you did teach your horse something: that trying to catch him is no longer a game. When you caught him, you whomped him—why would he *want* you to catch him?

Option #2: Using feed, try—by yourself—to cajole him to come close enough to slip the halter on him. If he won't let you catch him, give it one more try. If he still won't cooperate, fasten the halter and leadrope to the fence, go back to the house, and turn on the TV or your computer.

After a couple of hours, go back outside. Before you enter the arena, stop by the feed shed and fill a coffee can half full of sweet feed. You won't give him the whole amount—you mainly want the sound of the feed rattling in the can. Your horse has probably heard that sound at least once in his life, and he associates it with dinner and other warm, fuzzy feelings.

Now is the ideal time to teach your horse to come to you when you call him. Horses are capable of recognizing and responding to about twenty words and sounds, including the clucks and chirps and kissing noises most of us use to get a horse moving. To call your horse in to you, choose any word or sound you want. You can say "Come." You can say "Hey bonehead!" I whistle. Just be sure to use the same word or sound consistently, every time you want him to come to you.

Stand in the middle of the arena with your coffee can and rattle it. As you rattle it, call your horse. If he runs off, don't follow him. Rattle the can and call him again. Give him three chances. If he comes to you, give him a reward—a handful of feed. But instead of haltering him, slide the leadrope around his neck. *Then* slip his halter on. Most horses know when to stop acting silly. As you buckle his halter, tell him he's a good boy. *Say* "Good boy!" in a low, confident voice, and draw it out, so the sound is different (and longer) than the come-here command: "G-o-o-o-d boy!"

Have you taught your horse anything? Yes. Now he knows that you don't think tag is fun. How does he know that? Because you refused to play—you didn't chase him. He's also beginning to associate the sound you used when you called him with good things—like that handful of feed he's munching on.

But what happens if he blows all three opportunities and still isn't tired of playing tag?

Go back inside and balance your checkbook, answer your e-mail, or call a friend and make a date for a fishing trip or a movie. And wait.

Option #3: This option has a lot in common with #2, but you need some props and weather that's pleasant enough for you to sit outside for a while. Lacking either of these, your only remaining option is to try catching him again around dinner time. If your horse still won't come, leave him there overnight, without dinner. The next morning, make sure you have treats in your pocket when you open the arena gate. Your horse will probably run up to you and beg to be caught. He wants breakfast. But first, make sure he learns something. Ask him to come. When he does, tell him what a good boy he is, casually drape your leadrope over his neck (anywhere you can reach, but the closer to his head you are, the more control you have), and feed him a treat. *Then* slip his halter on and praise him. Even though this step may sound like unnecessary work, give it a try. Someday you might find yourself on a trail feeling sorry for yourself because your horse just dumped you, then stepped on his reins and yanked off his headstall—the one with no browband or throatlatch. The two of you face one another, each debating what to do next. All that separates you from catching your horse and riding home versus you *not* catching him and walking home could be your belt (or a rein, if it fastens with a snap and you can unsnap it in time) and your horse's willingness to let you approach him with it.

Back to Option #3. For props, you need a chair and a small table. Lightweight patio furniture is fine.

How to catch a horse who doesn't want to be caught: do something else. Prim has never seen me sitting in a patio chair before—note the raised tail and the position of her head. (Photo by Gina Cresse)

Since you're going to do some more waiting, you also need something to do—a cell phone, so you can call friends, a magazine to read, or this book. I don't recommend using your laptop—too much dust. Most importantly, you need that can of sweet feed. Put it under your chair with your halter and leadrope.

As soon as you walk through the gate carrying your props, your horse may charge around the arena, snorting and flagging his tail. He'll stay as far from you as possible because he's never seen a human carrying furniture before. Park the chair in the middle of the arena with the table next to it, if you brought one, sit down, and start reading. Don't even look at your horse.

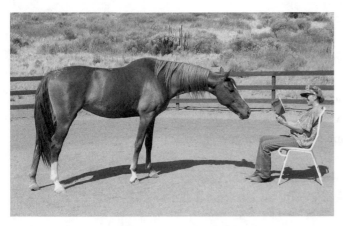

If you ignore your horse long enough—and you have food—he will come to you. (Photo by Gina Cresse)

Your horse will gradually edge closer to you—he's curious about why you're suddenly so much shorter than you were yesterday, and what these strange objects are. He can also smell the food. Sit as still as you can, no abrupt movements, and listen for soft, breathy snorts as opposed to short, vehement ones. They indicate that your horse is investigating you from a distance.

You'd think curiosity wouldn't be a useful trait in the wild. The horse who lingered behind to investigate what was rustling in the tall grass while the rest of the herd fled wouldn't stay alive long enough to pass his genes on to the next generation. But the fact remains: horses are curious. As long as you're not an obvious threat—waving your arms, jumping up and down, running at him or yelling at him—he will come closer and closer to you, neck extended, ears forward, sniffing.

How much time it will take your horse to approach you depends on his temperament. But sooner or later he'll extend his neck enough to sniff you at close range, still making those soft, breathy snorts. If you slowly hold out your hand with feed in it and call him, the horse will usually stretch his neck to the limit to nibble the feed from your outstretched hand.

What do you do next?

Nothing. The horse hasn't finished checking you out yet. He'll probably circle your chair, still sniffing, watching you carefully to make sure you don't suddenly spring at him. Or he may—not because of anything you did—suddenly take flight, usually with a loud snort. Resume whatever it was you were doing before he ran off. He'll be back.

The next time he approaches, he'll probably move closer to you than he did the last time, because you rewarded him last time. He wants to know if you'll do it again. Give him your "come" command and another handful of feed. While he's chewing, tell him he's a good boy.

After that, he may just wander away because he thinks he's figured you out. Phone another friend.

The next time your horse walks up to you, ask him to come. When he stretches his neck to eat out of your hand, praise him again using your voice. If he's relaxed—no snorts, no rolling eyeballs—stand up, the leadrope in your right hand. Slowly drape it over your horse's neck. He'll probably sidle away.

When he does, give him a food treat. (I have the halter in my hand, just in case.) (Photo by Gina Cresse)

Let him. Sit down again, but don't call your friend back. Your horse hasn't gone very far, and by the time you punch in the number he'll be standing in front of you again with his nose stuck out. Repeat the procedure: ask him to come, feed him, reward him, and *as you reward him* slide the leadrope over his neck.

You can restrain your horse to some extent by using the leadrope. If he decides to eat and walk away, for example, he can't do it as easily, although some horses will just keep walking. If yours does, tell him to "Whoa." This is another sound most horses have heard before, and he might slow down long enough for you to reach for the other end of the leadrope. As soon as he stops, halter him. If he doesn't stop, let him go. Since you've spent most of the morning talking on the phone and standing up and sitting down again, it will be hard to watch your horse walk off with the leadrope over his neck, tantalizingly just out of reach. Resist the temptation to lunge for it. You'll probably miss, and because you're behaving the way a predator would, your horse will run away from you. You've just added another twenty minutes to the training session. It will take you at least that long to re-establish your horse's trust in you.

Eventually patience pays off, and your horse will come close enough to let you capture him with the leadrope. (Photo by Gina Cresse)

If you *did* just let go, your horse will be back very shortly. He wants more food. This time he'll probably stand still while you drape the rope over his neck. Feed him another treat, praise him with your voice while you catch the loose end, and slip his halter on as he chews. Tell him he's a good boy again and feed him another treat. He's beginning to associate the two—those particular words and a treat.

This is why I advised you not to turn your horse out as soon as he arrives. He doesn't know you. He doesn't know where he is. As a result, he may not let you catch him. But given enough time to associate you with food, almost all horses will come to you.

You may have to repeat this lesson a few times to reinforce it (the process will be shorter each time), but now the buckskin is officially yours. He's learned to come when you call him.

FEED—THE BIG SWITCH

Your goal is to change your horse's diet from one type of feed to another with a minimum of fuss and upset to his digestive system during a seven- to ten-day time period. Once he's been in your care over twenty-four hours—which usually means the evening of the second day—start switching him over to his new feed.

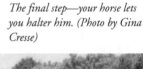

The final step—your horse lets you halter him. (Photo by Gina Cresse)

Dinner, therefore, ought to consist of about three-quarters of his usual portion of alfalfa cubes mixed in a bucket with three-quarters of the usual amount of sweet feed, and one-seventh of the recommended amount of stabilized rice bran. Empty the mixture into his feeder. Then add about a quarter of a flake of alfalfa/timothy hay.

For breakfast the following day, decrease the amount of cubes and sweet feed slightly, give your horse slightly more hay, and two-sevenths of the stabilized rice bran.

The following morning add a little of the vitamin/mineral supplement at the recommended dosage.

By the end of seven days, you should have no more sweet feed or alfalfa cubes left, and your horse should be happily dining on two-way hay, stabilized rice bran, and a vitamin/mineral supplement.

Once he's gotten used to the new routine, feed him slightly smaller portions of hay for dinner and breakfast, and start feeding him lunch.

Pasture

Suppose you have a pasture. Do you immediately turn your horse out the day he arrives, and leave him there? No, for two reasons. Reason one: we just discussed this. Don't turn your horse out anywhere unless you're absolutely certain you can catch him. Reason two: even if his previous owner kept him on pasture, introduce him to yours gradually, because the previous owner's pasture probably had an entirely different mixture of grasses and/or legumes than yours does.

If the previous owner pastured the horse but also fed him hay, wait until you've completely switched your horse's feed to timothy/alfalfa hay, and make sure he'll reliably come to you when you call him. The first day, feed him breakfast, but scale back a little. When he's finished, turn him out to pasture. After about thirty minutes, return him to his pipe corral. That's all the pasture for today. Feed him slightly less than the usual amount of hay for lunch and dinner.

The next morning, cut back a little more on the hay before you turn him out. Gradually leave him out longer and longer, but keep feeding him hay. By the end of a week to ten days, he'll be ready to stay in the pasture full time.

Feeding hay to a pastured horse is standard practice because otherwise many horses don't get all the nutrition they need. Unless your horse rates an unbiased #6 on the scorecard and your pasture is so lush he'll get fat if he eats another mouthful of *anything*, continue to feed him hay.

YOU SURVIVED!

This is how the first few days will typically play out. You'll notice that except for teaching your horse to come when you called him, I didn't encourage you to handle him much. That was deliberate; you don't know one another very well yet. You will tomorrow, when you test-ride your saddle and go for your first trail ride.

Meanwhile, do not tie your horse to the hitching rail and groom him. Too many unexpected things could happen, and you don't want to deal with any of them during this important getting-to-know-you phase.

For now, once you and your horse have agreed on how to go through gates and how to lead properly, repeat your "come" lesson once a day, and keep telling him what a good boy he is. That's all. Your goal is to build a relationship of mutual trust and respect with your horse, and you've already started the process by teaching him these simple, basic steps.

DAY 3

Go trail riding!

CHAPTER 12

THE WORLD ACCORDING TO HORSES

I stand in a grassy clearing ringed with eucalyptus trees, helplessly watching a lion charge me.

Less than a second ago the lion had been strolling nonchalantly in my direction. The next thing I knew he had flattened his body, lowered his head, and charged.

My mind has no direct communication with my feet. Otherwise I'd be running for my life, even though the lion is less than sixty feet away and it doesn't matter whether I run or not. A few more bounds and I'll be dead meat.

My mind does register the fact that the lion is inside a wire-mesh fenced enclosure, and that two other people stand between us. One is actress Tippi Hedren, diminutive even in high-heeled boots. The second person—a visitor, like me—has sunk to her knees, presumably to communicate with the lion on his own level. But even though my brain goes into fast-forward, conjecturing what will probably happen next, my feet still refuse to move.

First conjecture. Surely lions have charged people before, and the fence stops them. Doesn't it? If one of Tippi's big cats had broken out before, wouldn't I have seen a story on the five o'clock news, "Lion Escapes from Shambala, Kills Innocent Bystanders"?

Second conjecture. How high can a lion jump? High enough to clear the fence? And why has Tippi grasped the kneeling woman's elbow while saying urgently, "Stand up. *Please* stand up."

The lion is almost to the fence—one good leap and I'm history. I make a mental will. John has to promise he'll keep Prim until she dies. . . I want all my books to go to my friend Peggy Touchstone. . .

The crouching woman stands. Immediately the lion raises his head and slows to a walk, his movements as fluid as water running downhill. Before he even reaches the fence he slouches away in disgust. We're no longer worth his interest.

Half an hour later, when my blood pressure has returned to normal and I'm interviewing Tippi—famous for her starring role in Alfred Hitchcock's film classic *The Birds*—I depart from my questions list to blurt out, "Why did you ask that woman to stand up?"

"Because the lion saw her as prey," Tippi answers promptly. "You don't ever want a lion to think of you as prey."

For the same reason, Tippi herself—along with the cast and crew of a movie she was filming in Africa—were asked to stand when a lion handler strolled through the set with a full-grown male lion by his side. No leash. No fence, either.

What I remember best about that day at Shambala, the sixty-five-acre reserve for unwanted and abused big cats (many bought as cute, cuddly cubs by private owners) that Tippi Hedren calls home is this: faced with a predator that viewed me as dinner, I did exactly what many horses do. I froze, my mind a helpless captive inside a body that refused to cooperate. It was an experience I've never had before and hope never to have again.

Prim reacting to a perceived threat by snorting and racing around the corral. Now she's stopped to get a good look at it, head and tail raised. Note that Kyle's tail is raised too.

This is what reality is like for horses. They are constantly on the alert for predators or a movement that could indicate the presence of one. Eternally vigilant, they are eternally prepared to flee, fight, or freeze.

Such is life on the food chain.

FLEE, FIGHT, OR FREEZE

Like all animals that can't reason, horses carry their evolutionary history in their heads. In other words, they rely on instinct to keep them safe. The instinct that controls most of their behavior involves their status on the food chain. Throughout history—and horses have been around for about fifty-four million years—they were dinner on legs for

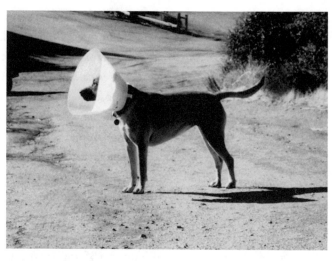

Chance, the "perceived threat," wearing an E-collar (short for "Elizabethan") so she won't chew herself.

big cats, wolves, and humans with big clubs. On this continent, they coexisted with the saber-toothed tiger, *Smilodon fatalis*—a feline with seven-inch fangs and such short legs it had to sneak up on its prey and ambush it. To minimize the risk of being ambushed, whenever horses sensed the presence of anything that *might* be a predator, they took to their heels. But occasionally a lone horse faced by a predator would freeze—exactly the way rabbits, hares, and humans do—in an instinctive attempt to blend in with the scenery, especially when the horse couldn't gauge how far away the predator was.

Since the modern horse, who has been around for approximately four million years, could outrun most of his predators—including a saber-toothed tiger, if he saw it in time—he

Your horse's worst nightmare: a saber-toothed tiger. (Drawing by Gina Cresse)

had only two additional ways to defend himself. Hard hooves were one. A well-aimed kick could kill or disable most predators, but first the horse had to swing his hindquarters around so the predator was directly behind him, and those precious seconds cost many horses their lives. Horses can also strike using their forelegs, but they seldom do so because that action would expose their vulnerable under-bellies. Although the horse has teeth and powerful jaws, his teeth are flat—good for nipping off and grinding coarse grass. He can't inflict a killing bite on another animal the way big cats and wolves do. Neither would he risk putting his head that close to a clawed feline.

For maximum protection, horses banded together in small groups the way cattle, sheep, buffalo, and other prey animals do, since they were less likely to be killed foraging with a herd than if they foraged solo. In spite of approximately 4,000 years of domestication, your horse's first response is to obey his instincts: he's a prey animal who can move from a standing position to a 35-mph sprint in a matter of seconds, and he belongs to a herd.

These two traits explain most of your horse's behavior.

HORSE HISTORY

Paleontologists, geneticists, and other researchers believe horses first evolved in North America and spread to Asia and eventually Europe by way of a land bridge across the Bering Straits. The earliest horse, once called *Eohippus*, the "dawn horse," had toes and stood at most five hands at the withers. Since horses left a nearly complete fossil record of their evolution on this continent, it should be easy to trace the development of *Eohippus*, recently renamed *Hyracotherium*, to the very different-looking *Equus caballus*, the modern horse. But as researchers have discovered, the evolution of today's horse is the result of a series of starts, stops, deadends, and periods of phenomenal growth spurts that allowed—on at least one occasion—five separate "horse" species to flourish on this continent.

Hyracotherium (or *Eohippus)* appeared in North America fifty-five million years ago. In addition to an arched, dog-like back, he had a short neck, a dog-like head, short legs, a small brain, and ate mainly leaves and fruit.

Seventeen million years ago, *Merychippus,* the first horse that actually resembled a horse, had evolved. He stood about ten hands at the withers and was smarter and faster than his ancestors. His back had lengthened, his head, muzzle, and legs had lengthened, and he ran on his raised middle toe. By now horses were foraging exclusively on wild grass tough enough to cut skin, and so dense with fiber that *Merychippus* had developed additional grinding teeth, or molars. Because the grass was so coarse, he wore his teeth down trying to eat it. To compensate, his teeth kept growing, the same way his hooves did. Another new development: to accommodate the deep roots of his new molars, his eyes moved farther back and to either side of his head.

Four million years ago, *Equus caballus*, the first true horse, was foraging in the grassy plains of North America. These horses stood about 13.2 hands. They had developed powerful, long legs (good for fleeing saber-toothed tigers), long necks, and wanderlust. Two million years later they entered the Old World. In Africa, they evolved into zebras. In Asia, North

Africa, and the Middle East, they branched off into donkeys and asses. A million years ago various *Equus* species roamed in large herds throughout Asia, Africa, Europe, North America, and South America.

But around eleven thousand years ago, *Equus caballus* disappeared from North America. (So did the saber-toothed tiger, and researchers still aren't sure why.) All that's left of fifty-five million years of evolution are two species of the genus *Equus*, a spectacular fossil record, the horny growths on the inside of your horse's knees and hocks (called chestnuts), and the brittle bits of cartilage that grow out of his fetlocks (called ergots). These chestnuts and ergots are physical reminders, the only ones that remain, of the first horse: they're what used to be toes.

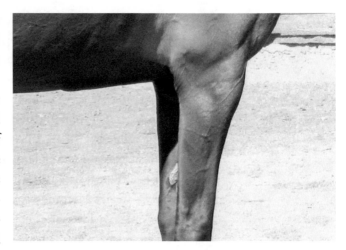

The chestnut on the inside of a horse's knee. He has four, one on each leg.

Domestication

Horses were a source of fresh meat until some early human recognized the potential benefits of riding one. The usual way humans domesticated animals was to kill a female for food, take her baby alive, hand-raise it, and then slaughter it, although some mares were kept for their milk.

But what flight of imagination prompted one nomadic Central Asian hunter to hop on the back of some strapping, hand-raised stud colt, and use him to find and kill other horses? And then to find and kill other humans? Horse skulls have been found at ancient settlements (4500–3500 BC) in Russia that show evidence of bit wear on the teeth. Some researchers say bit wear proves only that some horses had been *tamed*, but not necessarily domesticated. Until a species will reliably breed in captivity, it is not considered to be domesticated. In Asia, the horse was domesticated about 2000 BC. By 1000 BC horses were being used for warfare in China and parts of Europe. Probably because of their small size, they were used mainly to pull chariots. The Greeks, who took horses so seriously they meticulously recreated them in marble (see "Elgin Marbles" in the glossary), rode bareback or with a saddle cloth.

Humans created horseshoes once they realized that horses who worked hard wore their hooves down too fast to be useful. In Ostia, the seaport of ancient Rome and a flourishing trade center, the cobblestones are worn down in places by two-inch-deep indentations in the shape of horseshoes.

The modern horse—bigger, stronger, and faster than ever—reappeared in North America with the Spanish explorers. Shortly before his death in 1521, Juan Ponce de León brought fifty horses to present-day Florida. During the same time period, Hernán Cortés invaded Mexico and sent expeditions as far south as Honduras. Some horses escaped, others were left behind deliberately. Many were natural-gaited. Descendants of the Florida/Caribbean horses include the Paso Fino and Peruvian Paso.

When the British began shipping horses to their New England colonies two hundred years later, some were natural-gaited horses indigenous to the British Isles; a few were expensive purebred Thoroughbreds. Before long specific "types" of American horses, bred on American soil, began to emerge. As the frontier expanded westward, people who owned these horses removed them from the common gene pool and bred them only to mares of the same type to get more horses with the abilities they admired, such as speed in the Standardbred and comfortable gaits in the American Saddlebred. Morgans were particularly desirable because of their small size and tremendous strength. These sturdy horses could do the work of a draft horse, although they required much less feed; they also made excellent riding and driving horses. Today's Morgans are still widely used as carriage horses and in driving events.

Most saddle horses native to this country descend from Spanish and English natural-gaited horses, with deliberate outcrosses to Thoroughbreds and Arabians. Breeds native to this country include the Pony of the Americas, Appaloosas, Morgans, Quarter Horses, Paints, Florida Cracker Horses, Standardbreds, American Saddlebreds, Missouri Fox Trotting Horses, Racking Horses, Rocky Mountain Horses, and Tennessee Walking Horses. The last six breeds—out of twelve—are, or can be, natural-gaited.

KISSING COUSINS

In addition to *Equus caballus*, three related horse-like animals exist today: two species of the ass or donkey (a burro is a small donkey), three species of zebra, and *Equus Przewalski*, more commonly known as Przewalski's horse and the only other remaining species of horse left alive.

Donkeys

Donkeys, Asian donkeys in particular, are famous for their sprint and stamina—quick bursts of speed up to 44 mph and the ability to maintain a 15 mph gallop for up to two hours. Donkeys are usually mouse gray with long ears, loud voices, a pronounced dorsal stripe, and no withers. They have a more willing nature than either zebras or Przewalski's horses, although they have excellent memories and are famous for being stubborn—which means they have a reason for not doing as they're told, but their owner/rider/driver doesn't know what that reason is. Donkeys were domesticated much earlier than horses and have been ridden in the Middle East for centuries. But because of their size, they're used mainly as pack animals. They're much more surefooted than horses, and are often used in steep, rocky, or other precarious terrain. Wild donkeys still roam the arid salt flats of India.

Mules

Horses bred to donkeys produce mules. If the mule's sire was a horse stallion and his dam was a donkey, he (or she) is officially a hinny. If his sire was a donkey stallion (called a jack) and his dam was a mare, he's officially a mule. Mules are much more common than hinnies and are usually larger—although even their owners admit it's hard to tell them apart. Some mules bray, others whinny. Some have chestnuts on all four legs, as do horses; others have chestnuts only on their forelegs, like donkeys. While mules and hinnies are physically capable of reproducing,

A Mule Owner's Rule of Thumb:

Mules must be trained the way horses should be trained.

Heather Miliotti and Apples the donkey. Donkeys make excellent companion animals for horses.

A mule. Or maybe a hinny.
(Drawing by Gina Cresse)

both are sterile. Mules can do nearly anything a horse can, but because they have such good memories and tend to be more aggressive than horses, they have to be more carefully trained.

Zebras

With their bizarre black and white lightning-strike coats, zebras are fascinating to look at but impossible to ride. They won't tolerate humans on their backs and resist any attempt to train them to do anything. Horse/zebra crosses do occur, but so infrequently they have no common name. I only know of one such cross—a *zony* sired by a zebra out of a Shetland pony mare. Most offspring are, like the mule, sterile.

Przewalski's Horses

Przewalski's horses, the only other remaining species of *Equus*, look more like the modern horse than either donkeys or zebras.

Definitely a zebra! (Drawing by Gina Cresse)

Przewalski's horse, the only other remaining species of Equus. *(Drawing by Gina Cresse)*

They're very shy, and, like the zebra, have no desire to be ridden. If it weren't for zoos, which discovered how to breed them in captivity, they would be extinct; every Przewalski's horse alive today owes his existence to a mere thirteen ancestors.

Przewalski's horse stands approximately twelve hands, has a heavy build, a big head, a Roman nose, small ears and eyes, an upright mane, no forelock, a short back, and a dorsal stripe. They also carry sixty-six chromosomes, while all domestic horses carry sixty-four.

These horses once roamed throughout much of Asia, where they bred freely with local ponies. Their offspring were fertile, but the "Przewalski gene" diluted rapidly if the offspring were bred back to ponies. Some researchers believe that the horses painted by cave-dwelling artists in France and Spain are Przewalski's horses.

In the 1990s, some Przewalski's horses were re-introduced to their original homeland in the Mongolian steppes, where they appear to be thriving. Today, these small, dun-colored horses are the only truly wild horses in the world.

Equus caballus, the modern horse, differs from his kin in one extremely important way. At some point in the evolution of humans and horses, a man devised a bit and bridle and deliberately mounted a horse in order to run as fast as the horse did. That bargain of horses allowing themselves to be ridden and guided by humans—even in the noise and blood of combat—in return for protection resulted in the modern horse. But the bargain is a very recent one in evolutionary terms, and sometimes it's convenient for your horse to forget about it. Buried even deeper in his brain is the knowledge that he is a prey animal—and his ultimate safety depends on his herd and how fast he can run. Not on the human on his back.

HORSE SENSE

Today's horses depend on the same five senses humans do: sight, hearing, smell, taste, and touch. Horses use their senses mainly to identify predators and each other. How they behave *as a result* of what they see, hear, smell, taste, or touch give us insights into what they're liable to do next.

Sight: What's Up, Pussy Cat?

Do horses see the world the way humans do? No. The only animals who see the way humans do are other humans.

Three dimensional vision: The first thing most domestic horses do when something strange catches their attention, especially if it moves, is stop, raise their heads, and stare. After a few seconds the horses will usually exhale several soft, breathy snorts, take a few quick steps sideways or back, and stop and stare again. Because a horse's eyes are set on the widest part of his face (thanks to those deep-rooted back molars), he can't see the same way a human can. He prefers to view anything suspicious from several angles before deciding whether it's harmless or it's a saber-toothed tiger with bloodshot eyes and seven-inch fangs.

If you look your horse in the face, you'll notice that his head is almost triangular—a small muzzle that widens at the top of his head with his eyes on the widest part. Except for a small blind spot directly behind his ears and a larger one directly behind his tail, your horse can see almost everything around him. If you draw a circle over the top of his head, he sees what's in front of him, beside him, and behind him except for about 90 degrees in the very back of the circle. (A human's blind spot is 180 degrees.)

When a young or inexperienced horse sees you reach for his poll with a curry mitt, he may pull back or duck. Watch his eyes. They're usually rolled so far back in his head that you can see the whites of his eyes; he's straining to see what's in his blind spot.

Because of the position of *your* eyes, you have very little peripheral vision. Try closing your left eye. With your right eye open, how far to either side can you see? Not very far: your nose and eye socket get in the way. Now close your right eye and open the left one. Same problem. Because your eyes are in the front of your face, your range of vision is restricted to what's directly in front of you. Without moving your head, you can't see anything above you, below you, or to the side.

If you're observant, you noticed something else: the "picture" you saw out of your right eye was slightly different than the one you saw out of your left eye. In other words, with one eye closed, you no longer see in three dimensions. When you see one image with your right eye and another image with your left eye and have no way to focus—to merge the two images into a single, three-dimensional one—you have what's called monocular vision. This is pretty much how horses see the world. When humans have both eyes open, we have binocular vision because a mechanism in our brain enables us to resolve those two separate image into a single three-dimensional image.

The horse has the largest eyes of almost any land mammal.

While horses can see most of what surrounds them, they can't always see it clearly. Horses see part of the landscape in three dimensions, as we do. Because they're farsighted, they can see and focus on (three-dimensional binocular vision) objects that are miles away. While they *can* focus on objects directly in front of them, they can't do so easily or for very long. In addition, they have limited depth perception at close range, which explains why most horses are afraid of water. Without depth perception, they have no way of telling how deep it is.

Prim inspecting an oddity—a camera—at close range. Note her raised tail, vertical neck, and dilated nostrils. (Photo by Marilyn Dalrymple)

As my childhood friend Barbara Davis, an artist and dog breeder put it, "a horse's focal point converges too far for him to have the same kind of depth perception that animals with their eyes on the front of their face have."

Because your horse is a prey animal, seeing an unfamiliar object *move* is more important to his survival than knowing exactly how far away it is.

Color vision: For centuries researchers have believed that horses could only see black and white with a lot of gray tones. Old-time cowboys who spent their lives on horseback, and hunter/jumper judges and course designers like Jamie Alder, believe that horses can distinguish at least two colors: bright yellow and the more vivid shades of blue. That's why so many jumps have yellow or yellow-and-black-striped rails, and also why course designers like to include a water jump, especially one that features actual water dyed blue with Tidy Bowl. The latest research indicates that horses *can* see colors at the blue/green end of the spectrum, including yellow. If a horse saw a saber-toothed shape silhouetted against a blue sky, he didn't have to decide anything. He ran away.

Seeing in the dark: Horses have much better night vision than humans. When I was writing Old West articles for the now-defunct *Colorado Magazine*, I read more than one first-hand account of ranchers returning home on a moonless night by giving their horse his head.

Even though horses can see in the dark, if yours gets out during the night and you have to round him up on foot, take a flashlight with you as a precaution. Shine it on yourself every couple of minutes so your horse knows where you are and doesn't run over you.

Smell: One Sniff Tells All

While a horse's sense of smell is not as highly developed as a dog's, a horse can identify particular horses and humans by the way they smell. A horse can smell water. If he sees something new that's nonthreatening, he'll move closer to sniff it and find out what it is—dangerous or not dangerous, edible or not edible. If it's not dangerous and not edible, he'll walk away from it.

Like dogs, horses will stop along the trail to sniff the droppings of other horses. In the wild, stallions mark their territory by dropping a load of manure and then urinating on it. When he returns to that spot, if he discovers that another stallion has urinated on *his* manure heap, he will mark it again with his own scent. Mares will sniff but not mark.

Hearing: I Can't 'Ear You!

Horses also have very good hearing. This trait, together with their memory, makes them easy to train by using voice commands.

Before I met John, he trained horses at another stable where one of his owners had turned an old, retired broodmare out to pasture. The mare was blind, but the owner had bought her a companion—an elderly Shetland pony—and tied a bell to the pony's halter. The mare followed the pony everywhere; the two were inseparable. Because of the pony's bell, John and the barn crew always knew where to find the mare, and the mare always knew where to find dinner.

Prim's sense of smell tells her that bubbles aren't dangerous or edible. (Photo by Gina Cresse)

Neighs: Horses communicate with one another by various sounds. They neigh—the loudest noise they make—directly to other horses to indicate their presence or to remark on the other horse's presence. A mare in season will often neigh, even to geldings, to announce her sexual availability. When a horse neighs or whinnies, he opens his mouth and cuts loose at full volume. If you're on his back, you can feel the sound reverberate through his entire body.

Horses seldom neigh to humans in the same loud, assertive manner unless you show up very late to feed.

Nickers: Nickering back and forth is another way horses communicate. These are softer, breathier sounds than whinnies because while your horse does vocalize, he's mainly blowing air through his nose. A hungry horse will nicker at you as you step out of the hay shed carrying his breakfast. Sometimes the sound will be so soft you can't hear it, but you'll see his nostrils flutter.

Snorts: A horse confronted by something he hasn't seen before and isn't sure of will usually snort. Unlike the two previous sounds, he's not doing any vocalizing. Snorts are all air. There are loud, breathy snorts that end in an exclamation point. Softer snorts sound as though he's blowing his nose. Quite often he *is* blowing his nose. Long, low-pitched, breathy snorts communicate caution.

Getting to know you. The next step is usually a loud snort.

Squeals: Horses usually reserve squealing for encounters with the opposite sex, although often two horses who have never met and are getting acquainted over the fence by sniffing—usually nosebone to nosebone with arched necks and raised tails—will often end the introduction by squealing.

On the trail: When you ride, the position of your horse's ears is a very good way to evaluate what he's thinking—because he'll communicate the same information to you that he would otherwise communicate to his herdmates.

Are both ears pointed forward, but he's not tense? This is a good sign; he's interested and looking ahead to see what's out there. Are both ears pointed forward but now he's tense—he's raised his head and neck and his steps have quickened? This is not a good sign—something *is* Out There. Suppose one ear points forward but the other flicks to the side, then back to you, then forward? This is a very good sign. Your horse is indicating that he's knows you're on his back; he's acknowledging that he feels your aids and letting you know he's checking for predators. Suppose both ears are back—but not pinned back. Mixed signals here. His ear position could indicate nothing more than fatigue, boredom, or both. Or it could signify mild displeasure. You'll be able to tell more as you ride.

Most horses move their ears constantly. They want to know what's around them, friend or foe, although hot-blooded breeds react to their surroundings more emphatically than draft horses or warmbloods.

▲**Early Warning Sign**▼ While some horses are naturally lop-eared—both ears flop sideways, one at 9 A.M. and the other at 3 P.M.—a horse who habitually uses his ears but suddenly lets them flop may be feeling listless. Take his temperature.

Ears flattened against the skull: A horse with both ears back is warning other horses—or humans—to stay away, usually because he's protecting his food. Mares protect their foals the same way, particularly when the foal is very young. A horse with his ears pinned flat against his head is threatening to attack, especially if he's carrying his head low and swinging it from side to side. If he *is* ready to attack, he'll often bare his teeth.

I saw a mare knock a man down because he had approached her stall to see her new baby. He was so intent on the foal that he ignored the position of the mare's ears and her lowered head. She didn't bite him, but she swung her head into him so hard she knocked him off his feet.

Taste: The Molasses Factor

Horses need salt and will actively seek it out. Although sugar is not normally a part of their diet, they develop a taste for sweets very quickly. Their sweet tooth is the reason horses will eat their molasses-enhanced grain supplement with great gusto and then turn in resignation to their hay.

Carrots, one of the most common horse treats, are sweet. Some owners dump a few dozen carrots into their horse's feeder and call it lunch. Although unlikely, it *is* possible for a horse to choke on a carrot. If you want to feed your horse carrots, buy him the specially packaged mini-carrots—or bite off chunk-sized pieces so he can eat out of your hand—and feed him something else for lunch.

Many feed companies disguise the taste of their product by adding a sweetener, usually molasses, for "palatability." This means your horse won't eat it unless it contains molasses or another sweetener.

Touch: The Missing Magic

The last few years I owned Sinjun, John ran a training barn for the owner who had asked him to design and build one. Since our property abutted the Angeles National Forest, I usually headed for the woods when I rode. But one afternoon I decided to explore a trail behind our house.

As I turned a corner and looked down, I caught sight of a neighbor I didn't know we had—an elderly, very fat horse pastured in a small valley next to a small house. Sinjun and the other horse saw each other at the same time. Sinjun stiffened and gave a shallow, breathy snort that can usually be translated as, "Okay, what's *this*?"

The other horse responded with a long, heart-felt whinny. When his owners stepped out on their porch to see what was going on, I saw they were as elderly as their horse. I waved. They waved back. But the horse kept staring at Sinjun, even though he didn't utter another sound. What I'd heard was a neigh not only of welcome, but recognition and need. How many years had that horse gone without seeing or smelling another horse? For the first time I found myself wondering if isolating a horse, a herd animal, from other horses was a good idea.

■ Horses enjoy direct physical contact. When they're together in a pasture they spend a lot of time doing nothing. They graze. They stare off into the distance, thinking horse thoughts. They snooze, usually on their feet, but some will lie down for a daytime siesta. And more often than not they'll stand next to another horse, nose to tail, lazily swatting one another with their tails to discourage flies.

Most horses enjoy grooming, which is a form of touch. Most horses also enjoy being petted, although stroked would be more accurate. Don't pat-pat your horse on the nose or any other part of his body. He'll probably flinch because he isn't sure what happened or who did it—to him it felt like a poke. Instead, run your hands along his neck and sides, using long, smooth, even strokes the way you do when you groom him.

Petting, stroking, and grooming your horse all reinforce the idea that you do good things to him that he likes—he likes your touch. Many old-time horse whisperers depended heavily on touch to achieve their results.

Good vibrations: Hearing specialists are investigating the fact that the horse you're trail riding will often sense something—particularly something motorized that has a very low, rumbling sound—coming towards you, even though neither one of you can actually "hear" it. Some researchers have theorized that horses feel deep, bass sounds—reverberations—in their feet and bones. The soil acts as a conductor.

Body English: Neck, Head, and Tail Positions

Some breeds, such as Arabians, Andalusians, American Saddlebreds, Morgans, and Welsh Ponies, have a naturally high head-carriage—the natural position of their neck is vertical rather than horizontal. But most horses will raise their head and neck whenever they sense something new and potentially dangerous. A raised tail usually accompanies a raised head and pricked ears.

A raised tail can also indicate excitement. A high-spirited horse running and bucking in the arena often flags his tail by raising his tailbone until it's almost vertical. Since he's moving, the hair of his tail streams out behind him like a flag whipping in the breeze.

A horse with his tail clamped between his legs is frightened. A horse with a dead tail, one that rarely if ever moves, may have neurological problems. A horse who wrings his tail—switches it in circles—is usually irritated. ▲**Early Warning Sign**▼ If a horse who habitually uses his tail is suddenly too listless to swat away flies, he's not feeling well. Take his vital signs.

THE HERD INSTINCT

Most wild horse herds have two bosses, and one is usually a very pushy mare. She, not the stallion, decides where the other horses will travel, when to stop and graze, and when to move on. The stallion is usually on sentry duty. When the herd starts moving, he hangs back to urge on the stragglers.

There's only one top-dog stud in a herd, although he may allow a few juveniles from last year's foal crop to stay on until they either fight him for dominance or he runs them off.

If any horse in the herd thinks he sees, smells, hears, or otherwise senses danger and starts to run, the entire herd will join him without hesitation. But if the horses don't detect danger and something does sneak up on them, they immediately close ranks like a movie wagon train that just got word of an Indian attack. All young and vulnerable animals huddle in the middle, while the mature animals position themselves on the periphery, ready to kick and bite until they drive the predator away.

To your horse, home is where the herd is, or—more accurately—the herd *is* home. This is why, against all common sense (which means it's not how we humans think), if a blindfolded horse is being led away from a burning barn and the blindfold slips, he'll try to return to the burning barn.

If you're on a trail ride and come to a fenced pasture with horses in it, your horse might get excited. *How* excited depends on his breed, his own personality, and how often he sees other horses. Does he want to move closer to get a good sniff, nose to nose? If he does, be prepared for sudden squeals. If the other horses break into a gallop and race up and down the fence line, your horse may want to join them. Be prepared for takeoff.

When you're trail riding and your horse sees something strange that he suspects is a predator, he'll often shy, or jump off his feet. If he senses that *you*—the one he considers his herdmate (a very poor substitute for the real thing, but he's making do)—are afraid, he'll turn tail and head for home, usually at a racehorse gallop. Since horses evolved on open, grassy plains where the terrain was level, they fled without regard for rodent holes, rocks, trees, cliffs, or canyons—because there weren't any. It didn't matter where they went. It matters to the modern horse, but he doesn't know that.

When Prim sees something she can't account for, she stops suddenly, neck vertical, ears forward, her body rigid. If your horse reacts to a perceived danger this way, take two or three d-e-e-p breaths and concentrate on the inhale, then the exhale. On the final exhale, "let go" and allow your body to go limp in the saddle. The few times I've had to do this, I physically felt Prim's body soften as she relaxed under me. When she's frightened, I can feel her heart beating.

BUY YOUR HORSE A BUDDY

If you buy a horse, stable him by himself, trail ride alone, and never go to weekend horse shows, you may very well end up with a neurotic horse. He has no herd. All he has is you, and if you're like most owners, you're away at work at least part of the day. As a result your horse may start to weave, walk the fence line, lose his appetite, and/or lose weight. Weaving and fence-walking, long considered stable vices, are now recognized as the signs of a bored, lonely horse.

The solution? Buy your horse a friend. Having *any* kind of buddy will fill the empty hours of your horse's day and allow him to feel as though he belongs to a herd again.

In the wild, young stallions usually leave their herd at some point—but not willingly. The big guy, the head stud, has chased them out. Rather than forage alone, these young stallions will buddy up with other outcasts. One rancher observed a lone stallion buddying up with a lone male elk.

Civilized horses have sheep, goats, and other domestic animals for companions. High-strung Thoroughbred race horses often calm down when paired with a cat or chicken. Ponies don't always work because individual ponies can be so feisty they will steal your horse's hay and grain and defend the automatic drinker from him.

While the ideal buddy is another horse, many horse people claim that donkeys have a particularly calming influence on horses because their own nature is so placid.

If you buy a goat, make sure she's been nubbed, or dehorned.

If you buy a sheep, keep in mind that you have to shear it once a year.

If you buy a donkey, be prepared for a lot of noise. Some owners deliberately choose donkeys because they're very vocal watch dogs.

Glad to Make Your Acquaintance

Since your horse will probably throw a fit the first time he sees his new friend, introduce the two animals gradually. When I brought Kyle home, John and I left Prim alone in the corral—in other words, nobody tried to restrain her—while we took turns walking Kyle around the outside of the corral, stopping so they could sniff noses, then turning around and repeating the routine. We spent probably half an hour doing this. Our main concern was that if Prim didn't like Kyle, she could back him into a corner and kick the stuffing out of him.

But because we took precautions, when we led Kyle inside the corral Prim was curious about this new creature rather than afraid of him. He was a little afraid of Prim, but soon they were sniffing each other's tails and following other accepted "getting to know you" procedures, so we left them alone for the night.

The next morning Kyle still had both ears and no bite marks and wanted breakfast. Now, five years later, everybody in this canyon knows when I ride—because Kyle hollers his head off as soon as we disappear from sight. Prim, on the other hand, doesn't have any qualms about leaving her buddy—unless I take Kyle away from *her*. Then she trots along the fence in obvious distress, nickering. It's one of the few times I've seen her ignore food.

THE VALUE OF TRUST

One of the true joys of horse ownership is when your horse sees something that frightens him and tenses up and possibly even shies; but because he trusts you, he agrees to tiptoe past what he *knows* is a saber-toothed cat crouching in ambush. He won't pass it willingly, but he will pass it. The more frightened he gets, the calmer you have to be. Most riders develop this kind of confidence in their own ability very slowly, because we're influenced by other animals' behavior too—in this case, our horse's. "Staying calm" when your horse is having a panic attack requires courage—if your horse bucks you off, right here on this narrow mountain trail, you're history—and courage is a very hard emotion to fake.

But if you work with your horse consistently—at least every other day—and gain experience riding him, you'll develop more confidence. You'll also find that even a very spooky horse will settle down and shy less often.

A horse's most valuable assets are his memory, his ability to detect extremely subtle movements in his environment, and his speed.

As his owner, your most valuable asset is patience.

CHAPTER 13

TIME TO SADDLE UP AND HIT THE TRAIL

Y ou wake up at 6 A.M., *before* the alarm goes off. You're instantly suspicious. What's wrong? You never wake up this early on purpose.

And then it hits you. It's been four whole days since your horse first set foot on your property. He has adjusted to your yappy dog, the kid down the street who roars past on his motorcycle, and has made several new horse friends within whinnying distance. Yesterday you longed him, then put your saddle on him and longed him again. The saddle seemed to fit. Your horse even seems to recognize you, especially if you're carrying feed. And he's so relaxed he acts as though he's lived in your backyard all his life.

As for you, you're so eager to ride him that you've been counting down the days, hour by hour. The hour is now.

Toes tingling with anticipation, you hop out of bed, grinning. Your boots are in the guest bedroom closet—riding clothes too—because your husband or wife doesn't appreciate "horsey" smells as much as you do. If you ride Western, pulling your boots on won't be a problem. But if you ride English and opted for a pair of dress boots, pulling them on *is* a problem. Here's a tip that involves two plastic grocery bags, one for each foot.

After putting on whatever combination of socks or stockings you need, raise your lower leg until it's horizontal (I assume you're sitting down), slide a bag over it, and loosely tie the ends. Then, using boot pulls, slide your boot on *over* the bag. It's the only effective way to pull on new or very tight boots. After you finish riding, the bags will come off when the boots do.

As you finish dressing you think about your friend who lives in an old farmhouse a few miles away. She has agreed to meet you here at 7:30 for your first trail ride on your new horse, so you'll have company.

Today, your riding team (as opposed to your horse-care team) is you and your horse and your friend and her horse, out for a trail ride, destination unknown. The only thing you *do* know is that the trail will end where it started—in your backyard.

BUT FIRST—BREAKFAST

As you head for the barn, I suggest you think about breakfast. Your horse's, not yours. After you put some sweet feed, alfalfa cubes, and hay in your horse's feeder (by now you should be about halfway switched over to the new feeding program) go back inside and brew some coffee. By the time you finish your breakfast, your horse will probably have finished his.

Why am I making such a big deal out of breakfast? Because it's a big deal for your horse. *Any* time you feed your horse it's a big deal. Unless horses are pastured, they can't rustle up their own fixings. As a result, they're acutely aware of when the next meal is supposed to arrive. If you've been feeding your new horse three times a day, that's The Way Things Are (horse logic). What's more, he *anticipates* all three feedings.

Feed your horse before you ride him. If you don't, all he'll think about for the entire ride is the meal you didn't feed him. He didn't want to go trail riding in the first place. He wanted to stay home and eat, even though he's only been "home" four days. That's long enough for him to associate his corral—and you, of course—with the only reliable source of food since Mom left (more horse logic). If you ride during the time your horse would normally be eating, he'll dance and prance and jig sideways the entire time, trying to edge back to the barn, and you'll both have a miserable time. Your friend probably won't enjoy herself much either.

GETTING READY TO RIDE

After you finish your own breakfast, head out to the barn again. If your horse is still cleaning up the last of his feed, take the opportunity to clean his stall or corral. When you're both finished, slip a halter on him and lead him to your riding ring.

Longe Him

Turn your horse loose long enough to get the kinks out. In other words, you want him to buck *now*, not while you're on his back.

Since some horses don't expend energy unless they have to, you may have to longe your horse to get him moving, especially in hot weather. You may even have to get pushy about it. Unless your horse is sick or injured, he's holding out on you. In the deepest, darkest recesses of his brain is an image of a feline with seven-inch fangs that's looking at him and drooling. Most horses hold something in reserve for that one mad, desperate burst of speed that will allow them to outrun the predator behind them.

Know Your Knots

After you longe your horse, tie him to the hitching rail so he has *almost* enough room to turn his head and touch his shoulder with his nose. In other words, so his head is no more than three feet away from the rail. Use a quick-release safety knot (keep reading). If you give him more leeway, he can step on the rope. But if you tie him too short, he won't have any moving-around room. That may scare him, especially if he's young or inexperienced.

The majority of horses will stand willingly, without fussing and often without moving, while you groom and saddle them. But a few—for example the inexperienced horses I just mentioned—require more care. I strongly recommend that you use a quick-release safety knot every time you tie your horse, regardless of his temperament or how well he's broke. The reason I emphasized making your hitching rail out of two-inch galvanized pipe can be summed up in one word: safety. A terrified horse galloping down your driveway with a wooden rail attached to his leadrope that's banging his front legs with every stride is not a pretty sight. You have to restrain your horse somehow, so why not use a knot you can undo in a heartbeat if your horse suddenly panics and sets back? Just because he hasn't shown any signs of skittishness in the four days you've owned him is no guarantee he won't do something silly in the future.

Always use a leadrope to tie your horse. Forget all those Western movies where the cowboy tossed his reins over a hitching rail and his horse never moved—even when some guy shot the cowboy dead. That horse was a stunt horse. Never tie a horse by his reins.

I've seen three or four different quick-release knots; this one works for me. It works especially well when the leadrope is made out of nylon or some other limp, slippery material. Practice tying the knot a few times before you attach your horse to it.

- Step 1: Drape your leadrope over the top of the hitching rail so the *short* end—about eighteen inches of rope—is on the far side of the rail.
- Step 2: Use your left hand to pull the short end across the long end of the rope. (The short end will be your "quick release." Your horse will be tied to the long end.)

How to tie a quick-release safety knot. Step 1: Drape your leadrope over the top of the hitching rail so the short end—about 18" of rope—is on the far side of the rail. (Photo by Gina Cresse)

Step 2: Use your left hand to pull the short end across the long end. (The short end is your "quick release"; your horse will be tied to the long end.) (Photo by Gina Cresse)

Step 3: Loosen enough rope in the long *end (in your right hand) to form a loop. (Photo by Gina Cresse)*

Step 4: Push the second loop through *the first loop. (Photo by Gina Cresse)*

Step 5: Tighten the knot. (Photo by Gina Cresse)

- Step 3: Loosen enough rope in the *long* end (in your right hand) to form a loop, and use your left hand to create a second loop from the short end of the rope that's as big as the first loop.
- Step 4: Push the second loop (in your left hand) through the first loop.
- Step 5: Tighten the knot by pulling on the long end.

Even though the knot is securely fastened, all you have to do to release it is pull on the short end. The knot will release much more easily if the leadrope has a slippery texture—the reason I suggested it.

No Knots

Some horse owners prefer to tie a loop of some thin, easily broken cotton rope to their horse's halter and snap the leadrope to that, not directly to the halter. If something frightens the horse and he sets back, the rope is guaranteed to break. Yes, breakaway halters also work, but a horse has to thrash pretty hard to break one. The disadvantage of a breakable rope is that you now have a loose horse who's in totally unfamiliar surroundings—which is why you keep food treats in your pocket at all times and why you taught your horse to come.

Other owners prefer to take a single wrap around the hitching rail with the leadrope. As long as the rope doesn't cross itself, the wrap will simply pull apart if the horse sets back. The disadvantage of this method is that you now have a loose horse trailing his leadrope. You might be able to catch him more easily, but he can also step on the leadrope and trip himself.

A Horse Owner's Rule of Thumb:

Never tie a horse with a chain over his nose.

Good Grooming

Conscientious owners groom their horses before and after they ride. A daily brushing will do more to keep your horse's coat shiny than any supplement on the market, and frequent handling is a good way to get to know each other.

Here are two quick safety tips: since you don't know very much about your horse yet, whenever you work around his head—that includes brushing—untie him. For the same reason, when you brush your horse's tail, stand to one side of him and not directly behind him. He probably won't kick—he knows you're there—but do it anyway, just in case.

Most horses love to be "brushed" with cactus cloth. Since cactus cloth isn't as durable as a rubber curry mitt, a lot of riders save it for the horse's final grooming. I save mine for a final rub before I turn Prim loose.

Don't forget to clean his feet.

The Mane Idea

If your new horse has a long mane and you want to keep it that way, the inevitable tangles can turn into witch's knots. If you don't unsnarl them immediately, they'll curl around themselves until they resemble dreadlocks. In this case, prevention is the best—and as far as I know the *only*—cure: braid your horse's mane, at least the part that gets tied up in knots, and fasten each braid with an elastic band. But separate the knots by hand; if you use a commercial mane detangler, the elastic bands will slide off.

Witches' knots.

How to prevent them. The only reason I used bootlaces on the two braids closest to Prim's head is because I ran out of rubber bands.

Every few weeks, take out the old braid, pick it out by hand, and rebraid. When you encounter a snarl, don't rip through it—you'll pull out the hair. If you want your horse to have a long, flowing mane, think about how long it took to get to its present length. Yank enough hair out and he won't *have* a long mane anymore.

Saddling Your Horse

Despite the obvious differences between Western and English saddles, you place all four of them on your horse's back the same way.

- Put the saddle pad, or blanket, on first. Saddle pads come in hundreds of different fabrics, designs, shapes, and thicknesses; the ones favored by Western riders are usually square or rectangular and often feature traditional Native American designs. English saddle pads usually follow the outline of the saddle, although some are also rectangular.

- Lay the saddle pad on your horse's back so the edge closest to your left hand rests partially on his withers. Center the pad so there's an equal amount of material on both sides of his body. Some saddle pads have a strip down the center so you can visually match it against the horse's spine. (The strip should follow his backbone.) Slide the pad back slightly, towards his rump, so it moves in the same direction his hair grows. Then put the saddle on his back.

- If you accidentally positioned the saddle too far back, don't slide it towards his withers. If you do, you're literally "rubbing him the wrong way," and that minor irritation, in combination with an item of tack that hasn't been adjusted properly, or a bit that doesn't fit quite right, can grow into a major attitude problem. As a result, your first day of trail riding did very little except irritate your horse.

- Remove the saddle, pick up the pad, and replace it. This time, make sure the edge closest to your left hand is higher on the horse's withers than it was the first time. Place the saddle on his back again. Rock it gently from side to side until it's balanced. This time it ought to be in the right place.

- But before you tighten the girth, slide your hand between the horse's withers and the saddle pad. You should be able to do so easily; if the pad or blanket presses against his withers, it can rub a sore. Take the saddle off and try again, being careful to *raise* the front of the saddle pad slightly before you resaddle the horse.

- Before you bridle him, slide the flat of your hand under the girth, both sides, to check for pinched skin and to make sure the girth isn't *too* tight. Alternatively, pick up your horse's forelegs, one at a time, and stretch them forward.

Bridling Your Horse

You bridle a Western horse almost the same way you bridle an "English" horse, but because Western bridles have fewer parts, the process is easier to describe. (For the English version, see page 224.)

Bridling your horse—Western: First, untie your horse, remove his halter, and buckle it around his neck so you have something to grab if he starts to walk away. Then, so you can control him after he's bridled, slip the reins over his head.

- Some riders hold the bridle in their right hand about halfway up the cheekpieces. Others prefer to hold the bridle by the crownpiece using their left hand. How tall your horse is, and how tall *you* are, can also influence your bridling style.
- If you use the crownpiece method, raise the bridle until it's head-high and guide the bit to the horse's lips with your right hand. Most horses will open their mouths and accept the bit.
- Use your left hand to guide the crownpiece over the horse's head and your right hand to move his ears forward, one at a time, in order to slide the bridle over them without crumpling them.
- If your horse *doesn't* open his mouth to accept the bit, put the bridle aside. I want you to look inside your horse's mouth. Specifically, I want you to see where his bars are—the gaps in both sides of his jaw where the bit normally lies.

Lacking a halter, Brian uses one arm under Cowboy Justin's neck before raising the bit.

Once the bit is in the gelding's mouth, Brian raises the crownpiece of the bridle.

Using his right hand to move Justin's ear forward when necessary, Brian prepares to guide the crownpiece of the bridle over the gelding's head.

- Place your left hand over his nose to steady his head. Your right hand is under his chin, palm up. If your hand is big enough, use your thumb and middle finger, one on either side of his lower jaw, to feel along his gums. Make sure to keep your fingers *outside* his teeth. If your hand isn't big enough, use just your thumb. When you encounter the bars, most horses will open their mouth automatically. Once yours does, you'll see his bars. Since that's all you wanted to do, drop both hands and let him close his mouth.
- Pick up the bridle again. Hold it by the cheek pieces, the bit in your left hand. Using your right hand, raise the bridle until the bit encounters his teeth.
- If he won't open his mouth, steady the bit between his upper and lower teeth with your right hand. (Don't pull.) With your left hand, feel for the bars using your thumb or your thumb and middle finger. When you locate them, squeeze his bars with your fingers.
- At this point your horse will probably accept the bit. If he doesn't, slide a fold of his lip between the bar and your fingers. Squeeze again. Your horse will open his mouth.
- As soon as he does, pull the bit into his open mouth with your right hand as you slide the bridle up and tell him he's a good boy.
- When you reach his ears, use your *right* hand to swivel your horse's right ear frontwards. Cup your horse's ear with your hand and slide the crownpiece *over your hand*, not his ear. Once the crownpiece of the bridle is behind his ear, cup his left ear and slide the rest of the crownpiece over your hand.
  You have just bridled your horse with a minimum of fuss and trauma.

Bridling your horse—English. The process of putting an English bridle on a horse is essentially the same. The only difference is that you have extra leather—a browband, noseband, and throatlatch—to worry about. (See photos on pages 256–257)

- First, fasten your horse's halter around his neck. Use your right hand to move the noseband to the right side of the headstall (the browband will take care of itself) and hold the bridle in your right hand by the cheekpieces. When you ease the bit between your horse's teeth with your left hand, the noseband will be safely out of the way.
- As soon as your horse accepts the bit, raise the bridle and slide your left hand over his off, or right, ear to guide the crownpiece *over your hand*. Follow the same procedure with his left ear. Once the crownpiece is in place, straighten the browband and separate the straps of the noseband from the cheekpiece of the bridle.
- If the bit is the right size and the cheekpieces are correctly adjusted, you should see one or two folds of skin at both corners of your horse's mouth (the same with the Western horse).
- If you find that the noseband is higher on one side than the other, don't straighten it by pulling on the noseband itself. Your horse will feel the pull behind his ears. Instead, reach up to the browband. Holding the strap of the low side of the nose-

band, *push it up*. This movement will create slack in the strap on the other side. Pull *that* strap. Your horse's noseband should be level.

Mounting Your Horse

The process of mounting is basically the same in all four seats, although cowboys have two advantages: the saddle horn, and the fact that they ride with a longer stirrup than most English riders. As you raise your left leg to slide your foot in the stirrup, grab the horn with your left hand, push off with your right foot, and use the momentum to swing your leg over your horse's back.

English riders mount their horse using a similar method.

- First, gather both reins in your left hand, making sure there's equal tension in both reins. But don't shorten them—you horse might think you want him to back up.
- Since you don't have a saddle horn, grab some of your horse's mane with your left hand, the one holding your reins.
- Use your right hand to position your stirrup iron until it's at a right angle to your horse. Place your left foot in it.
- This next part is tricky, because it's not a good idea to grab the cantle while you haul yourself into the saddle—you'll pull the entire saddle off balance. Place the flat of your right hand on the right side of the saddle, anywhere that feels comfortable—the

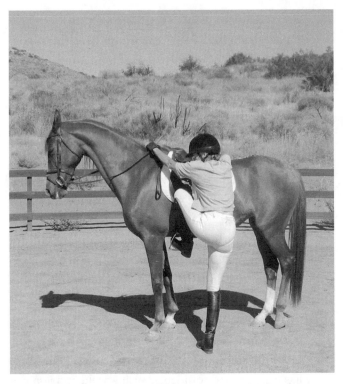

With a handful of Prim's mane in my left hand and my left foot in the stirrup, I'm ready to bounce into the saddle. This is why mounting blocks were invented. (Photo by Gina Cresse)

Both legs are now stirrup-level; this is what the process looks like from the off side. (Photo by Gina Cresse)

As you swing your right leg completely over your horse's rump, ease yourself into the saddle by using your right hand to brace yourself. This way your entire weight won't land on the horse's back all at once. (Photo by Gina Cresse)

Ordinarily you wouldn't stop at this point; you'd swing your right leg over the horse's back in one smooth movement. (Photo by Gina Cresse)

pommel, the seat itself, the bump over the stirrup leathers. To give yourself some momentum, bounce on your right foot and push off.

■ Both your legs should be fully extended on the near side of the horse, but only your left foot is in the stirrup iron. Lean forward slightly on your horse's back and shift your body weight to your right hand. As you swing your right leg over your horse's rump, move your right hand out of the way and *gradually* lower yourself into the saddle.

By using this method you have more control over your movements and will find it much easier to lower yourself into the saddle. Your horse will appreciate it.

If you use a mounting block, fasten the arena gate open before you get on, otherwise you'll have to dismount again in order to open it—unless your horse has been trained to sidepass or leg-yield and you can open and close gates from his back. Here's the correct way to mount a horse using a mounting block.

- Position your horse next to it but not touching it. Climb to the top step—that's the height most riders prefer. Then, instead of sliding your right leg over the horse's back and slipping both feet into the stirrup irons after you're seated, mount your horse exactly the way you would *without* a mounting block. The only difference is that you start from a higher altitude.
- In other words, place your *left* foot into the stirrup iron, swing your right leg over your horse's rump, settle yourself in the saddle, and slip your right foot through the right stirrup iron.

Short, Useful Exercises that Don't Seem Like Exercises

While you wait for your friend to arrive, get to know your horse. You don't have to do much—in fact this first time, I suggest that you just walk him. Do serpentines by walking your horse in big loops up and down the long side of the arena. Practice whoa-ing. Practice asking your horse to stand while you count to five (one thousand one, one thousand two, etc.) Practice your clucks—your horse should walk off instantly at the sound. If he doesn't, maybe his previous owner used another cue. Since you want your horse to respond to *your* cues, tell him to "Walk," and at the same time tighten your legs on him—in other words, squeeze his sides slightly with your lower legs. Reverse him and give him some slack in the reins and then take it back. Practice "Whoa" and "Walk" again.

A couple of weeks later, when you know your horse better and trust him more, ride without stirrups a few minutes before you set out. It's very good for your balance, and the better your balance is, the better your seat will be (see Chapter 19 for details).

Ring work doesn't have to be boring. All the exercises I've suggested will settle your horse down, improve your effectiveness as a rider, and increase your horse's responsiveness.

Exiting the Ring

Any horse you ride inside an arena should be willing to pass a gate, open or closed, without trying to stop. But some horses would much rather go *through* the gate and back to their corral. Have you ever ridden a horse—lesson horses get very good at this trick—who kept edging closer and closer to the gate and slowing down, even though the gate was closed? Annoying, wasn't it?

Teach your horse he can't go out that gate until you tell him to, and teach him that the very first time you ride him. If your horse starts to drift towards the open gate, ride to the opposite end of the arena so you can "pass" the gate without going near it. (Remember: don't pick fights with your horse.) When you leave the ring because your friend has arrived, halt your horse in the center of the ring, facing *away* from the gate, for a count of five. You now have two options. Use them interchangeably every time you ride in the arena, and soon your horse will wait for you to tell him what you want. Leaving the arena should always be your idea. Not your horse's.

Option #1 Dismount and lead him out the gate to the hitching rail or mounting block. Remount him and go for your trail ride. The next time you ride, do only ring work.

Don't trail ride afterwards. Exit the same way, by dismounting and leading your horse directly out the gate. The only difference is, the lesson is over. You don't want your horse to think he recognizes a pattern. If you dismount and walk him out of the ring, it doesn't mean he's finished work for the day.

Option #2 Stay on your horse's back, turn him until he's directly facing the gate, and exit by walking out in a straight line.

RIDING WITH A BUDDY

I can't guide you through your first trail ride tree by tree, rock by rock, or step by step, because everybody's experience will be different. Everybody's horse will be different. But do ask a friend or neighbor to join you the first time you ride your horse in open country—preferably a friend riding a steady, reliable, bomb-proof horse.

If your horse is young or inexperienced, his herd instinct will be just as strong as his instinct to flee if he thinks something is threatening him. Horses survived in the wild because they were willing to turn tail and run with the rest of their herd, *even if they themselves didn't see, hear, or smell anything.* But if the rest of the herd didn't see, hear, or smell anything worth running away from, an individual horse rarely decided to run away all by himself.

A horse unsure of his surroundings—or his rider, or both—will take his cues from any other horse in the area. (You know what I mean if you've ever ridden past a field of loose

Yes—riding with a friend on the same gentle horse. (Photo courtesy of the Arabian Horse Association and Ellen Johnson, photographer)

Riding with a friend in some pretty scenery—is there a better way to relax? (Photo by Gina Cresse)

horses.) If your friend's horse behaves like a well-trained, reliable citizen, so will your horse. As I've said before, horses have excellent memories. If your first trail ride is low-key, uneventful, and fun, your horse will look forward to the next one.

A Word about Whips

Most of the time, with most horses, it's prudent to carry a whip. It's definitely prudent the first time you ride your new horse. Buy a whip that comes with a wrist loop, so you won't drop it. I suggest buying the longest one you can find, so you can reach the horse behind the saddle.

Most riders pick up their whip just before they mount. Loop the whip over the wrist of your left hand, where it will lie unobtrusively against the horse's shoulder while you mount. Since your left hand will either be holding the saddle horn, the pommel of your saddle, or a big clump of mane, your horse won't see the whip as you swing into the saddle (useful if your new horse has been mistreated by someone using a whip on him).

People who show horses want the mane to fall to the right, and since any excess rein should also fall to the right, the logical place for your whip is in your left hand.

When to use a whip: Use it to reinforce any aid or cue or command you give your horse. For example, if you cluck and he doesn't move, cluck again and wait a split second to see if he'll react. If he doesn't, touch him just hard enough for him to feel it. Since all movement—a walk, a trot, a canter—originates from behind, I find a long dressage whip the most useful because I can reach my horse's hindquarters without changing my hand position.

■ Same thing with a leg-yield, which some Western riders call "moving the horse's hip" to one side. (The leg-yield I'm about to describe isn't necessarily how a dressage rider would do it, but for trail riding, it will do.) Suppose your horse is getting a little strong in the bridle and you want to slow him down. As your horse walks (don't go any faster your first time on the trail), tighten one rein slightly—just enough so you can see your horse's eyelashes and nostril. Let's say you tighten your left rein. At the same time, apply pressure with your *left leg* behind the girth by tightening your lower leg on your horse. By *tighten* I mean that your entire leg should be in contact with your horse—no daylight between your knees and the saddle. When you tighten your lower leg, you increase the contact. That's all. Don't *kick* your horse. Tighten your lower leg until he moves his haunches slightly sideways. As soon as he does, relax your leg and your inside rein and use your voice to praise him. If he doesn't, use your left rein and left leg a little more forcefully. If he still doesn't shift his hindquarters, ask again and wait a few seconds; if he doesn't respond, touch him with the whip on his hindquarters.

The leg-yield is a good illustration of why a long whip is more effective than a short one, Touching your horse on the shoulder has nothing to do with asking him to move his hindquarters. And if you try to use a short whip on his hindquarters without changing the position of your hands, you'll smack yourself on the leg.

The horse who backs up: Sinjun's favorite evasion was backing. If he spotted something he wasn't sure about—a big white rock on the side of the trail—he would immediately start to back without checking to see what, if anything, was behind him. Our barn was in the foothills near a lot of fire trails, but Sinjun and I very seldom rode on them unless we had company.

■ To stop a horse who uses backing as an evasion, cluck and tighten your legs on him to let him know you want him to move forward. Don't tell a backing horse to "whoa" because he won't know what you want—he associates "whoa" with stopping a *forward* movement. Cluck to him, instead. If he continues to back, ask him again and be prepared to apply the whip to his backside if he ignores the second cue.

When not to use a whip: If your horse spooks at something and you smack him to punish him, what just happened? He saw something he was unsure of and tried to get away from it—and you hit him. The next time he sees it, he'll *really* be afraid of it.

A Word about Spurs
Some of you may have shown as kids and were taught to gig your horse with your heels or spurs at every stride. That was then. This is now, and there's no need to gig a trail horse with your spurs every single time he takes a step.

Warning!
What follows is a discussion of some common problems that most riders encounter on the trail, and what you can do to protect yourself from them: big dogs, traffic, unsafe footing, and the unforeseen accident.

Big dogs: Big dogs can be dangerous. If you hear a dog barking but can't see him, you don't know whether the dog is loose and whether he might attack your horse. (Some dogs will.) Your friend should know. When in doubt, turn back.

Some dogs like to chase horses with no particular intent to hurt them, and can tell instantly if yours might run. I've seen a dog snooze while half a dozen horses and riders walked through "his" territory, only to wake up and growl at the one young, timid horse in the group. But because the other horses ignored the dog, the young one did too. Eventually the horse stopped being afraid of the dog, and the dog stopped growling.

Traffic: Paved roads, trucks, cars, and horses don't mix. But sometimes you have to cross a road to get where you're going. If your friend's horse will stand calmly while a cement mixer rumbles by at 50 mph, your horse will too—although he's apt to dance a little. Take a few deep breaths, and on the exhale make a conscious effort to relax in the saddle. Some horses will feel reassured if you close your legs on them a little. Do that by tightening the inner muscles of your thigh while you concentrate on feeling your horse's body the entire length of your leg. Don't increase the contact so much that your horse misinterprets what you want and moves forward. This advice also holds true for school buses, revved up muscle cars, and three motorcyclists riding abreast.

Whenever you're forced to ride on pavement, make sure your horse walks, and always walk *facing* traffic. It's a good idea to let your horse see what's coming. Many horses will bolt if they hear something behind them but can't see it—although if your friend's horse ignores the school bus, the muscle car, and the motorcyclists, your horse probably will too. It's also a good idea for *you* to see what's coming, because you might want to get off the road entirely until it passes. Ask your friend to come with you.

Bad footing: Your friend can tell you about the trails that turn into potential landslides because they're more like a collection of loosely packed stones than a trail, or which trails to avoid because they're riddled with rodent holes.

■ Trails that are part of a state or federal park system or wilderness area are usually well maintained and safe. But they're usually maintained for hikers, not horseback riders. Watch for low-hanging tree limbs. Some big boarding stables also maintain trails. Before you ride on one, find out whether the stable allows the general horse-owning public to use it. Your friend should know.

■ If your long-term goal is to leave the trails and go off-roading, find out about any natural or man-made hazards in the area. Terrain that looks lush and green may be swampy. Abandoned, unmarked mine shafts can be hidden by underbrush. If your friend doesn't know, find out if a local trail organization can provide maps containing this information.

■ Water crossings can be scary for some horses, especially if they're young or inexperienced. As you know, your horse has a wide *range* of vision but has trouble focusing on objects directly in front of him. Since horses are also very alert to movement, asking yours to walk through even a shallow stream can spook him. The water is moving, and since he can't bring

This horse isn't worried about getting his feet wet. Neither is his fearless young rider. (Photo courtesy of the American Morgan Horse Association)

it into focus—and even if he could, it's blurry—he can't tell how deep it is. Ideally, ask your friend to choose a trail that involves a water crossing. If your horse sees another horse splash across the stream, he'll probably conclude that he can safely cross too.

Don't be surprised if he jumps. He's not necessarily trying to jump the entire stream—although some horses will—he's trying to jump on, or next to, your friend's horse. For the same reason, *never* dismount and try to lead a balky horse through water. If he goes anywhere, he'll probably jump on the same rock you're standing on. *You're* safe—why not join you?

■ If you live near the beach, take advantage of it. One of the highlights of my life as a horse owner was riding Bachelor with Anne and her mare through the surf of the Pacific Ocean from Torrey Pines up the coast to the Del Mar race track. To get back on solid land we rode under the Pacific Coast Highway via a tunnel used by exercise riders from the track. Someone had thoughtfully left a bag of carrots within easy reach at the beach end—useful for bribing uncooperative horses.

Caution: if you ride with a standing martingale or tie-down, remove it before you swim your horse. Your horse *must* be able to keep his nose above water.

The unforseen: Trail riding is a relatively safe hobby, especially when you compare it to some other sports—stock car racing comes to mind. But accidents can happen, no matter how elaborately you plan to avoid them. The two safety precautions you can take as a rider are: wear a safety helmet, and carry a cell phone. The newer ones are so small they'll fit in your pocket. Others clip on your belt.

The exception to this generalization is children. Horses are big animals, and while some horses seem to have a built-in maternal gene, they have the potential to seriously injure children because they are so big. If your kids are still small, buy them ponies or small horses.

■ And *never* strap a child into a saddle. Suppose you're riding single file down a rural road with your daughters behind you one afternoon when the sprinkler system in somebody's hay field comes on. The hissing noise, the sudden movement, and the sheer scope of all that water spraying would cause almost any horse to jump off his feet—why not run now and decide later whether it's life-threatening? But it's easy for you, as an adult, to rein your horse in.

What's truly life-threatening is the horse who decides to run away first and ask questions later while one of your daughters is strapped to his saddle.

Strapping a child into a saddle is never a good idea, even if you're inside a ring in your own backyard. Don't do it.

Back at the Barn

Your friend may ride with you all the way back to your house, or if she lives along your return route, she might let you finish the ride by yourself.

The dismount. Ordinarily you wouldn't stop in this position and dig your knee into your horse. Instead, you'd take both feet out of the stirrups, swing your right leg over the horse's rump, and push yourself away from the saddle so both feet hit the ground at once. (Photo by Gina Cresse)

Either way, finish it at a walk. Even though your horse ate breakfast before you left, he'll probably try to speed up when you're close to home. Don't let him. Teach him this lesson the first day: *you* decide how fast the two of you will go. Not your horse.

Since your entire ride was conducted at the walk, and since you were careful to walk your horse home, your horse should have cooled himself out—in other words, you don't have a hot, sweaty horse to deal with.

■ Once you reach the hitching rail, dismount, and remove your saddle and saddlepad. Fasten your horse's halter around his neck and remove his bridle.

■ Here's a good opportunity to show your horse how enjoyable trail rides can be. Since he can't reach all the sweaty, itchy parts of his head—where the crownpiece of his bridle fits, his browband, his noseband, the corners of his lips—rub

As soon as I dismount, I usually remove Prim's bridle. Holding the crownpiece in both hands, I raise the bridle and slowly slide it forward until it clears her ears. (Photo by Gina Cresse)

With Prim's bridle over my shoulder, I rub the sweaty places on her face. (Photo by Gina Cresse)

those areas with both hands after removing his bridle. (Remove it by unfastening the nose-band and throatlatch, gripping the crownpiece with your right hand, and sliding the bridle over his ears.) As you rub his head, say "Good boy! G-o-o-o-d boy!"

But don't let *him* decide to use you as a rubbing post. Although it might seem endearing at first, a horse who persists in scratching his head against you, especially when you're not expecting it, can quickly become a nuisance. Tell him "No!" in a loud, firm voice. If he persists, tell him "No!" again and wait for a response. If you don't get one, elbow him in the neck.

■ Fasten your horse's halter and tie him to the hitching rail (using a safety knot, of course).

Since you don't have to cool him out by watering him and walking him, groom him.

■ Immediately rinse his bit off, so it's clean the next time you ride. (A pot-scrubber designed for nonstick cookware is perfect for this chore, since rinsing the bit rarely removes all the dirt and saliva.) Hang his bridle in the tackroom and slide his saddle on the saddle rack. Leave the saddle pad on the floor; you'll want to wash it. Then grab your grooming box, some rub rags, your three buckets, and head back outside.

Another Kind of "Hot" Horse

I have nothing against a brisk gallop—in fact I love the adrenaline rush almost as much as Prim does. (We have a built-in advantage: if I turn right when I reach the dirt road, it goes straight uphill. A horse galloping up a hill is much easier to stop than one galloping downhill.) But please—once you get to know your horse and let him gallop occasionally, walk him the last half-hour. And *always* walk him home. By then he should be cool enough to drink all the water he wants as soon as he wants it. But how do you know for sure?

There are two basic tests.

The first and most important is your horse's breathing. If he takes deep, shuddering gasps as he tries to catch his breath, and his nostrils flutter in and out so that you can see the glistening, shiny-pink lining, he's exhausted and probably dehydrated.

The second test: place the palm of your hand between your horse's front legs (his brisket). If he's hot, his hair will be wet and slick with sweat, and his skin will usually feel hotter there than other parts of his body.

■ Don't withhold water completely, as many of us were taught to do, because water is the very thing your horse needs right now. (Remember—over half of his body weight is water.) Even if he's so exhausted his sides are heaving, water him as soon as you dismount. Not all he wants—two or three gallons at a time. Since I have trouble visualizing what three gallons looks like, I count seconds (one thousand one, one thousand two, etc.) Let him drink about ten seconds. Then remove the bucket.

■ Some experts claim hot horses should only drink *warm* water. I don't quite follow the logic here. Very few natural water sources—streams, rivers, lakes, springs—are warmer than skin temperature. I'd go with tepid or chilly water because I do agree that drinking a lot of cold water all at once would be a shock to your horse's system, just as it would be to yours.

■ At this point, some owners like to use rubbing alcohol on their horse's legs as a brace. Cup your hand and pour some rubbing alcohol into it. As you wrap that hand around your horse's knee, front to back, the alcohol will spill out and run down his cannon bone. Rub it into his hair briskly with both hands to increase the blood circulation. Apply rubbing alcohol to all four legs, knee and hock to fetlock.

■ After letting your horse drink, fill your second bucket with water and use a wet rub rag to wash the sweat off him. Squeeze your rub rag almost dry before you wash your horse's face. Most horses don't like water dripping in their eyes and ears. (Remember—untie him first.) By the time you're finished you can give him more water. After he drinks another ten seconds, hand-walk him a few minutes.

Since drinking water speeds up the cooling process, your horse should be breathing normally by now, and the hair between his front legs should feel damp and no hotter than any other part of his body. Walk him a few more minutes and check his breathing and brisket again. That ought to do it. Return him to his corral, where he can drink his fill.

Electrolytes: Does Your Horse Need Them?

If you rode on a warm day and returned to the barn thirsty and sweaty with visions of Gatorade dancing in your head, you're probably dehydrated, and your body is telling you that you need electrolytes (and shade). Electrolytes are the minerals/salts inside your body that you lose through exertion and sweat. Horses need electrolytes too. According to Dr. Reynolds, they "maintain the fluid balance inside and outside of cells and regulate other body functions such as muscle and nerve contraction and oxygen and carbon dioxide transport."

When you yearn for Gatorade, your horse would probably appreciate an offer to replenish *his* electrolytes, too. They're available at your tack store. Mix according to the manufacturer's directions, but always give your horse a choice: one bucket containing plain water, the second containing water plus electrolytes. Your horse may be less dehydrated than you are, and prefer plain water. Never force-feed electrolytes to a horse, no matter how sure you are that he needs them.

Water Games

In warm weather, many owners like to hose their horse off. Start by wetting your horse's forelegs, from his hooves up to his knees. Don't let the water hit him full blast, especially if it's cold. Your horse isn't expecting it and might try to pull away.

■ Once you've hosed down his front legs to his knees, switch to his hind legs and repeat the procedure, hooves to hocks. Return to the front of his body and gradually move the water up to his brisket. At that point, direct the spray towards his backbone and move back towards his rump. Now that he's accustomed to the water, wet his stomach and between his hind legs. Stand behind him. Wet his tail, pick it up, and direct the water under his tail, between his haunches, and down to his hocks.

■ Lower the volume again and untie your horse. Holding him by the leadrope, move the hose up his neck. Direct the stream of water under his jaw. As I said earlier, most horses don't like water in their face. If yours doesn't, don't force the issue. Direct the water to his muzzle, being careful not to squirt it up his nose. Many horses will try to grab the end of the hose between their teeth. If your horse hasn't learned that game yet, guide the hose into the corner of his mouth the way you do when you worm him. Most horses enjoy the sensation of having their mouth "rinsed," and some will even swallow the water. When your horse gets tired of that, spray the sides of his face. If he tries to pull away again, stop immediately. When he's wet all over except for his head, wring out a rub rag and give his head a sponge bath.

I've watched amateur owners (although never trainers or well-brought-up grooms) blast their horse in the face with a hose, and watched the horse desperately try to avoid it. Why create an unpleasant situation when you have alternatives?

■ Once your horse knows he'll get hosed off after a ride (bathing requires soap and you do it to clean your horse, not dissolve sweat), he'll begin to look forward to it.

■ After hosing him off, don't let him just stand there and drip. Use your scraper to remove excess water. Start immediately behind his ears and scrape his neck, always working backwards, towards his rump, and down. Avoid the bony areas of his withers and backbone, and don't use it on his head or below his knees and hocks. Continue scraping alongside his back, sides, belly, and rump.

■ Then take a dry rub rag—preferably a face towel that still has some fluff left in it— and give him a vigorous rubdown starting with his head. Once your horse realizes how good it feels, he'll drop his head in your lap the second you approach him holding a towel.

TRAIL RIDING WITH A GROUP

Some riders prefer group riding because it gives them an opportunity to visit with old friends and meet new ones while they admire the scenery. Many organized rides include an activity—a trail-side barbecue, for example. One of the most memorable group rides I ever took was on a warm August night with a full moon.

Unless you live within riding distance of the trailhead, you need a horse trailer to get there, or somebody willing to pick you up and drive you back home afterwards.

Organized rides usually have a trail boss. This is the person who coordinates the ride and chooses the trails, always considering the safety of the least experienced horse and rider. But don't take a green-broke horse on an organized ride until you've ridden with friends often enough to be sure your horse will behave himself.

Before you sign up, contact the trail boss and ask for a description of the trails he's chosen. If you're afraid of heights, you won't enjoy three-foot-wide trails with a sheer drop on one side. Ask the trail boss about any other concerns you have: how long the ride will be, if you can bring your yappy dog (probably not), if stallions are allowed. Stallions of some breeds are very docile, but if your mare is in season, you might not want one behind you. Trail bosses who allow stallions usually request that they wear a yellow ribbon in their tail. A red ribbon

A horse with a red ribbon in his tail means he kicks—usually at other horses, but don't approach him from behind until you're sure.

indicates a horse who kicks. This horse usually brings up the rear. If your horse goes barefoot, ask whether that's a problem. Many trail bosses won't allow barefoot horses if the trails are stony.

If you have children, especially if they don't have much experience, ask the trail boss about that too. Many organized rides are for adults only.

Multi-Use Trails

In the past twenty years we've lost so much open land that in most parts of the country horseback riders share public trails with hikers, bicycle riders, and—regretfully—motorized vehicles, mainly motorcyclists and ATV riders. On the plus side, riding with a group along a multi-use trail, especially on a weekend, is a good way to safely introduce your horse to Real Life. If you're by yourself the first time your horse encounters hikers with backpacks, bicyclists whizzing by, and ATV off-roaders, he's going to get excited. But (the herd thing again) as long as he's with other horses, and as long as the *other* horses don't get upset, he won't either.

Everyone you encounter on a multi-use trail, including hikers, should yield to horses, but don't expect them to know that. Motorcyclists and ATV riders should stop and turn off their engines until the entire group is safely past, but don't expect them to know that either. If they do, be sure to thank them. A little courtesy goes a long way.

What to Take with You

If this is your first ride, don't overburden your horse or yourself. Strap on a fanny pack that includes a bottle of water, lunch (if stopping for lunch is on the agenda), several, large, sturdy plastic freezer bags, and a ten-foot leadrope. You've paid somebody who repairs tack—your tack store can direct you—to attach a similar snap on the other end of the rope. That way you can use the leadrope *as* a leadrope or as an extra set of reins.

Western riders have the option of bundling these items into a tote bag and using saddle strings to fasten it to their saddle. English riders have to be more creative. One option is to ride with a vest that features multiple pockets. Since many English saddles have small metal loops sewn into the off side of the cantle, you can, after you're more experienced, buy your horse his own fanny pack. Before you leave home, longe him with it so he knows what's bouncing up and down on his rump.

On the Open Trail

Before you set off from the trailhead, the trail boss will usually explain the policies regarding smoking, rest stops, and passing other horses. (If he doesn't, ask.) If passing is permitted, and your horse is a fast walker, always pass on the left, as though you were driving a car. Call ahead to the other rider to announce your intentions. If your horse is a slowpoke, keep to the right.

During the ride, let the trail boss know if you have to leave the group for any reason, or if your horse is acting up and you want to go on ahead. If your horse's bad behavior upsets the other horses, the trail boss may excuse you from the group. And don't decide to take a little gallop all by yourself, even if you've left the group. Speed is contagious; if your horse starts to run, so will the other horses—not a safe situation for children or beginning riders.

Whenever you have to ride single file, leave a horse's length between you and the horse in front of you so you won't run into him if he stops unexpectedly. When you pass under a low-hanging tree limb, warn the person behind you—who may be talking to somebody and not watching.

This is why you bought a trail horse. (Photo courtesy of the American Quarter Horse Association and America's Horse, *Becky Newell)*

A river break—snacks and stretching your legs are optional. (Photo courtesy of American Quarter Horse Association and America's Horse, *Becky Newell)*

The number-one reason why hikers and bicyclists are lobbying to ban horses from multi-use trails is horse manure. If your horse has to relieve himself, leave the trail. (You'll know what he wants because he keeps trying to stop and raise his tail.) If he's too fast for you, dismount immediately and turn one of your plastic freezer bags inside out. Pick up the road apples, reverse the bag, and zip it shut. Then zip it inside another plastic bag and dispose of it in a trash can at the end of the ride.

If you rode in with it (a soft drink, a candy bar), ride out with it—or at least with the container. Don't trash the trails, and don't clean the manure out of your trailer at the trailhead. If you want to remove it so your horse doesn't have to stand in it, shovel it into a muck bucket and take it home with you.

Serious camping—you sleep in portable housing, your horse sleeps in a portable corral. (Photo courtesy of the American Quarter Horse Association and America's Horse, *Becky Newell)*

CAMPING WITH HORSES

Horse overnights can be a lot of fun, but if it's your first time, go with experienced friends or as part of an organized group. There are too many things you don't know, and too many ways to get in trouble. For example: do you need a permit? (In some areas you don't need a permit unless you build a fire. But what good is a campout without a campfire?) How do you keep your horse from wandering off? (Put up a long, horizontal rope tied between two trees—ideally just above a limb, so the rope won't slide down the trunk—at the level of the horses' heads. Tie the horses far enough apart so they can't bite or kick one another.) Should you carry feed for your horse? (Yes. Carry what he's used to eating at home, except in smaller quantities. If you're on an organized ride that has a trail boss, one pack horse or donkey will usually carry cooking utensils and food for all the horses and humans.) Can you tie your sleeping bag behind you on the saddle? (Yes, but make sure to put something waterproof between the sleeping bag and your horse's rump. I learned that lesson by spending the night in a cold, damp sleeping bag that smelled like horse sweat.)

My recommendation: Trail riding in the wilderness is not the time to outfit your horse in leg wraps, tendon boots, shin boots, etc. The horses will kick up dust and all your wraps and boots will get dirty, with some of the dirt inevitably working its way *inside* the leg wraps, boots, etc. and irritating your horse. Take the leg wraps along if you like, but as first-aid equipment.

My best overnight camping tip: While it's usually a good idea to pack food items in plastic containers (glass is heavier and breakable), if you want fried eggs with your steak in the morning, buy a skinny jar of olives. Put the olives in another container and wash out the jar. Carefully break raw eggs into the jar. Screw the lid on tight, put the jar in a leak-proof zippered bag, and wrap it up in your extra clothes (which you'll wrap inside your sleeping bag). The next morning, heat your skillet—it too made the trip inside your sleeping bag—fry your steak, and pour each egg, yolk still intact, one at a time from your olive jar into your sizzling skillet.

TRAIL RIDING SOLO

For many owners, trail riding solo—just you and your horse—is the whole point of *owning* a backyard horse (my sentiments exactly). If you want to ride alone, particularly if you plan to off-road, start with the trails near your house. Once you know them, branch out a little farther each day. Whenever the trail forks, memorize a natural landmark—a dead tree, an unusual rock formation—to help you find your way back. If there *is* no unique natural landmark, dismount and build one by stacking flat rocks on top of each other.

Solo riding offers solitude, time for contemplation, beautiful country, and some one-on-one quality time with your horse. But it does have its drawbacks. While I don't want to dwell on them, you need to take them into consideration. If you ever kept your horse at a boarding stable, you know that getting bucked off and trudging back to the barn was almost a rite of passage. When you finally showed up, you got a lot of good-natured ribbing from the other boarders who knew you were coming because your horse arrived hours earlier, all by himself. But if you keep your horse in your backyard, he bucks you off during a trail ride, you sprain your ankle, and there's nobody home to notice that your horse came back without you—the situation's not so funny anymore.

But sometimes it's more fun to be alone, just you and your horse, cowboy and Cowboy.

(Photo courtesy of the Arabian Horse Association and Anne Young, photographer)

If you only plan to be gone for an hour or two, and you stay on the trails (no off-roading), many of these suggestions won't apply. On the other hand, better safe than sorry.

- Tell at least one person where you're going and when you intend to be back.
- If you like to ride far from civilization, carry a cell phone or walkie-talkie and your vet's emergency number as well as his clinic number. If you get hurt, call 911. If your horse gets hurt, call your vet. If you're in a remote area, tell the person who answers to contact your vet *and* the nearest Disaster Relief Team. (This team has various names and is usually affiliated with a local animal shelter.)

In case you and your horse part company, carry the phone with *you*. And carry it in a waterproof container in case you and your horse part company crossing a stream.

- A useful low-tech device easy to carry in your pocket—that's especially useful in remote areas where your cell phone might not work—is a mirror. The kind that comes with a woman's compact is perfect because of its sturdy backing. Use it to flash SOS signals (three short flashes, three long, three short) at any building you can see, and any aircraft.
- Carry a cigarette lighter, especially in cold weather, as well as an extra jacket or blanket, and a small, powerful flashlight. If you and your horse do part company, you need the cigarette lighter to start a fire. The blanket will keep your warm and the flashlight will help you identify things that go bump in the night. (Is one of them your loyal horse coming back to save you? Don't count on it.)

Dogs: While rottweilers, pit bulls, and German shepherds guarding the home fires pose an obvious threat, even small dogs can be dangerous if you're on their turf. Stay off their turf. Or, carry pepper spray—and before you use it, make sure you know which way the wind is blowing. Many riders solve the dog problem by riding with their own dog or dogs. Even a dog that chases horses is more interested in another dog than he is in your horse.

- Stray or feral dogs are rarely a threat, even if they run in packs. Since they have no territory to defend, they will usually avoid you. So will lone coyotes.
- But be careful if your dog comes with you; some coyotes hunt in pairs. One coyote will try to lure your dog into chasing him. If your dog falls for the ruse, the second coyote will circle back and come up behind him. The first coyote will turn around and both will jump your dog. Coyotes intent on your dog will ignore a screaming rider unless your horse is willing to wade into the middle of the fray. If you carry a whip, make sure you hit the animal you're aiming for.

Traffic: Avoid it as much as possible. If you ride along a public roadway, especially in town, and your horse relieves himself, dismount and clean it up.

- In rural areas, whenever you encounter hikers, bicycle riders, motorcycle or ATV riders, try to be courteous, even if they're not. If you see them approaching, leave the trail and turn your horse so he can see they're coming, and stay in plain sight so they can see both of you and slow down. If they do, thank them.

Footing: Never gallop your horse in unfamiliar territory, especially hilly areas. What to you looks like the gentle rise of a hill may end abruptly, and you'll find yourself teetering on the edge of a cliff while your horse scrambles frantically to keep his footing. The first few times you ride, especially if you ride by yourself, don't gallop your horse at all. Wait until you know one another better.

■ A dry, empty riverbed might look like the perfect place for an all-out gallop, but your horse can bow a tendon in deep sand. Watch how far his feet sink before you let him run.

■ When I was a kid growing up in New Jersey, I thought quicksand existed only in exotic, faraway places—until one spring when I was hiking through the woods with a friend. We were following a shallow streambed that had nearly dried up. Without warning both of us sank knee-deep into lique-fied sand—quicksand. Luckily it wasn't deep and we were able to escape. But if I found quicksand in suburban New Jersey, you can probably find it where you live. Don't ride in "dry" streambeds, especially in the spring. Every year I see a horse on TV that had to be airlifted out of quicksand because his rider thought the streambed was dry.

■ Abandoned mine shafts are a danger anywhere in the country where mining went on. Where the vegetation is lush, beware of abandoned wells. (Because they're very hard to see, the best way to do that is to ride on designated trails.) These old wells were originally covered with wooden plank-ing, but over time the wood rotted, the weeds took over, and

Don't gallop in unfamiliar ter-rain—note the dead tree.

eventually the area began to look like solid ground—until your horse stepped on it.

■ Another danger, particularly in cattle country, is barbed wire. Its color makes it hard to see, and whole strands of it can be just a few inches off the ground and remain invisible. Your horse can stumble into the wire and wrap it around his leg in seconds. Some horses will wait patiently for you to free them. Others won't. (This is why you vaccinate your horse against tetanus.)

The same dead tree from the op-posite side of the drop.

■ Most of these problems can be avoided if you stay on the trail. The exception is predators—real ones, like bobcats, bears, and cougars. Bobcats won't attack your horse—they're too small and you're too big. The safest way to cope with bears is to leave. A single cougar will probably not bother you unless your horse panics and bolts—in other words, be-haves like a prey animal. If you can control your horse, face the cougar and flap your arms to make you look bigger. Scream like the bloodthirsty predator you are. Take the of-fensive. *Don't* behave like prey.

■ Because of your horse's long neck and bony head, he car-ries most of his weight on his front feet. If you're in mountainous terrain and heading uphill, lean forward to help your horse keep his balance. Do not let him run up the hill—it's a bad habit that can catch you off-guard. Your horse will probably try it once or twice because it's easier than walking. When he goes down a hill, lean backward for the same reason—to help him balance.

■ Don't ride on private property without permission. If the property isn't posted and a gate blocks the trail, open it to ride through and close it behind you, especially if you're in cattle country. If you do ride in cattle country, it's smart to introduce your horse to a cow beforehand. Meeting a cow face to face terrifies most horses—even Quarter Horses who have never seen one before.

Another hazard of off-roading, especially in the West. Can you see the scroll of barbed wire? In time to keep your horse from stepping in it?

■ Rattlesnakes are a very real danger throughout the West and South (pygmy rattlers), and if you expect your horse to recognize one and whinny to warn you, you've been watching too many *Lassie* reruns. Contrary to what you may have seen in the movies, horses will not "instinctively" avoid rattlesnakes. On one trail ride, Bachelor walked right over a snake without breaking stride. I don't know whether it was a rattler or not—it was as big around as a Campbell's soup can, and so long I never saw either end. Should a rattler bite your horse, use your cell phone to call your vet. If your horse got it in the face, your vet will probably tell you to head for home in a hurry, while your horse can still breathe. As the tissue around the bite swells, it will constrict his air passages.

■ When you've ridden as far as you planned to go, turn your horse around and walk home. If your horse jigs and prances and in general behaves like an idiot (such horses are generally barn sour), here's an easy fix. When you reach his corral, instead of dismounting and unsaddling him, ride him in the arena for ten minutes. He won't like it; he's tired and here you are making him do extra. The next time he tries to run home, put him to work in the ring again. Pretty soon he won't be in such a hurry to get home.

■ I like to end every ride by hosing Prim down, weather permitting, or "touching her up." My definition of a touch-up: I rub the sweat marks out with a wet rub rag, rub a cactus cloth mitt over her, and clean her feet. They usually don't need cleaning, but I want to make sure she didn't pick up any stones.

I don't spend a lot of time grooming her at the end of my ride because like all beautifully groomed horses, as soon as I turn her loose, the first thing she'll do is roll. Your horse loves/likes/puts up with you, but don't expect gratitude.

CHAPTER 14

WHISPERING TO YOUR HORSE: BASIC TRAINING

Whether you were aware of it or not, you had a wish list in mind when you test-rode your horse, and you referred to it unconsciously while you evaluated how the horse looked and behaved.

Your wish list is probably just like every horse owner's wish list. You want the "perfect horse" who will (I'll explain the checkmarks in a minute):

✓✓ Let you catch him.

✓✓ Walk quietly next to you as you lead him.

✓✓ Walk through the gate of his corral or the arena without crowding you or pulling.

✓✓ Stand quietly while you groom him.

✓✓ Let you clean his feet without a fight.

✓ Let you bridle him without a fight.

✓ Stand quietly while you saddle him.

✓ Let you mount before moving off.

✓ Start moving when you cluck or tighten your legs on him.

✓ Stop when you say whoa.

✓ Back when you ask him to.

✓✓ Work in the arena without trying to sidle out the gate.

✓ Trot on the trail without getting strong in the bit.

✓ Canter on the trail without trying to run away with you.

✓✓ Return to the barn at a walk, without jigging.

But your wish list also has a flip side itemizing behaviors you *do not* want—although very few people think about them during the excitement of horse shopping. You don't want a horse who bucks, bites, bolts, or runs away with you, kicks, or rears. If you followed my suggestion about asking a trainer or your riding instructor to go horse shopping with you, you probably didn't buy one.

ON THE BRIGHT SIDE

Do you realize your horse already *knows* how to come to you, how to walk quietly on the lead line, walk through gates, stand quietly while you groom him and clean his feet, and how to work in the arena without slowing down at the gate? He does—that's why I double-checked those items. And who taught him? You did.

Teaching a horse rarely involves force. Good training progresses step by step, even though you probably didn't think of what you were doing as "training". As a result, you already have a solid foundation for teaching your horse how to do other things—and you did it without using force. Instead, you outsmarted your horse, and he now accepts you as the boss. Horses have lived in herds for millions of years; they're accustomed to being bossed around.

In this chapter I'll explain how to build on what you've already taught your horse so you can check off the rest of the items on your wish list. I'll also—and I want to do this first, to get it out of the way—identify which bad behaviors you can live with, and which ones you shouldn't.

BAD BEHAVIOR

After the honeymoon phase of horse ownership is over, you may realize that some of your horse's irritating little habits have gotten out of hand. What should you do?

First, call the horse's previous owner and explain the problem. Let's say your new horse bucks. If the owner *knew* the horse bucked, she was legally obligated to fess up.

On the other hand, some horses are very attuned to their riders. (Other, slightly more dim-witted horses, treat all riders equally.) These "attuned" horses can gauge, with astonishing accuracy, how well you ride and how confident you are on their backs. Should an attuned horse sense any weakness in you, he'll exploit it—just to see what he can get away with. If the previous owner is a competent rider, especially if she (or he) is a trainer, dealer, or small breeder, she may honestly not have known that your horse bucks. In other words, if your horse is attuned, he was probably a model of good behavior as long as the previous owner rode him.

Still, I suggest that you start by talking to the owner. Tell her you really like the horse, but what should you do about the bucking?

As I said earlier, most owners will try to work with you. Even if she won't, you have other options. Depending on the horse and the problem itself, it might be an easy fix; nothing that requires force.

Horses buck for many reasons. This one's only half a buck; Prim was kicking at Chance, who's running laps outside the fence. I don't allow dogs inside the ring; they chase horses. (Photo by Marilyn Dalrymple)

The Horse Who Bucks

Most horses buck because they feel good. Almost any horse will buck if you feed him grain or a sweetened feed supplement but don't ride very often. Horses always buck when the weather turns cool in the fall. They always buck on bright, frosty mornings. They often buck when the wind's blowing.

No more sweet feed: The easiest way to stop your horse from bucking is to eliminate the grain or sweet feed, replace it with good-quality hay, and ride him more often. (Another tip: longe him first. See Chapter 16 to find out how.)

Sometimes a horse will buck because, as the old saying goes, he "has a burr under his saddle." This horse bucks because, for example, he had a deer fly on his back and you swung a saddle blanket on top of the deer fly, and then you swung a saddle over the saddle blanket, and just after you swing into the saddle, the deer fly bites your horse. In other words, something about his tack isn't right, and he's bucking—or at least humping his back and threatening to buck—to alert you to that fact.

Pitching a fit: But what happens if you're trail riding when suddenly, out of the blue, your horse throws a bucking fit?

You have two options. One is to keep his head up (in order to buck, a horse has to bury his head between his front legs) and ride him through his fit to a standstill. The other is to dismount before he bucks you off and lead him home.

Some trainers discourage the second option because it rewards the horse. He wanted you off his back: if you dismount, he got what he wanted. If you have confidence in your ability to ride your horse to a standstill, you probably can—and the horse will sense and respond to your confidence. But if your instincts tell you that you *can't* handle this horse, he'll sense both your uncertainty and fear. Swallow your pride and get off.

Talk to a trainer: Consider putting your horse in training. Ask other horse owners what trainer they would recommend, and when you talk to him (or her), keep in mind that a trainer with a barn full of trophies isn't necessarily good. He's just successful.

Your best bet would be the trainer who helped you select the horse in the first place.

When you talk to the trainer, be very clear about your goals and what you expect him to do. Your short-term goal: you want your horse to stop bucking. Your long-term goal: you want a safe, reliable trail horse. Specifically, you want *the trainer* to ride your horse the first few times, so you can see whether you might be doing anything to encourage the bucking. Once your horse has stopped bucking with the trainer, you want to ride under the trainer's direct supervision while he teaches *you* how to let your horse know that every time he bucks, *this* unpleasant consequence will occur. After you've ridden your horse for several uneventful lessons while the trainer watches, you want to ride by yourself, still at the training barn but without supervision. The process shouldn't take more than two or three months, and when it's over, you'll probably have yourself a very nice horse.

Although it's rare, you'll occasionally bump into a mean horse. He's mean because that's his personality, the same way a horse can be lazy, cranky, stubborn, flighty, alert, etc. But more often than not, a mean horse was made that way by a human.

What follows is a cautionary tale about a problem horse I inadvertently bought, and how one person with a whip influenced one horse's destiny and the lives of four other people.

ASKING FOR TROUBLE

The horse had been mistreated, but since I rarely see mistreated horses, it took me longer than it should have to recognize the signs. Trouble (not his real name, but it will do) was a beauty, a long-legged light chestnut nearly sixteen hands, mostly Thoroughbred. I bought him from a small breeder who was planning to move to Colorado and didn't want to take all her horses. Since I had already ridden the gelding without incident, I wasn't paying attention as I longed him. Instead, I was listening to the seller explain that she'd had the horse in training—she had hoped to sell him as a hunter—but he didn't like jumping, so she brought him back home. I did note that every time I used the longe whip to ask for a change of gait, Trouble flattened his ears and aimed a cow kick at the whip.

But since he was easy to ride and handle, and the price was fair, I bought him.

Since John had stopped training horses to start his own business, and since our backyard wasn't suitable for horsekeeping, I arranged to board Trouble at a local stable.

The day he arrived, I led him to his new corral and fed him. The next day I took him out, tied him, brushed him, and then put him away and fed him again. No problem—he was very good about being handled. But the third day, when I longed him prior to riding him, I realized I had made a mistake. As Trouble cantered, something caught his attention and he stopped. He wasn't scared—a scared horse would have jumped back, away from the threat, his head up (and usually his tail), snorting. Trouble just didn't want to go past it. I clucked and popped the whip. No response. I popped the whip again. He pinned his ears and didn't move. I flicked him on the hindquarters with the whip. He kicked at it.

I walked up to him, coiling the longe line, and clucked again. Nothing. In case Trouble was misreading my intentions, I moved next to him so both of us faced forward and clucked again.

After waiting a second to see if he would respond (he didn't), I stepped back and pulled sharply on the longe line. Since I was so close to him, the pull caught Trouble off balance and he moved his front legs to keep from falling over. I told him "Good boy!" and clucked again. Grudgingly he picked up a trot and circled me. After trotting around me twice, his ears pinned the entire time, I ended the lesson; he'd done what I had asked him to. But when I walked up to him to stroke his neck and tell him he was a good boy and feed him a treat, he swung his head towards me, his lips drawn back.

You correct a horse who threatens to bite by slapping him hard on the neck, right behind the ears, if possible, with your open hand—he reacts to the sound as much as the contact—while telling him "No!" in a loud, firm voice. But Trouble's response was so openly aggressive I decided not to. In his view, slapping him could very well mean I wanted to fight back. I chose not to—wisely, as it turned out. Instead, I put the food reward I was holding back in my pocket—no treats for a horse who threatens to bite—and walked him back to his stall. Since he was still baring his teeth, I made sure to keep enough distance from him so I could defend myself with the longe whip if he went for me.

After grooming him the following day—I had no trouble catching or handling him—we went for a walk. Instead of a longe line I had him on a leadrope, but I held the loops in my right hand. Instead of a longe whip I carried a dressage whip in my left hand, which I held at my side. Since a dressage whip is longer than most other riding whips, I would be able to walk next to Trouble's shoulder with the whip in my left hand and sting him in the belly by reaching behind me if necessary to reinforce a "foreword" cue. This method usually works because the horse doesn't *see* you do anything. He misbehaves and gets stung—cosmic justice. You're innocent.

I walked Trouble all over the stable area. For the first ten or fifteen minutes our walk was uneventful; like most horses, Trouble was curious about his new environment. But then—just as he'd done on the longe line—he saw something he didn't want to go past and stopped.

I clucked.

Nothing happened.

Making sure both of us were facing forward and that I was standing close enough to him to reach him with the whip, I clucked again, giving him ample time to respond. When he didn't, I smacked him in the belly with the dressage whip. He danced away, ears flat against his head. Since he had technically "moved," I used my voice to praise him and started to walk again. Maybe Trouble didn't associate the whip with me. But he had already figured out that I wanted him to do certain things that he didn't want to do—maybe *I* wanted him to walk, but he didn't want to. He stopped again. I clucked, he ignored me, and I smacked him with the whip again.

This time Trouble stood straight up on his hind legs. When he came down, his front feet whizzed past my face by inches. I walked him back to his corral and put him away.

I'd made a mistake, all right. I owned a horse who kicked at longe whips, reared while being led, and threatened to bite.

I called his former owner. She said she hadn't ridden Trouble since he came back from the trainer, and the trainer hadn't mentioned having problems. Although she couldn't afford to take him back, she said I could exchange him. I asked her what else she had: Trouble's dam, a yearling, and a two-year-old. I thanked her for giving me the option but declined.

Since Trouble only acted aggressively when I carried a whip, I decided to switch tactics. Unlike his previous "trainer," I had no intention of working him over with a whip, but I couldn't explain that to him. Instead, I fashioned a longe whip like the ones some Saddlebred trainers use, made from the stock of a longe whip tied to several large plastic bags.

My new gadget got Trouble moving for exactly two days; he was a smart horse. These weren't saber-toothed tigers. These were grocery bags. The next time I shook the bags at him, he pinned both ears and reared.

I know my limitations, and I had reached them. I like to finish young horses—that is, to finish training them—but I don't break them to ride. That's for much younger people with faster reflexes. Nor do I retrain spoiled or abused horses. John could have helped me, but all his energy was directed at keeping his new business alive.

So I called Gayle Lampe in Missouri, although I was pretty sure I knew what she'd say. I was right. She advised me to get rid of Trouble before I got hurt.

I wasn't quite willing to do that yet. Somebody had done this horse wrong, and he deserved another chance. But he was the first horse I'd owned since putting Sinjun down, and I hadn't ridden in over a year. Somebody else was going to have the honor of riding Trouble before I did.

My next phone call was to a trainer I knew who made barn calls.

After another week of groundwork—consistently kind handling without whips and without improvement—the trainer decided it was time to ride Trouble. She had barely gotten settled in the saddle when the horse did exactly what Gayle had predicted he'd do. He stood straight up on his hind legs. As soon as Trouble's front feet hit the ground, the trainer urged him forward and was able to ride him in the arena about five minutes without incident. But it was too late. I was already composing For Sale ads in my head.

I sold Trouble, for a fraction of what I'd paid for him, to another boarder, and made absolutely sure she knew what she was getting. A week later I heard *she* had sold him. Her boyfriend had tried to longe Trouble with a longe whip to "teach him who was boss," and Trouble attacked him.

But with his third owner in as many weeks, Trouble got lucky. The woman who bought him rode him on the trail and never carried a whip. The last I heard they were living happily ever after.

I wish all abused horses could be that lucky.

If you bought a horse who rears—even a little—call a trainer.

The Horse Who Kicks

If you bought a horse who kicks, or threatens to, you'll find out about it when you walk into his corral. You have your halter and leadrope in hand, ready to lead your new horse to the arena and turn him out.

But instead of pricking his ears and looking at you expectantly—most horses' first reaction—your horse takes one look at you and swings around so that you're faced not with his head, but his rear end. If you attempt to walk around him, he'll shift his hind feet so you face his rump again. Look at his hind legs. If both of them are planted firmly on the ground, he's threatening to kick, but not very seriously. But if one hind leg is cocked—that is, if he's picked up one hind leg and is holding it under his body so the sole of his foot faces you—the threat level is much higher. Since you have food treats in your pocket, stop where you are, extend your hand, and use whatever word or sound you intend to use to ask him to come.

Once your horse decides your intentions are innocent, he may shift gears, turn to face you, and walk up to you for the treat. Don't take it personally—some horses threaten to kick because they don't want to leave their corral. But don't drop your guard; your horse might not want to longe or go for a trail ride, either.

What happens when you turn him out? Some horses, if the arena is on the small side, will buck and gallop off as soon as you remove the halter; in the process of bucking they may let fly with both hind feet—seemingly aimed at you. This horse isn't *necessarily* threatening to kick. He's bucking, and if he doesn't have enough room, he'll slew his hindquarters around and fling up his heels in your direction since he can't fling them anywhere else. The real question is, when you try to catch him, will he come to you or will he present you with his rump?

If he approaches you, give him his food treat, and praise him. Make a big deal out of it—you may have already solved your problem. Once you've groomed him, go into the tackroom for your saddle and bridle. If you walk out the door and the horse swings his hindquarters to you, maybe you haven't solved the problem—or maybe the horse is cold-backed and is afraid of the saddle. (I discuss saddling a cold-backed horse later in this chapter.) Give him the benefit of the doubt.

Note: a horse who stands with most of his weight on three legs—his two front legs and one hind leg, the toe of his other hind leg resting on the ground—is not threatening to kick. He's relaxing.

The Horse Who Bolts

If you're lucky, your horse will bolt while you're riding him in the arena instead of on the trail. First, make sure he's not running because he's scared. If he's scared, pull back on the reins— don't yank—and give him a voice cue. I use "E-a-a-s-y," or "So-o-o S-o-o." Whatever the sound is, use the same one to slow him down when you longe him. "S-o-o-o" works on a lot of horses because it sounds a lot like "whoa". Although your horse won't understand the meaning of the words, he'll hear the similarity between the two sounds and make the association. A horse running out of fear will usually stop.

The best way to handle a horse who isn't scared is to let him run. In fact urge him to run faster. Cluck to him. Cluck to him when he tries to slow down. Let him know he hasn't bluffed you or otherwise convinced you to get off his back—in fact you *want* him to keep running.

If you're on the trail and your horse bolts, you're more vulnerable. Unless you stop him, he'll run all the way back to the barn. (That's most bolters' intention.) If you ride well enough, stop him by bracing one hand against the swells using either your knuckles or your palm. (If you ride English, brace your hand against the pommel or the horse's withers.) Use your other hand to yank the rein backwards and up, so it shifts the position of the bit in the horse's mouth; it will get your horse's attention because it's uncomfortable. Some riders call this action the *pulling rein*; others call it the *emergency brake rein*. Whatever you call it, you're telling your horse you want him to turn, and this time don't release the pressure when he does. Keep pulling until your horse circles. Then release the pressure. Keep circling him until he slows down and stops.

Tim, the horse I bought for more money than I should have because the owner raised his price, turned out to be older and a little more experienced than she had claimed. Tim was a bolter; he bolted the first time I rode him at the barn where I was boarding him. He didn't head back to his stall, he just ran away—or tried to. I used my emergency rein and circled him.

After that we rarely went anyplace in a straight line. We leg-yielded (some old-time horsemen call this "braiding"—asking a horse to move one hind leg underneath himself instead of straight ahead) so that Tim moved sideways as well as forward. A horse can't push off his hind legs as easily as he can when you ride him straight forward; therefore it's hard for him to bolt. But sooner or later I'd forget why I was leg-yielding down the trail and relax. Tim seemed to enjoy catching me by surprise and bolting. No matter how many times I slowed him and circled, he'd try the same thing the next time I rode. He wasn't a mean horse—for him it was a game. For me it was an annoying habit, and even though I kept him for over a year until I bought Cassie, he was just a horse to me. Nothing special. No chemistry.

Looking back on the experience, I have to laugh at myself. When I compare Tim to Sinjun—who was mouthy, had an extremely short attention span, and would back up whenever he didn't feel like cooperating—I *should* have gotten along better with Tim. But horses are funny that way. Some go straight to your heart while others don't.

If your horse bolts and sticks his nose straight up in the air so it's hard for you to use your emergency rein, I suggest that you dismount—a horse with his head upside down can't see where he's going.

First, pick a landing spot. As soon as you see someplace reasonably level and free of rocks, brace *both* hands against the saddle or the horse's withers. Make sure both feet are out of the stirrups. Then, in a single movement, swing your right leg over his rump and shove your body out of the saddle to the left, or near side. Since you're accustomed to mounting and dismounting from that side, this dismount should be fairly easy. (Like riding without stirrups, this is another "practice this one at home" exercise.)

If your horse isn't going very fast, you'll probably land on your feet. If he's at a racehorse gallop, you might want to reconsider staying on. As long as you're on a trail and the footing is decent, you're probably better off staying astride him. Throwing yourself off the back of a horse at a full gallop is like throwing yourself out of a car traveling 30 mph. So he's running home—so what? He may get tired enough before you reach the barn that you can use the same technique on him that you did in the arena and *encourage* him to run.

Some bolters like to swap ends like a rodeo horse before they high-tail it home. This movement almost always leaves their rider without stirrups or reins. Unless you can reach down to get your reins back and circle him without stirrups, you might want to get off this horse too.

After you arrive home, you might want to phone a trainer.

The Horse Who Bites

Many horses are "mouthy" and like to nibble on whatever they can reach: their leadrope, the back of your shirt as you bend over to clean their feet, your hair. Other horses bite, or threaten to, when you saddle them. (As I said earlier, horses who threaten to bite only when you saddle them may be cold-backed.) With horses like Sinjun, being mouthy is part of their personality.

But other horses bite out of aggression. If they're show or performance horses, their vice is tolerated because they're good at what they do: they win prizes or outrun other horses. At home these horses usually wear muzzles, so they won't bite their grooms. A horse who has to wear a muzzle because he bites is not my idea of a friend.

Immediately call the horse's previous owner and find out what the story is.

ANNOYING BEHAVIORS

So much for troubled horses. Let's talk about the ones who only have annoying behavioral quirks.

A horse who doesn't want his ears touched, dances sideways and tosses his head when you go to saddle him, walks off before you've settled yourself in the saddle, and shies every fifteen seconds at butterflies has some annoying behavioral quirks.

Don't Get Near My Ears!

I'll start by discussing horses who are fussy about their ears because many horses *are* fussy about their ears. Since you have to touch their ears in order to slide the crownpiece into position, they don't like to be bridled. Trimming their ears is out of the question—and most of the time it's unnecessary. Your horse isn't a show horse. He needs the hair in his ears to keep the bugs out.

Some horses won't let you near their ears because they've been "eared" in the past— somebody twisted their ear to force them to do something, such as let a veterinarian pry their mouth open to examine their teeth—and every time you reach for their ear, they're sure you're going to twist it.

Other horses don't mind being bridled until you bridle them incorrectly—you bump them in the mouth with the bit and crumple their ears trying to slide the crownpiece over them.

Go back to the preceding chapter and practice the *right* way to bridle a horse. Once you teach your horse to accept a bit and bridle without fussing, you'll usually find you've also solved your horse's ear problem.

The Horse Who Flings His Head

But what happens if your horse starts tossing his head the instant he *sees* you holding a bridle? Or the horse who lifts his head w-a-y out of reach as you approach him?

Try treats (that's *treats*, not threats). Some owners claim that horses will readily accept the bit if you dip it in molasses first. When I tried that, by the time I got the horse bridled there was only a tiny amount of molasses left on the bit, whereas I had molasses all over my hand, my clothes, and the rest of the bridle.

■ Instead of molasses, I recommend grain or a pelleted sweet-feed. Some people claim they've had success using jelly.

■ Let's say you decide to use feed. Dig out a fistful and hold it in your left hand. Open your palm, place the bit in it, and offer it to your horse. (You should be holding the rest of the bridle in your right hand, as usual.) As he lowers his head, say, "head down." You can say "Rosebud." Just make sure you use the same cue every time and in the same tone of voice.

■ The horse was already lowering his head to eat the treat when you gave him the command. As soon as he wraps his lips around the bit (because it's on top of the treat, which is what he *really* wants), say, "good boy!" and ease the bit into his mouth. (As long as you use a snaffle or a curb with a low port your horse can eat with a bit in his mouth.) He'll probably stand next to you, quietly munching, while you slide the rest of the bridle on.

■ *Not* mashing his ears as you slide the crown piece of the bridle over them is crucial. Once the bit is in your horse's mouth, your right hand is free. To repeat what I said earlier: cup his off ear forward with your hand so you're actually sliding the crown piece over your *hand,* not his ear. Do the same with his near ear.

Since your horse is now bridled, and since you probably saddled him before you bridled him—that's the usual order—go for your trail ride.

How to bridle an "English" horse. I hold the bridle by the cheekpieces in my right hand while I ease the bit into Prim's mouth with my left. (Photo by Gina Cresse)

- When you come back, follow the suggestions I made in the previous chapter about rubbing your horse's head after you slide his bridle off (*without* clanking him in the teeth with the bit), and praising him.

- After you've gone through the bridling routine two or three times, your horse will figure out a few things: (1) If he lowers his head when you ask him to and accepts the bit, he gets a reward; (2) If he keeps his head lowered while you bridle him, you won't hurt his ears; (3) When you tell him "good boy," something pleasant will follow.

    End of lesson.

Once the bit is in Prim's mouth, I slide the crownpiece of the bridle over her cupped right ear. (Photo by Gina Cresse)

Saddling a Cold-Backed Horse

Some horses don't like to be saddled. A Western saddle, a hunt-seat saddle, even a bareback pad—it doesn't matter. What matters is that it's a saddle, and they don't want it on their back. When you do put it on their back, they fidget and duck instead of standing still.

Other horses object to being cinched up—sometimes by threatening to bite.

A third type dances away when you try to mount.

These behaviors are all specialties of a cold-backed horse. His back isn't colder than any other part of his body. His back is "cold" because his muscles are stiff or weak. You need to warm him up much the same way people who exercise warm up their muscles first.

Stretch His Back Muscles

A cold-backed horse is a good candidate for chiropractic stretches—in fact I suggest you start with them, preferably in the arena, before you groom him. (See Chapter 19.)

- After you stretch your horse's neck and forelegs and pull his tail—the tail pull is especially effective on cold-backed horses—curry him with a rubber mitt and brush him thoroughly, his back in particular. But don't clean his feet.

- Lay the saddle blanket across his back and saddle him slowly, so you don't sling forty pounds of wood and leather over his back and just drop it on him, especially if he's a youngster whose muscles are underdeveloped. If you can't control the saddle's downward momentum—in other words, if you have to sling it over his back and then let go because that's the only way you *can* saddle him—consider buying a lightweight synthetic saddle. At least until you've conquered the cold-back problem.

- Once the saddle is on your horse's back, cinch him up gradually and watch how he reacts. There's a little trick most horses seem to have been born knowing, and that is how to suck in a deep breath until their stomach is as round and tight as a barrel. If that's what your horse does, fasten the cinch as loosely as you can, barely touching him. If it's not what he does next, congratulations. You won't have to work quite as hard. Fasten the cinch very loosely.

- Slap the seat of the saddle with your hand a couple of times. Grab the horn in one hand and the cantle in the other and gently rock the saddle from side to side. If your horse did suck in air, these actions will usually help expel it. Tighten the cinch a little more.
- Clean your horse's feet. Tighten the cinch again, a little at a time.
- Since I always warm Prim up (there's that word again) on the longe line after I saddle her, by the time I'm ready to ride I can tighten the girth until I'm sure the saddle won't slip. You can do the same thing.

If you ride Western, always fasten the front cinch first, and fasten the rear cinch more loosely. It should graze the hair on your horse's belly—no more—but you shouldn't see daylight between the two, either.

Does the Saddle Fit?

Cold-backed horses are often afraid of being saddled and mounted because something about the process hurts them. In other words, your saddle might not fit—the tree is broken, or the saddle's the wrong size. The usual reason a saddle tree breaks is because the horse fell with it. Check the tree first. If it's intact, check the fit of the saddle.

The good news: your saddle isn't the problem. You've only ridden this horse two or three times; how could *your* saddle hurt him if the tree is okay and the saddle fits?

The bad news: your saddle isn't the problem. Somebody else's was. But how do you convince your horse that your saddle won't hurt him?

By making absolutely sure that every little wrinkle of the saddle pad is flat, nothing is poking or pinching him, and by putting some miles on him. Ride him every day or every other day, even if it's only ten or fifteen minutes. With gentle, repetitive handling, most horses grow out of cold-backed behavior as their muscles get stronger.

The Horse Who Threatens to Bite

Don't be surprised if your cold-backed horse threatens to bite when you tighten the cinch. Some horses will swung their head toward you, ears back. As with a kicker, there are levels of threat. This particular one is the lowest. As you cinch your horse up, keep an eye on him. If he swings his head towards you, his ears flat against his head, the threat level is higher and you need to correct it instantly. A horse who threatens to bite because he's cold-backed is entirely different than an aggressive horse like Trouble. Your immediate response to a cold-backed horse (but not an aggressive one) should be to slap his neck with your open hand and say "*No!*" very firmly. Never slap a horse in the face. It will scare him half to death (you just turned into a predator) and make him headshy without teaching him anything except to fear your hand.

In the days that follow, see if you can find a pattern in your horse's behavior. Does he only threaten to bite as you swing the saddle over his back? As you *place* the saddle on his back? As you tighten the cinch? Tying your horse so short he *can't* swing his head around far enough to bite is only a temporary fix and doesn't teach your horse anything. Here's a much more effective problem solver.

- Buy a pocket-sized container of breath spray at the drugstore. After you groom and saddle your horse, but before you clean his feet, tighten the cinch. Hold the spray, ready for instant use, in your left hand. As the horse swings his head around, spritz him in the nose. It will surprise him—although not enough that he'll try to run away—and the taste will puzzle him. Should he try to rub it off? Eat it? Spit it out? While he's deciding, cinch him up. If he swings his head in your direction again, squirt him in the nose again.

- While he rubs his muzzle against the hitching rail to get rid of it, pick up his front hoof—the one that's closest to you—and clean it. Then tighten the cinch a little more. If he swings his head around again, squirt him again. Then clean his hind hoof. Keep tightening the cinch, one hoof at a time, until your horse quits slinging his head around or until the cinch is as tight as you want it, whichever comes first.

- What have you accomplished? More than you might think. One, your horse's feet are clean. Two, your horse has blown out most of the air he sucked in to make his belly swell up. Three, by the time you mount, the cinch is tight enough that the saddle won't turn on you—because you tightened it gradually, while you cleaned your horse's feet.

Most importantly, your horse found out what will happen the next time he swings his head in your direction: *If I threaten to bite her, I get a snootful of spearmint.*

The Horse Who Takes a Hike

Some horses start moving as soon as your body meets the saddle—never mind that you haven't picked up your right stirrup yet. This habit isn't life-threatening, but it's definitely annoying. Don't let your horse get away with it.

- This behavior can also indicate the horse is cold-backed—you plopped your full weight into the saddle and his back muscles weren't prepared for it. But in this case, why he does it isn't as important as convincing him to stop.

- He should know what whoa means. If he doesn't, teach him how the next time you lead him into the arena. Instead of turning him loose, walk next to him. Without warning, say "Whoa" and stop. If your horse keeps walking, give one sharp tug on his leadrope and immediately release it. Even if he didn't stop he probably slowed down, so the release is his reward. *Don't* continue to pull on the leadrope. Snatch it once and let go. When your horse stops—and he will—praise him. (Don't forget the treat.)

- Your horse might get this concept much sooner if you thread a chain through his halter. Leather lead shanks come with a chain. Or you can buy one separately

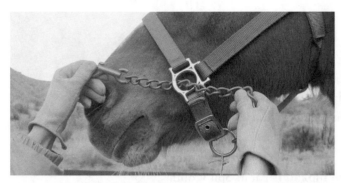

If your horse jerks you around, either on the longe line or when you lead him, use a chain over his nose. There are various ways to attach one; this method works for me. First, I slide it through the metal ring on the halter on Prim's near side. (Photo by Gina Cresse)

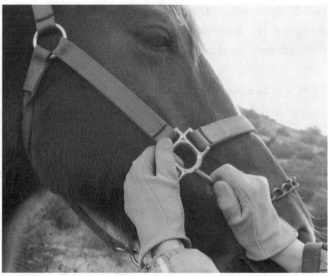

Then I pass the chain over Prim's nose and snap it to the ring on the other side of her halter. (Photo by Gina Cresse)

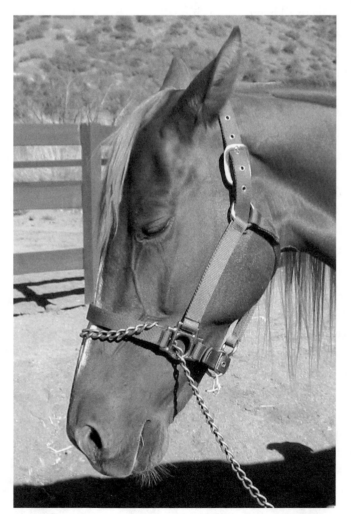

End result—a mare with a chain over her nose. Never tie a horse this way. If something startles him and he pulls back, the chain will tighten and he'll try to escape by pulling harder. (Photo by Gina Cresse)

(they're often sold as "stud chains") and snap it to the end of his leadrope. Any time you use a chain over your horse's nose, you *must* release the pressure instantly. Even though you may not have seen him respond, he did—usually out of surprise—although he may not have come to a complete stop. After three or four tries he *will* come to a complete stop because he's paying much more attention to you than he was a minute ago—before you put the chain on.

■ Once your horse will reliably respond to the whoa command on a leadrope, saddle and bridle him. Slide the reins over his head, so you can hold them the same way you held the leadrope—your right hand under his chin, the length of the reins in your left hand. Lead him around the arena holding the reins. Tell him "Whoa" and immediately stop walking. He'll most likely stop. If he doesn't, don't jerk or pull on the reins. He did probably slow down, or at least think about it, so give him another chance. Walk next to him—you can move up a little so you're next to his head instead of his shoulder—and say "Whoa." Wait a split second. If he doesn't stop, pull back on the bit without jerking it and immediately let go. He'll stop. Ask him to "Whoa" one more time and praise him extravagantly.

Teaching a horse to "whoa" from the ground is an effective method of communication. (Photo by Gina Cresse)

- Then mount your horse. Place your left foot in the stirrup, as usual, push off from the ground with your right foot the way I taught you to earlier, swing your right leg over his back, and *carefully* lower yourself into the saddle so your full weight doesn't descend on his back all at once. As soon as you're seated, pause a moment before you feel around for your right stirrup. Once you find it, slide your foot in and take up the reins.

- Why did I ask you to pause after you were seated? Because I want you to notice *when* your horse starts walking. Did he start when you moved your foot, trying to find the stirrup? "Feeling around" may be the source of the problem. Are you feeling around so vigorously that your horse mistakes it for a nudge, and tries to move off because that's what he thinks you want? If that's the problem, the remedy is obvious. Don't feel around so vigorously. Look down, see where the toe of your boot is, and slide it into the stirrup with as little fuss as possible. If your horse starts walking, just say "Whoa."
- Or did your horse start walking *before* you lowered your body into the saddle? This remedy is obvious too: be extra careful not to plop into the saddle. If your horse starts walking before you're settled, tell him to "Whoa."
- When he does, stroke his neck and tell him "Good boy." Once you have both feet in the stirrups, take your trail ride.

  Sometimes a horse will move off early because he's anticipating—he knows the two of you are going trail riding and he looks forward to it. Tell him "Whoa" until *you're* ready to go.
- When you come back from your ride, dismount as usual. Then remount your horse. Chances are that he's pleasantly relaxed from the ride and has no worries that you'll dig him in the side or plop down on his back—and no anticipation. In fact he wants this ride to be over, so he won't move. Praise him and dismount. Mount and dismount two or three more times, praising him each time.

Barriers

But if your horse persists in walking off, the next time you mount, face him into the outside of his corral or the riding ring. While he stands there, facing into the fence, shorten the reins until you have equal contact with his mouth in both reins, and mount—being careful about lowering your weight into the saddle and feeling for your stirrup. If he starts to move, say "Whoa."

- Since he's facing the fence, he *can't* move forward. Go for your ride, and when you come back, practice mounting and dismounting again.
- Or, enlist the help of a friend. Ask him (or her) to stand in front of your horse. If your horse moves to the left when you mount, your friend should move to the left too, still facing him. If the horse moves to the right, the friend should move to the right. Don't let the friend grab your horse's reins to "help" you. His job is to act as a barrier, nothing more. Since your horse isn't used to anybody pulling straight down on the reins, he might panic and do something really stupid, like rear.
- Once you're mounted and have both feet in the stirrup and your horse is still waiting for a cue, thank your friend profusely—maybe his horse is tied to the hitching rail so he can go with you—and hit the trail.
- When you return home, practice dismounting and immediately remounting your horse a few times. He'll probably be too tired to move off. Pat him on the neck and

tell him he's a good boy and a damn smart horse, and that you're going to do this—dismount and remount—one more time, just so he remembers. Then do it. Dismount, immediately remount, praise him, and get off.

End of lesson.

The Horse Who Shies

When a horse shies, his entire body slants to the side, and immediately after that—it's part of the same movement—he jumps sideways. If you fall off, or if you communicate your fear of the *prospect* of falling off by clamping your legs around the horse's sides and tightening your reins, he'll conclude that you agree with him: he's in mortal danger and it's time to leave. You don't want him to do that. Trying to stop a runaway isn't fun.

If your horse encounters something scary on the trail and shies, your smartest move is to take a deep breath and make a conscious effort to relax. No gripping with your knees. No rigidity anywhere in your body. No yelling about how stupid he is. Some people like to talk to their horse, but if the only time you talk to him is in tense situations, he'll begin to associate the sound of your voice with tense situations. Instead, squeeze your lower legs against his sides just a *little,* to remind him you're still on his back, while you jiggle the bit a *little* (use your ring and little fingers) to remind him you're still holding the reins. In other words, reinforce the idea that *you* are one who's riding and guiding him.

Backing

If you trail ride seriously, having a horse who responds to leg-yields or sidepasses and backs on command can come in handy. (You won't have to mount and dismount to go through gates.)

You backed your horse—in the show ring it's called a *rein-back*—once, before you bought him. Do you remember how you did it? If you do, ask your horse to back. If *he* remembers, he will. But if either one of you is confused, teach him how *you* want him to do it. The most effective method I know of is to halt your horse in the arena, before you set out for your ride. Slide the reins through your hands until you can feel your horse's mouth. Then close your legs on him and tell him to "Back." Normally you tighten your legs to ask him to go *forward*, but because you have him on such a short rein, he'll probably figure out that you don't want him to do that. Most horses will take a tentative step backwards, instead. Immediately give him some slack in the reins and relax your leg contact—that's his reward—and praise him with your voice. Don't ask for much at first. If he gets tense, even shifting his weight back is worth praising him for. The next day he'll probably take a complete step backwards. Reward him immediately. By the end of the week he'll back four or five steps before you sense any reluctance on his part. Immediately relax your rein contact and your legs and praise him.

HORSE LOGIC

When John first left the horse business, I kept Sinjun at a boarding stable where I watched a girl ride her horse in the ring one afternoon, trying to get him to step over some ground poles. The horse was unsure about these striped things lying half-buried in the sand and tried to sniff them. The girl yanked his head up and kicked him to get him going. But because she had yanked him in the mouth, the horse decided there was definitely something suspicious about those stripes. He had no intention of stepping over them and exposing his vulnerable underbelly if there was any possibility that they were alive and planning to attack. That's why he wanted to smell them: to see if they were alive, and if so, if he could identify them.

Impatiently the girl kicked him again. When the horse planted all four feet and refused to move, she used her whip on him. He refused to go forward. She used her whip harder. He didn't move.

If I had tried to help the girl—and her luckless horse—she might have been grateful, but more than likely she would have told me to mind my own business. Sinjun and I walked off so I wouldn't have to watch any more.

A few days later, I happened to be saddling him up for another trail ride when I saw the same girl in the ring with the same horse, except this time she wasn't riding him. She was leading him, and she didn't have a whip. She was obviously going to try a different tactic— *leading* her horse over the ground poles.

Her horse continued to refuse. After a few minutes of walking him in circles, she enlarged the circle until the horse had to step over the ground pole (an excellent tactic, but in this case the horse was too smart to fall for it). Instead, he pulled back, walked *behind* the ground pole, and continued the circle. Once again I rode away, but this time it was because I was laughing.

Why did the horse refuse at first to step over the poles? Because they were new to him, and since they weren't moving, the horse was curious rather than frightened. But when he tried to identify them, something hurt him—first in the mouth when the girl yanked his head up, then on the rump when she hit him. When she tried to lead him over the poles, he wasn't curious about them anymore. He remembered exactly what had happened the first time he'd seen these poles, right in this same spot. The *poles* were dangerous: *they* had caused him pain. Why should he go anywhere near them?

Completely logical, once you think about it from the horse's point of view.

WHAT YOU'VE ACCOMPLISHED

Teaching your horse manners can be very frustrating. But if you go back to your original wish list, you'll realize you can double-check every item on it. Your horse *will* let you bridle him without a fight. He'll stand quietly when you saddle him, let you mount without moving off, move when you tell him to, stop when you ask, and back up. If your horse will do all that, he would never dream of getting strong in the bit and fighting for his head even if you do gallop on the trail; he remembers too vividly what happened when he tried to run away with you. Be patient, keep trying, and above all, don't get into a fight with him.

Instead, teach yourself how to think the way he does—like a horse.

CHAPTER 15

WHISPERING TO YOUR HORSE:
LONGEING AT LIBERTY

No time to longe your horse?

Neither do I, but I *must* longe Prim to exercise her and before I ride. Free longeing is the answer your "no time" dilemma—it's fast, effective, and no-frills. Sometimes called liberty training, free longeing doesn't require a longeing cavesson or a longe line.

Even if you have all the time in the world, remember that horse owning should be a learning affair as well as a love affair. Why not teach your horse to longe at liberty just so you know how? Then you can show him off to your horse-owning friends who will gasp, clap, and demand, "Who taught him that?"

That's your cue to smile modestly and say, "I did."

There's also a practical reason for teaching your horse to free longe before you complicate his life with a longeing cavesson, longe line, side reins, and a surcingle. A horse who's never been longed before may regard all these accessories with alarm. Are you planning to attack him? Can he escape? He'll probably try to, especially if you snapped the longe line to the top ring of the longing cavesson to control his head. Flight is typical prey behavior, except this time the horse is dragging what he thinks is the predator (you and the longe line) behind him. Other horses prefer fighting to fleeing and will buck, rear, or spin around—anything to get rid of whatever is on his nose that prevents *him* from deciding which way to go next. These behaviors, especially spinning, are hard to correct on the longe line. But you can side-step most of them by liberty training your horse first.

Teaching a horse to longe at liberty is as easy as walking—take it one step at a time. The only equipment you need is a longe whip and bell boots for your horse's front legs to protect his fetlock area and keep him from scalping himself. I like the ones that fasten with a hook and loop (Velcro) because they're easy-on, easy-off.

Don't forget the horse treats.

OUTSMARTING YOUR HORSE

What follows is a discussion of the techniques I used to teach Prim to free longe. Most I developed by working with my previous horses, but since each horse's personality is unique, my techniques have varied from one horse to the next. Although Prim takes fright easily, she listens and she tries. But she also has pronounced dislikes. If I nag her to do something she finds boring, such as ring work, she loses her temper—flinging her head around and humping her back. Because I don't like to fight with horses, we do ring work only once a week, immediately before a trail ride. Since I spend most of the day in front of my computer, I take ten minutes to retrain my body position by riding without stirrups. To make sure Prim cooperates and stays alert, I keep the repetitions to a minimum and do a lot of transitions. If she can't anticipate, she won't get bored.

When I bought her as a three-year-old, I had two goals. I wanted to teach her the basics of dressage, and I wanted to apply them to trail riding. Now that she's sixteen and *knows* the basics of dressage, my goals have changed. I longe her to take the edge off her, to make her more reliable on the trail, and to make her more responsive in general.

With Thanks

First, I'd like to acknowledge my gratitude to the late Glenn Randall, Hollywood horse trainer, and his son Corky. Glenn Randall taught generations of movie stars how to ride, from matinee idol Errol Flynn to William Shatner, a.k.a. *Star Trek*'s Captain Kirk. Glenn trained Roy Rogers' horses (there were three Triggers) and, with Corky's help, did the horse work for many films, including the screen adaptation of Walter Farley's classic kid's book *The Black Stallion*. Glenn insisted on the humane treatment of movie horses and taught them how to take a fall instead of shackling them with a running-W and yanking their feet out from under them. He referred to his predecessors—the running-W users (the practice is now illegal)—as "wires and pliers" guys. His masterpiece was the brilliant stunt work in *Ben-Hur* with its unforgettable chariot race.

I won't give away the tricks of Glenn Randall's trade—his son and daughter-in-law still do film and television work and re-educate "problem" horses like Trouble. But I don't think he'd mind if I repeat something he told me in an interview. He said he got the idea of using the *position* of the whip as a visual cue from watching horses being broke to drive without bridles. "Point your whip to the right, they'd go to the right. Point your whip to the left, they'd

Glenn Randall at seventy two, still training "picture horses." This black Arabian had the starring role in the 1979 film The Black Stallion. *(Photo courtesy of* Horse & Rider.*)*

Glenn's son Corky, left. (The waxed mustaches are a family tradition.) Corky's assistant, Rex Peterson, doubled for Robert Redford in The Electric Horseman. *(Photo courtesy of* Saddle Horse Report*)*

The Randalls use two whips in their training; each serves a specific purpose. Corky teaching the Arabian how to bow. (Photo courtesy of Horse & Rider*)*

go left. And I got to thinkin', why couldn't that be used for pictures? Directin' a horse at liberty and having full control over him? So I developed my technique out of that."

I decided if Glenn Randall could improvise on other people's methods, I could too.

THE ONLY ESSENTIAL—A LONGE WHIP

You can't free longe a horse without a longe whip, and it's essential to buy a longe whip and not a driving whip, which has a long stock (the stiff end) but a very short lash. Most tack stores carry longe whips. The stock generally measures five-and-a-half feet and the lash measures six feet. On the end of the lash is a tassel called a popper that sounds like a firecracker when you flick your wrist correctly. The noise can be as effective as actually touching the horse with the whip.

Some people get the hang of popping a whip by holding it upright, snapping it down, and then briefly flicking their wrist up at the last minute. Others get it by using the whip in a quick sideways movement with a last-minute flick of the wrist in the opposite direction. Practice.

Since most longe whips are less than twelve feet long, you can't actually touch your horse with it—you're too far away—unless you extend the lash. Tie a length of any thin, tightly braided rope (sashcord works) to your whip above the popper. If you want a new popper, tie a knot about two inches from the bottom of the sashcord and fray the ends.

When you longe a horse, you want him to go around you in a circle while you stand in the middle. Picture yourself holding a dog on a leash. Now picture the dog about twenty feet away from you, still on the leash. Now picture the dog walking around you in a circle, and you're not moving. You're longeing your dog.

Now forget about the leash. You won't need it until Chapter 16.

HOW DO YOU DO?

Before you longe your horse for the first time, introduce him to the whip. You do this by leaning it against the fence and turning your horse out in the ring. When he's finished kicking up his heels, buckle his halter on and feed him his treat.

While he munches, shift the leadrope to your left hand, if you're right-handed. With your right hand, slowly pick up the longe whip. Move away from the fence. Hold the whip upright, the stock end in the dirt, so that the entire whip is vertical and resembles a stick-figure. Using your left hand (the one now holding the leadrope), dig another treat out of your pocket and offer it to your horse with your arm extended.

At first he may be suspicious of the whip. Let *him* come to you—and he will, to get the treat. You don't want him to think you're chasing him with the whip. If he backs up, lower the whip until the tip is in the dirt. Make sure to keep your whip arm relaxed and by your side—the whip looks much less threatening that way. If your horse pulls back, don't try to stop him. Instead, let out that first loop in your leadrope, so he won't feel trapped. The point is to get him used to the longe whip, not scare him with it.

Introducing your horse to the longe whip. (Photo by Gina Cresse)

When your horse stops backing up (back him into the fence if you have to) raise the tip of the whip again so the whip is vertical. Don't move it around, and keep your left hand—the one holding his leadrope and the treat—outstretched. Eventually your horse will come close enough to eat the treat. Then he'll sniff the whip.

When he's finished sniffing, move the whip around a little. Move it *slowly*, and keep it away from his head. (Remember—you're on his near side.) Starting with his chest or shoulder, touch him with the whip and move it down the outside of one front leg. If your horse is very apprehensive, he may know about whips from unpleasant first-hand experience and flinch. But even a horse who hasn't seen a longe whip before may flinch the first time you touch him with it. Because you're moving the whip so slowly—and because your horse knows there's another treat in his future—he'll probably conclude the whip isn't life threatening. Slowly move it up to his withers and along his back and side. *Gently* touch his croup and move the whip down his hind legs.

When you're done, repeat the procedure on his off side. Then go through the entire routine one more time, making sure to slide the whip down the *inside* of his front legs, *under* his belly, and down the *inside* of his hind legs. Horses can be touchy about their hind legs.

If your horse acts afraid—shifts from foot to foot, or tries to back up when you run the whip under his belly—gain his confidence by moving as slowly as possible. Be patient with him. You may have to repeat the entire procedure tomorrow. But before you go any further, he has to understand he has no reason to fear the whip.

Slowly move the whip over your horse's body until he gets the idea it won't bite. (Photo by Gina Cresse)

Conclude the introduction by touching him lightly with the whip on some part of his body where he doesn't mind being touched—on most horses, that's usually the chest or shoulder. When he stands without fretting, reward him with a food treat and your voice; use exactly the same words you used the first time he let you catch him in your arena, the same words you use every time he does something correctly: "Good boy! *Go-o-o-o-d* boy!"

But if your horse reacts aggressively—pins his ears, swings his lowered head towards you and bares his teeth—stop at once. You may have Trouble on your hands.

SHORT AND SWEET

Remember that you're trying to teach your horse to do something he's not sure how to do— let another animal that isn't a horse (you) decide where he'll go, how fast, and how long he'll keep going. Losing your temper won't help him learn. You'll accomplish much more if you keep the training lessons *short*—no longer than ten minutes per session, and no more than one session per day.

If after ten minutes your horse hasn't gotten whatever it is that you're trying to teach him, end the session anyway. But—as I've said earlier—be sure to end on a positive note. Choose something your horse already knows how to do, such as stopping when you say "Whoa." You may be surprised to feel your own frustration melting away as you praise him for at least one job well done.

In the information that follows, I'm not saying your horse should master Step 1 on the first day, Step 2 on the second day, etc. Individual horses, like individual children, learn at different rates of speed—and some horses have a shorter attention span than others. The steps are just a way of keeping track of the information you need to teach your horse to free longe. He must be able to perform Step 4, for example, *every time you ask* before you move on to Step 5.

FREE LONGEING

In order to longe your horse you need a fenced arena, preferably a round one. Horses can evade you too easily in corners. Even better is a bull ring completely enclosed with high wooden panels, including the gate. Horses tend to learn fast in a ring like this. Since they can't see what's happening outside, and you're the only other living thing inside, the horse *has* to focus on you. Most professional trainers use a wood-paneled bull ring.

But any fenced arena will do, and if yours happens to be square, I suggest that you buy four fifty-gallon plastic barrels and put one in each corner. Your horse will find it much harder to evade you or spin around that way.

Turning Your Horse Loose

I'll start here because unless you work with your horse daily, he can overpower you when you turn him loose in an arena. In fact it's the main reason I keep insisting that you longe your horse at least every other day.

A bull ring with high, wood-paneled sides, so the horse can't see out.

Your horse yanks you off your feet when you turn him loose? Try this method. First, give him a food treat. While he's munching it, take off his halter. (Photo by Gina Cresse)

This is what I mean by *overpower*. Most well-fed horses kept in confined quarters are impatient to stretch their legs and run. You, on the other hand, are a little apprehensive, because sometimes you hardly have time to slip your horse's halter off before he pivots and takes off bucking. He may have even pivoted on your foot a time or two. You also aren't crazy about the time you didn't get the halter all the way off before he spun around, and he pulled you so hard you ended up on your hands and knees.

Food treats: Food rewards are essential. Choose something you can fit in your pocket and dole out one at a time, like baby carrots or handfuls of your horse's favorite pelleted feed. Make sure he knows you have them. (You should have fed him something when you walked into his corral.) Now that you're standing with him in the arena, feed him another treat. While he's chewing, take off his halter. A funny thing will happen. Your horse will not go berserk. In fact he probably won't go anyplace. He'll look at you, instead, because he's wondering if you have any more treats. Of course you do. So give him one.

Mission accomplished. When you turn back to the gate, he'll run off bucking.

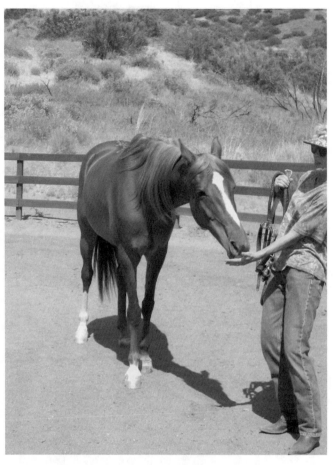

Your horse has a decision to make. Run off? Or hang around to see if you have another treat? (Photo by Gina Cresse)

Food is a great motivator. Your horse decided to hang around—and you rewarded him. Your horse won't yank you off your feet anymore. (Photo by Gina Cresse)

Calling Him In

Getting your horse to come to you is crucial. Although I discussed this process in detail in Chapter 11, and you should have been using it consistently since the day your horse arrived on your property, I'll summarize it again here.

Voice cues: Decide on a command. I tend to be very unimaginative when it comes to voice cues and simply tell Prim what I want her to do. If I want her to walk I say "Walk." To call her in to me I whistle, using the same two-tone sound every time.

Outsmart him: Walk into the ring, make the sound or say the word you've chosen, and extend your hand. In your outstretched hand is—you guessed it—a treat. Since your horse ate one when you turned him loose, he'll remember the smell. Chances are he'll walk towards you. He's also curious about why you're sticking your hand out.

If he turns tail and runs, reread Chapter 11 and be prepared to spend some time on this.

Once you've introduced your horse to the longe whip and can safely turn him out and reliably call him in to you, he's ready for Step 1.

First, put on his bell boots.

STEP 1

Remove your horse's halter and leadrope and put them someplace within easy reach. (I buckle Prim's halter to the top rail of the fence by the gate.)

Trotting to the Left

It's not easy to teach a horse how to longe at the walk, either at liberty or on the longe line; there are too many other things he can do instead. So we'll begin with the trot.

You've just called your horse to you and fed him a treat. Make sure your horse is facing left, or counterclockwise. You want to be on his near side, where you'd be if you were leading him.

- Step back, away from your horse, the whip in your right hand, and move forward, so you're facing the same direction that you want your horse to face. This is your basic position: if the two of you were walking, you'd be next to his croup.

The longe whip held shoulder high, so the stock is horizontal. This is the "trot" aid, along with your voice cue and body position. (Photo by Gina Cresse)

- Raise your whip to shoulder level (yours). Before your horse has a chance to follow you—most horses' first reaction, because they're used to being led—cluck to him or tell him to "Trot." If he persists in moving towards you, walk towards *him*, making sure to stay slightly behind him with your body facing forward, and say "Trot" again. He'll probably retreat to the fence because he's not sure what you want him to do.

- What you want him to do is trot going to the left. That means you reposition yourself behind him with your body facing forward, but not *directly* behind him. Eventually you want to form a triangle with your horse, although you won't have the third angle until you add the longe line.

- Cluck to your horse again, or use the "Get going" word you decided to use. Your horse may give you puzzled glances. Keep telling him to "Trot" and keep walking towards his rump with your body facing the same direction his is—forward. As long as you keep moving, he will too. And the faster you go, the faster he'll go—but don't chase him (the predator thing again).

  Make sure you're not inadvertently giving him "Stop" signals by facing him, and make sure to keep your whip at shoulder level.

- These three factors in combination—your body position, your voice, and the position of your whip—will eventually enable your horse to figure out what you want, and he'll hesitantly trot. (He'll figure it out faster if you're in a bull ring.) Immediately praise him—tell him "Good boy!" or whatever words or sound you chose to let him know he did the right thing. Praise him using the same words every time you feed him a treat, so he associates being praised with the treat.

- As you tell your horse he's a good boy, be prepared for him to slow down. Any time you say *anything* to a moving horse he will interpret it as "Slow down." If he does, crouch slightly, move the whip towards his rump, and say "Trot." Why the crouch? Predators crouch; it gives you a slight air of menace.

■ Chances are that your ten minutes are up. Just because your horse caught on so quickly, don't be tempted to continue the lesson. Horses learn more with a nickel's worth of training a day than they do in half-hour sessions that leave you both exhausted.

How to Stop Your Horse and End Every Lesson

Drop your right arm, the one holding the whip, to your side and lower the whip so the tip rests on the ground. The whip in this position will signal your horse that you're going to ask him to do something different: ask for a different gait, ask him to reverse, ask him to stop.

■ Next, slide the stock through your right hand so you're holding the whip upright, the same way you did when you introduced your horse to the longe whip, and tell your horse to "Whoa." He may ignore you. If he does, move so that you're standing slightly ahead of him, facing him. Raise your *left* hand until it's shoulder high, palm vertical (pretend you're directing traffic), and repeat your voice command. Since you're in his way, your horse will probably stop. Nearly all horses will slow down.

■ That's good enough for the first time you ask for Step 1. As soon as your horse slows down, call him in. At first he may approach you hesitantly because of the whip,

Your horse's reward for doing the right thing: a food treat, a "Good boy!" and much petting. (Photo by Gina Cresse)

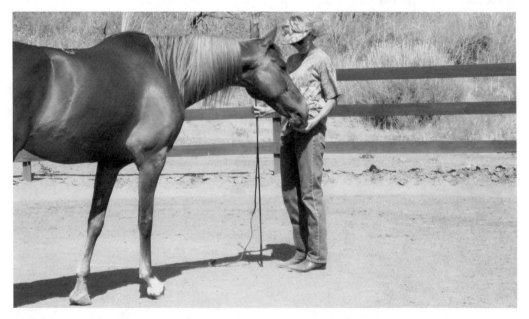

When your horse approaches you for his reward while you're holding the longe whip, you know *he trusts you. (Photo by Gina Cresse)*

but once he's sure you have a treat for him, he'll come. While he chews, either drop the whip completely or lean it against the fence, and halter him. Be sure to move very slowly and confidently. Confidence begets confidence.

What Just Happened?

As you walk your horse back to his stall or to the hitching rail in preparation for a trail ride, ask yourself what your horse learned in the past ten minutes.

Ideally, he learned to trot to the left when you asked him to. Why did he trot? Because you asked him to. And every time he didn't trot, you asked him again. As I said earlier, your horse has much better peripheral vision than you do. Because of how his eyes are positioned on his head, he *saw* you point the whip at his rump. He *saw* where you were standing and which way you were facing—and both of those facts told him to move forward. He also probably figured out that you wanted him to trot because nothing else he did seemed to satisfy you. In other words, your horse *should* have learned to associate the word "Trot" with the position of your body and the whip, and to associate all three with the physical act of trotting.

If he did—congratulations. If he didn't, repeat Step 1 tomorrow.

STEP 2

Before you ask your horse to trot going to the right, or clockwise, you have to turn him around. Reversing your horse will illustrate how crucial body language is.

Reversing

As your horse trots to the left, step *forward* in order to face him and say "Whoa." Immediately drop your arm so the tip of the longe whip touches the dirt.

Reversing your horse: use your body position to tell your horse to slow down. Note my lowered whip. Also note that Prim has turned her head to look at me—she isn't sure what I want. (Photo by Gina Cresse)

Still looking at me, Prim has almost stopped. At this point I pass the whip from my right hand to my left in front of my body, so she can see me do it. (Photo by Gina Cresse)

- As soon as your horse stops, pass the longe whip across the front of your body from your right hand to your left hand *so your horse can see it*. As you raise your *left* arm— the one that now holds the whip—to shoulder level, say "Turn around." (At least that's what I say.)

- Immediately assume the same position that you did when he was trotting left, so you're standing beside him and almost-but-not-quite behind him. Both of you should be facing right. Say "Trot."

    But because your horse isn't used to a human standing on his off side, he might keep trying to turn back to you. Respond by positioning yourself farther behind him while you drive him forward with the whip, away from you. (Yes, there's a difference between *driving him forward* and *chasing him*. And both of you know it.) Keep re-positioning yourself and repeat the word "Trot."

- What happens if, out of confusion or excitement, your horse starts to run? Immediately lower your arm and whip and move towards him. Raise your *right* hand to the level of your shoulder and say "Easy." String it out. "E-e-e-z-e-e, boy." Your horse will most likely drop down to a trot because your body language, your raised right hand, the position of your left hand (the one with the whip), and your verbal cue all tell him the same thing—you don't want him to speed up.

Prim reverses because the position of the whip (in my left hand), the position of my body, and my voice aid ("Turn around") all tell her that's what I want her to do. (Photo by Gina Cresse)

Again in response to my cues, Prim starts trotting to the right, clockwise. (Photo by Gina Cresse)

After several false starts your horse will figure it out—although he might surprise you and get it right the first time.

STEP 3

You want your horse against the fence, or rail. Once he trots on command, he'll probably try to drift away from the fence, towards you, and make smaller circles. Or he may leave the rail because he sees something outside that he mistrusts, so he'll move towards you just to play it safe. (He's less apt to do either of these things in a bull ring.)

You Don't *Want* Smaller Circles

Without moving your body, point your whip at his *shoulder* and say "Out!" If he persists, repeat your cue and act more aggressively—crouch slightly and tell him "Out!" in a strong, firm, commanding voice. He'll go back to the rail, although he'll also probably speed up. (Predators that crouch mean business.) But you just completed Step 2, so you know how to slow him down.

How to Count Strides

Now is a good time to start counting strides, so you can time how long you longe your horse. The trot is the easiest gait for you to see where he puts his feet.

■ Remember that the trot is a diagonal gait, and a complete stride has two beats. One is when your horse's *left* hind leg and *right* foreleg hit the ground. The second is when his *right* hind and *left* fore hit the ground. In the middle of the trot is a hard-to-see moment when the horse is airborne—all four feet are off the ground. It's called the moment of suspension, and you can also see it when he canters.

STEP 4

After you've counted, let's say, fifty complete trot strides in the first direction, you want your horse to canter. Still maintaining your basic body position, crouch slightly and raise your whip. Bring the whip forward, up, and back to make a C in the air. As you do, cluck or say "Canter" or use whatever voice cue you've decided on.

Most horses will simply trot faster.

If yours does, slow him down by straightening your body and saying "Easy, boy" in a calm, soothing voice. Remember—if you move fast, so will your horse. The reverse is also true: if you want your horse to slow down, slow your own movements. Once your horse is doing a steady, relaxed trot again, repeat what you just did, except exaggerate it. Crouch lower. Paint a slightly bigger C. Speak in a louder voice.

If your horse still doesn't get it, slow him down again. Then give him the verbal cue and the body English and wait half a second to see if he'll canter. If he doesn't, pop the whip behind him.

If that doesn't work, try again—except this time, don't pop the whip. Touch the horse on the rump with it. Don't *hit* him. Just touch him lightly with the whip—once. You probably won't have to go that far, especially in a bull pen, and especially since he tried to canter at the trot but you wouldn't let him.

■ Once he's cantering, raise the whip so it's significantly higher than shoulder level, and keep it in that position until you ask your horse to do something else. Some people claim that holding a whip in this position is "threatening" to a horse. If you beat him with it then yes, the position is threatening. The only reason to raise your longe whip is to give your horse a visual cue that's different from the one you use to ask him to trot.

■ Instead of cantering, what if he cross-canters? The stride originates *behind*—in other words, a horse on his left lead (going counterclockwise) will begin by pushing off with his *right* hind foot. A horse on the correct lead always leads with his inside legs, not the legs closest to the fence. As you watch a horse who's cantering counterclockwise on the correct lead, you'll see him raise his *left* hind leg higher than his right hind leg, and it will hit the ground first. To complete the stride, he will raise his *left* foreleg higher than his right foreleg, which will also hit the ground first. The sequence of footfalls for a horse cantering on his left lead is: right hind (one beat); left hind and right foreleg together (second beat); and left foreleg (third beat). If a horse is cross-cantering, he's picked up the left lead behind, but in front he's leading with his right leg (see photo on page 294). Most horses that cross-canter will correct them-

A good canter on the correct inside (right) lead. (Photo by Gina Cresse)

Holding the whip in the "canter" position. Notice my arm is still shoulder-high, but the whip itself is higher, so the horse can see the difference between the "canter" and "trot" cues. (Photo by Gina Cresse)

The moment of suspension at the canter, when all four legs are off the ground. When she completes the stride, Prim will be on the correct (inside) lead. (Photo by Marilyn Dalrymple)

selves because they feel unbalanced. If yours doesn't, correct him by asking him to drop back to a trot. Then ask him to canter again.

▪ Some horses will cross-canter going to the right but not to the left. Others will cross-canter to the left but not the right. Many horses never cross-canter. Count your blessings. Correcting a horse who persists in cross-cantering is tedious work.

STEP 5

To reverse a horse who's cantering, bring him down to a trot and then stop him. If you ask him to reverse without stopping first, it's easy for him to interfere with himself, especially when he feels good or the weather's chilly.

Always lower your whip before you ask your horse to reverse. He will probably swing away from the fence in order to look at you, to see what you want. As soon as he sees you switch the whip from one hand to the other, he'll know.

STEP 6

Teaching your horse to walk to the left is a lot like teaching him how to jog to the left. Some horses will try to follow you as you move away because they're used to following you on a leadrope. Use your whip to keep your horse moving forward. But this time, relax your whip arm (your right arm) so the tip touches the ground, a position that your horse is used to thinking of as a cue to transition into another gait or speed. Scratch the whip around in the

The third basic whip position with the tip in the dirt. The lowered whip tells the horse I'm going to ask for something different—a transition to another gait, a change of direction, etc. (Photo by Gina Cresse)

Teaching your horse to walk at liberty can be very frustrating. Technically Prim is doing a very slow jog as she transitions into the walk. (Photo by Marilyn Dalrymple)

dirt a little—nothing too attention-getting. As soon as you move the whip, your horse will probably start to jog. Reposition your body and tell him "Easy" to slow him down.

You may have to repeat this lesson a few times. Some horses need a ten-minute schooling session every day for a week just to figure out that they can walk in a circle by themselves without you next to their shoulder as an escort. But eventually, your horse will get it.

Walking to the Right
Teaching a horse to walk to the *right* can be even more frustrating than teaching him to walk counterclockwise, which is why I saved it for last—so your horse already knows the basics.

- To begin, stand in your basic position. As you did earlier, point the whip *down*, to indicate a transition, and say "Walk." Your horse will probably stay planted like a tree right where he is; he's not used to being "led" from this side.
- Repeat the verbal cue and tell him to "Walk" again. If he moves at all, it will probably be to edge towards you. Immediately reposition yourself so you're slightly behind him and repeat "Walk."
- If he *still* doesn't do anything, tell him to "Walk" and wait a heartbeat to see if he'll respond. If he doesn't, pop the whip.
- If your horse does anything, he'll move off at a slow, very hesitant jog. Tell him "Whoa" and start over. Move a little closer to him and repeat everything you just

did. If he's still confused, *gently* touch his rump with the whip. He'll probably duck his tail and lurch forward. As you reposition yourself, tell him "Good boy!" He *did* walk, never mind where or how fast.

■ But if ten minutes come and go and your horse still doesn't know what you want, call him in to you so you can reward him for doing *something* right. Then call it a day.

■ Whatever you do, don't take your frustration out on your horse. The reason he won't walk to the right, or lope to the left without cross-cantering, is because he doesn't understand that's what you want. He's not deliberately disobeying. He just doesn't get it. If you hit him with the longe whip because he can't figure out what you want, who's being stupid?

COMPLETELY FREE LONGEING

Once your horse knows the basics of free longeing, you can use less obvious cues to achieve the same results. When you longe your horse to the left, tuck the whip behind your left shoulder and the crook of your elbow (so it's upright and the horse can still see it) and use your right arm the way you previously used the whip. Because you replaced your whip with your arm, the position of your body becomes increasingly important. Be sure to face the same way your horse is facing to keep him moving forward. As soon as you turn your body to face his, your horse will attempt to stop or reverse. To ask for the trot from the walk, or the canter from the trot, crouch slightly. Use exactly the same voice aids. You might have to move closer to your horse at first, until he gets the idea.

Next, get rid of the whip entirely and see how much you can communicate to your horse through the position of your body and an occasional voice cue. You may find that your horse is less distracted by what's going on outside the ring than he used to be. That's because as your cues become less obvious, he focuses more on you as he tries to figure out what you want.

This technique—using various cues to ask for what you want and then when you get that, replacing the cues with progressively more subtle ones—works just as well in the saddle as it does from the ground.

YOU AND YOUR LIBERTY HORSE

Once your horse will perform all three gaits, reverse, stop, and come to you—no tack, no longe line, no whip—you can feel justifiably proud of yourself. You trained your horse to do something he didn't want to do: give up his autonomy and let you direct his movements. That's an impressive accomplishment.

Invite your friends over for a demonstration and be prepared for a lot of ooohing and ahhhing. When you longe a horse at liberty, he's paying such close attention to you that he seems to be reading your mind.

CHAPTER 16

WHISPERING TO YOUR HORSE: LONGEING TO SOLVE PROBLEMS

To most riders, longing a horse is almost as exciting as watching leather soak up neats-foot oil. But you'd be surprised how many of your horse's less-than-desirable habits you can get rid of by longing him.

When you tell him to "Giddyup," does he ignore your clucks and chirps and keep plodding along at the same, snail-like pace—or balk entirely and refuse to take another step?

Longe him.

When you pull back on the reins and tell him to "Whoa," does he fling his nose in the air and fight you?

Longe him.

When you're out on the trail and urge him to go faster, does he unload you instead and hightail it back home without even a backwards glance to see if you're okay?

Longe him.

LONGEING—AN OVERVIEW

I once watched a cowboy longe a horse with a halter and leadrope to cool him out after a trail ride. Even though the horse's circles were pretty small, the idea was the same. And while I wouldn't recommend it as a training technique, I once longed Prim using my reins instead of a longe line, and the palm of my hand instead of a whip.

I had ridden her up the road to visit our neighbors, the Jimminks, because they have an arena bigger than my house and have been gracious enough to let me use it. All four of their kids are deeply involved in 4-H, so they have plenty of chickens, steers, lambs, goats, and pigs. The pigs are in a big pen covered with a blue plastic tarp. If you've been trail riding for any length of time, you know what horses think about blue plastic tarp flapping in the wind. To make matters worse, Hobbs, Rick Jimmink's horse (a Los Angeles Police Department retiree), lives in a pasture adjoining the arena. Hobbs was so excited to see Prim that he galloped figure-eights around his pasture, neighing.

Between Hobbs and the blue tarp, Prim was so worked up by the time I reached the arena that I knew I was going to end up on the ground—or in Cincinnati—unless I did something to calm her down. (Fortunately she's a forgiving horse who will gallop full-out for sixty seconds but flat walk on a loose rein immediately afterwards.)

Do not try the technique I'm about to describe at home. It was a one-time solution to a one-time problem, and I knew my horse well enough to predict how she would react.

Longeing cavesson. (Drawing by Gina Cresse)

Once inside the arena, I dismounted and longed Prim at a trot, using my reins and smacking her on the rump with my hand whenever she tried to slow down. For the first few minutes she ran circles around me with her nose in the air. But gradually, as I kept insisting that she focus on *me*, not Hobbs or the blue tarp, she calmed down. Then I turned her around so she circled me at the trot going the other direction. Once I was sure I had her full attention, I halted her with her rump to Hobbs, so she couldn't see him, and remounted. I won't claim she was Old Shep for the next half-hour, but I didn't end up in Cincinnati either.

LONGEING—THE REAL DEAL

As you've probably discovered, free longeing has one built-in disadvantage. Since your horse isn't physically connected to you, it's easy for him to move in one direction while he stargazes—turns his head away from you because something outside the ring distracts him.

How do you keep his focus on *you*?

You buy the following equipment.

Longeing Necessities

You need a longe whip, which you already have, a longeing cavesson, a thirty-foot longe line, a surcingle, and side reins.

The cavesson: A longeing cavesson is preferable to a halter because it has a ring on top of the noseband as well as

A longeing cavesson fits higher and tighter on a horse's head than a halter. (Photo by Gina Cresse)

on either side, so you have direct control of the horse's head. Unlike halters, cavessons are designed for a very snug fit. If you use a halter to longe your horse, it will slide all over his face and distract him from what you're trying to teach him.

The only other difference is that a cavesson has a padded noseband that won't scratch your horse. Although you *can* buy beautifully made leather and brass longeing cavessons lined with real sheepskin, they're not necessary. The inexpensive nylon kind with synthetic padding work just as well and last just as long. (Unless you're scrupulous about cleaning the brass every time you use the longeing cavesson, the brass will turn green.)

Many of the newer longeing cavessons have rings that swivel, allowing you to reverse your horse on the longe line without having to walk up to him, unsnap the longe line, turn him around, and reattach the longe line. If you buy the swivel type, make sure to attach the longe line to the ring at the center of the noseband. Otherwise you *will* have to walk up to your horse and disconnect him before you reverse.

■ Please note that longeing cavessons fit too snugly to allow your horse to chew. That means no food treats. When you feed your horse to reward him for a job well done, loosen the noseband first, or remove the cavesson entirely.

The longe line: You can make one out of whatever unbreakable, rope-type material you have handy, as long as it's sturdy and you can coil it. I've seen longe lines so flimsy they look as if they were designed to gift wrap presents, not work a horse. This is not time to be frugal. Buy the expensive heavy-weight kind, and make sure the line is at least thirty feet long.

Storebought longe lines are flat and have a snap on one end and a loop on the other to use as a handle. Don't slip your hand completely through the loop to your wrist, the way you would a dog's leash. You can grip better that way, but that's the problem. If your horse, in his excitement, yanks you off your feet, you'll have a hard time letting go of the longe line. Instead, hold it as though you intend to pick up a suitcase by clenching your hand in a loose fist around the *end* of the loop. Your horse can still yank you off your feet if he hits the other end hard enough, but all you have to do to free yourself is let go.

How not *to hold a longe line.*

Holding it with your fingers will give you all the control you need.

The surcingle: This is a girth or cinch *without* a saddle that completely encircles your horse. You can adjust most surcingles from both sides by tightening the straps the same way you'd tighten your girth or cinch.

For my money, the best surcingles are made of leather and canvas with wool-stuffed pads designed to fit snugly on either side of your horse's withers. Surprisingly, these sturdy leather surcincles are often less expensive than the nylon kind padded only with "fleece" (usually synthetic) that flattens with use, and the exposed edges of the nylon can rub sores on your horse.

Most surcingles have at least two metal rings on each side, plus one directly on top of the surcingle. You don't need the top one; you *do* need the side rings. The best surcingles—the leather ones—have three rings, and the third is placed lower than the last ring of most nylon surcingles. It's the one you'll use most often because that position is how most horses carry their heads.

Side reins: Leather side reins will keep your horse's head straight and prevent him from stargazing. Snap one end to a side ring of your longeing cavesson and the other end to the lowest ring of the surcingle.

For additional give, especially with young horses, I add a short length of surgical tubing, tied off at each end with duct tape and ending in a metal ring. Snap the side rein to a ring on the cavesson, and snap the other end to a ring on the tubing. Use a double-ended snap to connect the tubing to a ring on the surcingle. Most side reins are leather and have some natural give, but not much. Nylon side reins have no give at all. Recently I've seen side reins made with a rubber donut that will also provide your horse with additional give.

The only tricky part about side reins is adjusting them correctly. You don't want them dangling, but you don't want them too tight either. (Finding a happy medium is easier if the side reins include something that stretches—like surgical tubing.) If your horse refuses to move, or moves only with reluctance, they're too tight. Loosen them a couple of holes. You're not trying to set your horse's head. You're trying to teach him to move forward while carrying his head in whatever position is natural to him. When you find the correct length, the horse will move forward.

HOW TO LONGE YOUR HORSE

If you don't have a bull ring, longe your horse in some kind of fenced enclosure, at least until you both know what you're doing. Otherwise it's too tempting for your horse to decide he's had enough, he's outta here.

After you adjust the cavesson, snap the longe line to the ring on top of the noseband. Make sure to keep the longe line high enough and taut enough that your horse doesn't step on it and trip, or put a foreleg over it and wrap it around his shins. Also make sure to keep the longe line looped in your hand (some owners prefer to loop it over their hand) so you can let out additional line when you need it and reel it back when you don't.

Hang your horse's halter and leadrope on the fence until you need them. (Photo by Gina Cresse)

Coil the longe line in your hand so additional line spools off from the top. In other words, when you coil the longe line to use it, start with the hand-hold and make loops. The snap should be on the outside; it's the first part of the longe line you'll use. (Photo by Gina Cresse)

Expect the Unexpected

If your horse gets tangled up in the longe line, he'll be convinced that some saber-toothed tiger has finally bushwacked him. Many horses will struggle frantically to free themselves, thereby tangling themselves up even more. Others will freeze, panic-stricken, and wait for you to help them. To my surprise, Prim freezes. Why was I surprised? Because a dressage trainer unaccustomed to hot horses once urged me to get rid of her, telling me Prim had "no sense of her own physical safety" and would endanger my life if I rode her on the trail.

The easiest way to untangle a horse caught in a longe line is to approach him slowly and talk to him soothingly while you unsnap the line from his longeing cavesson. Use the cheekpiece of the longing cavesson to lead your horse forward, out of the snarl, and lead him to the rail where you keep his halter and leadrope. (You need the leadrope to hold on to him while you untangle the longe line.) Otherwise you're going to have to persuade your horse to stand still long enough for you to free each leg separately. Once everything's sorted out and you know your horse isn't hurt (he shouldn't be hurt, just very apprehensive), snap the longe line to his cavesson again and pick up where you left off as though nothing had happened.

Longeing Your Horse at the Trot

I'll use the trot as an example of what might happen the first time you work your horse with a cavesson and longe line. Don't attach the side reins; I'll discuss them when you need them, and right now you don't need them.

Your position: Now that you've added the longeing cavesson and longe line, your basic position vis-a-vis your horse is a true triangle with all the connecting lines in place. Stand facing left, the same direction your horse is facing. Your right arm—the one holding the whip—is shoulder-high, and the whip points to a spot immediately behind your horse's tail. (Although he can't see the lash end of the whip, he can see your arm and the position of the stock.) As a result, the first line of the triangle is the whip extending from your raised right arm. The second line is the horse's body, tail to head. The third line runs from the cavesson's noseband through the longe line to your left hand.

■ Because you've longed your horse at liberty, he knows what to do when you say "Trot." Very few horses will fail to understand what you want simply because they're wearing new headgear. But most horses will fail to grasp the idea that *because* of the new headgear, you now control their head. They haven't tested it yet. They will.

With a longeing cavesson and a longe line, you can control your horse's head. Note the protective bell boots. (Photo by Gina Cresse)

Get his head back: If your horse turns his head to look at something outside the ring, pull it back. Pull slowly and don't jerk. But pull forcefully enough to move his head back where it belongs—in front of his body. Your horse will probably be very surprised because you've never repositioned his head from the ground before. He may toss his head or try to stop. Holding your whip shoulder-high, ask him to "trot." Even if your horse tried to stop, he will probably resume trotting when you ask him to. If he doesn't, he's not one hundred percent sure what you want him to do. Since you want him to trot, make sure you're facing the same way he is and repeat your verbal command.

Remember: ten-minute sessions.

What Else Can Go Wrong?

Several things: Once your horse discovers that you control his head, he may—out of confusion, anxiety, or temper—suddenly rear, strike at the longe line, take off at a gallop, or buck. What do you do?

Nothing. If your horse wants to throw a tantrum, let him. Even though rearing and bucking might look like a thousand pounds of exploding dynamite to you, they're normal reactions for some horses. Your horse won't hurt you, and the special effects are only temporary. If your horse is a docile soul, he might not act up at all.

The important thing is to keep enough tension in your longe line to make sure your horse doesn't get his forelegs tangled in it. As soon as he settles down, praise him with your voice and ask him to trot again. In other words, ignore his bad behavior. You can't prevent it, and if you punish him for it, he won't understand why.

■ Some horses throw a tantrum by changing directions in mid-air. These are the spin-and-reverse artists, and in this case you have to intervene—as quickly as possible, so your horse associates being turned around by hand with a voice command. Since your horse is accustomed to reversing at liberty, he'll most likely turn into the fence to change direction instead of turning to face you. Some horses can spin so fast that by the time you realize what happened, the horse is going right instead of left and the longe line is pressed against the side of his face and neck.

Immediately drop your whip and tell him "Whoa." Walk directly towards your horse's head so you face him. He's familiar with these cues from being longed at liberty, and will either stop or slow down. Keep saying "Whoa" and keep the tension in your longe line (still in your left hand) by using your right hand to feed loops into your left hand. Tell him "Whoa" until he stops.

Once you reach him, grasp the longe line over his nose with your right hand and say "Turn around." As you say it, *lead him around you* in a half-circle (the horse should always be between you and the fence) until he's facing left again. As soon as that happens, back away from him, pick up your whip, re-establish your basic triangle position, and tell him to "Trot."

Don't praise him. And don't throw a temper tantrum of your own and yank on the longe line or smack him with the whip. Just keep asking for what you want.

You'll probably have to ask more than once. A horse who reverses unexpectedly can be very frustrating, but remind yourself that your horse is even more frustrated than you are. He reversed for a reason—even though you and I, as humans, have no idea what that reason was.

■ I can't predict exactly how your horse will react because I don't know your horse. Most horses will exhibit one or more of the behaviors I just described. Others will stop dead in their tracks and refuse to move. A few will try to find safety by edging towards you.

Or, your horse might react by trotting all the way around the ring without doing one thing wrong. Praise him. Lavishly.

■ End this lesson the same way you end all longeing lessons: ask your horse to "Whoa" and call him in to you. When he does, drape the leadrope over his neck, remove the longeing cavesson, feed him his treat, and tell him what a good boy he is. Before you halter him, rub the sweat marks on his nose and behind his ears where the longeing cavesson rested and praise him again.

Prim cantering on the correct lead, facing the same direction she's moving in. (Photo by Gina Cresse)

At the canter and the walk: Following the same procedures you used when you taught your horse to longe at liberty, teach him to canter in both directions and then to walk in both directions. Even though the first lesson your horse learned on the longe line—that you control his head—may have been a little dramatic, most horses settle down very quickly and figure out what you want them to do much faster than they did when learning to longe at liberty.

And reverse: After a few weeks of uneventful longeing, most owners want to teach their horse to change direction by himself, so they don't have to walk up to him and turn him around by hand. Since your horse knows what "Whoa" and "Come" mean, teaching him to reverse on the longe line should be easy.

- Let's say your horse is walking left and you want him to reverse. First, tell him to "Whoa." Since most horses anticipate—especially when they know there's a food treat in their future—your horse will probably stint on the "Whoa" part and immediately swing around and begin to walk towards you.
- Your longe line is still in your right hand your whip is in your left. *As you switch hands* so you hold the longe line in your left hand and your whip in your right (the tip of your longe whip should be in the dirt), tell your horse to "Turn around." Most horses will stop and look at you in bewilderment.

Prim cross-cantering. To pick up the correct inside (right) lead, Prim's right hind *leg should be in front of her left hind. She* is *on the correct lead in front. I'll bring her down to the trot and ask for the canter again. (Photo by Gina Cresse)*

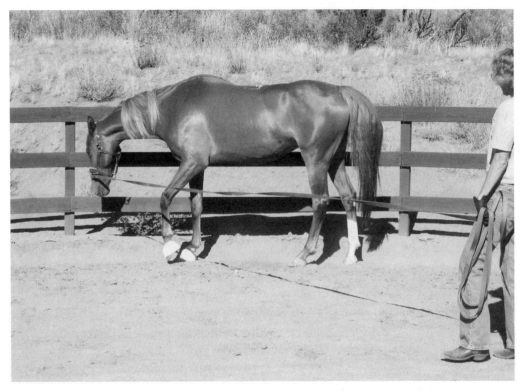

At the walk. A stronger contact on the longe line would straighten Prim's head. (Photo by Gina Cresse)

- Take a few steps back, so you're facing right—the same direction you want your horse to face—repeat your verbal command, and raise your whip slightly. Because you reverse him at liberty using exactly the same cues, he'll probably put it together pretty fast and break into a trot or canter. Since he's moving in the correct direction—to the right—don't try to slow him down immediately. Too many commands all at once will confuse your horse. Unless he's relying completely on instinct, he's a straight-line, cause-and-effect thinker. Let him get at least halfway around the ring before you ask him to "Walk." After he's walked around the ring a time or two, halt him—he'll probably be tentative about stopping because of what happened the last time you said "Whoa"—and say "Come." He will. End of lesson.
- Tomorrow, repeat the lesson by reversing him to the right to reinforce the idea. But this time, after he's done it correctly, reverse him to the *left*. He'll probably do it without hesitation since he knows (from free longeing) what to do when you switch hands.

PROBLEM SOLVING ON THE LONGE LINE
Remember the three scenarios I laid out at the beginning of this chapter? Here's how to re-educate the horse who doesn't want to go, the horse who doesn't want to stop, and the horse who throws a fit.

A Wake-Up Call For Lazy Horses

Most so-called balkers are just plain lazy. A balky horse has chosen to ignore what a cluck means. Smacking him with a whip doesn't help. Spurs don't get his attention, they merely irritate him.

Barn sour: Some horses don't want to leave home because they're barn sour—home is where the hay is. Re-educating a barn-sour horse is pretty easy and works on nearly all horses. I discussed how to do it in chapter 12.

■ Other horses are reluctant to go forward because they're fat, the same way overweight people would rather plop down in front of a TV than go hiking.

■ Underweight horses may have a similar problem—they're not enthusiastic about trail riding because they lack energy. Some owners deliberately keep their horse on the thin side for that very reason, especially if the horse is high-strung or unpredictable.

■ Or is your horse "lazy" because his feet hurt? Check for lameness while you're in the saddle; see if his strides steady and evenly spaced. When you get back home, longe him at the trot, the same way you did when you were considering whether or not to buy him. Close your eyes—you should hear a distinct two-beat rhythm. If you think you can detect even a slight lameness, call your vet.

If you vet determines that your horse isn't lame, he'll probably suggest putting him on a diet if he's too fat, and feeding him more hay if he's too thin.

While you wait for your horse to lose or gain pounds, longe him—unless, of course, your vet tells you not to. This time, attach the side reins. Longing your horse consistently, using your longe whip when necessary to reinforce your voice and body position, will usually change his outlook on life. Suddenly he's in a herd situation, and you're the boss. Every step he takes reinforces the fact that what *he* feels like doing is irrelevant. *You're* in control, and *you* want him to move forward.

The next time you ride your horse, you'll probably see a big improvement in his attitude.

Human to Horse—Are You Listening?

A horse who ignores your attempts to stop by tossing his head or tucking his nose into his chest may be one of those attuned horses I discussed earlier. He's figured out your weaknesses as a rider and keeps looking for ways to exploit them.

But before you longe him, take a look at his mouth. Then take a look at his bit. There are several reasons why your horse might over-react to rein pressure. Three of the most common: your horse needs his teeth floated; he's grown wolf teeth; the bit is too severe.

■ A horse who lets half-eaten feed spill out of his mouth or takes longer and longer to finish eating probably needs his teeth floated. Or he might have other dental problems. Sniff his breath. It should smell fresh and grassy, very much like the hay you feed him. If it doesn't—if it actively smells bad—call your vet. A show horse I once knew had a sinus infection. The infection had remained undetected for so long that it had started to destroy the bones of her face before anybody discovered it. (An abscessed tooth can cause similar problems.) How did somebody discover it? The mare had bad breath. Healthy horses don't have halitosis.

Schedule a field call so your vet can check for dental problems. Ask him to look at your horse's tongue too. Sometimes a horse will fight the bit because of an injury to his tongue.

■ Ask yourself why you're using this particular bit. If your horse is well trained and you have good hands, a curb with a mild port and short shanks shouldn't bother him. A snaffle shouldn't either. But if you're heavy-handed, any bit can be severe. It's also possible that your horse's problem might have nothing to do with you. You may be seeing learned behavior, particularly if the horse is mature. In other words, your horse *expects* pain when you exert pressure on the reins, and he fights you to avoid it.

Consider re-educating him on the longe line with either a solid-mouth bar snaffle or a smooth, fat, jointed snaffle. (The thicker the mouthpiece, the milder the bit.) Your goal is to show your horse that he can take contact with the bit and move forward without hurting himself.

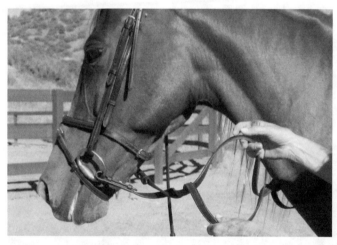

So the reins won't slip down your horse's neck where he might step on them, leave the throatlatch undone and criss-cross the reins under his neck. (Photo by Gina Cresse)

Slide the throatlatch under one of the reins and buckle it. (Photo by Gina Cresse)

This is how the reins should look when you're finished. (Photo by Gina Cresse)

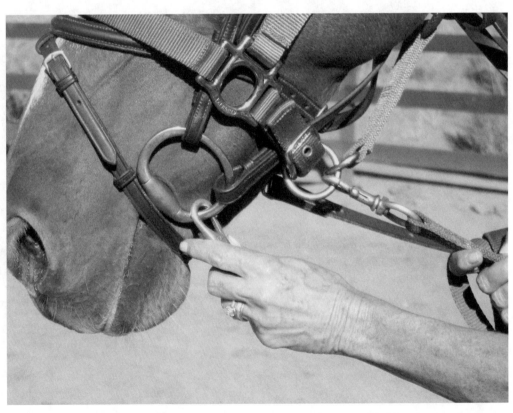

To longe a horse with side reins fastened to his bit, buckle his halter on and snap one end of the side reins to his bit under the bridle reins. Snap the other end to the lowest loop on the surcingle. (Photo by Gina Cresse)

Prim at the trot, moving forward into the bit. (Photo by Gina Cresse)

He already knows how to longe at liberty. This time, fasten the surcingle and then bridle him. Criss-cross the reins under his neck three or four times, slide the throatlatch through one of the loops, and fasten the throatlatch. Then attach the side reins by snapping one end to the lowest ring on the surcingle and the other to the ring of the snaffle. Remember—when the side

Moving forward into the bit at the canter. (Photo by Gina Cresse)

reins are correctly adjusted, your horse will move forward willingly.

■ Re-educating a horse like this takes a lot of time, patience, and repetition. Vary your routine—jog him twice around the arena, for example. Just before you reach the gate, ask him to stop. Ask him to jog around the arena twice more, but this time ask him to stop *after* he passes the gate, just in case he's anticipating. Then ask him to walk. Halfway around the ring ask him to jog again. After he's jogged around the ring three times and *before* he passes the gate, ask him to lope. In other words, keep your sessions as interesting as possible by throwing in a lot of halts and changes of gait, and asking him to jog or lope slowly and then faster.

When your ten minutes are up, ask your horse to do something he does well—and by this time most horses respond to "Whoa" very, very well.

■ Your horse's learned behavior may be so deeply ingrained that you can never completely convince him to stop fighting the bit when you ask him to halt. If that's the case, consider using a mechanical hackamore, even if you ride English. If your vet discovered that your horse injured his tongue somewhere along the line, I also suggest that you try him in a hackamore. Some horses are happiest when they don't have a bit in their mouth, and when they're happy, they're a lot more fun to ride.

The Horse Who Bucks

Most owners longe their horse before they ride to take the edge off him. A hot horse can be fun because he's a challenge, but you don't want a trail horse who jumps off his feet at things only he can see—fretting, worrying, dancing sideways, and crow-hopping. As my friend and neighbor Rick Jimmink put it, "I ride because I want to relax. I don't want *Fear Factor.*"

Nine times out of ten, if your horse bucks you off, he's not doing it because he's mean. He bucks because he feels good. If you fall off, that's your problem and has nothing to do with him (horse logic). Longe him—especially when the cool weather sets in and nights get chilly. If you ride without longeing him first, your horse will probably throw in a buck or two when you ask him to canter, just because he feels good.

If I haven't ridden Prim for a while I longe her twice, even though she's a senior. I free longe her to take the edge off her. Once I've saddled her and we're ready to ride, I longe her a second time, to make sure she's paying attention to me.

If your horse is pastured outside with other horses, you probably won't have to longe him to take the edge off him. He has no edge. He spends his days almost the same way he would in the wild, bickering with other horses about which weeds and seeds belong to him and which ones don't.

Longe him anyway, just to remind him who's calling the shots.

SOME PARTING ADVICE

There are several different ways to teach a horse to longe. You can get results from almost any method as long as you consistently use the same cues, longe your horse at least every other day, and keep your lessons short.

CHAPTER 17

HORSE CHORES: WHAT AND WHEN

Even if your tackroom doesn't have electricity and you don't spend much time there, I suggest you tack a calendar and/or a cork board to one wall. Computers are incredible inventions, but unless you have one in your tackroom, it won't help you keep track of the last time you wormed your horse, or if it's time to reorder fly predators. I also suggest that you keep a pencil handy. Ink doesn't run uphill, and if you're trying to write a note to yourself on your wall calendar, your pen will quickly stop working.

As an owner, you should have one designated area where you can keep track of paperwork involving your horse, vet work, feed, the hay shed, corral, etc. How much hay did you buy last time, and how long did it take the feed store to deliver it? Where *did* you put the phone number for the poison-control center? The simplest way to stay on top of what needs doing and when is to move an inexpensive desk and chair into your tackroom and hang up a calendar.

CHORES

You should perform some horse chores daily, without even thinking about them. They're a habit, like brushing your teeth. Once-a-week chores are a little harder to keep track of—and a little easier to postpone. A few chores are not done on a specific date; for example, you spring-clean your tack room once a year, sometime in the spring. Other owners prefer to clean theirs by getting ready for winter.

Since I went over many of these chores in detail in earlier chapters, I won't repeat the information here. Use these suggestions as a timeline. The chores I haven't discussed before, such as how to clean your tack, I'll discuss here.

Chores You Do Several Times a Day

Feed: You feed your horse in the morning and clean his stall or corral, and turn him out before you feed him dinner. If you feed three times a day, that too becomes part of your routine.

Once you set a precedent with your horse, stick to it—especially if it involves feed. If you *are* feeding three times a day, don't go on a two-week vacation and arrange for somebody to feed twice a day. It's not fair to your horse, physically or psychologically. But since finding a responsible person willing to feed three times a day can be difficult, at least arrange for a double ration of breakfast hay.

Cleaning: Clean your horse's stall and/or corral once a day. Many owners and most training barns clean once in the morning and again in the afternoon. Manure attracts flies, especially if you stable your horse outside. Flies bite, and some carry disease. You can help your horse by removing the manure. Standing in manure and mud isn't good for him either. If you keep him outside and it's raining, pull on your rubber boots and muck out the manure. Then clean his feet and apply an anti-thrush product.

Water: Whether your horse lives indoors or out, check his drinker whenever you feed. Is the drinker working properly? Nothing's broken or clogged up? Always check the

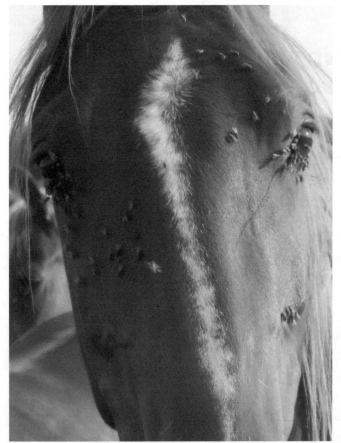

Pastured horses are hard to keep fly-free. Try a combination of insect repellent rubbed directly on the horse's face, and fly predators. Prompt manure removal helps too.

When the water in your horse's drinking barrel looks like yesterday's coffee, time to scrub it clean.

water in a stock tank or other outdoor waterer. All kinds of strange things can fall in and potentially contaminate an outdoor waterer, but you won't know about them unless you look. How long, for example, do you want that dead kangaroo rat in there?

Once-a-Day Chores

Turn your horse out, longe him, or ride him once a day. If I turn a horse out or longe him, I brush him and pick out his feet before putting him away so I know his feet are clean. When I ride, I groom him and clean his feet before and after. The rides don't have to be long—just enough to exercise him and keep him interested, and enough for you to enjoy them.

■ Here's how I like to groom a horse. First I go over him with a rubber curry mitt, then brush him with a stiff-bristled brush. In good weather, when I groom after I ride, I keep a bucket of water handy—the same bucket I use to clean tack—and I dunk the brush every few strokes. After shaking the excess water off, I groom the horse again. Frequent dunkings clean the brush, and the wet brush digs deep to remove dirt.

■ After every ride, I clean my horse's bit with an abrasive pad designed to clean non-stick cookware. If he hasn't broken a sweat—my saddle and bridle are still dry, in other words—I go over them with a clean, dry cloth. To clean the girth, I dampen a cloth with a spray-on liquid glycerine saddle soap. (I also use it to clean my boots when I get back to the house.) If the leather is sweaty in spots, particularly the bridle, I clean it using warm water, a small amount of a mild dish soap like Ivory liquid (some riders prefer Murphy Oil Soap), and a soft-bristled brush. There's no need to clean the entire saddle and bridle; spot-cleaning it will stop the scurf buildup and you won't face a major cleaning project once a month.

■ Before putting my horse and my grooming box away, I knock the dirt out of my curry comb by banging it against a wall, post, or the fence. Since I usually use a soft brush on a horse's face, I rub it against the stiffer brush to loosen the dirt from both. Then I dunk them both in water and shake off the excess.

Every Other Day

If you absolutely do not have time to turn your horse out, longe, or ride him once a day, do it every other day. Brush him and check his feet. Clean your bit if necessary and touch up your saddle and bridle.

Twice a Week

Some horses on a maintenance level of a supplement like psyllium, for sand colic, should be dosed twice a week. Pick two days and stick to them. If you can't remember whether you actually *gave* your horse the supplement, mark your calendar.

Once a Week

- If your horse is pastured, check for suspicious new plants or flowers; you don't want to accidentally grow an invader that's toxic to your horse. When in doubt, pull it out (and wear gloves).
- If you don't clean your tack every time you ride, set aside one day a week to do it. Write it down on your calendar.

  - Most horse owners who keep their horse indoors put down fresh bedding as needed. If you keep your horse outdoors in a pipe corral and are still trying to establish a base, you may have to add bedding every week. Once you've established a base, you'll only need to add two or three bags of shavings a month.
  - Do you clip your horse's bridle path so the crownpiece of your bridle doesn't flatten it? Your job will be much easier if you run your clipper over it once a week. And if your horse fusses because he doesn't like you working around his ears, he'll relax much faster once clipping becomes part of his routine.

- Do a general cleanup. Use a broom to sweep up and remove the dirt and spilled feed from your tackroom floor. Hose down the rubber pads by the hitching rail. Empty your trash.
- If your horse lives in a corral with an automatic drinker, use your pot-scrubber to clean it. In the summer you'll have to scrub it more often because of the algae.

Most conscientious riders and all professional grooms clean tack immediately after it's been used. This groom likes saddle soap and a natural sponge. For how to clean and condition Western tack using neatsfoot oil, see pages 308–310.

After soaping the saddle right-side up, the groom turns it over and soaps it upside down. Sawhorses come in handy for this job. (Notice the towels protecting the cantle.)

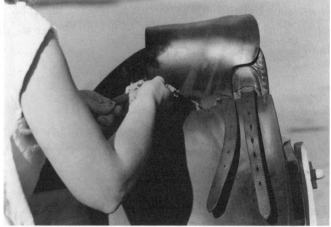

She soaps every piece of leather on the saddle, including the underside of the skirt.

- If you use a barrel or other nonautomated drinker, how long you can go before cleaning it depends on the construction of the waterer, your horse's eating habits, and the weather.

Some owners like big rubber waterers because algae doesn't cling to the sides the way it does to galvanized tubs. As a result, rubber tubs don't need cleaning as often. Many horses like to rinse their mouths with water after eating. Bits of whatever they just ate will float for a few hours, then sink to the bottom. Because algae thrives in direct sunlight, your horse's water can turn dark and unappetizing overnight in hot weather. While a thirsty horse will drink almost anything, if the water is dirty he'll drink only enough to slake his thirst.

- Here in the high desert, we're overwhelmed every spring by small, dusty-gray moths that drown by the dozen everyplace there's water—the bird bath, the dog's outdoor water bowl, and of course the horse's water barrel. The powder on their wings washes off and leaves a grayish residue behind. Not only is the surface of the waterer littered with dead moths, but the water is cloudy. During moth season, I clean Prim's waterer every three or four days.

The bottom line: make sure your horse has fresh, clean water available to him at all times.

She cleans the bridle the same way—one piece of leather at a time. This is why you bought a tack hook.

How to Clean a Horse Waterer

If you habitually postpone scrubbing your horse's waterer until you can't see the bottom, you'll have to scour it—a tedious and time-consuming chore, especially if you use bleach. Wouldn't you rather be riding?

Here's what it takes to clean an outside horse waterer. The night before, don't add water—unless, obviously, the barrel or tub is empty.

Without bleach: The next morning, take a lightweight plastic bucket into the corral with you. Bail out as much water as you can, leaving only an inch or so on the bottom. Using your pot-scrubber, scrub the bottom of the tank or waterer and up and down the sides.

- Do not use small, fine-grade steel pads. They're are unbeatable for their intended purpose, but their intended purpose is to scour pots and pans—not horse waterers. While you can easily rinse the metal residue down the drain of your sink, it's almost impossible to rinse it out of something as big as a horse waterer. Do you want your horse to drink tiny particles of metal? Do you want them to collect in his gut? Can you spell c-o-l-i-c?

- Scour the drinker until it's clean, then tip it over to empty the remaining water. Pull on heavy leather gloves for this step, and don't grab the bottom rim of the waterer until you're absolutely sure that nothing lives there. Snakes and black widow spiders find such crannies irresistible.
- Once the waterer is completely empty, set it upright and refill it with water.

With bleach: The only product that will kill algae is bleach.

- Follow the same steps I outlined previously until you reach the final "refill" step. Then pour in two gallons of water plus half a cup of bleach and scour the waterer thoroughly. The dicey part about using bleach is making sure you get it all out—otherwise you're asking your horse to drink diluted chlorine. If people swallow too much of it, they get sick. So will your horse.
- After you pour the water out, rinse the waterer by filling it about halfway with fresh water—no bleach. Scour it again, making sure to rinse your pot-scrubber first. Empty the waterer a second time. Fill it halfway up with water. Scrub again. Empty.
- Let it stand in the sun until it's completely dry, two or three hours. Of course you have put a full bucket into your horse's stall or corral in case he gets thirsty. Once the waterer is dry, fill it to the top with fresh water. You're done.

Once a Month
A buying spree: Take an inventory of your feed and anything in your grooming box that you're running low on. (Depending on the size of your hay barn, you may want to shop more often.) Some people spend hours hanging around tack stores, checking out the new products while they talk to the owner or manager. If you don't have that much leisure time, write down the items you need on a shopping list, then attach it to your calendar. Colorful Post-It Notes were born for this job.

Every Six to Eight Weeks
A shoeing spree: If your horse wears shoes, he needs new ones every six to eight weeks, depending on how fast his feet grow. If your horse goes barefoot—which is better for his feet, provided he has good feet to begin with—he'll need a trim every six or eight weeks too.

Every Six Months

- If you have a young horse, an accident-prone horse, or an elderly horse who's not "maintaining" as well as you'd like him to, a twice-yearly vet check is good preventive medicine. The vet will take your horse's vital signs, check his teeth, ask how much he's eating and drinking, the amount and quality of his manure, etc. and give you suggestions for improving his overall health.

■ If you feel the urge to clean your tackroom (most people feel it in the spring or fall; others never feel it). Clean the floor and windows and—depending on your opinion of spiders—use the broom to get rid of cobwebs. Having a clean tackroom is an incentive to *keeping* it clean.

■ Dig some old, well-dried horse manure/shavings into your riding ring and drag it to improve the footing. A good time to do this is right after a gentle rain, when the ground is damp but not saturated.

As Needed

Parasites: If your horse doesn't spend much time around other horses, it may not be necessary to worm him as often as the directions on paste wormers tell you to. Ask your vet for his recommendation. If your horse doesn't shed his winter coat completely or his coat looks rough any time of year and you can see his ribs no matter how much you feed him—especially if he has a pot belly and acts lethargic—he probably needs to be wormed.

Stall maintenance: Even if you line your horse's stall with rubber pads, you'll have to strip the stall periodically, i.e. when it starts to smell. Remove all the bedding, pull out the pads, and scrub them with soap and water. While they dry, add powdered limestone (often called agricultural lime and available at garden stores) to the wet spots in the stall. Once the pads are dry, drag them back to the stall and lay down new bedding.

■ If the stall really stinks, remove the bedding and pads and dig up the entire stall. (Move your horse into the arena and hand-water him for a couple of days. Feed him while he's tied to the hitching rail, so he can nibble leftovers off the pad, not the bare ground.) Add lime liberally to the stall floor, work it in, and wait a day or two while the soil dries. Tamp it down, add DG (decomposed granite), scrub the mats, return them to the stall, bed with shavings, and move your horse back in. By adding DG, you shouldn't have to strip your horse's stall as often.

General cleanup: Periodically wash all your brushes, curry combs, and other grooming tools. If the bristles of your brushes have flattened or are falling out, buy new brushes. Wash your grooming box, too.

Every Year

Call the veterinarian: For your horse's health, have your vet inoculate him against whatever bad-guy germs and viruses lurk in your neck of the woods. It's cheap insurance. The vet will also give your horse a thorough physical, and before he leaves will give you a copy of his findings for your records. File it in your desk and write a note on your calendar to schedule another vet visit next year. Some people schedule medical checkups—even visits to their own doctor—by choosing a date that has some personal significance. It might be their birthday, the week after New Year (and all those resolutions), or Ground Hog Day.

■ If your vet tells you he wants to check your horse again in six months to see if his teeth need floating, jot that down on your calendar too.

Chores by the Season

Some chores can't easily be categorized as weekly or monthly. Even if you live in a part of the country that only has two seasons, rainy and dry, you can probably still key your chores to the following four-season breakdown.

Spring Chores

■ Spring chores always include helping your horse shed his winter coat. Once you notice he's losing hair, use a shedding blade to help him get rid of it. (Don't use it on a horse who hasn't started shedding yet.) Make sure not to use it too vigorously on horses with thin skin. They'll protest.

■ Once you're sure the cold weather is over, wash your horse's blanket or blankets (if he wears them) and store them in plastic tubs in the tackroom. Clean blankets are ready for instant use as soon as the nights start getting chilly next fall. Many tack stores offer a laundry service, or you can wash the blankets yourself.

Deep-clean your tack: For you procrastinators—those of you who haven't cleaned your tack since you stopped riding last winter—it's time. Here's how to deep-clean and recondition leather tack.

■ Wait for a warm, sunny day—your tack will appreciate it.
■ You need saddle soap or a mild dish soap. Jack McCloskey, a Western-saddle maker I know, uses Palmolive Antibacterial soap. You also need pure neatsfoot oil, some way to heat it, and a leather conditioner.
■ Jack heats neatsfoot oil to 180°–200°F in a crock pot. Hot, even warm, neatsfoot oil will penetrate the saddle leather, whereas cool oil will sit on the surface without sinking in. The next time you ride, you'll be wearing it.
■ A *neat* is an archaic word for cow, and neatsfoot oil is rendered from the feet of dead cattle. If this fact bothers you, use a good brand of light olive oil instead. Heat it, but only to about 100°F. Olive oil breaks down under high heat and darkens.
■ You'll also need several pails of warm water, a sponge, and a pot-scrubber. Don't use the same pot-scrubber you use to clean your horse's waterer; buy another one and keep them separate. You don't want a greasy, oily residue on your horse's drinking water. Some owners prefer to use rags or cloths instead of sponges, which tend to disintegrate.
■ A double-pronged tack hook suspended from a beam in the tackroom comes in handy.

- So does a sawhorse, particularly for cleaning heavy Western saddles.
- Rubber gloves are optional but very helpful. (Have you ever looked at the hands of a professional groom?)

To clean your bridle: Start by taking it apart. If it consists of more than one piece—in addition to the reins, you might have a browband and a flash noseband, for example—number each piece of leather and jot down what other pieces of leather it's connected to.

When I bought Bachelor, the cowboy who owned him was still using a bosal. Under his direction, I replaced the bosal and mecate with a bridle, a jointed snaffle bit, and a running martingale, which many Western trainers use on young horses to teach them to lower their heads. I took the bridle and martingale home with me one afternoon to clean them and didn't bother to draw a diagram. Cleaning them took me fifteen minutes. It took me about five minutes to put the bridle back together and forty-five minutes to reassemble the martingale. If you've ever used one, you know it only has three or four pieces of leather. What was so hard about reassembling it?

The buckle. Instead of being stitched to the leather, as most buckles are, it was a floater, and I kept putting it on backwards or on the wrong side of the keeper.

Step 1. Wet your sponge or rag and squeeze out as much water as you can. Work the soap into your bridle. The pot-scrubber is especially helpful on those areas that collect greasy black scurf, like the inside of your reins and the cheekpieces of the headstall. Or you can use a toothbrush or other small brush with stiff bristles. The sponge will get dirty very quickly—keep rinsing it. Change the water whenever it turns gray. Don't *soak* any part of your bridle with water—you just want to remove the dirt. Before going to the next step, dry it completely, away from direct sunlight.

Step 2. Once your bridle is clean and dry, go over it with a light coating of hot/warm neatsfoot oil, preferably using a pad of natural lamb's wool. The leather may need more than one coat, but several light coats are better than one heavy coat. Avoid saturating the leather; there's no way to remove excess oil once it soaks in.

- If you don't have a crockpot in your tackroom, warm the neatsfoot oil by putting it in a metal pie tin and setting it out in the sun.

Step 3. Once your bridle is pliable—letting it absorb the oil overnight will help—apply a light coating of leather conditioner to restore and protect the natural shine.

To clean your saddle: Follow the same sequence of steps. When you apply the neatsfoot oil, use a circular motion similar to the one you use when you curry your horse.

■ Pay special attention to the billets and stirrup leathers of an English saddle. They take a beating every time you ride.

■ If the seat of your Western saddle is suede, cover it with plastic and masking tape to protect it. Remove both cinches. But when you clean and oil the tops of the stirrup leathers, pull the fenders down. Don't pull them *out*; they're hard to replace.

■ If the skirt, fenders, or other areas of your Western saddle have dried out over the winter, apply the hot/warm neatsfoot oil using a paintbrush. (Put down newspapers to protect the floor.) Let your saddle "set" overnight. The next day, check the leather for pliability. If it needs more help, heat additional neatsfoot oil and give it another light coat. That ought to do it. Once the leather has softened, apply a conditioner.

Insect control: Throughout most of the country, fly season begins in early spring and ends with the first hard frost. Order fly predators as soon as you see the pesky kind.

Once your horse's fly mask rips, it won't keep flies off his face. Need another reason to replace it with a new one? Horses can easily scratch their ear with a hind foot; you don't want your horse to snag his shoe in his fly mask.

■ Buy your horse a new fly mask; they seldom last longer than one season.

■ If biting flies are a problem, spray those parts of your horse's body they seem to like. Some flies go for your horse's lower legs and leave dozens of tiny, bleeding bites that immediately scab over and are no larger than the period at the end of this sentence.

■ Most people use fly spray on their horse every day; others use it only when they ride. Check the directions. Some sprays don't have to be applied as often as others.

■ Instead of spraying insect repellent directly on your horse's face, spray a cloth and rub his face with it. If you're going to ride, stuff the cloth in your pocket so you can reapply the repellent during your ride.

Colic prevention: If you have good, grassy spring pasture, start turning your horse out to graze, but limit the amount of time you keep him there. Gradually, over the course of a week, leave him out longer and longer.

Spring grass is often called water grass for good reason. Your horse might get fat on it, but it's a temporary "hay belly."

Summer Chores

Cleaning your gelding's sheath: How do you know whether he needs it cleaned? I don't usually answer a question by asking one, but have you ever wondered about that strange sound you hear, especially at the trot, that sounds like a combination of a bouncing basketball and a fish sloshing around in your gelding's belly? That's the sound of your horse's penis rubbing against a dirty sheath. Since the sheath is like a pocket, dirt, shavings, and other foreign matter can get trapped there along with a black, waxy secretion called smegma. A buildup can cause more than funny noises; it can cause infections.

- Using warm water and a mild soap (Palmolive Antibacterial would be a good choice), gently rub a cloth or rag over your horse's belly, starting at the girth area. Your horse should be calm—don't choose a day when it's windy or he's nervous or excited.
- Move your soapy cloth over his sheath. If he's relaxed, he'll let you. Then slide your hand and the cloth inside his sheath and gently tug on his penis until it extends. He'll allow you to do this if he's sure you won't hurt him. Otherwise he would never have let you get this far.
- Soap his penis gently and thoroughly to remove the black flakes of smegma, and keep rinsing out your cloth. When the rinse water stays clean, you're done.

Cleaning your mare's genitals: Mares excrete smegma around their teats. The first time the weather's warm enough, lather a wet cloth with warm water and soap and clean her underbelly. When you reach her teats, you'll probably see black, rubbery flakes on your cloth. That's smegma—rinse it off. Continue to gently move your soapy cloth over the area until no more black flakes rub off. Rinse thoroughly and move slowly and confidently and carefully. For most mares this area is very sensitive, and some of them have to get used to the idea that you want to clean them there. Others cow-kick first, then ask questions.

Colic alert: If you garden, don't be tempted to feed your horse lawn trimmings.

Fall Chores

- Fall chores involve getting your horse ready for winter. If you blanket him, and many owners do not, take his clean blanket out of storage and make sure it still fits him by putting it on him and running your hand under it, particularly the front. Your hand should slide easily, with no tight areas (over his withers and in front of his shoulders in particular). No blanket should restrict your horse's shoulder or tail movement.
- Some owners prefer to keep a flighty, high-strung horse on the thin side over the summer, when they do most of their riding. If I just described your horse, it's time to feed him more hay. A horse with an acceptable level of body fat on him (see chapter 8) will weather a long, cold winter much more easily than a thin horse, blanketed or not.
- Make sure your barn and/or tackroom and other outbuildings are ready for winter too. Does your hay shed need a new roof, but you kept postponing it because some other repair always took priority? Replace it *now*, before six inches of snow settle on it. To keep rodents from wintering in your tackroom, make the necessary repairs or stop by the local animal shelter and adopt a couple of kittens.
- Now is the time to toss that two-year-old fly spray that was barely doing its job over the summer. Throw out everything you haven't used for the past twelve months.

Unscheduled Events

You go out one morning to feed only to discover that your horse's automatic drinker has clogged up, or that the family member who fed last night forgot to fill your horse's water bucket. The end result is the same—your horse has been without water all night, and has possibly been without water since dinner yesterday. Do you fill a bucket and let him drink as much as he wants, as fast as he wants to?

No, not even if the water is tepid.

■ Water him the same way you would water a sweaty, thirsty, dehydrated horse—that is, water him gradually and walk him. Fill one bucket with tepid water and a second with tepid water plus electrolytes. Allow him to drink the same three-gallons worth of whichever bucket he chooses, pull his head out, and walk him for five minutes. Give him more water and walk him again—ten seconds worth of water for every five minutes of walking until he stops trying to drag you over to the buckets every time you pass them. At that point you can let him drink his fill before you return him to his corral and figure out what's wrong with his drinker.

■ How long the process takes depends on several factors: how long he's been without water, if he first ran out during the day or at night, and the outside temperature.

■ If your horse has only been without water for a couple of hours—say he had water when you fed him breakfast on Saturday, but by the time you fed him lunch the drinker was empty—do you still have to do the whole electrolyte walking/watering routine? No, unless your horse repeatedly nuzzles the broken drinker. Under most circumstances, your horse probably doesn't *know* he's been without water. Use the pinch test. If he's dehydrated, you have to go through the electrolyte walking/watering routine. If he's not, fill a bucket with water and let him drink his fill.

Winter Chores

Some owners seem to think they can stop grooming their horse over the winter. If you ride him, groom him. Yes, it takes longer for a horse's winter coat to dry than his summer coat. For that reason alone winter isn't a good time to bathe your horse or hose his legs.

Cold-weather grooming: Here's what I do when I come back from a ride if the outside temperature is above forty degrees. First I loosen the girth. But I leave the saddle on the horse's back so he stays warm and his blood circulates freely until he's completely dry between the front legs.

■ Next I remove the bridle. Using a *damp* cloth, I wipe the horse's face, particularly where it came in contact with the bridle. Most horses sweat profusely around their ears, so I'm careful to rub the hair that was under the crownpiece.

■ I rub his face dry with a clean, dry towel.

- After rinsing my cloth and wringing out as much water as I can, I rub any sweaty areas on the horse's body; for most horses, that means their brisket, between their hind legs, and under their tail.

- I toss the dirty water and refill my bucket. After removing the saddle and pad, I use a clean damp cloth to rub the sweat marks out of the horse's sides, particularly the girth area. I towel the area dry and rub the entire horse all over.

- Then I brush his tail and mane.

- I pick out his feet and, if necessary, apply hoof dressing or anti-thrush medication.

- I like to end each grooming with a brisk rubdown with the cactus-cloth mitt; other owners prefer to brush their horse. Either method helps evaporate any remaining moisture, and separates and fluffs up the hair to provide better insulation against the cold. By now the horse is completely dry, and I return him to his corral or pasture.

- Follow this procedure even if your horse lives inside in a stall.

- Some owners who ride during winter don't use water at all. Instead they use rubbing alcohol, and spray it directly on the horse. The alcohol dries sweat faster than water does. Be careful about spraying it on your horse's face and ears. Spray some on a clean cloth and rub him dry, instead.

Below freezing-weather grooming: If you like to ride when it's this cold, you probably already know what to do when you're finished. Here are a few tips.

- Most owners remove their horse's saddle and bridle immediately, usually in a sheltered indoor area, and rub the horse down with thick, clean, dry towels to remove as much sweat as possible.

- Then they wrap the horse in a cooler from poll to tail. If the cooler doesn't have ties, they slide the top portion under the crownpiece of his halter. The best coolers are wool or wool blends that wick moisture from a sweaty coat; it reforms on the outside of the cooler.

- If the cooler gets wet on the outside but the horse isn't dry (owners slip their hand under the cooler and feel his coat), they replace the cooler with another one.

- They clean the horse's feet and brush his mane and tail.

- While they wait for the horse to dry completely, some owners like to feed—usually a pelleted, grain-based feed supplement—and water their horse. The act of digesting food generates warmth, as you probably know from your own experience.

- When the horse's coat is completely dry, they remove the cooler, brush or curry him or go over him with a curry mitt, and turn him out or return him to his stall.

THE THIRD GREAT DEBATE: BLANKETING YOUR HORSE

You may have noticed that in neither method of cold-weather grooming did I mention the word *blanket*. That was deliberate. In my opinion, as well as the opinion of many trainers and veterinarians, most healthy horses don't need blanketing.

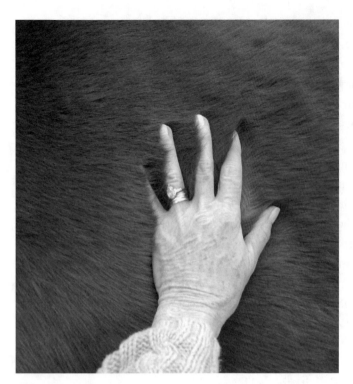

Although winter hair growth is triggered by the amount of daylight (nights get longer, days get shorter), horses in very cold climates tend to be woollier than horses living in mild climates.

Some definitions: There are four main types of blankets.

- *Sheets* tend to be lightweight and are designed to be used in summer weather, particularly to deter flies. Only horses kept in stalls need sheets.
- As the weather turns cool, some owners replace a summer sheet with a heavier, more durable *stable blanket.* As the name indicates, these blankets aren't for outdoor horses either—particularly horses pastured with herd mates.
- *Turnout blankets* were designed for horses who live outdoors, or horses who wear blankets while in their stall but need sturdier protection when turned out. Most of the time these blankets too are unnecessary.
- A *cooler* is a rectangular blanket used to cool a horse out after strenuous work. While the horse is hand-walked, the cooler, which covers the horse from ears to tail (some are hock length) and draws the sweat away from the horse's coat. Coolers have just this one use; don't use them as stable blankets. There's no foolproof way to fasten them.

Indoor horses: Show horses spend the winter in blankets because they're body-clipped, and they're body-clipped because they're worked every day. Since you don't own a show horse, you have no reason to clip *or* blanket him.

- Some stalled horses, usually at the whim of their owners, wear a fly sheet in summer and a stable blanket in the winter. Because these horses are kept blanketed, they rarely grow a heavy winter coat. Researchers believe that actual exposure to the cold determines the coat's thickness.

    My colleague Gail Lofdahl, who grew up in Minnesota, remembers riding horses with "six-inch-deep winter coats; riding them was like riding on a bearskin rug." These horses spent the day outside but were brought in at night, not blanketed.
- If you do blanket your indoor horse, keep a spare on hand. If the blanket you removed before you rode is so dirty you don't want to put it back on, use the spare.
- Don't leave a horse who has grown little or no winter coat unblanketed overnight, especially if the temperature is below forty degrees. He's not accustomed to it, and by tomorrow you're likely to have a sick horse.
- Healthy horses stabled indoors who carry some body fat, particularly those who don't wear a sheet in summer, rarely need a blanket in winter. Their winter coat— and extra hay—provides them with all the protection they need.
- Some show-horse owners take their horses out of training at the end of the show season and turn them out "to be horses." Are the horses clipped? No. Are they blan-

keted? Rarely, unless they're elderly or on the thin side. Sometimes all the horses are brought indoors at night, particularly if the weather turns nasty.

Horses outside in a corral: If your horse lives outside in a pipe corral, the temperature shouldn't get much colder than the temperature inside your barn, as long as the barn's properly ventilated. The only difference is that the indoor horse is protected from extremes of wind, rain, and snow. But even horses kept in a corral seldom need a blanket. They grow their own when they need one, and when the weather warms up again, they shed it.

- Do not clip an outdoor horse. If you clip him, blanket him.
- The other exceptions are elderly horses, thin horses (but yours shouldn't be, with all the feed supplements available), and those with health problems. As long as the weather is good—the sun's out and the temperature isn't below freezing—turn these horses out during the day and bring them inside at night. Unless they refuse to grow a winter coat and/or they shiver, these horses seldom need blankets. If the bad weather continues without let up for days (temperatures below freezing, wind, and any form of moisture are the worst combination), keep the horses inside. If that's not possible—you don't have a barn—buy your shivering horse a water-and-wind resistant blanket guaranteed to *breathe*.

Pastured horses: Healthy outdoor horses who grow a good, thick winter coat do very well in below zero temperatures. Even in a blizzard, as long as the horses are sheltered from the wind by trees or the side of a hill, they'll turn tail to the storm and wait it out. Many East-coast owners build their outdoor horse a three-sided run-in shelter. Some horses will use it, others will not.

- If your pasture doesn't have trees, plant some to form a natural windbreak. Depending on your climate zone, you should be able to find trees that are fast growers—up to eight feet a year, in some cases. By the third year you'll have your windbreak. If the trees are deciduous and lose their leaves in the fall, plant them close together. If they're evergreens, leave room for them to spread out as they mature.
- No pastured horse should be kept in a stable blanket. There are too many ways he can snag, it, rip it, or pull it completely upside down. If he has herdmates, the horses are always nipping and biting at each other. The only reason to put a turnout blanket on a pastured horse is if he's thin, sick, or very wet.
- As long as the horse is healthy and not shivering, don't put a *turnout* blanket on your pastured horse either.
- The bigger your pasture is, the more opportunity your horse has to decide for himself where to hang out when the wind blows or the rain comes down in sheets.

Doing right by your horse: Most owners blanket their horse because that's what other horse owners do. Since they don't want to be seen as uncaring, they buy their horse a blanket too—even though he doesn't need one.

■ How do you know whether your horse needs a blanket? If your horse is already wearing a stable blanket, slip your hand under it. His coat should feel dry and smooth. If he's sweating, he's overheated. Either remove the blanket or replace it with a lighter one.

■ If your senior horse doesn't grow a winter coat for some reason—sometimes elderly horses, particularly if they're hot-blooded, won't grow much of one—feed him more hay; if you haven't started him on a senior feed, do so now, and buy him a traditional tan and blue-plaid horse blanket. They're expensive but worth it. Because they're contoured to hug your horse's body, they rarely slip. In addition, they're made out of a tightly woven fabric that keeps your horse warm while it wicks away moisture from his skin—in case he works up a sweat about something.

■ How about a senior horse who lives outside? He *should* be in a corral, where you can keep an eye on him, and not wandering around in a pasture. Even in a corral you're faced with the problem of protecting him from the elements. This horse is a candidate for a plaid blanket, or a turnout blanket that resists rain but is made out of a breatheable fabric. Check under the blanket periodically; a turnout blanket may be too warm for him.

■ Under no circumstances should you buy a completely rainproof blanket. If you've ever worn a rainproof raincoat, you know how uncomfortable they can be if you sweat, because the material doesn't breathe. In other words, it can't wick away the heat and moisture trapped beneath it.

How to measure your horse for a blanket: Few horses will stand still for tape measures. Use your leadrope, instead. Start at the center of your horse's chest and walk back to the farthest point of his haunches. Measure him again. If you get the same measurement both times, lay the leadrope against a measuring tape.

■ Horse blankets are sold in two-inch increments. For example, if you measure your horse twice and come up with seventy-one inches both times, round the number *up* and buy him a seventy-two-inch blanket.

All blankets except coolers come with an adjustable chest strap or two, and two belly straps, also adjustable, that cross under your horse's stomach. Fasten the belly straps so there's space visible between your horse's coat and the straps. If you leave more space, he can get a hoof through it too easily. If you tighten them too much your horse will think they're bucking straps like the ones rodeo broncs wear and will act accordingly. Most stable and turnout blankets have additional fastenings that criss-cross between the horse's hind legs and help to secure the back end of the blanket.

First-timers: If you've never blanketed a horse before, or are worried about how your horse might react, roll up the blanket the way you would a beach towel, back to front, and approach your horse with it while he's in the arena. Hold his leadrope in one hand with the blanket over your other arm. He'll probably want to sniff it. After he finishes his inspection, slide the roll slowly over his withers. Once the blanket is in place, unroll it over his back. Check to make sure there's an equal amount of blanket on both sides. Fasten the chest straps first, then the belly straps. Save the straps between his hind legs for another day.

Walk your horse on the leadrope so he knows what the blanket feels like when he moves. Once he's become accustomed to it, unfasten his halter and use your longe whip to longe him at liberty a minute or two.

One more successful introduction.

CHAPTER 18

SHOWING OFF

Your dream of keeping your own horse in your own backyard has come true. Taking care of him isn't as hard as you thought. You *enjoy* feeding, grooming, and exercising him, medicating him when necessary, and loving him. Your spouse doesn't share your passion, but he (he's usually a "he") is smart enough to feed your horse when you can't and can even recite your vet's phone number by heart. After watching your horse gallop up to the fence and whinny the instant you open the back door, your husband teases you that it's cupboard love: of course your horse loves you; you feed him. You retort by asking him if that's why he loves you. Then you go for a trail ride.

For many backyard owners, that's as far as it goes. They have real lives—usually involving paychecks—and their horse is their relaxation and reward.

Other people find themselves being drawn into the local horse community. A neighbor talks you into attending a meeting of Equestrian Trails, Inc. (ETI) to discuss how to keep motorized vehicles off the fast-disappearing trails in your area. The next thing you know you just volunteered to organize the food concession for their upcoming horse show.

Or your teen—who has dyed his purple hair shoe-polish brown, lost the nose ring, and is growing a mustache—announces at dinner that he doesn't want to start his own band anymore. You blink and take in the fact that he's wearing jeans that fit. No more gang-member pants that allow any passerby to read who manufactured his undershorts. When you ask what he *does* want, he says he thinks roping is pretty cool and could he, like, have a *reata* for

Christmas? You exchange looks with your husband. Maybe this adolescent from hell hurtling towards adulthood is really your flesh and blood after all.

Or maybe *you* want the *reata*.

Sooner or later, the horse show bug bites most owners. For some it remains a lifelong passion. Other owners go to one or two shows, shrug their shoulders, and never enter a show ring again. A few will compete every once in a while, as a hobby, no better or worse than any other. Just more expensive.

But even going to one or two shows requires planning. For example, how do you get your horses to the show?

THE FOURTH GREAT DEBATE: DO YOU NEED A HORSE TRAILER?

Many backyard owners get along just fine without a horse trailer. If all you want to do is head for the hills with your horse after a stressful day of work, your smartest option would be to rent a trailer if and when you need one. It's certainly your cheapest option, if you know your towing vehicle can handle the weight, know how to hitch a horse trailer correctly, and know how to haul a horse. Check Equipment Rentals in the yellow pages of your local phone book; most keep a horse trailer or two in the yard.

But before you make the decision to buy or rent, call a family get-together. You need to discuss a few things.

Pros: You need a horse trailer because:
- Somebody in your family (no names, please) has gotten hooked on horse shows.
- Having your own trailer is crucial in an emergency.

A couple of horse trailers (and the vehicles towing them) at a small local show.

Cons: You don't need a horse trailer because:

- Nobody knows how to drive one.
- They're expensive.

All are valid arguments, and I'll discuss them in reverse order.

Trailers—How Much Do They Cost?

No doubt about it, a horse trailer is expensive—and, like a Western saddle, the more extras you want, such as a built-in bunk bed, the more it's going to cost.

But first, think about how you're going to pull this trailer. Even if you decide to buy a one-horse (a trailer big enough to haul just one horse), you need a pickup or an SUV. Most passenger cars aren't heavy enough to haul a horse trailer. Do you already own a pickup? You should, because hauling your hay home from the feed store is cheaper than asking the feed store to deliver it—to say nothing of bags of shavings, feed, etc. For ease of discussion, I'll assume you own either a pickup or some other heavy-duty vehicle.

Size: Do you want a one-horse trailer or a two-horse? How about a no-frills slant-loaded stock trailer that can carry one horse or an entire herd?

Construction: Do you want a trailer made out of aluminum, fiberglass, or steel? The first is lightweight but breakable and hard to repair. It also corrodes. Fiberglass is best used in combination with other materials. Steel is heavier (which means you need a truck with some horsepower under the hood) but sturdier (which is why it's used to build cars). The best trailers usually have a steel frame and chassis with aluminum and/or fiberglass for the exterior.

Other options: Do you want a trailer that attaches to your pickup with a ball hitch and safety chains? Yes. If you own only own or two horses, forget about a gooseneck trailer. It's not worth the extra money.

- Make sure the trailer has its own brake system. In addition, a breakaway brake is a smart investment; it's a steel cable that mechanically activates your trailer brakes if the trailer pulls away from your truck. Some states *require* breakaway brakes. (When you hitch up your trailer, make sure the cable is longer than your safety chains. Otherwise you defeat the purpose of the breakaway brake.)
- Sway bars or stabilizer bars, which minimize the sideways movement of the trailer, are also useful.
- You want a trailer with a back gate that swings down to form a ramp, so your horse can walk directly into the trailer. Your only other option is a step-up, which means the horse has to climb into the trailer one foot at a time. Most horses load with much less fuss if they can walk up a ramp. Yes, a horse can slide off the side of the ramp and skin his leg up, but he can do the same thing in a step-up. In my experience, horses find walking up a slope easier and more natural than climbing stairs.

- Which direction do you want your horse to face? Many professional haulers swear that horses relax sooner in a slant-loaded trailer. They face slightly sideways, instead of straight ahead, the way they do in a regular trailer.
- If you have a tall horse—sixteen hands or over—the trailer's interior height is another consideration. Some aren't very high, and a tall horse will bump his head. You can buy your horse a padded hood, but they're a mixed blessing. They tend to make horses sweat, and in hot weather some horses will try to rub them off. If your horse succeeds, he's also succeeded in slipping his halter, since you fasten the halter *over* the hood. Now you have a loose horse in your trailer—not a good scenario.
- If you plan to show, do you want to sleep in the trailer? Some of the fancier models sport a built-in bed. Since you don't have to pay for a motel, your only remaining expenses will be entry fees, a stall fee for your horse, his feed and bedding (unless you bring your own from home), and your meals.

New versus Used

Do you have to buy a new trailer? Of course not. You can find some very good deals on used trailers if you know what you want and are willing to wait until you find it.

Usually you can tell how well the former owner maintained the trailer by its appearance—the paint's not old and faded, the trailer itself has no dings or dents, the tires are new, the tail and brake lights work, and you don't see rust spots. Check the hinges on the rear door; it should open smoothly and without squealing. Check all the other hinges. Double-check the flooring. Along with a sturdy new ball hitch and safety chains, the floor of the trailer is your most important consideration because that's all there is between your horse and the highway.

Before You Decide

Look at a lot of trailers, new and used. Compare prices and warranties. Decide which extras you want and which ones you can live without. Narrow the field down to a few makes and models and find out how much each one weighs. Then go home and read the fine print of the owner's manual of your pickup to see if it has enough under the hood to pull the trailer *and* the weight of a thousand-pound horse or two.

If you decide on a used trailer, tell the owner you'd like to take it to a mechanic and have it checked out. Then do it.

How to Haul a Horse

As long as you can drive a car, you can drive a pickup with a horse trailer hitched to it.

Here are a few tips.

What's your driving style? Buy a twenty-four-pack of any popular canned soft drink, sometimes called a suitcase. Put it in the bed of your pickup, up front. If you haven't bought a pickup yet, put it in the trunk of your car and make sure it's the only thing in there. Turn the air conditioning and the radio off.

You're at a stop. Do you punch the gas the second the traffic light turns green? If you didn't already know that about yourself, you'll know it when that twenty-four-pack slams from the front of your pickup, where you put it, into the tailgate.

Do you hit the brakes at the very last second? Listen as the twenty-four-pack skids from the tailgate towards the window behind your seat.

Do you race through turns? Listen for the sound of shifting soft drinks—and feel what happens to your truck when the load shifts.

Most soft drink cans weigh twelve ounces. A twenty-four-pack weighs approximately eighteen pounds. Imagine driving with fifty-six of these suitcases behind you, and add that number to the weight of the trailer itself. That's what hauling a thousand-pound horse feels like.

■ Once you know your weaknesses, work at not hearing those cans slide. Ease through intersections when the light turns green, and pick up speed gradually. When you approach an intersection, slow down in case the light turns red and you have to stop. When you're hauling horses, you have to stop both the truck and the trailer, which—if you're going even slightly downhill—is pushing *against* your truck. Any time you brake, do it gradually and steadily to give your "suitcase" time to brace himself. Make your turns slow and wide—you don't want to hear those cans move.

■ When you succeed, hitch an empty two-horse to your truck and ride around town again. First, back your truck up to the tongue of the trailer. Until you gain experience, this is a two-person job, with the other person—preferably an experienced horse hauler—standing by the trailer using hand gestures to indicate whether you should keep backing, turn right, or stop. Your buddy will be particularly helpful the first time you try to back up with the trailer hitched behind you.

■ The first time you actually haul a horse, having a helper is a must. A confined horse, even one snugly haltered, can still move around. If you bought a two-horse and opened the partition so your horse can balance himself around turns (that's what most people do because it's more comfortable for the horse), expect to feel it in your steering wheel every time he shifts his weight. If you don't know how to compensate for that, the helper riding shotgun can talk you through it.

Getting Your Horse in the Trailer

One reason to buy a registered horse of any breed is that he's probably been handled since infancy, particularly if you bought him from a breeder. Most breeders show their horses because if they win a lot, it's good advertising. Many shows have halter or in-hand classes, which involve leading and posing the horse but not riding him. These classes are mainly (but not exclusively) for weanlings and yearlings.

For a weanling's first couple of hauls, he's usually "helped" into the trailer by two people standing behind him, their arms linked behind his tail. Sometimes the foal's dam is already loaded and will nicker at him in encouragement. Whether the foal wants to go to or not, the handlers walk him up the ramp and into the trailer. Two humans can physically outmaneuver a horse this young, and the foal's reward for cooperating is instantaneous: he's reunited with his dam. Cause and effect. Good training.

My point: If you bought a three-year-old with papers from the person who bred him, he's probably been in and out of trailers a dozen times. As a result, the owner can probably toss the leadrope over the horse's neck and he'll walk to your trailer, march up the ramp without hesitation, and head for the nearest vacant space with a hay bag.

Easy loaders: Most horses seem to *want* to trust people, even if they just met you and they haven't been loaded and unloaded since infancy. As long as you're confident and keep walking, most horses will follow you up the ramp and into the trailer the first time you try.

■ Once the horse is all the way inside, with his chest against the chest board of the trailer, your hauler buddy will snap the butt bar in place. Make sure to do that first, before you tie the horse. Otherwise he can set back, break his halter, and run backwards or fall out of the trailer. Tie his head with enough slack that he can look sideways, but not all the way around. Make sure he has a flake of hay to keep him occupied during the trip. (You brought it with you.) Back out the escape door and immediately close it—some horses will try to follow you—close up the end of the trailer, and walk around to the driver's seat. You're ready to roll.

To unload a horse: Play the movie backwards. Open up the back of the truck, leaving the butt bar in place. Untie the horse and drape the leadrope over his neck. Then, standing to one side so you can jump to the ground, unsnap the butt bar. As your horse backs down the ramp, grab his leadrope.

Uneasy loaders: If the horse has any doubts about the situation, it can be very hard to persuade him to walk into a small, enclosed place he's never seen before, especially if he thinks there might be something in there that likes horseburger. Although the method I'm about to describe takes two people, you can easily do it by yourself once you learn how. A cowboy taught me this little trick—the cowboy I bought Bachelor from. In fact it was Bachelor we were loading.

■ Using a longe line, the cowboy snapped one end to a welded metal loop in the left side of the trailer. (Nearly all trailers have them.) I held Bachelor by a leadrope snapped to his halter, both of us facing the ramp. The cowboy's next step was to walk behind Bachelor so the longe line was behind Bachelor's tail—snug enough not to slide, but not tight. When the cowboy reached the right side of the ramp, he told me to lead Bachelor up the ramp, both of us facing forward.

■ Every time Bachelor took a step, the cowboy took up the slack in the longe line. As long as the horse kept walking, the longe line didn't bother him. But when he paused, debating whether to balk or run backwards (most horses' two favorite evasions when loading) the cowboy tightened the longe line.

■ Bachelor walked up the ramp and into the trailer and snatched a mouthful of hay out of the hay bag.

- This technique works because the pressure of the longe line against the horse's rump is usually enough to stop him from backing. (The butt bar works on the same principle.)

Friendly persuasion: Some horses actively balk at loading. There are a couple of ways to encourage him to walk inside a trailer and think it was his idea. If you have the acreage, drive a horse trailer with hay in it into the pasture and leave the trailer there overnight. Remove all the other horses, and if you unhitch the trailer, put blocks under all four corners so it won't tip when the horse steps into it. The next morning, carry in more hay. Within a couple of days your balky horse will be walking in and out of the trailer the way you walk from one room of your house to another.

If you have the time but not the acreage: Many owners swear by this method, although you do have to get the horse in the trailer first. It works best if you do it around feeding time.

- After the person helping you has attached the butt bar, stay in the trailer with your horse for about ten minutes, praising and petting him while he eats his reward. Then unsnap the butt bar, back the horse out of the trailer, and immediately load him again. He'll probably go willingly because he's still hungry. Feed him, praise him, and repeat one more time. Then lead him to his corral or pasture, remove his halter, and turn him out with the rest of dinner.
- Because you rewarded him at all the right times and ended the lesson on a positive note, you'll probably be able to lead him right up the ramp the following day—also around feeding time. Unload him, reload him, and feed him. Repeat. Load and unload him every day, right before feeding time, for the next three or four days. After that, you should be able to toss the leadrope over his neck and he'll walk himself up the ramp.
- Never turn to face a horse you're trying to load. Without intending to, you're confronting the horse—your body English tells him to stay away from you. If you pull on the leadrope, you're reinforcing his fear that there really *is* something to be afraid of inside that trailer, and he'll pull back. End result—a scared horse and a frustrated, frazzled owner wishing he (or she) had a whip—maybe even a new horse.

Some last-minute safety tips: Most people who trailer horses do it for years without a mishap. But if the weather's bad—it's raining so hard you can hardly see, or there's ice on the road—be extra careful, especially when you stop or start. Some people are reluctant to drive cars, let alone horse trailers, under those conditions.

- Even though the odds are against it, it is possible to jackknife your trailer. If you feel yourself losing control, take your foot off the accelerator. Do not step on the pickup's brakes. Instead, gradually apply the *trailer* brakes. Your trailer will straighten out.

■ Whenever you haul a horse by yourself, make sure to carry your cell phone and flares or other emergency markers, especially if you drive at night. Should something go wrong, pull off the road as far as possible and stop. Use your cell phone to call for help, set up your flares, and climb back in the truck until help arrives. Never leave your horse unattended, and *never* unhitch the trailer from the truck while the horse is in it.

EMERGENCIES

Back to your to-buy-or-not-to-buy decision. Many owners who never show and don't care about organized trail rides, endurance riding, or any other form of competition will buy a horse trailer anyway, and practice loading their horse and taking him for a ride now and then.

Why? If your horse turns up lame one day and your vet wants him at the clinic to run some tests, you can drive the horse there yourself. But if you have a medical emergency and your horse needs help *now*, call before you load up your horse. Your vet may prefer to come to you.

Like all horse people, John and I live with the constant threat of natural disasters—wildfires, in our case. Other areas of the country are vulnerable to floods, tornados, and hurricanes. Some owners buy a horse trailer for this one reason: in case they have to leave home in a hurry.

My recommendation: Even if you own only one horse, buy a two-horse trailer. It won't cost *that* much more, and you might want to buy your friend a buddy one day. A new two-horse trailer costs from $4,000–$12,000, but you should be able to find a good, sturdy used one for $1,000 or less.

Another reason to buy your own trailer: in an emergency like floods, for example, law enforcement officials might tell you to evacuate. If you have a two-horse, you can drive your own horse to safety as well as the pony that belongs to your neighbor's eight-year-old daughter—a shaggy, Roman-nosed runt she loves more than life itself.

WARNING: SHOWING HORSES CAN BE ADDICTIVE

If you're like most horse lovers, you've probably been to a few shows. You know the heart-pounding adrenaline rush they can generate. If you've ever felt an urge, even a tickle, to be in that ring yourself, on *your* horse, competing for that blue ribbon—give it a try. All you have to lose is your entry fee.

People who ride Western also find reining competitions fun, or rodeo events like roping or barrel racing. Nearly everything I say in this section about showing horses also applies to these events. Other Western riders show in classes for their particular breed, and the classes are the same ones found in English classes—pleasure and equitation, leadline classes, and so on—although Western horses and English horses don't compete in the same ring together.

Think Small, Start Local

Local shows are much more informal than the big, A-rated, United States Equestrian Federation-sanctioned shows—and often a lot more fun. And since "local" is where you live, you'll have a chance to meet other horse owners with similar interests.

Some shows are put on by an individual barn or riding stable. If you see a show or gymkhana advertised, call and find out about it. Many welcome both English and Western riders. Others are either/or. Make sure you're eligible to show—many one-day shows are strictly for kids—and whether you have to belong to the organization that's sponsoring the show. Some insist that you do; others aren't as picky. Earlier, I mentioned ETI, a California grass-roots save-our-trails organization that recently went national; they don't care if you're a member or not.

Gymkhanas: These are usually for kids (including teens—even teens with dyed purple hair), and most classes, especially for young children, are games on horseback. The more competitive gymkhanas use a point system that encourages riders to show throughout the season. At the end of the year, awards are given to the high-point winners. One gymkhana in my area is dedicated to Western pattern riding, with events like pole bending, the keyhole, quadrangle, cloverleaf, and barrel racing.

But I've been to gymkhanas put on by local riding stables that welcomed all riders, regardless of seat affiliation or age. If you've ever watched adults compete in events like musical squares, relay races, and egg and spoon races, it sometimes seems as though they're having more fun than the kids.

The leaky roof circuit: These one-day shows, usually held on a Saturday, are mini-versions of the week-long A-rated shows, except they don't offer as many classes. Horse people often refer to them as *showing out of your trailer* because that's exactly what happens. Your

One of the timed events at a gymkhana. The horse is wearing a romal.

The communal hitching rail at a local show. The communal drinking trough is on the right.

Emily Travis, Christina Swan, and Brooke Hasselbach riding home from the gymkhana. Why bother with a trailer when you can ride to the show?

Showing out of your trailer.

trailer turns into a tackroom for your horse (who's usually tied to the trailer resting his weight on three legs and looking bored) and dressing room for you.

Sponsoring organizations: Most groups that put on shows for kids also do a very good job of educating them about all aspects of horse care, not just riding. For contact information, see Appendix II.

- United States Pony Club membership is open to children of both sexes who ride hunt seat and dressage and is patterned after the original Pony Club in Great Britain. The Pony Club UK (the one in Britain) has over 137,000 members in sixteen countries and is the largest association of riders in the world. The focus is on jumping, dressage, and three-day eventing.

A 4-H showmanship class. One of the many types of in-hand classes.

- 4-H. Although best known for teaching youngsters how to raise and exhibit livestock—steers, goats, sheep, swine, etc.—4-H also has a Horse Project division open to both English and Western riders. The focus is on promoting horsemanship and good horse management. Local groups also sponsor shows.

- Equestrian Trails, Inc., a group I mentioned earlier, is a non-profit organization for children and adults. Dedicated to acquiring new trails and preserving existing ones, ETI also promotes good horsemanship and participates in legislation pertaining to horses. Open to riders of any seat, this organization has hundreds of local "corrals" that put on a variety of events including shows,

A chestnut mare with a flaxen mane and her impeccably-dressed young rider.

gymkhanas, classes for mules and donkeys, driving classes, trail rides, and overnight camping.

■ To find similar groups in your area, ask your horse-owning friends.

Inside the Show Ring

Suppose you decide to enter your horse at a one-day show sponsored by a local organization and held at a member's barn. See if you can talk a friend into going with you. Four hands are usually better than two, especially if this is your show-ring debut. If it is, be aware that there are posted rules and unposted (and unspoken) rules. The posted ones say things like, "Dogs Must Be Leashed," and "No Stallions." Find out about them beforehand by contacting the show manager.

Here are some of the unspoken rules.

Arrive early: You want your horse to get used to the sights and sounds of a show. Also, you can pick a good parking spot—under a tree during a summer show is pleasant. (Keep the position of the sun in mind, so you'll still be shaded in the afternoon.) If you didn't longe your horse before you left home, and there's a designated warmup ring on the premises, longe him and/or ride him now. Then ride him all over the grounds. He'll probably spook at things—picnic tables shaded by awnings, a noisy old truck pulling a rattletrap old trailer—but that's the whole idea. By the time your class is scheduled to enter the ring, you want him too comfortable, or too tired, to spook at anything.

Arriving early and walking your horse around the showgrounds is a great way to introduce him to other horses, moving cars, blowing candy wrappers, etc.

No fast moves: At a show, there's no need for frantic, hasty movements. Keep your voice down and move slowly, especially when you're close to other horses. Deal with pre-show jitters by practicing stress-management techniques at home—deep breathing, visualizing your class hoofbeat by hoofbeat, whatever works. Don't yell at your horse, even if he does something stupid. Don't yell at your friend, either.

Safety first: Approach a strange horse slowly from his near side. If he's green or new to showing, he might not expect to see you on his off-side. If you absolutely must pet him, ask the rider for permission. You don't know anything about this horse—he could be headshy, he could bite, he could strike at you. If the rider is agreeable, use your whole hand to stroke the horse's neck. *Don't* pat his nose.

Once your own horse is saddled and bridled, don't walk him by leaving the reins over his neck as though you were still in the saddle. Slide them over his head and grasp them under his chin as though you were leading him with a halter and leadrope. You have more control this way. If you didn't slide the reins over his head and he shies at something, you probably just lost him—you didn't have enough rein to hold onto. A loose horse is dangerous, particularly an inexperienced one. He's frightened and not watching where he's going. Your safest bet is to fasten a halter over his bridle (criss-cross the reins through the throatlatch, the way I taught you to in chapter 16) and snap a leadrope to his halter.

Listen to the announcer: Keep track of what class is in the ring. If it's the one immediately before yours, be ready to enter as soon as the riders exit through the out-gate and the runner, or ring steward, tells you to. Here's where a friend really comes in handy. After making sure you're in the saddle, he or she can flick the dust off your boots and hiss, "Keep your heels down!" as you ride through the in-gate.

As you enter: Once you're through the gate, turn right. Follow the rail so it's next to your right elbow and you and your horse are traveling counterclockwise. This is the *first direction*, and the judge will usually ask for whatever she (or he) wants you to do—walk, trot, canter—going the first direction, then ask you to reverse and go clockwise, the second direction.

In most classes, you reverse by turning your horse to the inside, so he faces the center of the ring. Don't reverse into the rail.

Showing has a lot in common with driving on a highway. Stay in your own lane (keep to the rail). If you want to pass the horse in front of you, do it on the inside. Don't try to squeeze between the horse and the rail.

If your horse won't settle down: If he spooks at shadows and kicks at other horses, you should have longed him before you left home—or you should have gotten here earlier and worked him harder. Ask the judge to excuse you from the class before the other horses get riled up too (the herd thing again). If you don't, the judge will probably excuse you.

If somebody else's horse won't settle down: Slow your horse to a walk and stay away from the horse long enough for the rider to get him safely out the gate.

At the end of the class: The announcer will ask you to line up in the center of the ring. If he asks you to line up nose to tail, do so. If he doesn't, the horses usually line up shoulder to shoulder, facing the same direction. Most judges will walk the lineup, looking at each horse individually. Occasionally, especially if it's a class for younger riders, she'll offer encouragement or advice to each rider. Usually that's all she'll do, but sometimes a judge will ask each rider to back his or her horse. Make sure your horse knows how to back *straight*, without colliding with another horse.

If you win a ribbon: The runner (ring steward, or back gate-man) will usually hand it to you while the announcer tells the audience your name and the name of your horse.

If you win a *blue* ribbon, total strangers will clap and cheer, and all the time and money and effort you invested—including the trailer you're still paying off—that led up to this one moment will be worth every cent.

When your last class is over: Unsaddle and unbridle your horse, water him, rub him down, and walk him a little. Collect all your trash. Some shows have a designated manure pile or dumpster. If not, and if your horse leaves droppings behind, scoop them into your muck bucket and take them home with you.

Should *You* Host a Horse Show?

Since I don't know anything about your facilities, I can't answer that question. But I can offer a few suggestions. Before you commit yourself, discuss it with your spouse. If he or she is agreeable, schedule a meeting with your attorney. Schedule another one with your insurance agent.

Serious about Showing

Weekend shows offer bigger audiences than little one-day shows and a wider variety of classes. The entry fees are also higher, but some shows have cash paybacks in addition to the ribbons and trophies. If you walk off with enough championships, you can probably win back your entry fees and maybe even your road expenses.

What to look for: On the entry form, sometimes called the prize list, you'll see dozens of classes for people who ride hunt seat, Western, saddle seat, even lower-level dressage. You'll see driving classes. You'll see trail obstacle classes, but if your horse has a thing about blue tarps (especially if they're on the ground—they look too much like water—and he doesn't want to walk a bridge to get over one), enter a pleasure class.

Feel out of place? If you feel silly competing against kids half your age, look for "Jack Benny 39 & Over" or "rusty stirrup" classes.

Stall rentals: Many weekend shows are held at fairgrounds or other public arenas with permanent, bleacher-style seating. Often they have stalls or pipe corrals available, so you can keep your horse in one over the weekend—for a price, of course. If you want to sleep in the trailer, go ahead. But don't even think about asking your poor horse to spend two nights in it. A trailer is too small for him to move around freely or lie down. Rent him a stall.

■ If you don't want to sleep in your trailer but you do want to keep an eye on your horse, rent two stalls. Use the second one to store hay and bedding and to stow your tack. Set up a cot and/or a sleeping bag, with your cell phone, a battery-powered alarm clock, night light, and radio within easy reach. If you have electricity, you can hook up a hot plate and do your own cooking. But check with show management first—some won't allow this because of fire hazard.

Specialty Shows

Some shows are devoted specifically to what the horses and their riders *do,* regardless of breed. At a hunter/jumper show, they jump fences. At a rodeo, they rope cattle.

Other shows are breed-specific. There are associations at every level, from neighborhood to national, that put on shows for Quarter Horses, Icelandic ponies, Pintos, or Hackney horses driven in tandem pulling antique carriages.

With a good horse you can win serious money at some of these shows. To find them, contact your breed registry.

On the Road Again

When John trained horses for a living, we followed the West Coast summer show circuit. Beginning in February with the Aid to the Zoo show in Phoenix (everybody called it the A to Z show), we went to a show a month until the grand finale—the Grand National in San Francisco in late October. Packing gets very monotonous after a while. So does doing laundry.

But life on the road has its moments. John and I were on our way from the hotel to the show grounds at A to Z once when he realized he was wearing one blue sock and one brown

A young rider and her alert, attractive horse take a fence in a hunter class.

As good as it gets: the 1984 Olympics, when the U. S. jumping squad won the team gold.

Riding in the rain. John won this class too. (Photo by Jack Schatzberg)

sock. I protested that his socks wouldn't show in a photograph—he was driving a fine harness horse—but he was so confident he would win that he drove back to the motel. While I stayed in the car and fumed, he found a matching blue sock.

He won the class.

And then there was the night I watched Zsa Zsa Gabor ride her plantation Tennessee Walker, My Darling. (Plantation Walkers don't show wearing stacked heels.) Zsa Zsa, who had put on a few pounds since her movie star days, rode in a lipstick-red saddle, dressed entirely in black, without gloves—all the better to blind the audience with the paperweight-sized diamond on her finger. Since it was a championship class, the horses had to be stripped (their saddles were removed) while the judge walked the lineup and assessed their conformation. Zsa Zsa did a tummy-slide off her horse and stood demurely with her back to the judge so he could read the number on the back of her riding coat. Then, while her trainer resaddled My Darling, a groom ran into the ring carrying a stepladder. Zsa Zsa turned, marched up the ladder, and settled herself in the saddle.

She brought down the house and won her class, too.

Other Options

If showing doesn't appeal to you but you'd still like to do *something* competitive with your horse, you have plenty of options.

Endurance riding: Look into the Tevis Cup, or the Levi Strauss Ride & Tie competition. Both attract serious athletes, which means you and your horse have to be in top-notch physical shape. If you're a beginner, scale down to smaller, less demanding rides before you tackle either of these.

Or, you can use your driving skills to take your kids for a pony ride.

Driving competitions: Depending on your interest and level of expertise, you can drive one horse or a hitch of six. You can show in trail or obstacle classes, or participate in cross-country events. If your passion is restoring old carriages, you can drive in parades that let you show off your handiwork as well as your horse.

Vacations on Horseback

Maybe you don't like *any* kind of competing. Maybe you just like to ride your horse and enjoy the scenery. If that's the case, why not plan a vacation around scenery you've never seen before?

Suppose your best friend, another horse owner, lives in Oregon, but you live in upstate New York. The two of you decide to take a leave of absence from civilization and go camping on horseback. You meet in Cheyenne, Wyoming (population 53,000), each of you trailering your own horse. You spend the next two weeks in high-country heaven, experiencing nature at its finest—unencumbered by people, their trash, or their telecommunication devices.

It's also possible to vacation on horseback when you're out of the country. Suppose your spouse wants to see London and has a day-long trip to the British Museum in mind, and another at the Tate Gallery. Museums are not your thing, so you compromise. For every day you spend indoors in a museum, your spouse has to accompany you on a day-long pony trek in the moors. (Look for Holidays on Horseback listings in the back of horse magazines.)

SHOW GROOMING

In many competitions where athletic ability is more important than looks—endurance riding, for example—your horse's grooming or lack of it isn't essential. But in a show ring, grooming is everything. The blue ribbon occasionally goes not to the best horse or rider, but to the best turned-out horse with the cleanest tack, and the neatest, best-dressed, I'm-trying-as-hard-as-I-can rider. Judging a horse show is very subjective, particularly in any class where quality counts as much as ability—especially big classes. Even the judge may not know why she awarded the blue ribbon to this horse instead of that one. But a beautifully groomed horse wearing spanking clean tack with a neat, well-dressed rider (you) all tell the judge that you take showing seriously enough to spend the time to present yourself and your horse at your best.

One thing most judges agree on: a horse's entrance into the ring is what initially catches their eye; how he looks, his "brilliance." That first impression stays with them until the end of the class. Most of a performance horse's brilliance is the result of careful training, but a handsome, glossy, buffed-up coat definitely plays a part.

Here are some tips from professional show-horse grooms for how to catch the judge's eye the second you enter the show ring.

Manes and Tails

Show horses, English and Western, traditionally wear their manes on the right side of their neck. If your horse is like most horses, half his mane falls one way, a third falls the opposite way, and he rubbed the rest out on the fence.

To train a mane: Brush it thoroughly and wet it. While it's still wet, pull all of it to the right and braid the parts that don't want to stay there. After two or three days, untie the braids and brush the horse's mane. Whenever it shows signs of reverting, rewet and rebraid.

- The smaller the braid, the kinkier your horse's mane will be.
- The longer his mane is, the easier it will be to train (gravity works in your favor).

If your horse's mane is long and snarled, use your fingers to unsnarl it, and try not to break the hairs. It took a long time to grow a mane that long, and it will take a long time to regrow any hair you pull out.

Once your horse's mane will lie flat, don't braid it wet unless you're showing the next day and want it to have ripples.

Picking a horse's tail out, hair by hair. (Photo by Gina Cresse)

A show hunter with his mane and forelock braided. (Drawing by Gina Cresse)

Tails, you win: The best way to groom your horse's tail is to brush it thoroughly to remove the snarls, shampoo it, rinse it, then rinse it again with two cups of vinegar diluted in a bucket of water to remove all the soap scum. When his tail is so clean it squeaks, add some human hair conditioner. Rub it in thoroughly and rinse again. As his tail dries, pick the dry stands apart hair by hair. It's boring work, but it will add volume to your horse's tail. As any judge will tell you, a long, full tail looks better than a short, scruffy one.

Western classes: In these classes you show your horse with a full mane and tail. For a neater appearance, clip your horse's bridle path. Lately I've seen tails—and not only in Western classes—that have been braided wet in sections (other sections are straight), then brushed out before the show. The result is an eye-catching rippled tail that matches your horse's rippled mane.

Don't braid your horse's wet tail and leave it that way over the winter—the braids can rot and the hair will fall out. If you braid his tail to keep it from snarling, braid it *dry* and take it apart and inspect it every so often.

Hunter/jumper and dressage classes: In these classes your horse's mane must be short, and often both his mane and tail must be braided and tied. If you don't know how, ask someone to show you, or hire a freelance braider at the show.

Saddle seat classes: In these classes you show your three-gaited (walk, trot, canter) American Saddlebred with a roached mane, but you show your five-gaited Saddlebred—and most Morgans, Arabians, Andalusians, etc.—with a full mane and tail. The bridle path is usually longer than the one on Western horses, to accentuate your horse's refined throat-latch.

How to Clip Your Horse

To look his best—to show off his bone structure and way of going—your horse should be clipped. Electric clippers do a better job than battery-powered ones. Because they won't quit on you unexpectedly, they're also more reliable. But some horses are afraid of the cord, and many shows have portable stalls that lack electrical outlets.

Clip here: Clip your horse's bridle path and the long hairs around his muzzle and under his jaw. The easiest way to remove the long hairs around his eyes is to pull them out by hand, one at a time, with a quick jerk.

Clip your horse's ears by folding both ends over as though you were bending a playing card, and trim only the edges. Unless you keep him in a stall year-round with a fly hood that has little white cotton ear-protectors on his head, your horse needs the hairs inside his ear to keep out dust and insects.

Trim the hair around his coronary band and neaten up his fetlocks front and back. On his front legs, trim the long hairs along the tendon that runs from the backs of his knees to his fetlocks.

The bridle path, that part of the horse's mane where the crown-piece of the bridle fits, is trimmed on show horses for a neater appearance. (Photo by Gina Cresse)

■ If your horse has white on his legs, clip the hair as high as the markings go, both on his forelegs and hind legs. And do this three or four days before the show, at home, or your horse will look as though he's wearing long pink stockings. Just before you enter the ring, rub baby powder or dry cornstarch into the white markings.

Other owners like to smear a cornstarch and water paste on the horse's legs the night before. If the horse rolls or urinates and splashes his legs, the cornstarch gets dirty. At the show the next morning, they wash the dirty cornstarch out and towel his legs dry. Then they repowder him before he enters the ring.

Clip your horse's chin whiskers and the long hairs under his jaws. (Photo by Gina Cresse)

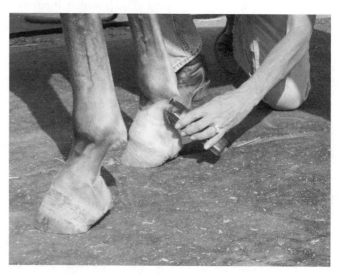

Use clippers to neaten up his fetlock area. (Photo by Gina Cresse)

How to Bathe Your Horse

Give your horse the full treatment, a soap and water bath *at home* at least a day before you leave for the show, to give the natural oils in his coat time to come back (soap removes them). Use a shampoo formulated especially for horses and follow the directions. Rinse his coat with vinegar and water to get rid of the soap; dried soap itches.

Once your horse is dry, groom him scrupulously—and make sure your grooming tools are as clean as he is. The easiest way to do that is by bathing them along with him. Before you put him away, blanket him. You know from experience what he's going to do the instant you turn him loose.

When you groom him at the show, rinse your stiff body brush in water every half-dozen swipes to wipe any remaining dust particles out of his coat. Allow yourself enough time to rub him dry before you saddle up. Then go over him with a soft-bristled brush for added shine, and spray him with one of those products guaranteed to add even more shine without attracting dirt. Don't spray your horse's back with it because the saddle will slip. If you save this step for after you saddle him, cover your saddle. If you don't, *you'll* slip.

What to Wear

Your tack must be spotless—which means a lot of drudge work, also done before you leave home (see Chapter 17).

The correct tack: If you normally ride your horse using a running martingale, for example, or use a breastplate on your Western horse, make sure they're allowed. If they're not, the judge will excuse you. The class requirements—including what tack is expected or prohibited—should be spelled out in the prize list. If you show on a regular basis, you'll usually get a prize list/entry form in the mail. If you're new to showing, call the horse show manager and ask him (or her) to send you one.

The correct dress: Make sure *you* know what to wear. Most one-day and weekend shows are pretty relaxed about the rider's attire, and you can show Western wearing generic blue jeans, a cowboy (or fancy cowgirl) shirt, boots, and a hat. If you ride hunt seat, you'll probably be proper wearing breeches, knee-high black dress boots, a long-sleeved white shirt, and a black velveteen safety helmet that looks like a hunt cap.

The "A" list: But if you show at the big A-rated shows conducted under the auspices of the United States Equestrian Federation (USEF), be prepared to follow the letter of the law, because that's what the judge will follow. Join USEF—you have to be a member in good standing in order to show—and familiarize yourself with the laws contained in the current *Rule Book.*

■ If you ride in Western classes, you can show any horse that stands 14.1 or over, and you should be wearing a Western hat, pants, boots, and a long-sleeved shirt. In some classes, riders are required to wear a necktie, bolo, or neckerchief. Chaps are required in some classes but not in others, and sweaters, jackets, and vests can be worn at the rider's discretion. As of this writing you can ride using a romal or split reins, and a curb bit with shanks no longer than eight-and-a-half inches. You must use either a curb chain or a leather chin strap—no rolled, braided, or rawhide curb straps. Snaffles and bosals are allowed on junior horses, i.e., those five years old or younger. Gag bits are prohibited.

If you want to show in reining classes, the rules might be different.

■ At a hunter-jumper show, you're expected to enter the ring wearing a scarlet or dark jacket (technically a coat), a white shirt with a white stock (necktie), and white, buff, or canary yellow breeches. The saddle must be a particular type, and so must the bit. A smooth jointed snaffle will get you through almost anything unless it's a gag snaffle—check *before* you leave for the show. Also check to see what types of nosebands are allowed.

Ladies, you need a hairnet under that cute little cap.

■ If you show Arabians, American Saddlebreds, Morgans, and the other show horse breeds, you'll be wearing a riding suit, jodhpur boots, and a specific kind of hat—unless you're female and you're driving a fine harness horse. Disgruntled male drivers complain that they weren't beaten by another harness horse; they were beaten by a woman whose slit sequined gown inched so far up her thigh that the judge couldn't take his eyes off her long enough to look at the other horses.

■ Lower-level dressage exhibitors usually wear what hunter/jumper exhibitors wear. For the rider, that means a short coat in a "conservative" color, a tie or stock tie, and boots or jodhpur boots. You need a hunt cap, but if you really want to, you can wear a top hat. As for your horse, you can ride him using any kind of English saddle as long as it has stirrups. Most of the nosebands available in tack catalogs are permitted; martingales are not. And don't tie ribbons in your horse's mane the way saddle seat riders do; they're not permitted either.

Although these particular dress codes are in force today, by the time you read this chapter they may have changed. The best way to avoid being excused from the ring because you wore spurs or forgot to wear spurs is to join the USEF and check the current *Rule Book*.

My recommendation: Remember to breathe!

Junior horses, those five years old and under, can compete in most Western classes in a smooth, jointed snaffle or a bosal. Individual breeds—Morgans, for example—also offer hackamore classes for young horses. (Drawing by Gina Cresse)

CHAPTER 19

YOU AND YOUR HORSE

Riding is good exercise, but to enjoy it to its fullest, you should be in good physical shape yourself. When you ride, you use your body in ways you normally wouldn't; you sit in the saddle differently than you sit in a chair, for instance. To be an effective rider, you have to strengthen your stomach muscles—which help support your back—and you have to develop more stretch in your legs.

For a long and healthy life, you need physical strength, flexibility, balance, and endurance.

YOU

Here are a few exercises designed specifically for riders that will help you develop and maintain all four. (Hint: yoga makes your entire body more limber, and people who practice yoga tend to be more in tune with their bodies.) If you do these exercises once a day, they'll not only make you a better rider, they'll make you *feel* better.

Strength

For riding, upper-body strength (i.e., your shoulders and arms) isn't as important as your balance and flexibility, although it has a place in your overall health program. Physical therapist Patty Jakobi-Stopper, CSCS (the initials stand for Certified Strength and Conditioning Specialist), suggests that you stop by a local gym, explain what you want, and let a trainer

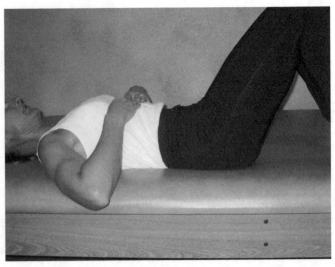

These exercises are for you. Patty Jakobi-Stopper, licensed physical therapist and backyard horse owner, demonstrates the pelvic tilt. First, find the natural hollow in your lower spine (where Patty's hand is).

Your next step is to flatten that hollow (remove your hand first) so you can feel the entire length of your spine against the floor.

customize a weight-training program for you. Patty believes that strengthening your abdominal muscles, or stomach muscles, is crucial to riding. Her backyard horse is a 16.3-hand Oldenburg jumper named Dakota.

The exercises that follow strengthen your quadriceps (the muscles in front of your thigh that tie into your knee) and your lower abdominals.

The pelvic tilt: A very effective exercise that strengthens your lower abdominal muscles and stretches your lower back. If you do it in a chair, nobody has to know you're exercising. If you do it on the floor, people will probably notice. You can even incorporate the exercise into your daily routine—while you sit at the table, your desk, or in a car, as long as you're not driving. You can even do it on an airplane to ease a backache caused by economy seating.

■ I'll start with the floor version because it's easier to describe. Lie on your back, arms outstretched at your sides and at right angles to your body, knees up, feet flat on the floor. Pay attention to where your backbone is. You should be able to slide one hand into the space formed by the natural curve of your lower back and the floor. Once you know the space is there, remove your hand. Then flatten your lower back so the space isn't there anymore. You do this by tightening your lower abdominal muscles. If you don't know where they are, cough. Better yet, laugh. Hold for a count of ten (one thousand one, one thousand two, etc.). Repeat three to five times as you gain muscle strength.

■ Here's the chair version. Sit in a straight-backed chair with your backbone straight and both feet on the floor. Don't lean against the back of the chair. Tighten your lower abdominals and hold for a ten-count. Relax. Repeat three to five times.

For riders, the chair version is more effective because you have to balance your upper body over your pelvis to do it correctly, the same way you sit in the saddle.

Crunches: To ride with a balanced seat—no matter which seat it is—you need strong abdominal muscles. (They help your posture even when you're not riding.) Weak abdominal muscles also contribute to lower back pain, so if you strengthen your abdominal muscles, you're less likely to have a bad back.

A riding instructor taught me how to do crunches while we sat in the grass watching a mutual friend work her horse.

- Step 1: Sit down—in the grass, on the floor, whatever's handy—so that your upper body is straight, your legs are bent at the knee, and the soles of your feet are flat on the floor. Hold your arms out to the side at shoulder level.
- Step 2: Slowly tilt your upper body backwards by moving your arms behind you. Allow your feet to come off the floor so you're teetering on your sacrum (the end of your tailbone).
- Step 3: Slowly tilt your upper body forward. This time your feet won't touch the floor because you draw your knees up towards your face. Loosely embrace your

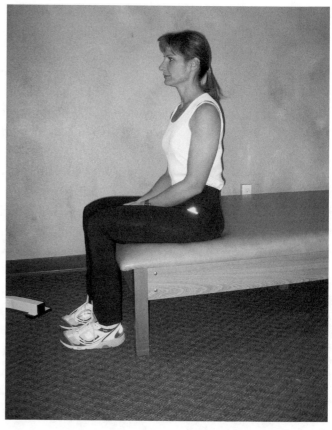

The chair version of the pelvic tilt. Some people grasp the concept more quickly when told to "tighten your buttocks."

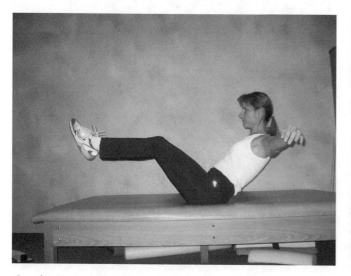

Crunches. You want to see-saw on the end of your tailbone. Back . . .

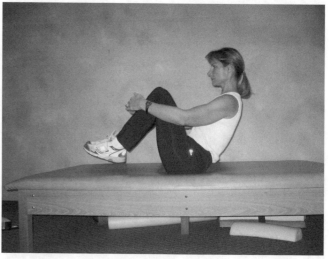

. . . and forth. This exercise firms (no more tummy flab) and strengthens your abdominal muscles.

knees with your arms, then move them behind you again the way you did in Step 1, without allowing your feet to touch the floor. Work up to twenty crunches at a time.

Quadricep strengthener: To me this is the kitchen exercise, because the long wood panels of my kitchen cabinets are smooth enough that I can press the small of my back against them. This exercise strengthens your quadriceps. Since you don't want your feet to slide out from under you, do the exercise barefoot or wearing skid-proof shoes.

■ Stand with your back against a wall or other flat, smooth surface. Allow your body to sink down until your lower legs, from the knee down, are perfectly straight and at a right angle to your upper leg from knee to thigh. Either count twenty seconds out loud or set a timer. In the beginning you probably won't be able to hold this position much longer than twenty seconds. Build up to sixty seconds.

Flexibility

Since your inner thigh muscles get a workout when you ride, some people use this next exercise as a warmup before heading for the barn. It also helps your balance.

To stretch your adductor muscles: Stand with your feet two to three feet apart, toes out. Bend forward from the waist and allow your body to sink between your bent knees. Hold your hands on your thighs, palms down, although you may find it easier to balance

Flexing your adductor (inner-thigh) muscles. As you continue to do this exercise and your muscles get stronger, you'll be able to lower your body until your rear end is closer to the floor. Patty demonstrates the beginner version.

Next, stretch your other leg. This exercise also helps your balance, and doing it together with crunches can make a big difference in how sore you are the day after you ride.

yourself if you hold both arms straight out in front of you. Keep your head aligned with your spine—don't stick it up like a turtle. Hold the stretch for a count of twenty.

- Maintaining the same position, shift to the right so your weight is supported over your right foot. Hold the stretch for ten seconds. Then shift to your left and hold that stretch for ten seconds. Do three stretches on each side, and make sure that the foot that *isn't* supporting your weight stays flat on the floor—especially the heel.

- Once you develop some muscle tone you can allow your weight to sink until your rear end nearly touches the floor. But if you feel any strain in your lower back, go back to the easy version.

To stretch your hamstrings: This yoga stretch helps to relax tight muscles and is a good cool-down after you finish riding.

- Stand with your feet side by side. Slide your right foot forward about two feet, so it's directly in front of your left foot. Bend down from the waist, reaching for the floor with both hands, one on either side of your bent right knee. You should feel your rib cage touch the top of your right leg. Use the tips of your fingertips to balance yourself. If you don't feel the stretch in your right leg or want more stretch, try to touch the floor with your palms—or, as Patty suggests, "pull your toes towards your nose." Keep your left leg straight and make sure both heels are on the floor. Count to twenty. Change legs and repeat.

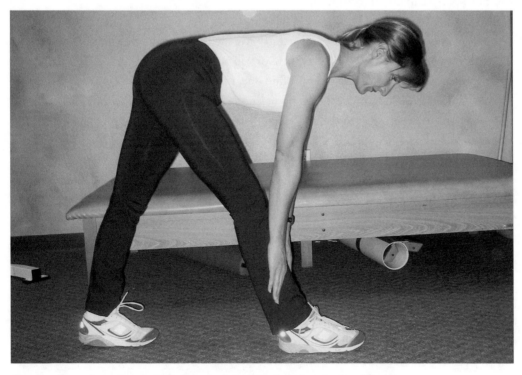

If you stretch your hamstrings, you'll find it easier to keep your heels down in the saddle.

Balance

Stand perfectly still so you're facing forward, your legs are slightly apart, and your weight is evenly distributed on both feet. It helps if you look out the window and focus on an object—a bird bath, a tree, your horse.

■ If you're right-handed, do this exercise by raising your left leg first, because your right leg is probably the stronger of the two and will support you better while you try to figure out if you're doing this exercise correctly. Raise your knee until it almost touches your chest. Clasp the leg with one hand around your ankle and the other just below your knee, and count to three. Don't be discouraged if you can't balance yourself on one foot for the entire three-count in the beginning.

■ Put your left leg down and pick up your right leg. Do exactly the same thing. Stay relaxed—be particularly aware of the small of your back—and focus on that birdbath. Soon you'll be able to hold each leg up for a five-count. Repeat the exercise five times.

Except for the following exercise, I do mine in the morning, after I feed but before I eat breakfast. I usually start with additional stretching exercises—a little yoga here, a little deep breathing there.

Bedtime

Since the next exercise relaxes you, it's also a good cool-down exercise. I like to do it before I go to bed at night, since I tend to lie awake itemizing everything I didn't get done during the day and will have to do tomorrow.

■ You need a prop—an inexpensive thirty-five inch-long foam roll with a diameter of six inches. Most medical supply stores carry them or will order one for you. Or look for a company that sells them on the Internet. If you can't find one, roll some beach towels into a cylinder.

■ With the roll lengthwise on the floor, sit down on one end, so the roll is between you and the floor. Scoot your rear to the very edge (these things aren't very long), one leg on either side of the roll, knees bent and feet flat on the floor. Then slowly *lie down* on the roll so you can feel every vertebra of your backbone touch it. You should have just enough room on the other end to lower your head on the roll. Lift both arms over your head and rest them on the carpet so they're parallel, knuckles down. (You'll probably feel the small of your back leave the tube. For right now that's okay.)

■ Since people like me clench our teeth without knowing it—and then wonder why we can't fall asleep—my first step is to open my mouth as wide as possible and make faces, flicking my tongue in and out to relax my jaw muscles.

■ If you choose not to stick your tongue out and make funny faces, go directly to the next step.

■ Take a few deep breaths from your diaphragm; you should see your lower abdominals expand as you breathe in. Breathe out through your mouth, holding your lips as though you were sipping on a straw.

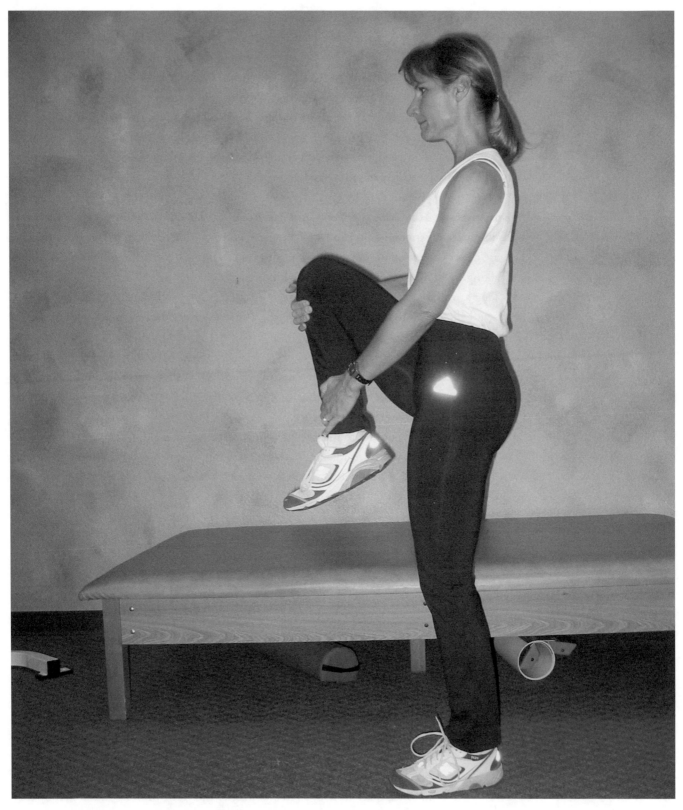

Doing these exercises in front of a mirror can help. This one is good for your balance.

Congratulations—you just learned how to do a yoga belly-breath. When you do this exercise on a foam roll, it will open your chest muscles, stretch the muscles of your back, and relax your entire body. Continue to breathe in and out as you count to thirty.

■ Next, move your arms to the side until they're shoulder-level, your palms on the floor so your arms are at right angles to your body. You should be able to feel the entire length of your spine touch the roll. Concentrate on how heavy your body feels. Think about you and the roll sinking slowly into the carpet as you continue to take slow, rhythmic, deep breaths.

When I've inhaled and exhaled twenty more times, I sit up—making sure every vertebrae in my back touches the roll—and go to bed.

Endurance: Hey Mister Trampoline Man (with Apologies to Bob Dylan)

As important as strengthening and stretching are, exercises that build endurance are crucial to those of us who are climbing, or have already crested, the hill. I'm talking bone density here. Walking, swimming, riding a bike—any kind of aerobic exercise will keep you physically fit as long as you do it actively enough to breathe hard. Oxygen is the fuel that feeds your muscles and allows you to move. The more oxygen you can breathe in and out of your lungs, the more stamina you'll have.

■ I do aerobics on a trampoline that's forty inches in diameter. You can buy one over the Internet, where John bought mine, or at a discount store. The one I have takes up one small, inconspicuous corner of my office.

■ I like to do aerobics to music—anything with a good, solid beat. Because I'm in my own home, I don't have to wear leotards, watch myself in the mirror, or pay an instructor. Set to my favorite music, doing aerobics to the trampoline's bounce makes me feel as if I'm dancing, not exercising.

YOUR HORSE

Believe it or not, there are exercises your horse can do without you on his back. The chiropractor I talked about in Chapter 6 suggested these basic stretching exercises.

Range of Motion—Neck

If you do this one using a bribe—preferably something large, like a whole carrot (one big enough so your horse can snap off bite-sized pieces)—you won't have any trouble getting him to cooperate. In the beginning you might have trouble with him backing up. He's trying to see what you have in your hand, and it's hard for him to focus on something that close.

■ Once your horse knows the carrot doesn't have fangs, move it to his right shoulder so he has to bend his neck in order to reach it. Let him take a bite. Another reason to choose a carrot is because it will take him a second or two to bite a piece off—and, as we all know, it takes time to stretch a muscle. But don't prolong the stretch by teasing him and moving the carrot away. He did his job. Do yours.

These exercises are for your horse, and this first one flexes his neck. Stand slightly behind or at his left shoulder (older horses aren't always as limber as younger ones) and offer him a carrot. You want him to stretch his neck; if he has to shift his hindquarters to reach the carrot, move forward. Repeat on his right side. (Photo by Gina Cresse)

Ask your horse to stretch his head down, again using the carrot as a bribe. Most horses will see it at knee level, but if you hold the carrot between his front legs, they'll lose sight of it. Use your hand to guide your horse's head down and towards his knees if not actually between them. (Photo by Gina Cresse)

- After he swallows, stand by his left shoulder and repeat the exercise.
- Lastly, crouch down and hold the carrot slightly below knee level *behind* his front legs. You want him to stretch his neck straight down and between his legs in order to eat it. You'll probably have to show it to him first, because otherwise he won't be able to tell what it is.

Range of Motion—Shoulder

As long as your horse is fit, this exercise is a good way to limber up his shoulder area.

- Standing next to his shoulder on the right side, ask him to pick up his right foreleg. He should do this instantly because you taught him how in Chapter 7.
- Holding your horse's hoof in both hands, back up until his leg is almost straight. Hold for a count of three and gently return your horse's hoof to the ground.
- Repeat on his left side.

Stretch and Relax

Tie your horse to the hitching rail and walk behind him, trailing your hand along his back and rump so he knows where you are. When you're directly behind him, grasp the middle of his tail with both hands. Holding both arms

Shoulder stretch to the front. Don't raise or extend your horse's leg beyond what he's comfortable with. When Prim was younger, I could easily hold her leg so her forearm was horizontal. (Photo by Gina Cresse)

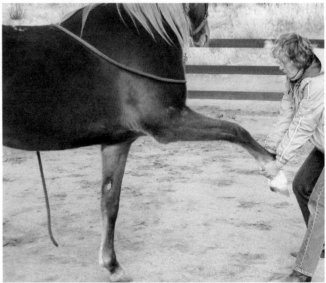

straight, pull straight back, using your body weight to brace yourself for a count of five. Then release his tail.

■ This exercise has several benefits, especially if your horse is so reluctant to have you brush or otherwise touch his tail that he immediately clamps it between his hind legs. If your horse behaves this way, grasp his tail fast, before he can activate those muscles—they're strong enough to trap your hand. By pulling, you relax those muscles. Most horses will allow you to pull their tail because it feels good. In fact after you do it two or three times, your horse will probably allow you to brush his tail without any fuss whatsoever.

■ It's important to pull straight back. Watch your horse as you pull—many horses will shift their feet to balance themselves. Release his tail when his weight is evenly distributed over all four feet, no longer than a count of five.

The tail pull. This exercise helps free up your horse's entire spine. Prim is clamping her tail muscles and resisting me. (Photo by Gina Cresse)

■ Do these exercises only once a day, and if your horse is arthritic or has other physical problems, check with your vet first.

YOU AND YOUR HORSE

Here are a few exercises you can do while you're riding. It's helpful to have a friend longe your horse at the walk so you don't have to worry about where he's going, although if you have a small, circular ring and your horse will walk following the fence, you can do these by yourself. If you're not sure of your horse, do these exercises while he's stopped and facing into the fence.

One: With your reins lying on your horse's neck, raise both hands over your head and stretch them as high as you can. Hold for a count of five. You'll feel the stretch in your rib cage, and when you lower your hands, you should be able to feel your body balanced in the deepest part of the saddle. Your weight is supported by the triangle of your sacrum (your tail bone) in the center of the saddle with one of your seatbones on either side of it.

Two: Lower both arms to shoulder level and move them to the sides so they look like airplane wings. Hold them there for a count of three. Don't do this next part if you're not sure of your horse. He'll catch glimpses of movement over his head and may shy. On the other

The rest of these exercises are for you and your horse—which means you do them mounted. Here, Ally does an arms-over-the-head stretch that will improve her position (and her mare's disposition) in the saddle. In other words, it will help Ally achieve a good, deep seat.

This "airplane" exercise helps your balance because the tug of gravity on your outstretched arms also settles your seatbones deeper into the saddle.

hand, if he didn't react to the first exercise, he probably won't react to this one. Swing your right arm in front of your body and reach for your left arm, which is still extended. Hold the position for a count of five and then repeat it by turning left so your left arm reaches for your right one. The exercise will improve your range of motion and make you more flexible.

Three: Place both hands against the small of your back, palms out, one hand over the other. Sit up straight in the saddle—no slouching—and hold for a five-count. When you withdraw your hands, think about where your shoulders are. For maximum balance, ride with your back and shoulders in this position.

If you're riding on the trail and discover yourself slouching, roll your shoulders in a tiny half-circle, front to back, as though you were going to turn your palms up. That's how to hold your upper body.

Four: Because this exercise may seem strange to your horse, prepare for the fact that he might shy. But if he's still calm—and most horses will be—he probably won't react to this exercise either.

If you put the backs of your hands against your own back, your shoulders will be in the correct position.

Raise your arms the way you did for the second exercise, so they're at shoulder level. Using your right hand, reach across your horse's withers and attempt to touch the toe of your left boot. Unless you're very limber, you might not be able to. Do not contort your body attempting to touch your toe. The exercise is meant to increase your range of motion and your flexibility, and it won't do you any good if it pulls your body out of alignment. As soon as you feel *any* discomfort in your lower back, stop immediately. The next time you do the exercise, reach for an area just below your knee.

Riding without Stirrups

This is probably the most valuable exercise you can do on horseback. I always longe Prim before I ride her, and I ride her in the ring without stirrups for about five minutes before we hit the trail.

You want your legs to hang straight down from your seat so that if your horse suddenly disappeared from under you, you would still be standing. In other words, you want to feel that your legs are under you and you're sitting straight, with your entire body balanced over your horse.

Many people, including some riding instructors, insist that you keep your legs and feet in exactly the same position you use when you ride with stirrups, which means keep your heels down. In my opinion forcing your legs into this position is useful only for advanced riders, particularly those in equitation classes (where only the rider is judged, not the horse) who already *have* leg muscles and a good, balanced seat.

Ally can touch her toes. Provided your horse is as agreeable as hers, feel free to bend and stretch in the saddle. You'll gain confidence by finding out what you're physically capable of doing on horseback.

What I'm about to describe will help you *achieve* a good, balanced seat.

At the walk: Take your feet out of the stirrups and let them relax, even if your toes hang lower than your heels. You want a little slack in the reins, just in case, so don't throw them away and ride on the buckle. As the horse walks, push your heels down until you can feel a pull that begins in your Achilles tendon (the long, vertical tendon just above your heel) and goes straight up the back of your leg. Hold that position for a count of twenty. Relax. You want to *stretch* those muscles; you're not trying to stay on by gripping with your legs.

■ While you relax, shift your attention to the way your horse is moving. Don't close your eyes—riding with your eyes closed isn't a good idea under any circumstances—but concentrate on how your body, especially your legs, moves as a result of how your horse moves. Because you're completely relaxed, you'll probably notice that your right leg bumps his side slightly during one step, while your left leg bumps his side when he takes the next step.

■ While you're still relaxed, regain your stirrups without looking down. If you can't, sneak a peek and locate the stirrup irons. Then try again.

At the trot: If you ride English, I suggest that you cross your stirrups over the horse's withers before you trot. In other words, take your feet out of the stirrup irons. By sliding your hand down the leathers, pick up the stirrup iron on your off-side and lay it across your horse's withers so the stirrup iron is on the near side. Do the same thing with the other stirrup iron. The trot is bouncy, and loose stirrup irons banging against your shins can hurt. But if you cross them over your horse's withers, they'll hardly move.

- This time, forget about stretching your heels. Instead, concentrate on not making your body do anything. Riders who lack confidence in their seat will try to grip with their legs. Don't be tempted to do that: keep them limp as dishtowels.
- Allow your balance to take over. At first you'll feel very insecure, as though somebody greased the saddle. But if you refuse to tighten your muscles and grip, you'll stop sliding around.
- When you get tired, or when you've passed the gate five times, slow your horse to a walk and pat his neck. He thinks exercises are boring too.

■ Once you're able to sit to the trot half a dozen times around the ring, stop your horse, uncross your stirrups, and post to the trot. When you post, you allow the thrust of the horse's hind leg to push your body out of the saddle. The muscles of your inner thighs act as shock absorbers for the first one-two beat of the trot stride. By the second beat, you're back in the saddle.

■ Next, try to tell what diagonal you're on without looking down. (You can—it just takes practice.) When I say *diagonal*, I'm referring to the fact that a horse has four legs. If he's trotting, he has two diagonal feet on the ground (for example the right front and the left hind) and two in the air (the left front and the right hind).

- When your horse raises his left hind leg and his right front leg (the one closest to the rail if he's going counterclockwise), your body should be out of the saddle. The horse is on his right diagonal, and you should be posting on the right diagonal.

- To check your diagonal, glance down at your horse's shoulders. If you're on the wrong diagonal (your body rises as his left shoulder comes up) sit down in the saddle for one beat and pick up the correct diagonal on the second beat. Anybody who shows English must know how to post to the trot on the correct diagonal.

- Even if your future plans don't involve showing, learn to post anyway. If you're trail riding at a nice, brisk trot, it's much easier on your horse's back if you post. Be sure to change your diagonal every so often so your horse doesn't have to bear the weight of your body on the same two legs during the "down" phase of the trot.

At the canter: Spend a lot of time trotting without stirrups before you try cantering. Since the canter is a smoother gait than the trot it's actually easier to ride, but because the horse is moving faster, it may not feel easier.

- Leave your stirrups crossed over your horse's withers. Relax your legs—in other words, don't clench your leg muscles.

- It's important to know what lead your horse is on when he canters. I've only fallen off twice (as opposed to getting bucked off), and the first time it happened, the horse fell with me. I was riding Bachelor in a Western saddle. He was on his right lead, but I wasn't paying attention and turned him left. Bachelor obliged, tripped over himself, and fell with me under him. Neither of us was hurt—just rattled—and I immediately got back on. Don't ask a horse to turn left unless he's on his left lead.

- Even though the push for the canter stride comes from the horse's hind legs, exactly the way it does at the trot, watch your horse's shoulders to see what lead he's on. If he picked up the lead with his right hind leg (you're going counterclockwise again), his left foreleg is leading—in other words, his inside foreleg. His left shoulder will be slightly in front of his right.

- If you can't feel your own left shoulder tilt very slightly in response, you'll have to look down at your horse's shoulder to make sure. Once you know what lead he's on, concentrate on feeling it.

- When you have a good, balanced seat, you'll be able to tell what lead your horse is on without looking.

- Once you feel comfortable cantering without stirrups, uncross them and try to get your feet back in the irons without looking. It's harder than it was at the walk because the stirrup irons are swinging. But one reason you want good balance is so you'll stay on your horse if he shies. Another reason: if he shies and you lose a stirrup, it's helpful to know how to get it back.

RIDING WITH A DISABILITY

I have a neurological disorder called cervical dystonia. (When I was first diagnosed, most specialists called it spasmatic torticollis, but it's the same thing.) To learn more about it, I subscribed to newsletters, attended symposia, seminars, and self-help groups. I noticed almost immediately that the happiest people were the ones who refused to let their medical condition define them. The level of pain associated with dystonia causes many people to feel angry or depressed, often both. At first I felt that way myself, but eventually I realized I already *have* a life. I'm more than what's wrong with me. I'm a person—and as a person, I'm passionate about three things: my husband, my writing, and my horse.

Dystonia is classified as a neurological movement disorder. In my case, muscles in my neck and shoulders keep trying to turn my head to the left. In response, the muscles on the right side of my neck and shoulders, back, and hips try to pull my head back where it belongs. This constant tug of war takes its toll, and by now—I've had dystonia for over twenty years—most people resign themselves to the inevitable. They *let* their head twist to one side and walk sideways, so they can see where they're going.

I prefer not to. I exercise every day and ride whenever I can.

(Photo by Gina Cresse)

(Photo by Gina Cresse)

Riding doesn't have to be strenuous to be fun, and people of most levels of ability or disability can enjoy it. I know a blind woman who rides. I know people with heart conditions, hip problems, spine problems, arthritis—they all ride. I know a woman who took up riding *because* she had cervical dystonia and wanted some form of enjoyable physical activity to take her mind off it. Until she bought a horse, she had never ridden before.

If you have a disability but want to ride, or continue to ride, run it past your doctor.

But some passions are too strong to fade quietly away, even under doctor's orders. In fact I believe that our *passions* define us, not our illnesses. Since my neurologist has never forbidden me to ride—I'm not even sure he knows I have a horse—I intend to ride as long as I can.

Life is a one-way ticket to an unknown destination. Why deprive yourself of passion when he's standing right in front of you, eyes luminous with trust, nuzzling your hand for carrots?

APPENDIX I

A GLOSSARY OF HORSE TERMS

All words and expressions in **boldface** are defined in this glossary.

A

    aids (refers to a rider)—Parts of the rider's body, or extensions of those body parts, used to control and guide the horse. The **natural aids** include hands, arms, legs, seatbones, body position, and voice. **Artificial aids** include the **bit**, reins, **martingales, whips**, and spurs. Some owners call a specific aid a **cue**.

    aired-up—An eager, excited horse; neck arched, tail **flagged**, ears pricked.

    anticipate (refers to a horse)—To sense a pattern in his owner's behavior and act prematurely. When the owner cleans the horse's feet, for example, and always picks up the **near** front **hoof** first, then the near hind, then the **off** hind, and finally the off right, the horse will anticipate his owner by picking up the next foot in the rotation before the owner reaches for it.

    arena—An enclosed space where the owner or rider turns the horse out for exercise. In this book I use the word **arena** interchangeably with the words **ring** and **riding ring**.

    artificial aid—See **aid**.

B

    baby-sitter—A horse so trustworthy a toddler could ride him through a 4th of July fireworks display. Similar expressions include child-broke, push-button, and **bomb-proof**.

bales—Hay and straw are sold in bales. The weight of individual bales can vary widely.

bald-faced—A horse with a very wide blaze that covers one or both eyes (which are usually blue or **glass**) and nostrils (which are pink).

balk (refers to a horse)—To resist moving forward or to stop; his rider can't convince him to get going again.

barefoot—An unshod horse. Some horses have such good, sturdy feet they don't need shoes. Such horses are rare.

barn sour—A horse reluctant to leave his stall or corral and tries to turn around and run home at every opportunity.

barrel—The horse's rib cage. Some horses, because of the degree of arch of their ribs, have much rounder barrels than others. The word can also refer to a fifty-gallon barrel used as a **waterer**.

bars—The spaces in a horse's mouth where he has no teeth, only the underlying bone covered with skin. He has two empty spaces in his upper jaw between his incisors and molars, and two corresponding empty spaces in his lower jaw. The bars are where the **bit** lies.

bat—A short English riding **crop**. See **whip**.

bay—A brown horse with a black mane and tail and black **points**.

bearing surface—The area of the horse's hoof that comes into direct physical contact with the ground.

bedding—Any material that makes the floor of a stall or corral more comfortable for horses. The most commonly used bedding is wood **shavings**, although some owners prefer **straw**.

behind—The horse's hind legs. For example, "That horse is lame behind." See also **in front**.

bell boots—Circular rubber "cuffs" that protect the horse's **coronary** area. Used mainly to **longe** a horse. (See **coronet**.)

billets—Part of a **saddle**; the straps that attach the girth to the saddle.

bit—The detachable metal part of the **bridle** that goes in the horse's mouth. See the illustrations in Chapter 2.

bite (refers to a horse)—To grab an object (another horse, a mouthful of grass) using his teeth. The second meaning of the word refers to the shape of the horse's mouth. A **parrot-mouthed** horse has an overbite; other horses have an underslung or **undershot** jaw. Both horses have such a bad bite they cannot nip off pasture grass or chew an apple.

blanket—Refers to a covering for the horse's body, usually to provide warmth or protection from bad weather. Also refers to the coat pattern of some Appaloosas.

blaze—A solid white marking on a horse's face that extends the length of his nose. See **bald-faced, snip and a stripe**, and **star**.

blind spot—While most horses have excellent peripheral vision because their eyes are on the sides of their head, they can't see anything directly behind them and have trouble focusing on anything directly in front of them. The size of the blind spots depends on the exact position of the horse's eyes.

body-clip—To shave a horse, using clippers, from forelock to tail to remove his winter coat. Show and performance horses are routinely body-clipped during the winter because they're worked every day and blanketed afterwards. See **blanket.**

bolt (refers to a horse)—To break into a sudden gallop for no apparent reason and refuse to slow down or stop. (See **vice.**) The second meaning of the word also refers to a horse—to swallow some or most of his feed without chewing it.

bomb-proof—See **baby-sitter.**

bone spavin—A generalized lameness in the **hock** usually caused by wear and tear.

bosal—A bitless **bridle** that works by exerting pressure on the horse's nose. The rider controls the horse with braided rope reins called a **mecate.** See **hackamore.**

bowed tendon—Inflammation of the tendon that runs down the back of the horse's legs, primarily the forelegs. Usually due to an injury. If the bow is severe enough, the horse will pull up lame.

brace—Any astringent used to increase a horse's circulation after a hard ride.

breast collar—A piece of **tack** that keeps the **saddle** from slipping back. Useful when riding in rough terrain.

bridle—Consists of a **bit**, reins, and a **headstall.** An English bridle has additional parts. See illustrations in chapter 2.

bridle path—The area behind the horse's ears where the **crownpiece** of the **bridle** rests. A show horse with his bridle path clipped presents a neater appearance than one who hasn't been clipped.

brisket—Part of a horse between his front legs. (The usual test for a hot horse is to feel the heat and wetness of his brisket.)

broke—A horse of any age who can be safely ridden at all three gaits (or at his natural gaits if he's natural-gaited). For example, an ad might read, "Welsh pony gelding, eight years old, broke to ride and drive." See **green-broke.**

broodmare—A mare retired from the show ring or race track whose sole purpose in life is to produce offspring.

browband—Part of a **bridle**, usually English but occasionally Western. See illustration on page 26.

buck (refers to a horse)—To work off energy or unload his rider by lowering his head between his front legs and kicking up his heels.

buckskin—A horse with a tan, yellow, or pale gold coat, black mane and tail, and black **points.** If the horse has papers, he's a *registered* Buckskin.

bulbs—The sensitive heel area of a horse's hoof that lies directly beneath his **coronet** and is separated by his **frog.** See illustration on page 118.

bull pen—See **bull ring.**

bull ring—A circular pen, fifty to sixty feet in diameter, with solid wooden sides high enough that the horse can't see over them. Also called a **bull pen.**

burro—See **donkey.**

bute—Phenylbutazone. An anti-inflammatory medication for the horse's bones, joints, and painful conditions.

C

canter—A three-beat **gait** that's faster than a **trot** but slower than a **gallop**. Western riders call it a **lope**, although a true lope is slower than a canter, and the horse usually carries his head lower.

cantle—part of a **saddle**. See illustrations in Chapter 2.

cast—A horse who is down and can't get back up because he's too close to the wall (an indoor horse) or has wedged his feet through the rails of a corral (an outdoor horse).

cavesson—The **noseband** of an English **bridle**. A **longeing** cavesson is a **headstall** similar to a **halter**, used specifically to **longe** a horse.

cereal grains—Grain-bearing hays that are cut with the grain still on them; they provide the horse with nutrients in addition to **roughage**. The cereal grains include oats, wheat, and barley.

cheek piece—Part of a **bridle**. See illustrations in Chapter 2.

chestnut—A shade tree that bears horse chestnuts (which are poisonous to horses). The second meaning of the word describes a horse with a reddish **coat** and a mane and tail the same color or slightly lighter; sometimes called a **sorrel**. The third meaning refers to the hard, scab-like protrusion on the inside of a horse's knees and hocks. Like **ergots**, chestnuts are evolutionary tagalongs.

choke—Results when a horse's food lodges in his esophagus. Choke can be life threatening.

cinch—The part of a Western **saddle** that keeps it on. The cinch slides under the horse's belly from one side and fastens on the other. Most Western saddles have two cinches, but English saddles have only one, called a **girth**.

cloth—See **rub rag**.

cluck—A voice **aid**. The smacking or kissing noise most riders make to get their horse moving.

coat—The hair on a horse's body. For example, horses grow a winter coat that they shed as soon as warm weather arrives. The word also refers to a horse's basic body color. His mane and tail can be the same color as his coat, or they can be different.

cob—A specific size of halter or **bridle**. A cob-sized halter will fit most horses. Bigger horses, such as **warmbloods**, need a larger size.

coffin bone—One of the three small bones in a horse's foot. The position of the bone can change as the result of chronic **founder.**

cold-backed—A horse reluctant to be saddled, usually because something about the procedure hurts him. Such a horse will often back away when the rider approaches carrying a **saddle**, threaten to bite as the rider tightens the **girth**, and hump his back when the rider first mounts.

colic—A potentially life-threatening intestinal condition caused by indigestion (gas), a twisted intestine, or a physical blockage.

colt—See **foal**.

complete feed—Horse feed sold in bags instead of bales. Complete feeds are designed to replace both hay and grain. Usually fed to older horses who have trouble chewing.

confirmed—An older horse with a long-standing (and hard to correct) **vice** like **bolting**.

conformation—How the horse is built. A horse with good conformation is preferable to one with poor conformation because how the horse is built determines how he moves.

contact—Refers to the amount of tension between the rider's hands and the horse's mouth. The second meaning of the word describes the thickness of the saddle; many riders prefer a close-contact saddle to one with a lot of leather between them and the horse.

coronary band—See **coronet.**

coronet—The part of the horse's lower leg where the skin and hair of his **pastern** end and the **wall** of his hoof begins. Also called the **coronary band**.

corral—A horse's fenced, outdoor living quarters. In this book I use the words **pipe corral** interchangeably with **paddock** and corral.

corrective shoeing—A specific type of shoeing that protects injuries or corrects deformities of the horse's foot.

cow kick (refers to a horse)—To kick sideways with one hind leg. See **kick**.

cracks—See **sand cracks**.

crib (refers to a horse)—To clamp his jaws around something—a rail, the lip of his feeder—and suck in air. Such a horse is called a cribber or wind sucker. One of the **stable vices**.

crop—See **whip**.

cross-canter—To canter on one **lead in front** and the other lead **behind**.

cross-tied (refers to a horse)—To stand in the aisleway of the barn tied between two ropes, or ties while being brushed and/or saddled.

croup—Part of the horse. See illustration on page 179.

crow-hop—A teasing, semi-serious **buck** that may or may not turn into a serious, get-off-my-back buck. The horse jumps forward stiff-legged with both front feet together, the way crows and ravens hop.

crownpiece—Part of the bridle that fits behind the horse's ears. See illustrations in Chapter 2.

cue—See **aid**

cull—A horse, usually a purebred, who doesn't conform to the standards of the breed and can be bought cheap.

curb—A specific type of bit with shanks and a **curb chain** or strap. Used mainly by Western riders unless it's part of a **double bridle**. See illustration pages 24 and 28.

curb chain—See **curb**.

curry comb—A grooming item riders use to deep-clean a horse's coat. Especially useful for removing mud and dead winter hair.

cutback saddle—A type of English **saddle** with a notch in the **pommel** so the pommel won't rub the horse's **withers**.

D

dam—A horse's mother. See also **sire**.

diagonal—Which legs the horse is using at the **trot**. The word also refers to the position of the rider's body in the saddle at the trot. A horse who trots has two diagonal feet on the ground and two in the air at any given time except for a brief **moment of suspension** when all four feet are off the ground. In a **riding ring**, when the rail (or fence) is on the right, English riders **post** by letting the thrust of the horse's hind leg push them out of the saddle. When the horse raises his *left* hind leg and his *right* front leg (the one closest to the rail), the rider's body should be out of the saddle. This horse is on his right diagonal, and his rider is correctly posting on the right diagonal.

dished—A horse, usually an Arabian or old-fashioned Thoroughbred, with a wide jaw and forehead tapering to a small muzzle is said to have a dished face. See also **Roman nose**.

donkey—One of several species of ass, a horse-like animal. A **burro** is a small donkey. See also **Przewalski's horse** and **zebra**.

D-ring snaffle—See **snaffle**.

dorsal stripe—The line that runs down some horses' backbone. All **donkeys**, **buckskins**, **duns**, and grullas have dorsal stripes, as do individual horses of many other breeds. The stripe is often black but can also be darker than the horse's **coat** color.

double bridle—An English **bridle** fitted with two **bits**, a **curb** and a thin **snaffle**. The rider has four reins.

Dutch door—A stall door that has a top half and a bottom half. Each half has hinges along one side, so the door can swing out. Most owners keep the lower half closed and the top half open, so the horse can look out. Usually seen in older barns.

dun—A horse having a red to tan **coat** with a mane, tail, and **dorsal stripe** a shade or two darker. Can be registered as a Buckskin, which is a color registry. (A grulla can also be registered as a Buckskin.)

E

ear—Part of a horse's body (see illustration on page 179). The word (refers to humans) also means to twist a horse's ear to distract him from something else taking place at the same time that the horse would not normally allow—such as a veterinarian trying to look inside his mouth. See **twitch**.

easy keeper—A horse who thrives on relatively small portions of feed without losing weight; he's not a picky eater and requires very few nutritional frills.

edge—A ready-for-anything horse, usually because he hasn't been exercised lately. Some competition horses are fed and trained to develop such boldness.

electrolytes—Salts/minerals naturally present in the horse's body tissues; he loses them through sweat and urine. Available in packaged form from tack stores.

Elgin Marbles—Ancient Grecian sculptures originally adorning the Parthenon, many celebrating the beauty of the horse. Taken from Athens to London by Thomas Bruce, the seventh Earl of Elgin, in 1806. Now on display at the British Museum.

enterolith—A physical blockage in the horse's gut. Usually caused by a foreign object the horse accidentally swallowed, such as a tiny piece of wire. With the gradual buildup of minerals around the object, it can eventually become a stone big enough to require surgical removal.

equitation—A class at a horse show where the rider's form is judged, not the horse's ability. Usually for riders under the age of eighteen.

ergot—A bony protrusion on the horse's **fetlock**. See **chestnut**.

evasions—Behaviors a horse develops because he doesn't want to do what a human has asked him to do. A pastured horse who doesn't want to be caught will evade his owner by running away.

F

farrier—The person who trims and shoes a horse's feet. Some horse people call them **shoers**, but be careful who you call a blacksmith. A blacksmith works with iron; he or she does not necessarily shoe horses.

feeder—A container that holds hay and grain (or pelleted grain supplements) and salt. Also called a feeding bin or manger.

fender—Part of a Western saddle. See illustration on page 14.

fetlock—Part of the horse. See illustration on page 179.

filly—See **foal.**

finished—A completely trained or broke horse. At the other extreme is the **green-broke** horse.

flag (refers to the horse)—To raise his tail. A high-spirited horse who's "feeling his oats" often raises his tail when he runs. It resembles a flagpole with the hair streaming behind it.

flank—Part of the horse. See illustration on page 179.

flat saddle—An English **saddle**. Its profile is flatter than that of a Western saddle.

flat walk—A true, **lateral**, four-beat **gait** with the following sequence of footfalls: *left* rear, one beat; *left* front, second beat; *right* hind, third beat; *right* front, fourth beat.

flaxen—A chestnut horse with a blond mane lighter than his coat color is said to have a flaxen mane. Some chestnuts have flaxen manes and tails that are nearly white.

float—To file a horse's teeth to ensure a good **bite**, so the molars are level with no sharp edges.

foal—A young horse of either sex. A **filly** is a female and a **colt** is a male until they turn three. At that age fillies become **mares** and colts become horses—**geldings** if they're castrated, **stallions** if they're not.

forelock—The part of a horse's mane that falls between his ears onto his forehead.

forge—See **interfere.**

forgiving—A horse who doesn't hold grudges, even when an inexperienced rider bumps him in the mouth or bounces all over his back.

founder—A painful inflammation of the horse's feet, although the actual cause of the inflammation may have nothing to do with his feet. See **laminitis**.

free longe—A type of longeing that dispenses with the **longe line** and the **longeing cavesson.** Instead, the owner relies on the position of his or her longe **whip**, voice **cues**, and body English to tell the horse what to do.

frog—The V-shaped wedge in the bottom of the horse's hoof. See illustration on page 118. The texture of the frog should be rubbery and yield slightly to the touch. The **sole** that surrounds it is much harder.

full-cheek snaffle—See **snaffle**.

G

gag bit—A **snaffle** bit attached to a **headstall** that is one continuous piece of leather from the **crownpiece,** down the **cheek pieces**, and though the rings of the bit to the reins themselves.

gait—How the horse is traveling. Since a horse has four legs, he can put them down in a variety of sequences, unlike humans, who are stuck with left foot, right foot. Most horses naturally **walk**, **trot**, **canter**, and **gallop**. **Natural-gaited** horses do not trot; instead they **single-foot**, **rack**, or **pace**.

gallop—The horse's fastest **gait**. Seen more often at a race track than in the show ring or on the trail. A high-speed, four-beat **canter**.

gelding—A castrated male horse. See also **mare** and **stallion**.

girth—See **cinch.**

glass eye—A blue or amber eye. Most horses have dark brown eyes. But a **bald-faced** horse, or any horse with white around his eyes, can have one glass eye and one normally colored eye, or two glass eyes, depending on how much of his face is white. Also called a wall eye or clock eye.

grade—An unregistered, non-purebred horse. If he were a dog, he'd be a mutt.

green-broke—A horse, usually young, who has been taught to lead, has been ridden at all three **gaits** (but not for very long or very often), and knows how to start, slow down, stop, and turn. What he mainly needs is mileage.

groom (refers to a human)—To clean and brush the horse, **forelock** to tail, nostrils to feet. A professional who grooms horses for a living is called a groom or caretaker.

ground manners—How the horse behaves when handled by a human. Ground manners include how the horse leads, whether he allows his feet to be picked up and cleaned, and whether he stands quietly to be saddled and bridled.

gullet—The part of the underside of a saddle that is raised to clear the horse's spine.

gymkhana—A morning-long or day-long competition, mainly for kids, that involves competitive games on horseback.

H

hackamore—A bitless bridle that works by applying pressure on the horse's nose. There are two types, a **bosal** and a **mechanical** hackamore. The latter has a **headstall**, reinforced noseband, shanks, a **curb** strap or chain, and reins.

halter—A piece of **tack** designed to fit securely around a horse's head so a human can handle him.

hand—The unit of measure that determines a horse's height at the **withers**. One hand equals four inches.

hand-walk (refers to a person)—To walk a horse by hand rather than put him on a mechanized **hot-walker**.

hay—The horse's natural feed, but dried and packaged in **bales**. **Hay** in its naturally occurring form is grass.

headshy—A horse who has probably been hit in the face. Since he doesn't know why he was hit, he can be very defensive about being brushed on the head or bridled. Requires gentle, patient handling.

hay hooks—Two hooks, one for each hand, used to move hay bales.

headstall—The basic **bridle**, i.e., the **crownpiece** and **cheek pieces**. For Western riders, that's all they need by way of a bridle. English headstalls usually include a **throatlatch**, **noseband**, and **browband**. See **bridle** and the illustrations on p. 24 (Western) and p. 26 (English).

high-strung—See **hot**.

hinny—See **mule**.

hock—Part of a horse. See illustration on p. 179.

hoof—Part of a horse. See illustration on p. 118.

horn—Part of a Western saddle. See also **pommel** and illustrations on pp. 14 and 26.

hot—A flighty, high-strung horse. The second meaning of the word refers to the temperature of the weather. The third meaning describes the horse's temperature after exertion.

hot-walker—A machine that walks horses, either to exercise them or cool down **hot**, sweaty ones that have just been worked. The horse is snapped to an overhead line and the machine "leads" him in large circles. See **hand-walk**.

I

in front—The horse's forelegs. See **behind**.

in season—An ovulating mare.

interfere (refers to a horse)—To hit one leg with another leg because of his conformation, shoeing, or fast footwork. A horse who **forges** hits the sole of his front foot with the toe of his hind foot. A horse who **scalps himself** steps on the heels of his front feet with his hind feet.

in training—A horse being taught by a professional trainer at the trainer's barn for a specific purpose, for example, so he can learn to jump, race, cut cattle, or overcome specific **vices**.

J

jack—A **donkey** stallion. See **mule**.

jig—A series of short, fast, jittery steps. Most tense or high-strung horses will jig.

jog—The Western horse's **trot**. It's faster than the **walk** but slower than the **lope**. (A jog is slower than a trot.)

jump off his feet—See **shy**.

K

    kick (refers to a horse)—To use his powerful hind legs to protect himself from other horses and occasionally from humans. If he defends himself with his front legs, he uses them to **strike**. See also **cow kick.**

    knee—Part of a horse. See illustration on page 179.

L

    laminitis—See **founder**.

    lateral gaits—See **single-foot** and **pace**.

    lead—Which foreleg the horse is leading with at the **lope** or **canter**. In a riding ring, he should lead with his **inside** foreleg—the one closest to the inside of the ring as opposed to the rail (or fence) side.

    lead shank—A type of leadrope that's usually a flat piece of leather, like a belt, with a chain and snap on one end.

    leg-yield—When the horse steps under himself with one hind leg and as a result moves sideways as well as forward. An English term used primarily in dressage. A similar Western term is **sidepass,** although the horse moves only to the side, not forward.

    longe (refers to a person)—To exercise a horse without riding him. The horse is attached to a longe line held by the handler, and circles the handler at various **gaits**.

    longeing cavesson—Headgear similar to a **halter** but designed specifically to **longe** a horse.

    lope—A leisurely, three-beat **gait** used by Western horses. English riders call the same gait a **canter**, although the canter is usually faster. See also **lead**.

M

    maintenance—How much an owner feeds a horse to keep him from losing or gaining weight.

    mare—An adult female horse. See also **stallion** and **gelding.**

    martingale—One of the **artificial aids.** See **running martingale** and **standing martingale.**

    mecate—See **bosal.**

    mechanical hackamore—See **hackamore.**

    moment of suspension—That moment during the **trot** and **canter** when all four of the horse's feet are off the ground.

    muck out (refers to a human)—To clean a stall or corral.

    muck bucket—A bucket, usually plastic with handles on both sides, that the person who's mucking out uses to deposit manure. Some owners prefer them to wheelbarrows.

    mule—Any cross between a horse and a **donkey**. Technically, a mule results from breeding a donkey **stallion** to a **mare**. When a horse **stallion** breeds a female **donkey**, the result is a **hinny**.

    mustang—America's "wild" horses. A few are directly descended from horses ridden by Cortés and his men when they invaded Mexico in the 16th century. Most are recently descended from feral horses.

muzzle—To put a safety device on a horse that prevents him from biting. The second meaning of the word refers to the lower portion of the horse's face: lips, jaw, and nostrils.

N

natural aid—See **aid.**

natural-gaited—A horse who **single-foots, racks,** or **paces** naturally, without training.

navicular—One of the three small bones in the horse's foot. Poor conformation and working the horse on hard surfaces can cause navicular disease, a serious lameness.

near—The left side of the horse as both horse and rider face the same direction. Riders always mount and dismount a horse from the near side. The ancient Greeks are thought to have originated the practice because they carried their swords on their left hip—the better to grab the hilt with their right hand once they were mounted. See **off.**

nerved—A procedure, now seldom used, to help a **navicular** horse by severing the nerves that send pain signals from his foot to his brain. **Bute**, joint supplements like glucosamine and chondroitin sulfate, and **corrective shoeing** have replaced nerving.

noseband—Part of a **bridle.** See illustration page 26.

O

off—the right side of the horse. See **near.**

on the buckle—A horse so trustworthy the rider can "throw the reins away" and ride with the reins completely loose. If the horse is wearing an English bride, the rider holds only the buckle of the reins.

overbite—See **bite, parrot-mouthed,** and **undershot.**

P

pace (refers to a horse)—To move **laterally** instead of **diagonally.** When a horse paces, his right foreleg and right hind leg are in the air at the same time, while his left foreleg and left hind leg are on the ground. Usually seen only in racing Standardbreds and camels.

pad—A solid rubber pad under an outdoor horse's feeder is good insurance against sand **colic.** The word also refers to padding under the saddle. See **saddle pad.**

paddock—See **corral.**

papers—A horse with papers is registered with a breed association—for example, the American Quarter Horse Association. His papers document that fact.

park saddle—Used by saddle **seat** riders (one of the three English seats). See illustration on page 19. The saddle is characterized by an extremely low **pommel** and an even lower **cantle.**

parrot-mouthed—See **bite.**

pastern—Part of a horse. See illustration on page 179.

pick out a horse's feet—To clean a horse's feet using a hoof pick.

pick out a horse's tail—To separate each strand of hair in a horse's tail by hand.

pins his ears (refers to a horse)—An angry horse with his ears flattened against his head. Pinned ears usually indicate the horse is ready to bite. Sometimes it's a bluff, sometimes not.

pipe corral—See **corral.**

pitchfork—Any long-handled metal or plastic-pronged fork used to separate manure from the horse's bedding.

points—Horses with black legs from the knees and **hocks** on down. Some horses (bays, for example) can have white socks or stockings on their lower legs in addition to black points.

pole barn—A wooden barn built by sinking wooden posts (or poles, hence the name) into the ground.

poll—Part of a horse. See illustration on page 179.

pommel—Part of an English saddle. See illustration on pages 14 and 19.

pony—Any "horse" who measures 14½ hands or less. Some ponies belong to specific pony breeds; others are small versions of horse-sized breeds.

port—The part of a **curb** bit that resembles an upside down U.

posting trot—See **diagonal** and **sitting trot.**

Przewalski's horse—The only truly wild horse left in the world. Although they will breed in captivity, they have never been used as draft animals or for riding. See also **donkey** and **zebra.**

put down—To have a horse humanely euthanized by a veterinarian.

Q

quarter crack—See **sand crack.**

quirt—See **whip.**

quittor—A chronic inflammation of the horse's foot below the **coronet**, characterized by pus-filled sores.

R

rack—See **single foot.**

rag—See **rub rag.**

rain rot—A fungal condition usually found on the back of a horse's **pasterns.**

rear (said of a horse)—To stand on his hind legs; usually an **evasion.**

reata—A rawhide rope used by many tradition-minded cowboys to rope cattle and horses. Other cowboys prefer a nylon or polyester rope they can tie directly to the saddle horn without taking dallies.

riding crop—See **whip.**

riding ring—See **arena.**

ring—See **arena.**

ring work—A rider works his or her horse inside a **ring** with the intent to improve his or her riding skills, or to teach the horse how to do something.

roach—To shave a horse's mane down to the skin. In a human it would be a buzz cut.

road apples—Slang for horse manure.

Roman nose—A horse's nose that is slightly convex instead of straight. Often considered a sign of inferior breeding or a stubborn horse, or both.

roughage—The fiber in the horse's feed that keeps the feed moving through his gut, where the friendly bacteria break it down.

round corral—A small, circular **arena**, fifty to sixty feet in diameter, used mainly for training the horse on the ground. Not for riding. Also called a **round pen**.

round pen—See **round corral**.

rub his mane out (refers to a horse)—To rub a section of his mane out on a rail or pipe, either because his neck itches or because it's spring and the grass is greener on the other side. Result: a horse whose mane is all one length except for a bald spot.

rub rag—A **cloth** used to clean horses. Also called **rags** or cloths. Many owners prefer them to **sponges**.

Rule of Thumb—A truism all savvy horse owners—cowboys, and fox hunters—know for a fact.

runaway—A horse **galloping** out of control.

running martingale—A piece of **tack** designed to teach a horse to keep a lowered head (often used on young horses). Since the martingale is connected to the reins, the horse bumps himself in the mouth whenever he raises his head too high. See also **standing martingale** and **tie-down**.

S

saddle—Four different **seats** are recognized by the United States Equestrian Federation (USEF). Each seat has a particular saddle that is different in shape and purpose from the other three. See **seat**.

saddle blanket—A blanket used by Western riders who place it on the horse's back before they saddle the horse. English riders call it a **saddle pad**.

saddle pad—See **saddle blanket**.

saddle strings—Leather strings found on most Western trail and pleasure saddles. See illustration on page 14.

sand colic—A type of **colic** caused by an impaction in the horse's gut, in this case sand.

sand crack—A vertical crack in a horse's front **hoof**. Cracks that start at the **bearing surface** and split up the hoof are less serious than those that start at the **coronary band** and split down.

scald—Small, oozing sores around the horse's pastern that scab over, then reappear. When the scabs are removed, the horse's hair comes with them. Scald and **scratches** commonly occur when the horse stands in wet bedding or mud.

scalp—See **interfere**.

scratches—Similar to **scald** but the horse's hair doesn't come out when the scabs are removed.

scurf—An oily, scabby buildup on tack that results from lack of cleaning.

seat—The rider's position on a horse; his or her form. For the second meaning of the word, see **saddle**. The third meaning refers to that portion of the **saddle** where the rider sits.

seatbones—The rider's pelvic bones, one per leg, that come in direct contact with the **seat** of the **saddle**.

sedentary—A mature horse not ridden at all or ridden only lightly.

serpentine—An exercise on horseback to refine the rider's **aids** and the horse's responsiveness. The horse is guided through a series of big, snake-like loops, usually back and forth across a rectangular **arena**.

set back (refers to a horse)—To panic and pull back while tied. The horse throws the full weight of his body against the leadrope while shaking his head from side to side as he attempts to free himself.

shank—The lower portion of a **curb** bit where the reins are attached.

shavings—See **bedding**.

shoer—See **farrier**.

shy (refers to a horse)—To **spook** or **jump off his feet** because he's frightened—a full-body **evasion**.

sidepass—When a Western horse moves sideways. See **leg-yield**.

side reins—Two pieces of leather and/or surgical rubber tubing with snaps on both ends. Side reins connect the rings of the **snaffle** with the rings on a **saddle** or **surcingle**.

single-foot—To **rack**, a natural gait for many horse breeds (Rocky Mountain Horse, the Racking Horse, and some American Saddlebreds). The gait is **lateral** with a rhythmic, one-two-three-four cadence. Also called a stepping **pace** or a broken pace.

sire—A horse's father. See also **dam**.

sitting trot—When the horse trots, the rider does not **post**. Instead, he or she stays in the saddle, absorbing the "bounce" of the trot by using his or her abdominal muscles.

skirt—Part of a saddle. See illustrations on pages 14 and 19.

snaffle—A type of English **bit** with many variations. The basic types are a straight **bar** snaffle, a **D-ring**, **eggbutt**, **loose-ring**, and **full-cheek** snaffle.

snip and a stripe—The white markings on a horse's face. A **snip** is usually between the nostrils and a stripe is a narrow **blaze**.

sock—A horse with white on his legs has either **socks** or **stockings**. Socks are shorter and usually stop just above the fetlock. If they extend to the knees in front and the hocks behind, they're stockings.

sorrel—See **chestnut**.

sole—The bottom of the horse's **hoof**. See also **frog**.

sound—A healthy horse with no injuries or defects.

sour-eared—A horse who habitually keeps his ears back but not **pinned** when the rider works him. Such horses are usually bored or unhappy.

sponge—Used to clean a horse. Some owners prefer **rub rags**.

spook—See **shy**.

stable vices—Bad habits that a horse can develop, particularly if he lives in confined quarters and isn't given enough exercise. Some common stable vices are **cribbing**, **weaving**, reluctance to stand still while being groomed and handled, reluctance to being saddled (see

cold-backed), reluctance to leave the barn area, and, once the rider convinces him to do so, trying to return to it before the rider wants to (**barn sour**). See also **vices**.

stallion—An adult male horse, uncastrated. See also **gelding, mare**, and **stud**.

standing martingale—See **tie-down.**

star—Any small white marking on a horse's face, usually between his eyes. See also **blaze** and a **snip and a stripe**.

stick—See **whip**.

stirrup leathers—Parts of an English saddle that hold the **stirrup irons**. The tops of the leathers are attached to the stirrup bar under the **skirt**. See illustration on page 19.

stirrup irons—See **stirrups.**

stirrups—Where the rider's feet go when he or she is in the saddle. The stirrups on a Western saddle are wide from front to back because they're designed for people riding with high-heeled boots. If you ride English, you call them **stirrup irons.**

stock tank—See **waterer.**

stocked up—When a horse's hind legs fill up with fluid because of inactivity.

stocking—See **sock**.

stone bruise—When a horse, usually traveling on rocky ground, bruises the **sole** of his foot and pulls up lame. A horse who recently had his feet trimmed is vulnerable to stone bruising.

straw—The dried and baled stalks of certain grasses. Used mainly for bedding.

stretch—Some show horses are taught to move their forelegs forward at the halt so they're easier to mount and less apt to **walk** off while the rider is still half in the **saddle**. Also refers to the positions a horse assumes to stretch tight and tired muscles.

strike (refers to a horse)—To **rear** and use his forelegs defensively. Horses **kick** with their hind legs and strike with their forelegs.

stud—A **stallion** used for breeding is called a stud. See also **mare** and **gelding**.

supplement—Literally means "something added," and most owners use it in a very broad sense: "I supplement my horse's hay with grain." Other owners consider a supplement to be a specific addition to their horse's diet, such as a vitamin/mineral supplement.

surcingle—Also called a belly band. A strap made out of leather and canvas and/ or synthetic material that completely encircles the horse's **girth** area. Many owners use a surcingle instead of a saddle to **longe** their horse because it's easier and faster than riding him.

T

tack—the horse's **saddle**, including the **girth** (a **martingale** or **breastplate**, if he wears one), and all the parts of his **bridle**, including the **bit** and anything that attaches to it. See illustrations in Chapter 2.

tail wringing—When a horse is agitated or angry, he'll jerk his tail back and forth and sometimes switch it in a circular motion. Usually accompanied by **sour ears**.

tandem—When two or more horses or ponies are harnessed to a conveyance (carriage, jog cart, sleigh, etc.) in single file.

thin—To pull a few strands of hair at a time from a horse's mane. Usually done by English riders to make the mane easier to braid. Since no horse likes having his hair pulled out, most backyard owners don't do it.

thrifty—Describes a healthy, active, low-maintenance horse. See **thrive.**

thrive—If a physically healthy horse maintains weight, he is said to thrive. See **thrifty.**

throatlatch—Part of a **bridle**, most often an English bridle. See illustration on page 26. The word can also refer to part of a horse where the throatlatch is fastened. See illustration on p. 179.

thrush—An infection that affects the horse's **hoof**, particularly the **frog**. The condition is caused by standing in wet, dirty footing, and is characterized by a foul smell.

tie-down—A piece of **tack** designed to keep the horse from raising his head above a certain height. English riders call it a **standing martingale.** See **running martingale.**

top dressing—Any feed or feed supplement the owner scatters over the horse's main course, which is usually hay.

trace minerals—Various minerals available to the horse in four-pound bricks or fifty-pound blocks. They usually contain sodium chloride (salt), cobalt, copper, iodine, iron, manganese, and zinc.

transition—A change of the horse's **gait**, speed, or direction. For example, most Western riders will signal to their horse that they want to **lope** by leaning slightly forward in the **saddle** before giving their horse a lope **cue.**

tree—The foundation of every **saddle**, English or Western, over which the saddle maker cuts and forms the saddle leather. The tree determines a saddle's size and shape.

trim—When a horse has outgrown his shoes, or a barefoot horse's hooves get too long, they need their hooves shortened and leveled. Most horses require trimming every six to eight weeks.

trot—A **diagonal gait** that's faster than a **walk** but slower than a **canter**. The Western **jog** is similar but slower.

turnout ring—A fenced area big enough to turn a horse out in so he can exercise.

twitch—A device that goes over the end of the horse's nose and tightens to prevent unruly behavior. There are several versions; the best are lightweight metal and look like nutcrackers. Since many nerve endings are located in the horse's nose, a twitch is an effective way to control a rambunctious horse. Vets often carry their own twitch.

U

undershot—A horse whose upper front teeth have no direct contact with his lower front teeth. Also called having an underslung jaw. See **bite.**

V

vet check—A prepurchase physical examination by a veterinarian to test the horse for soundness.

vices—Bad or self-destructive behavior once thought to be deliberate on the horse's part. Horse owners now recognize that these behaviors can also be caused by boredom, lack of exercise, loneliness, or stress. See **stable vices.** Such a horse can be a **fence-walker, weaver, barn sour,** or a **cribber**. A horse with more serious vices will **rear, strike out** with his forelegs, **kick, bite,** or **bolt**.

W

walk—The slowest of the horse's natural **gaits**. Depending on the breed, the other natural gaits are the **trot** (or **jog**), and the **canter** (or **lope**).

wall—The outer portion of the horse's hoof that's visible when his foot is on the ground.

warmblood—Any breed of European sport horse who is bigger-boned and heavier than an American riding horse. They are the result of systematically breeding indigenous draft or carriage horses (cold-blooded) to Thoroughbred and/or Arabian (hot-blooded) horses.

waterer—Any container that holds water for an outdoor horse. It can be a fifty-gallon **barrel**, an old, claw-footed bathtub, a rubber or metal **stock tank**, etc.

weanling—A three- to six-month-old **foal** old enough to be separated from his **dam** and nibble grass instead of nursing.

weave (refers to a horse)—To constantly and rhythmically shift his weight from one side of his body to the other. See **stable vices**.

whip—One of the **artificial aids**. A whip is used immediately after a **natural aid** to reinforce it if the horse doesn't respond to the natural aid. Most English riders call their whip a **bat** or **stick**; Western riders call theirs a **quirt**.

white line—The division between the **sole** of the horse's foot and the outer **wall** of the hoof.

withers—Part of a horse. See illustration on page 179.

wobbler—A horse with a neurological condition that affects his coordination.

wolf teeth—Small teeth that sometimes grow in the **bars** of a horse's mouth. Because they make wearing a **bit** uncomfortable, most owners ask a vet or horse dentist to extract them.

X

Xenophon—the ancient Greek horseman who wrote what is considered the first how-to book about riding.

Y

yearling—A horse who has passed his first birthday. After next year's birthday he'll be a two-year-old.

Z

zebra—One of several species related to the domestic horse.

zebra stripes—Zebra **duns** have horizontal stripes across their knees and hocks.

APPENDIX II

ADDITIONAL SOURCES OF INFORMATION

I. CHAPTER NOTES

Chapter 1

For questions about property requirements and zoning restrictions for backyard horse owners:

- Contact information for Los Angeles County, California, Department of Regional Planning: phone (213) 723–4475; Web site, planning.co.la.ca.us
- Contact information for Fullerton, California Planning Department: phone (714) 738–6317; Web site, www.ci.fullerton.ca.us/dev_serv/animlreg.html
- Contact information for the County of Orange, California, Planning Department: phone (714) 834–5146; Web site, pdsd.oc.ca.gov
- Contact information for Charles County, Maryland Planning Department: phone (301) 645–0627; Web site, www.charlescounty.org

In many counties, animal control is shared by the American Society for the Prevention of Cruelty to Animals (ASPCA) and/or the Humane Society. If all you get are recorded messages, busy signals, or endlessly ringing phones, contact either of these organizations. For local branches, check your phone book.

- The American Society for the Prevention of Cruelty to Animals (ASPCA), Headquarters in New York: phone (212) 876–7700; Web site, www.aspca.org
- The Humane Society of the United States, headquarters in Washington, D.C.: phone (202) 452–1100; Web site, www.hsus.org

Chapter 2

Recommended reading for riding Western:

- *The* reference book for how to ride like a cowboy is *Western Horsemanship* by Richard Shrake (Colorado Springs, Colorado: Western Horseman, Inc., 1990). Well known as a teacher and clinician, Shrake has written a book that's clear, easy to follow, and accentuates the positive. He wants his riders to *like* what they're doing and provides solid information for riders of all levels, from beginning to advanced.
- Ed Connell's *Hackamore Reinsman* (Cisco, Texas: The Longhorn Press, 1952). The book I have is the 11th printing. Connell also wrote *Reinsman of the West: Bridles & Bits, Vol. II* (Livermore, California: Lennoche Publishers, 1964). These books (I don't have Vol. I of *Reinsman of the West* but I assume there is one) are the real thing. Written by an honest-to-goodness working cowboy who's been there and done that, the books explain how to take a green horse, put him in a hackamore, and develop him into a finished reining horse with a mouth that's a soft as a silk scarf.
- Another source—long out of print but worth checking for at used bookstores (or Amazon.com (http://www.amazon.com)—is Sydney E. Fletcher's *The Cowboy and His Horse* (New York: Grosset & Dunlap, 1951). This exceptional book, with an introduction by historian Joseph Henry Jackson, was intended for children. But the information, Fletcher's artwork in particular, is so accurate and presented in such an engaging style that anybody hankering to learn more about the old West will fall in love with it. Pretend you bought it for your kids for Christmas.
- Robert W. Miller's *Western Horse Behavior and Training* (originally published in 1974 by Big Sky Books and republished by Doubleday). Full of practical tips, interesting information, Western lore, and informal studies regarding horses' behavior.

Recommended reading for riding hunt seat:

- Go directly to the master, George H. Morris, whose *Hunter Seat Equitation* (New York: Doubleday, 1990), now in its third edition, covers the basics of hunt seat for pleasure riders as well as those interested in hunting and the show ring. Morris, the youngest rider to ever win the ASPCA Maclay and the AHSA (American Horse Shows Association) Medal finals, has coached riders to national and international wins, including a team gold for the American show jumping team at the 1994 Olympic Games.

Recommended reading for riding dressage:

■ *The Beginning Dressage Book*, by Kathryn Denby-Wrightson and Joan Fry, explains what tack you need, the basics of longeing, how to ride with a balanced seat, and how to use your aids to ask for your horse's cooperation at the walk, trot, and canter. Originally published in 1981, this classic was published in a new format with new illustrations by The Lyons Press (Guilford, Connecticut) in 2004. Its easy-to-follow, informal style makes this one a keeper.

Recommended reading for riding saddle seat:

■ Gayle Lampe's *Riding for Success Both In and Out of the Show Ring* (St. Louis, Missouri: Saddle & Bridle, 1996) lives up to its title. Crammed with astute observations from Gayle's thirty-five years as saddle seat program director for the Equestrian Science Department at William Woods University in Fulton, Missouri, this book is a must-read for anyone riding show horses. Gayle holds judges' cards for nine equestrian disciplines and has judged shows from Madison Square Garden to South Africa.
■ It's no accident that all four books share a lot of very basic information—how to lead a horse, saddle a horse, control a horse, or ask a horse to perform a maneuver he would seldom use in the wild (such as side passing or leg-yielding)—thereby proving what you suspected all along: good horsemanship is good horsemanship, regardless of breed or seat.

For more information about tack:

■ State Line Tack puts out a catalog for hunter/jumper and dressage tack and a separate catalog for Western tack, although both catalogs overlap. Contact information: phone (800) 228–9208; Web site, www.statelinetack.com
■ Dover Saddlery carries tack for hunter/jumper, dressage, and Western riders. Contact information: phone (800) 989–1500; Web site, www.doversaddlery.com
■ Libertyville Saddle Shop carries park saddles and the full bridles that go with them as well as hunter/jumper, dressage, and Western tack. Contact information: phone (800) 872–3353; Web site, www.saddleshop.com
■ Country Supply puts out a catalog specifically for Western tack. Contact information: phone (800) 637–6721; Web site, www.countrysupply.com

Chapter 3

For more information about breed associations and registries:

■ *The Horse Industry Directory.* Updated each year by the American Horse Council, this useful spiral-bound booklet lists contact information for every breed registry in this country—at least the ones that want people to know about (e.g., Quarter

Horses, the Florida Cracker Horse, the American Buckskin Registry Association, Cleveland Bays, etc.).

The Directory also includes information about state Extension Specialists (who can in turn give you the phone number for your local 4-H organization) and national "Show and Sport" organizations such as the National Reining Horse Association. Contact information: phone (202) 296–4031; Web site, www.horsecouncil.org

Recommended Reading:

- *Simon & Schuster's Guide to Horses and Ponies*, edited by Maurizio Bongianni (New York: Simon & Schuster, 1988), is crammed with gorgeous color photographs and odd and interesting facts. Expect some surprises: Did you know that the exotic-looking Akhal-Teké horses—with their long legs and greyhound-thin bodies (a desert breed native to Russia) are so hardy they have been known to travel for days without water?
- Another useful guide is *The Observer's Book of Horses and Ponies* by R. S. Summerhays (Frederick Warne & Co. Ltd., 1961). The book was originally published in England but is long out of print. Even though the evolutionary information is out of date, the book contains many first-person sightings of indigenous horses and ponies on their own turf, and some wonderful old photographs that show, for example, what *Equus Przewalski* looked like half a century ago (exactly the way he looks today).

Chapter 4

For questions about how to build your own barn:

- Colorado horsewoman Cherry Hill has written several books about barn design and construction. Contact information: Web site, www.horsekeeping.com

For questions about modular barns:

- At least a dozen companies—some local, some national—will build you the modular barn of your dreams. Since they advertise in all major horse magazines, they're easy to find.

Chapter 5

See notes for the previous chapter.

Chapter 6

For questions about horse health:

- Dr. Mark Williams suggested these books. *How Be Your Own Veterinarian (Sometimes): A Do-It-Yourself Guide for the Horseman* by Ruth B. James, DVM (Mills, Wyoming:

Alpine Press, 1985), and *Understanding Basic Horse Care: Your Guide to Horse Health Care and Management* by Michael Dall (Berkeley, California: Eclipse, 1998). If you can't find or order these books from a bookstore, try one of the tack store catalogs, www.amazon.com, or horse-related Web sites that sell books, such as www.roundpenmagic.com.

- The Morris Animal Foundation funds a variety of health studies involving companion animals, a category that includes horses. They publish a very informative newsletter, and according to one of the most recent, they're currently funding two horse-related studies. One involves a three-year study of "Gene Mapping in Horses." The principle investigator, Dr. Ernest Bailey of the University of Kentucky—working with researchers at Texas A&M University, the University of Minnesota, and Cornell University—plans to "identify and map 20,000 horse genes. The study results will lead to new diagnostic tests [to identify a tendency towards certain diseases], new methods of disease management, and improved therapies for horses." Contact information: phone (303) 790–2345; Web site, www.MorrisAnimalFoundation.org

  Additional reading: *The Illustrated Veterinary Encyclopedia for Horsemen*, edited by Don M. Wagoner (Dallas, Texas: Equine Research Publications, 1975). Considering how far veterinary medicine has advanced in the past decade alone, this book is surprisingly up to date. Intended for readers with some medical background, the information is presented so clearly that the book has been reprinted numerous times and is still in print. Its special merit is the illustrations—at least one photograph per page and sometimes four or five, plus drawings. If you can't identify a founder stance, or want to know what an advanced case of thrush looks like, buy this book.

- On the Internet, take a look at www.thebarnbook.com. Based in Florida, it contains valuable information about how to prepare your horse for natural disasters such as hurricanes. For example: put your name, phone number, and address in a small, waterproof bag and attach it to your horse's halter in case you're separated. Do *not* include a copy of a negative Coggins; that makes it too easy for thieves to ship him out of state.

Chapter 7
For questions about hoof care:

- Used as a textbook in many farrier schools, Doug Butler's *The Principles of Horseshoing* (LaPorte, Colorado: Butler Publishing, revised edition, 1985) is still the last word on how to shoe a horse. Butler, who holds two PhD degrees from Cornell University (one in Veterinary Anatomy and the other in Equine Nutrition) writes in clear, nontechnical language that accurately describes potentially serious hoof conditions without alarming readers. Contact information: Web site, farrierfocus.com, or cowboycode.com. Another useful source is the American Farrier's Association. Contact information: Web site, www.americanfarriers.org

Chapter 8
For questions about horse feed:

- See the section that lists magazines and newsletters at the end of this Appendix.
- Check some of the general sources that I've already suggested or the Internet.

Recommended reading:

- Lon Lewis, *Feeding and Care of the Horse*, 2nd ed. (Hagerstown, Maryland: Lippincott, Williams & Wilkins, 1997). According to nutritionist Dr. Judith Reynolds, this book is, "the best single nutrition text available."
- *Nutrient Requirements of Horses,* 5th ed. (Subcommittee on Horse Nutrition, Committee on Animal Nutrition, Board on Agriculture, National Research Council, Washington, D.C.: National Academy Press, 1989). This book is the gold standard of horse nutrition, providing nutritional guidelines still in use today; Lewis draws on them heavily in his own book. Try the library or amazon.com for a used copy. (The information is presented in fairly technical language. For the average owner, Lewis' book is far more reader-friendly.)

For questions about horse nutrition, including free advice about feed:

- Ask nutritionist Dr. Judith Reynolds, PhD, PAS Contact information: phone HELPLINE (800) 680–8254; Web site, www.admani.com

For questions about horse feed manufactured by Purina Mills:

- Contact information: phone (800) 227–8941; Web site, horse.purinamills.com

Chapter 9
For questions about elder-horse nutrition:

- See notes for the previous chapter.
- Articles about caring for elderly horses are available from most of the sources mentioned in this Appendix; specifically, see the section on magazines at the very end of this Appendix.
- Check the Internet.

Chapter 10
For questions regarding horse abuse:

- The American Society for the Prevention of Cruelty to Animals (ASPCA): check your local phone book.
- The Humane Society of the United States: check your local phone book.

For questions about acquiring a horse from a rescue organization:

- For organizations in your area, contact your local Humane Society or ASPCA.
- The Equus Sanctuary at www.equus.org/
- Equine Protection of North America (E.P.O.N.A.) at eponarescue.org
- Also check into the Exceller Fund, although they mainly provide information about retired Thoroughbred race horses. Contact information: Web site, www.exceller fund.org/links.htm

Chapter 11
For questions about what's "normal" delivery-day behavior:

- One of the smartest guides about how to partner up with your new horse and what to do if things don't go exactly as planned is Fran Devereux Smith's *First Horse: The Complete Guide for the First-Time Horse Owner* (Colorado Springs, Colorado: Western Horseman Inc., 1995). What the author has to say about horse owning and handling is applicable to any owner, riding any breed of horse, using any seat— whether it's your first horse or your fifth.

    English riders, pretend you're not seeing spots and big hats. The information pertains to *all* owners.

Chapter 12
For questions about the evolution and behavior of horses and their kin:

- The Institute for Ancient Equestrian Studies at users.hartwick.edu/iaes
- The Equine Behavior Lab at www2.vet.upenn.edu/labs/equinebehavior/index.htm
- Dorothy Russell Havermeyer Foundation Workshop Horse Behavior and Welfare at www2.vet.upenn.edu/labs/equinebehavior/hvnwkshp/hv02/levine.htm

Recommended reading:

- Sue McDonnell's *A Practical Field Guide to Horse Behavior: The Equid Ethogram* (Lexington, Kentucky: Eclipse Press, 2003). This one-of-a-kind book provides a wealth of information about horse behavior and has the photos to illustrate it (an ethogram is a catalog of behaviors). Dr. McDonnell founded the Equine Behavior Program at the University of Pennsylvania School of Veterinary Medicine.
- *Western Mule Magazine*. Contact information: phone (417) 859–6853; Web site, www.westernmulemagazine.com

Chapter 13
For additional information about your first trail ride:

- See notes for Chapter 11.

- *The Trail Rider* magazine. Contact information: phone (800) 448–1154; Web site, www.trailridermagazine.com
- For additional tips, go to roundpenmagic.com.

Chapter 14

For questions about basic training and problem horses:

- Word of mouth is your most reliable source. Start by asking your vet, trainer, and/or riding instructor.
- Other possibilities: books and videos by horse behaviorists (a.k.a. horse whisperers) such as Monty Roberts, Tom Dorrance, Mark Rashid, John Lyons, his son Josh Lyons, and Pat Parelli. But do not try to emulate their methods on your horse. Use what they have to say as guidelines to decide: (1) whether your horse's "problem" is fixable; (2) whether you're contributing to it; (3) whether you should seek advice from a professional trainer.

Recommended reading:

- *First Horse* (see notes for Chapter 11)
- Stephen D. Price was the editorial director for this one-stop source book about everything equine; writers are Barbara Burn, Gail Rentsch, and David A. Spector. *The Whole Horse Catalog: The Complete Guide to Buying, Stabling and Stable Management, Equine Health, Tack, Rider Apparel, Equestrian Activities and Organizations . . . and Everything Else a Horse Owner and Rider Will Ever Need* (New York: Simon & Schuster, 1998). As its low-key subtitle indicates, I could have listed this book as recommended reading for any of the preceding chapters. If it has to do with horses, it's probably in this book; the volume covers everything from how to make a manure pit to what to wear when playing polo.

Chapter 15

For questions about how to longe a horse at liberty:

- Check the book section of your local tack store.
- Check the Internet.

For questions about how to train a horse for the movies:

- See www.joanfry.com for an insider's account of the making of the 1979 film classic *The Black Stallion*, with Mickey Rooney.

Chapter 16

For questions about how to longe a horse:

- Entire books have been written about this subject. See the book section of your local tack store or tack catalog and/or check the Internet.

Chapter 17

For questions about what needs doing when:

- Most of this information is available from horse magazines. If you subscribe to one long enough, it will eventually get around to barn chores. Or check the Internet.

Chapter 18

For questions about showing your horse:

- USEF (United States Equestrian Foundation) is the organization that replaced the old American Horse Shows Association (AHSA) and governs most A-rated shows; it is also our national liaison with the FEI (Fédération d'Equestre Internationale), the international Olympic organization. As a member, you're eligible for various year-end awards depending on your seat or division (hunter/jumper, dressage, saddle seat, and reining) in your area. For children and adults. Contact information: phone (859) 258–2472; Web site, usef.org
- 4-H. Although this organization is best known for its emphasis on market animals, local groups sponsor horse projects for interested members. For riders aged five to nineteen. Contact information: Web site, www.4-h.org.

  4-H is a branch of the Cooperative Extension Service, which is a program of the United States Department of Agriculture. To find a group near you, look up the phone number for your local Cooperative Extension Office, then ask for the County 4-H Extension Agent.
- United States Pony Clubs. Open to riders under the age of twenty one. Contact information: phone (859) 254–7669; Web site, www.ponyclub.org
- Equestrian Trails, Inc. Now nationwide, ETI is open to riders of all ages. Contact information: (818) 362–6819; Web site is pending.

Recommended reading:

- Have you considered driving your backyard horse? Read the revised edition of this practical guide by Marilyn C. Childs and Rick M. Wallen, *Training Your Colt to Ride and Drive: A Complete Guide for Pleasure and Show* (North Pomfret, Vermont: Trafalgar Square Publishing, 1993). If you've ever hankered to drive a team of horses down a snowy country lane, this book will tell you how.

Chapter 19

To find fitness programs for you and your horse:

■ This information is available from books (look through your tack store's selection), catalogs, horse magazines, and the Internet.

II. MAGAZINES, NEWSLETTERS, AND BOOKS FOR GENERAL HORSE CARE INFORMATION

■ *John Lyons' Perfect Horse.* Although Lyons is a cowboy and proud of it, the information in this newsletter will interest and help all riders. He over-relies on some methods—for example, a horse has to be pretty well broke in order to slow him down by displacing his hips (leg-yielding), but Lyons' down-home style and step-by-step photos are easy to follow. In addition to the usual training tips, health updates, and how-to articles, *Perfect Horse* is perfectly free of advertising. That fact alone makes me open it before any other horse magazine that arrives in the mail. Contact information: phone (800) 424–7887; Web site, www.perfecthorse.com

■ *Western Horseman* is the granddaddy of Western horse magazines and still going strong after sixty-eight years of publication. It contains practical advice in every issue, much of it applicable to owners who ride English. The magazine also showcases the work of Western artists. Contact information: phone (719) 633–5524; Web site, www.westernhorseman.com

■ *Horse & Rider.* A useful, all-round general interest publication for Western riders and owners. Contact information: phone (877) 717–8928; Web site, www.equisearch. com/magazines/horseandrider/contacts

■ *Equus.* This health-oriented magazine is strongly pro-Arabian and pro-sport horses (dressage, jumping, three-day eventing) and rarely contains articles about gaited or Western horses. But the medical information—which includes nutrition, hoof care, and the latest medical breakthroughs—is up-to-date and accurate; nearly everyone on the editorial advisory board is a veterinarian. Contact information: phone (800) 829–5910; Web site, Equusmagazine.com

■ One of the most informative hunter/jumper/dressage magazines on the market is *Practical Horseman.* As its name implies, it's a practical guide to horse owning and riding and offers riding, training, barn, general safety, and trailering tips for the English rider. Contact information: Web site, www.equisearch.com/magazines/ practicalhorseman/contacts

■ Although *Practical Horseman's Book of Horsekeeping*, edited by M. A. Stoneridge (Garden City, New York: Doubleday, 1983) is out of print, I strongly recommend that you look for a used copy. This book provides commonsense information about common topics by questioning the experts: trainers, barn managers, horse haulers, etc. It also contains the only photos I've seen of what a horse looks like when he shies.

■ For saddle-seat riders, *Saddle & Bridle* is tough to beat. Its readers are mainly people who own, ride, train, and/or compete on American Saddlebred show horses, but the magazine also covers Morgans, Hackney and Shetland ponies, Standardbred road-sters (or road horses), and other show breeds. In addition to show results, each issue carries general-interest columns on training, horse health, books about horse care, etc. Contact information: phone (314) 725–9115; Web site, saddleandbridle.com

- Also for saddle seat exhibitors, *The Saddle Horse Report* is a weekly newspaper con-taining mainly show results. *Horse World*, a monthly magazine published by the same company, has general-interest features including interviews with trainers and owners. Contact information: phone (931) 684–8123; Web site, saddlehorsereport.com

III. INTERNET SOURCES FOR GENERAL HORSE-CARE INFORMATION

- The following on-line source is provided by the publisher of *Equus, Dressage Today, Horse & Rider,* and *Practical Horseman*; the Web site offers accurate and up-to-date information about horse health, training tips, horse and stable care, tack tips, etc. (www.EquiSearch.com).
- For horse health and nothing but horse health, there's the one and only *The Horse: Your Guide to Equine Health Care*, a monthly magazine. The on-line version contains over 5,000 veterinarian-approved articles (www.thehorse.com/).
- For additional sources, see also the Internet sites in Part I of this Appendix.

INDEX